# Azores

## the Bradt Travel Guide

**David Sayers**
**With Murray Stewart**
*Foreword by Ben Fogle*

edition
6

www.bradtguides.com

Bradt Travel Guides Ltd, UK
The Globe Pequot Press Inc, USA

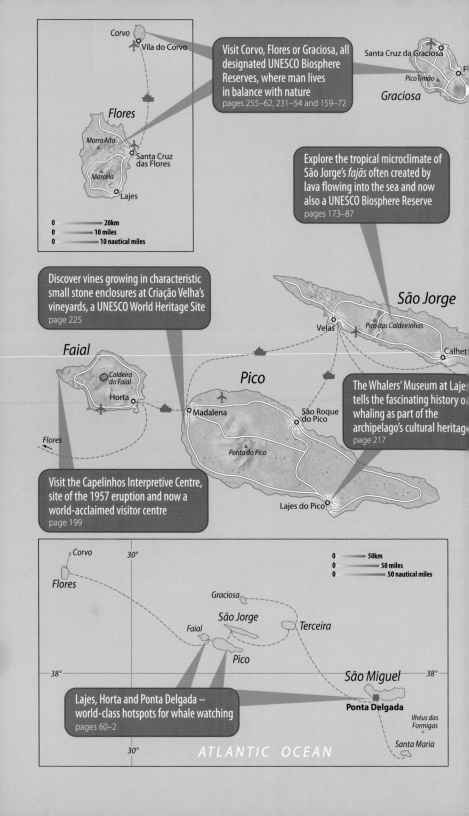

Visit Corvo, Flores or Graciosa, all designated UNESCO Biosphere Reserves, where man lives in balance with nature
pages 255–62, 231–54 and 159–72

Explore the tropical microclimate of São Jorge's *fajãs* often created by lava flowing into the sea and now also a UNESCO Biosphere Reserve
pages 173–87

Discover vines growing in characteristic small stone enclosures at Criação Velha's vineyards, a UNESCO World Heritage Site
page 225

The Whalers' Museum at Laje tells the fascinating history o whaling as part of the archipelago's cultural heritag
page 217

Visit the Capelinhos Interpretive Centre, site of the 1957 eruption and now a world-acclaimed visitor centre
page 199

Lajes, Horta and Ponta Delgada – world-class hotspots for whale watching
pages 60–2

Corvo
Vila do Corvo

Santa Cruz da Graciosa
Pico Timão
Graciosa

Flores
Morro Alto
Santa Cruz das Flores
Marcela
Lajes

0 — 20km
0 — 10 miles
0 — 10 nautical miles

São Jorge
Velas
Pico das Caldeirinhas
Calhet

Faial
Caldeira do Faial
Horta

Pico
Madalena
São Roque do Pico
Ponta do Pico
Lajes do Pico

Flores

Corvo            30°
Flores
Graciosa
São Jorge            Terceira
Faial
Pico
São Miguel
38°                                38°
Ponta Delgada
Ilhéus das Formigas
Santa Maria
30°
ATLANTIC OCEAN

0 — 50km
0 — 50 miles
0 — 50 nautical miles

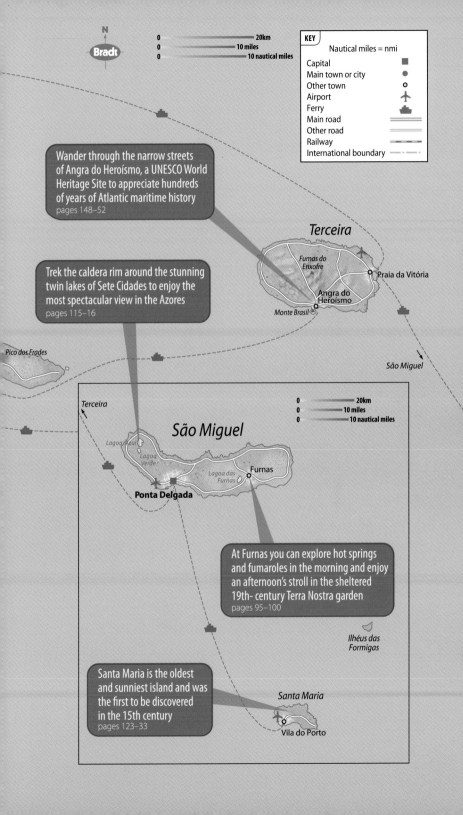

Wander through the narrow streets of Angra do Heroísmo, a UNESCO World Heritage Site to appreciate hundreds of years of Atlantic maritime history
pages 148–52

Trek the caldera rim around the stunning twin lakes of Sete Cidades to enjoy the most spectacular view in the Azores
pages 115–16

At Furnas you can explore hot springs and fumaroles in the morning and enjoy an afternoon's stroll in the sheltered 19th- century Terra Nostra garden
pages 95–100

Santa Maria is the oldest and sunniest island and was the first to be discovered in the 15th century
pages 123–33

KEY

Nautical miles = nmi

- Capital ▪
- Main town or city ●
- Other town ○
- Airport ✈
- Ferry ⛴
- Main road ——
- Other road ——
- Railway ——
- International boundary ——

Bradt

0 ——— 20km
0 ——— 10 miles
0 ——— 10 nautical miles

Terceira

Furnas do Enxofre

Praia da Vitória

Angra do Heroísmo

Monte Brasil

Pico dos Frades

São Miguel

Terceira

São Miguel

Lagoa Azul
Lagoa Verde
Lagoa das Furnas

Furnas

Ponta Delgada

0 ——— 20km
0 ——— 10 miles
0 ——— 10 nautical miles

Ilhéus das Formigas

Santa Maria

Vila do Porto

# Azores
# Don't miss...

### Small-scale charm
Little chapels or *impérios* like this one on Terceira act as the hub of the island's exuberant religious festivals
(AT/S) pages 26 and 28

### Climbing Pico
Pico mountain in the warm evening sun (RUDS/D)
pages 220–1

## Awe-inspiring views

The coastal path on the west of Flores reveals a rocky shoreline (MS)

pages 241–7

## Tranquillity and timelessness

Farmers still use ponies to bring the milk churns down from the higher fields (SS)

## Whale and dolphin watching

Some 25 species of cetaceans have been sighted off the Azores, making the archipelago one of the world's viewing hotspots

(PJ/S) pages 60–2

# Azores in colour

*above*    Pico's wines were once sent to the Russian Tsar; now the vineyards are a UNESCO World Heritage Site and are still producing good wines (RG/S) page 225

*left*    The sometimes isolated *fajãs* of São Jorge island create striking landscapes (ABB/S) page 174

*below*    Tiny Corvo is the remotest island in the archipelago (MdA/APUA) pages 255–62

_above_    On São Miguel, many roads laid down in the early last century were landscaped with plane trees, hydrangeas, azaleas and roses (HD/S)

_right_    Beautiful Flores is renowned for its jaw-dropping waterfalls (H/D) page 243

_below_    A Faial-type windmill on Pico (RD/FLPA) page 27

## AUTHOR

**David Sayers** is a horticulturist who studied at Kew and overseas, and has spent a lifetime exploring the world for plants. Abandoning gardening after 20 years and graduating in social sciences, he worked in social policy and corporate planning, at the same time using annual leave to lead adventure/botanical holidays to the Himalayas for Thomas Cook and others. In 1982, he formed a company specialising in botanical and garden travel and for 26 years arranged and led tours worldwide. In 1984, he offered the Azores for the first time and led the first ever tour group to climb Pico and to visit São Jorge, Flores and Corvo. He now writes on botanical travel.

## UPDATER

Since giving up his career as a corporate restructurer with a global firm of accountants, **Murray Stewart** has twice updated Bradt's North Cyprus guide, updated the guide to Cape Verde and written the very first edition of *The Basque Country and Navarre*, published in April 2016. He has also been published in national travel magazines, written blogs on various destinations, contributed prize-winning travel articles online, recovered €11 million of bank debt in Spain while working as a restructuring consultant, volunteered at the Olympic Games and Commonwealth Games, worked on the National Census and taught both English and Spanish. In previous years, he visited over 55 countries, teaching English in Mexico and Chile, been interviewed by Radio Ecuador in the midst of a civil insurrection and been threatened with a beating in Bulgaria; twice he has walked over 1,000km on the Camino de Santiago pilgrims' route in France and Spain, in the process raising thousands of pounds for charity and gathering material for a future travelogue.

## ILLUSTRATOR

**Hedvika Fraser** comes from Prague and has lived in Britain for the past 40 years. Formerly a science editor and translator, a childhood fascination with orchids led to painting them in watercolour, and the charm of the Azores led her to the line drawings illustrating this guide.

## PUBLISHER'S FOREWORD    *Hilary Bradt*

Many years ago I used to visit bookshops in Europe to sell the early Bradt guides. There was (and still is) one in Brussels with the mysterious name L'Anticyclone des Azores. That was the first time I'd heard of the Azores and its climate-influencing weather patterns. Now this archipelago is known and loved by the many visitors who come for the whale watching or to walk in the green, flower-covered mountains. I've known David Sayers for almost as long as I've known that Brussels bookshop and he has had a distinctly bright and sunny influence on our island coverage! He's handed over the reins for the sixth edition to Murray Stewart, a trusted Bradt author with several of our guidebooks to his name, and Murray has done his usual meticulous job of ensuring everything is updated beautifully. I'm proud to be publishing the latest version of this successful book.

Sixth edition published November 2016. First published 2001.
Bradt Travel Guides Ltd
IDC House, The Vale, Chalfont St Peter, Bucks SL9 9RZ, England.
www.bradtguides.com
Print edition published in the USA by The Globe Pequot Press Inc,
PO Box 480, Guilford, Connecticut 06437-0480

Text copyright © 2016 David Sayers
Maps copyright © 2016 Bradt Travel Guides Ltd
Illustrations copyright © 2016 Individual photographers and artists (see below)
Project manager: Claire Strange
Cover image research: Pepi Bluck, Perfect Picture

ISBN: 978 1 78477 023 5 (print)
e-ISBN: 978 1 78477 168 3 (e-pub)
e-ISBN: 978 1 78477 268 0 (mobi)

**British Library Cataloguing in Publication Data**
A catalogue record for this book is available from the British Library

**Photographs** AWL Images: Maurício Abreu (MA/AWL), Alan Copson (AC/AWL); Azoresphotos. visitazores.com: Maurício de Abreu/DRT (MdA/APVA), Tourism Açores (TA/APVA); Carina Costa (CC); Dreamstime.com: Jaime Debrum (JD/D), H368k742 (H/D), Paweł Opaska (PO/D), Anibel Trejo (AT/D), Robert Van Der Schoot (RVDS/D); FLPA (www.flpa.co.uk): Reinhard Dirscher (RD/FLPA); 4Corners Images: Günter Gräfenhain (GG/4C); Gerby Michielsen (GM); Shutterstock.com: ABB Photo (ABBP/S), AMA (AMA/S), ArjaKo's (A/S), Henner Damke (HD/S), Rafal Gadomski (RG/S), Andrea Izzotti (AI/S), mrfotos (M/S), Anibel Trejo (AT/S); Murray Stewart (MS); SuperStock (SS)
*Front cover* View to Fajazinha, Flores Island (GG/4C)
*Back cover* Small church on Pico island (M/S); sperm whale swimming near Pico (HD/S)
*Title page* The village of São Mateus da Calheta, Terceira (H/D); Império da Caridade, Angra da Heroísmo (AT/D); Lagoa do Fogo volcanic lake, São Miguel (A/S)

**Illustrations** Hedvika Fraser

**Maps** David McCutcheon FBCart.S; includes map data © OpenStreetMap contributors

Typeset by www.dataworks.co.in
Production managed by Jellyfish Print Solutions; printed in India
Digital conversion by www.dataworks.co.in

# Foreword

*By Ben Fogle*

For me the Azores represents a bite-sized piece of a national identity. The islands offer a taste of Portugal wrapped up in their own unique Atlantic geography and geology. The island archipelago has been described as like heaven and hell: defined both by a lush green environment and by the fiery belly of the earth.

It's a heady mix that can overwhelm the senses. Birds, plants, whales and dolphins, combined with Portuguese architecture, are akin to heaven; sulphurous water bubbling up from deep underground, thick volcanic ash and pumice that blanket vast swathes of land, and black lava flows, frozen like fossils that dip into the turgid Atlantic Ocean, are all reminiscent of hell.

It is truly astonishing to think that these islands emerged from the ocean relatively recently in geological terms and that all the flora and fauna are immigrants, migrating halfway across the Atlantic, borne on the ocean current or in the wind.

The Azores is a hauntingly beautiful chain of nine islands spread over more than 600km of ocean, halfway between Lisbon and New York. In some ways the Azores is to Portugal what the Outer Hebrides is to Scotland – a remote archipelago many miles offshore – but there the similarities end. Where the Hebrides are flat, sandy isles, the Azores islands are rugged and volcanic, dominated by their geology and influenced by the warm Gulf Stream that has created an ecosystem unlike anywhere else.

The Azores High is responsible for the unique ecology of this archipelago. This area of high pressure is semi-permanent and ensures the islands are more tropical than you might expect. It combines with the warm ocean currents of the Gulf Stream, creating a subtropical climate.

Ponta da Ferraria must rate as one of the greatest places in the world for a saltwater swim. A natural swimming pool formed by lava lies next to the ocean but is heated by a bubbling spring that pumps water into the pool at 61°C. Indeed, the water in the pool is too hot to swim in at low tide and is only cool enough when it mixes with crashing Atlantic waves that tumble in at high tide, bringing the temperature down to a comfortable 28°C. It is the perfect combination of exhilaration and relaxation.

One of the most memorable experiences for me was my first visit to Terra Nostra Garden on São Miguel, the main island. In 1770, Thomas Hickling built a summer house on a small hill overlooking a thermal-spring swimming pool. Thirty acres of rich gardens were planted in the ensuing years, and now there are more than 2,500 trees, abundant ferns, a formal flower garden, a garden devoted to cycads and another to camellias. The garden thrives in the subtropical climate and it is now simply breathtaking.

Not far away is Furnas where boiling pools and steaming vents offer a portal to Middle Earth. For decades, if not centuries, families have come here to cook the famous *cozido nas caldeiras* in huge pots buried in the volcanic sand; prized cooking spots are passed down from generation to generation. Holes about a metre deep have been dug into the hot earth into which a container is lowered. Filled with different meats, sausage, vegetables, kale, potato and cabbage, the pot is left to cook gently for seven hours. The long, slow simmer ensures that meat becomes tender and flavours meld. This simple form of cooking, in my eyes, is symbolic of how the land and the geology have shaped the unique culture and heritage of these islands.

Volcanic activity has, of course, cast, moulded and created these unique islands, and Faial is an example of how the Azores has been changed by the power of the earth. The western tip of the island exemplifies this, its entire landscape formed by the great eruption in 1957–58. Walking on this moon-like terrain is like stepping onto another planet. On the face of it, it is a bleak, soulless place, but it takes on a gritty beauty that overcomes most visitors.

Perhaps one of the most iconic activities in the Azores is to climb the summit of the tallest peak, Pico mountain, at 2,351m. The 5km journey begins at Cabeço das Cabras at 1,231m. The difficulty of the ascent varies according to the weather, but the views from the summit are well worth the 6-hour round trip. No matter how many mountains you have climbed there is something utterly mesmerising about looking out over thousands of miles of ocean and cloud below.

Most people associate the Azores with whales. Indeed, the ocean around the islands offers one of the best habitats in the world for marine mammals and more than 24 species have been identified off the coast. For many years, until the 1980s, sperm whales were hunted commercially in the Azores from small boats with hand-held harpoons. Fortunately, today whale hunting has been replaced by whale watching. Short-finned pilot whales and sperm whales are the most common in the Azores and can be seen all year round.

Early one morning on my last trip I headed out to sea in a fast rigid inflatable boat. Dressed in wet-weather gear to protect me from the ocean spray, I travelled out deep into the Atlantic Ocean. The boat leapt from wave to wave, directed from the same observation huts used by the hunters of previous decades. The difference was that I was armed with a camera rather than a harpoon gun.

There can be few sights as moving as that of a breaching sperm whale. These marine mammals can measure up to 20m and are surprisingly elusive considering their size. Persevere, however, and you will be rewarded with an experience that will, quite literally, take your breath away.

Whale watching, swimming, bathing in hot springs, eating volcano-cooked food, mountain biking, kayaking, walking, birdwatching, visiting tea plantations, island hopping … the list of eco-friendly activities available on the Azores is endless. In an era when more and more people are looking for something different from their holiday, the islands of the Azores really are at the forefront of the 'natural' travel movement.

*Ben Fogle*

# Acknowledgements

I am much indebted to Albano Cymbron and increasingly to his daughter Catarina, of the Melo Agency in Ponta Delgada, for facts, insights and contributions about Azorean life and history and for their unstinted time and practical support. Also to them go my thanks for invaluable introductions to kind and generous people throughout the islands who have helped me in so many different ways. To Helena Carvalho and Cristina Valcorba in the Melo office for their continuing help. Finally to this stalwart team, my thanks for making all my travel arrangements.

For invaluable textual contributions to this guide and for their time and interest I am most grateful to Dr Isabel Soares de Albergaria from São Miguel who contributed the pages on art and architecture and thus revealed some of the treasures that might otherwise have remained hidden; to António Pedroso from São Jorge for providing many cultural anecdotes; to Monique Cymbron from São Miguel for her Azorean kitchen; to Luis Silva for delving into the history of the Azorean cow; and to geologist Pedro Freire of Geo-fun in Ponta Delgada who generously gave his knowledge and time to steer me through the lava flows of volcanic history.

Vital practical support was given by the Azores Regional Directorate of Tourism in Horta, whose continuing interest in this guide I gratefully acknowledge. I am indebted to Sunvil for international flights, to Azores Airlines for domestic flights, and to hoteliers for their generous hospitality throughout the islands and especially Hotel Talisman in Ponta Delgada and Casa do António in Velas. Following earlier editions I remain amazed and thankful at the patience of Sandra Dart of the Azores Regional Tourism Office for her continuing prompt replies to my many emails. My thanks also go to the local tourism officers on Pico, Santa Maria, Flores and Graciosa, and especially to Rui Costa on Terceira for unfailing help and long friendship. Also to Katt Rita on Corvo.

For all the illustrations and for her indulgent support at home during my many and often extended visits to the islands, I express heartfelt thanks to my partner Hedvika Fraser.

Lastly, and central to the whole project, the ebullient team at Bradt Travel Guides.

*David Sayers*

To many, many Azorean islanders, I am greatly indebted for unstinting assistance in the update of this book.

First of all, however, a big thank you to David Sayers for providing such a wealth of knowledge and expertise in the first five editions of this guidebook to the Azorean archipelago. His sterling work is reflected in the fact that much of the text regarding geology, botany and history remains blissfully untouched in this latest edition.

For effortlessly pulling together a complex logistical schedule and supporting me in my research, I would like to thank Ian Coates and Dilys Riley at Archipelago Choice in the United Kingdom. On the islands themselves, too many people to list enabled me to quickly absorb the island culture and its nuances. For special assistance on São Miguel, let me express my gratitude to Maria João Gouveia, Carina Costa, Gerby Michielsen and Pedro Freire; on Graciosa, to Marta Quadros; on Terceira to Tiago Fortuna; António Pedroso on São Jorge; Stefano Folgaria on Flores; Manuel and Kathy Rita on Corvo; Serge Viallelle on Pico and Alan Vittery and Miguel Henrique on Santa Maria. Thanks also to the various tourist offices across the islands and the various hotels that so kindly supported me.

At Bradt, many thanks to Adrian Phillips and Rachel Fielding for the opportunity and to Tom Jordan and Claire Strange for editorial expertise.

And of course, a huge thanks to my dear friend Sara Lister for her support throughout.

*Murray Stewart*

## FEEDBACK REQUEST AND UPDATES WEBSITE

At Bradt Travel Guides we're aware that guidebooks start to go out of date on the day they're published – and that you, our readers, are out there in the field doing research of your own. You'll find out before us when a fine new family-run hotel opens or a favourite restaurant changes hands and goes downhill. So why not write and tell us about your experiences? Contact us on ☏ 01753 893444 or ✉ info@bradtguides.com. We will forward emails to the author who may post updates on the Bradt website at www.bradtupdates.com/azores. Alternatively you can add a review of the book to www.bradtguides.com or Amazon.

# Contents

## LIST OF MAPS

## KEY TO SYMBOLS

| | | | | |
|---|---|---|---|---|
| ═══ | Expressway | | † | Church/cathedral |
| ══ | Main road | | ⅄ | Campsite |
| ══ | Other road | | ✽ | Garden etc |
| ------ | Track/4x4 | | ► | Golf course |
| ·········· | Featured footpath | | ⚲ | Lighthouse |
| ·········· | Other footpath | | ⤢ | Beach |
| ⫟⫠⫟ | Tunnel | | ⤴ | Swimming |
| ------ | Ferry route | | ⤳ | Birdwatching |
| ⛴ | Passenger ferry | | ⌒ | Cave/grotto |
| ✈ ✈ | Airport (international/domestic) | | ≋ | Waterfall |
| ⛟ | Taxis | | ♣ | Woodland |
| ⛽ | Filling station/garage | | ▲ | Summit (height in metres) |
| ℹ | Tourist information | | ⌣ | Fortifications/city walls |
| ⚱ | Museum/art gallery | | ⊙ | Volcanic crater |
| ⊞ | Important/historic building | | ⊛ | Stadium |
| ⛫ | Castle/fortification | | ⸽⸽ | Runway |
| ⊠ | Post office | | ⸬ | Protected area/reserve |
| ⊞ | Hospital/clinic etc | | ⣿ | Urban park |
| ✚ | Health centre/pharmacy | | ▨ | Market |

# Introduction

*by David Sayers*

It is perhaps strange to think there is a cluster of nine small islands, isolated but thriving, lying between Lisbon and New York and surrounded by the great Atlantic Ocean.

Very much part of Europe and members of the European Union, they have many of the accoutrements of modern life: the latest fashion trainers, cars, second homes, and the very latest communications technology connecting home computers with the internet.

Yet few people are aware of the existence of the Azores and many of those who are hold an image of dry, sun-baked volcanic islands like Lanzarote in the Canaries. And they almost always assume they belong to Spain.

The Azores are Europe's best-kept secret: verdant, tranquil, diverse, exquisitely beautiful, always welcoming. Further south and close to the African coast lies Madeira, Portugal's more familiar Atlantic island; sunnier and with less rain and cloud but considerably more developed for tourism, and famous for its well-promoted flowers and gardens. It was going to Madeira that aroused my curiosity about those other far-off islands; a flight from Funchal took me to Ponta Delgada, and back to an ambience that possibly could have been found in Madeira half a century ago. One needs to take the Azores at their own speed. Fight it, and you will be frustrated; relax along with it and you will return a different person. Old-World courtesy prevails, a reminder of the many tiny niceties of life that have been sacrificed to the exigencies of faster lifestyles.

Since they were first settled in the 15th century, each island has developed at a different speed, depending upon the quality of its harbour, terrain, crops, and its distance from the others. Today this is reflected in their diversity, each island offering the visitor its own individual character that makes the Azores such a varied entity.

All the islands are green, the flowers are mostly sophisticated and subtle, the gardens are steeped in history and, like the flowers, are more cerebral than flamboyant. While some main towns have their roads and traffic, just a short distance away men ride horses to their pastures and pony carts filled with milk churns clatter over cobbles. Flashing neon lights are rare, streets are narrow, shops modest and in keeping with the streetscape, coffee bars are numerous while nightclubs are few. The islands reflect their turbulent geological past and offer rural landscapes enhanced by rocky or precipitous coasts surrounded by an often travel-brochure-blue sea. Religious and secular festivals riot through the calendar and touch the lives of every island and islander. There are sailing regattas, golf tournaments, big-game fishing tournaments, cycle races, car rallies and other events that come as rather a surprise and largely leave the non-enthusiasts in happy oblivion. There is so much to explore, so much to experience; these islands should be savoured like a rare wine.

*David Sayers*

For me the Azores were an immediate *coup de foudre*. The scenery is very beautiful, I could never tire of walking the hills, there is an interesting flora, the geology is fascinating, the natives are extra friendly, and there is blissful peace. I was spending months each year in distant countries where travel is hard work, and to suddenly find all the natural attractions with the wonderful bonus of good coffee, excellent wines, a comfortable bed and easy flight seemed a paradise. It still does, even after 30 years. The long-established Azorean travel agent Albano Cymbron and I pioneered a series of walks (and even marked the routes with blobs of red paint), and in 1991, wrote and jointly published a modest guide to six of the islands. We sold 2,000 copies. A year later I was invited to advise on the restoration of the Terra Nostra garden in Furnas, one of the great gems of Azorean heritage. This developed into a major project, and from there came two more garden restorations, this time for the Ponta Delgada Municipality. Friendships have matured over the years, and the islands remain as lovely as ever – what more could one wish for. Now three entire islands have been recognised by UNESCO as Biosphere Reserves for their balance between man, nature and sustainable development. Someone else must have fallen in love with the Azores!

I hope this guide will help you discover some of the hidden delights of this little-known cluster of islands, and that you will have a memorable holiday. And maybe go back again!

## A NOTE ON MAPS

**KEYS AND SYMBOLS** Maps include alphabetical keys covering the locations of those places to stay, eat or drink that are featured in the book. Note that regional maps may not show all hotels and restaurants in the area: other establishments may be located in towns shown on the map.

**GRIDS AND GRID REFERENCES** Several maps use gridlines to allow easy location of sites. Map grid references are listed in square brackets after the name of the place or site of interest in the text, with page number followed by grid number, eg: [70 C3].

On occasion, hotels or restaurants that are not listed in the guide (but which might serve as alternative options if required or serve as useful landmarks to aid navigation) are also included on the maps; these are marked with accommodation (🏠) or restaurant (✗) symbols.

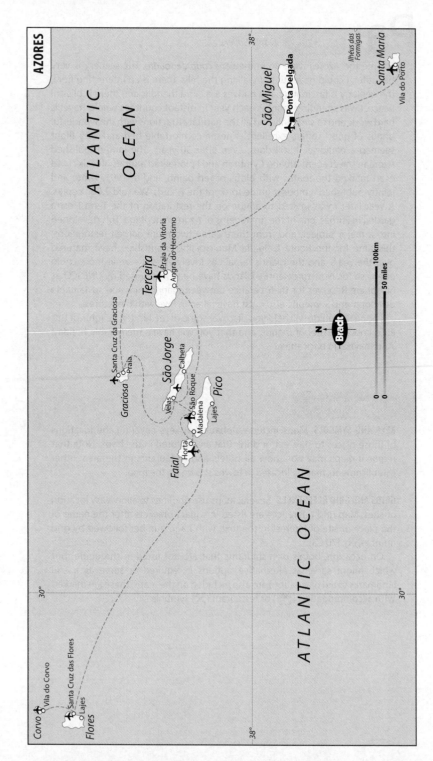

AZORES

ATLANTIC OCEAN

ATLANTIC OCEAN

Corvo ✈ Vila do Corvo
Flores
Santa Cruz das Flores ✈
Lajes

Graciosa ✈
Santa Cruz da Graciosa
Praia

São Jorge
Velas ✈
Calheta
São Roque
Madalena ✈
Pico
Lajes
Faial
Horta ✈

Terceira
Praia da Vitória
Angra do Heroísmo

São Miguel
Ponta Delgada ✈

Ilhéus das Formigas
Santa Maria ✈
Vila do Porto

N

Bradt

100km
50 miles

38°

30°

30°

38°

# Part One

## GENERAL INFORMATION

**Islands** São Miguel, Santa Maria, Terceira, Graciosa, São Jorge, Faial, Pico, Flores, Corvo

**Location** In the Atlantic Ocean, approximately 1,500km from Lisbon and 3,900km from the east coast of North America

**Size** Nine islands varying in size from 17km$^2$ (Corvo) to 746km$^2$ (São Miguel), spread across some 600km of ocean

**Climate** Temperate, maritime climate with agreeable temperatures ranging from 13–14°C in January/February to 22–23°C in July/August. Rain throughout the year; light cloud common.

**Status** Autonomous region of Portugal

**Population** 247,000 (census 2011)

**Economy** Major earners are beef, dairy products, fishing and tourism

**Language** Portuguese

**Religion** Roman Catholic

**Currency** Euro

**Rate of exchange** £1 = €1.18, US$1 = €0.90 (September 2016)

**Time** GMT −1; 4 hours later than US Eastern Standard Time

**Electricity** 220 volts

**International telephone code** +351

**Flag** Blue and white block colour. At the centre is a goshawk, with nine golden stars, one for each island. In the left corner is the national coat of arms.

**Coat of arms** The shield is silver with a red border, and includes a goshawk and nine golden stars.

**National anthem** *Hino da Região Autónoma dos Açores* (*Anthem to Autonomy*)

**Motto** *Antes morrer livres que em paz sujeitos* ('Better to die free than live enslaved')

**Public holidays** See page 57

# 1

# Background Information

## GEOGRAPHY AND CLIMATE

**LOCATION** The nine islands of the Azores – the westernmost point of Europe – are spread over some 600km of ocean (the Economic Free Zone is about 940km²) and are located roughly 1,500km or two hours' flying time from Lisbon and about 3,900km or five hours from the east coast of North America. Running along a southeast to northwest axis, they lie on either side of the line of latitude that links Lisbon with New York, and are between latitudes 36–39°N and longitudes 25–31°W. The total population is approximately 247,000. The islands separate conveniently into three groups: the Eastern Group of São Miguel and Santa Maria; the Central Group of Terceira, Graciosa, São Jorge, Pico and Faial; and the Western Group of Flores and Corvo. The islands closest to each other are Pico and Faial at just 6km apart. In area, they range from Corvo at 17km² to São Miguel at 746km². Highest altitudes vary from 412m on Graciosa to 2,351m on Pico.

**CLIMATE** For small islands the weather, especially when in the middle of a large ocean, is all-important. For the busy city worker, as everywhere, the weather impacts little on a daily basis, and for the visitor rain is but a passing nuisance. However, for Azorean farmers even a relatively short dry period causes problems because the volcanic soils are very quick-draining, while a rough sea means the coastal fishermen cannot go out, there is no income for them, and no fresh fish for the villages.

The Azores have a mild and equable climate, surrounded as they are by a huge expanse of sea and influenced by the warm Gulf Stream. This means that the temperature is pleasant at any time of year. The average winter temperature is 13°C, only sometimes dropping to around 4°C at night; frosts occur only above 1,000m. In summer, the average temperature is 23°C, with a maximum of 27°C.

Rain can and does fall in every month, but it is seldom persistent; and one can drive from rain through a world of rainbows into sunshine. If it is raining in the morning, do not despair – there could be clear skies and sunshine by lunchtime. Of course, the reverse is often true! The annual rainfall increases westwards and ranges from 700mm in Ponta Delgada on São Miguel to 1,600mm in Santa Cruz on Flores. Average humidity is around 80–85%, but can go up to 100%. Flowers love it! Many days are still or with a gentle breeze. However, winds can occasionally be strong and this is especially noticeable on exposed mountains. A winter gale can also bring an invigorating chill, but the scudding clouds and turbulent seas can be inspiring for the visitor. Snow can sometimes be seen on Pico's summit, even in April.

For swimmers, the sea temperatures also vary relatively little and you will often see people bathing off the beaches throughout the winter, when the lowest sea temperatures are 15–16°C in February and March. The highest are in August and September, with an average of around 22–24°C, and are still a welcoming 21°C in October.

**AVERAGE MINIMUM TEMPERATURES IN °C**

| Jan | Feb | Mar | Apr | May | Jun | Jul | Aug | Sep | Oct | Nov | Dec |
|-----|-----|-----|-----|-----|-----|-----|-----|-----|-----|-----|-----|
| 11  | 10  | 11  | 11  | 13  | 15  | 16  | 17  | 17  | 15  | 13  | 12  |

**AVERAGE MAXIMUM TEMPERATURES IN °C**

| Jan | Feb | Mar | Apr | May | Jun | Jul | Aug | Sep | Oct | Nov | Dec |
|-----|-----|-----|-----|-----|-----|-----|-----|-----|-----|-----|-----|
| 16  | 16  | 16  | 17  | 19  | 21  | 23  | 25  | 24  | 21  | 18  | 17  |

**AVERAGE SEA TEMPERATURE IN °C**

| Jan | Feb | Mar | Apr | May | Jun | Jul | Aug | Sep | Oct | Nov | Dec |
|-----|-----|-----|-----|-----|-----|-----|-----|-----|-----|-----|-----|
| 16  | 16  | 16  | 16  | 17  | 19  | 22  | 23  | 23  | 21  | 19  | 18  |

Source: www.weather2travel.com

# NATURAL HISTORY AND CONSERVATION

It was not until the middle of the 19th century that the first studies of the flora, fauna and oceanographics took place, when the Azores were frequently visited by scientists. In 1841 and 1845, the British war vessel HMS *Styx*, led by Captain Vidal, undertook hydrographic studies of the Azores, drawing up the first map where the islands appear correctly surveyed and with their positions correctly given. HMS *Beagle* stopped in Terceira and São Miguel on its return from voyaging round the world, enabling Charles Darwin to make shore excursions. In 1850, HMS *Rattlesnake*, on the way home from a four-year voyage surveying the Coral Sea and the New Guinea coast, sailed into Horta for six days' recuperation. It had taken almost nine weeks to travel from the Falkland Islands, their last landfall, and the islands' plentiful supplies were much needed for the health of the crew and passengers. The ship's assistant surgeon and naturalist was Thomas Huxley, who later famously defended Darwin and his theory of evolution; during their week in port, he made the ascent of Pico. Prince Albert I of Monaco (1848–1922) stayed several times on the islands making oceanographic studies, then a new scientific discipline, and exploring the caldera on Graciosa. There are references to these studies in the Oceanographic Museum in Monaco.

Many of the remaining patches of native vegetation are now in protected zones and you might see notices to this effect. The vegetation of the islands, particularly on Pico, Terceira and São Miguel, is interesting not only because it represents communities that were once widespread in parts of Europe millions of years ago, but also because very few aspects of its ecology and biology have been studied and the opportunities for simple observation and research are considerable. There is a desire to know what is happening in amongst the evergreens. Many stretches of coastal cliff are protected zones, mostly for seabirds; again you might see the signs. The marine environment is similarly protected.

You may be curious to know what the yellow plastic traps are for that you may see around the islands. These are pheromone traps for the rather colourful iridescent copper and green Japanese beetle, a very serious pest about 15mm long and 10mm wide. Not a problem in its native Japan, where there are natural predators, it was accidentally introduced into the USA in the early 1900s and in the 1970s arrived in the Azores, thought to be from a military aircraft landing at Lajes on Terceira.

The larval stage is mostly spent in lawns and pastureland feeding on roots, and the adult eats the foliage of many plants including vines, roses, oak and fruit trees.

**GEOLOGY** The archipelago is formed from the upper sections of volcanoes. In the mid-Atlantic, tectonic plates are pulling apart on the ocean bed. The gap between them is filled by molten volcanic material that rises from the Earth's mantle and continuously forms new oceanic crust. This extrusion wells up and forms an enormous underwater mountain chain or mid-ocean ridge, and the sea floor spreads. The **Mid-Atlantic Ridge** runs from the Arctic to the Antarctic, meeting on its way the Indian Ocean Ridge off the southern tip of Africa. Along its length lie Iceland, the largest landmass created from oceanic crust, the Azores, Ascension, Saint Helena and Tristan da Cunha islands. Mid-ocean ridges occur beneath all our major oceans, and only in exceptional cases are there so many eruptions that they build up to appear above sea level and form islands. Much more frequent activity occurs under the ocean's surface on the seabed than is seen on the surface of the islands. Seamounts constantly rise and fall, and new lava pressure ridges are formed.

In the Azores, giant linear ridges have been created, conspicuously Pico and São Jorge, and these are among the largest such volcanic ridges actively forming anywhere on our planet. With the ocean floor roughly between 1,000m and 3,000m below sea level, it is fun to try to imagine the landscape that would confront the traveller if the Atlantic Ocean could be emptied.

The situation is more complicated because, near the Azores, three plates meet in a T-shaped triple junction. The North American, African and Eurasian plates meet at a point between the Western and Central groups of islands, between Flores and Faial. Flores and Corvo are on the North American Plate. The Mid-Atlantic Ridge forms two legs of the 'T' and the other islands are alongside a spreading centre called the **Terceira Rift**, formed about 36 million years ago. It is not certain on which plates, African or Eurasian, the remaining islands belong or whether some might be on an Azorean microplate.

The seismic tremors felt in the islands are mostly caused by magma flowing up through the cracks left in the Earth's crust as the plates separate. At times these

## A DICTIONARY OF AZOREAN TERRAIN

For newcomers to the Azores, translation of a few key words that regularly appear on maps may help to understand the geography. Here are the most common:

*caldeira* – caldera (volcanic crater)
*canada* – path, trail
*furna* – cave, grotto
*fajã* – piece of flat coastal land (created by lava flow or landslip)
*gruta* – cave, grotto
*lajes* (plural of *laje*) – lit rooftops
*lomba* – ridge (of mountain)
*miradouro* – viewpoint
*pico* – summit of mountain
*praia* – beach
*quinta* – manor house, farm, estate
*ribeira* – small river, stream
*serra* – mountain range

Of the few things generally known about the Azores, the 'Azores High' probably tops the list. This is an area of high pressure or anticyclone that is semi-permanent.

Very simply, warm moist air rises over the tropics leading to low pressure there; this warm moist air then moves north towards the subtropical latitudes and cools. It then descends, increasing the pressure over the subtropical latitudes, at the same time becoming drier and resulting in largely clear skies. This tropical/subtropical circulation varies little in position; in summer it is more northerly, in winter and spring more southerly, usually lying to the south or southwest of the archipelago. This high-pressure belt is part of the global circulatory system and is called the Hadley cell. In the north Atlantic it is centred close to the Azores for most of the time, hence the 'Azores High'. The reason it is centred there is because the Azores lie roughly midway between the influence of the African and American continents. Landmasses distort the process and strong summer heating at these latitudes can cause, for example, low pressure in the northern summer over southeast Asia and India and bring monsoon rains. Surface layers of the ocean do not heat up in the same way as the land does, and therefore allow the high-pressure belt to persist.

Sometimes the 'Azores High' extends northeast towards the British Isles, especially when they have a good summer. In winter it can sometimes recede southwards, if the jet stream is also further south. Occasionally it disappears altogether to be replaced by low pressure, while often, at the same time, high pressure dominates northern Europe, giving cold weather in winter and hot, often eventually thundery, weather in summer.

In the Azores the weather is influenced by the strength and location of this high, particularly in summer. A strong high gives pleasant, warm weather with

tremors, measuring less than 5.0 on the Richter scale, will occur with surprising frequency. Six of the islands have all been subject to **eruptions and earthquakes** within recent history, but the remaining three, Santa Maria, Flores and Corvo, are now considered inactive.

Of the central and eastern islands, Santa Maria was the first to rise above the sea some five million years ago but changes in sea level and tectonic activity caused it to submerge. A million years later, the Formigas islets and what is now the eastern end of São Miguel rose above the sea and Santa Maria reappeared. It was during this period of submergence that the island acquired its marine fossils, the only island to have them. The oldest part of São Miguel is around Pico da Vara in the east; at the far western end, Sete Cidades began around 290,000 years ago, at the same time as Água de Pau started out from the ocean bed. Thus São Miguel was once two islands, only becoming united when the Picos region north of what is now Ponta Delgada began a long series of eruptions starting 50,000 years ago. Terceira, Graciosa, São Jorge and Faial are all younger than a million years, Pico being the youngest at a mere 300,000 years or less. The two western isles, Flores and Corvo, lie on the western flanks of the Mid-Atlantic Ridge; the oldest rocks on Flores date to around 2.5 million years and are below sea level; the youngest are about 3,000 years old.

In 1811, about a mile off the coast of São Miguel opposite Ferraria, a new island appeared. One hundred metres tall and about 1.5km long, it took about a month to create. The British frigate *Sabrina* was in the area and her commanding officer, Captain Tillard, landed on the still-steaming island, planted a Union Jack, named the island '**Sabrina**' and claimed it as British territory! Unfortunately for his little wind. A weak high gives weather that is changeable and wet, and you can tell when a depression is coming by a sudden drop in the barometer and a southerly wind, veering from southwest to northwest. A low approaches with steadily lowering and thickening cloud. The wind increases, bringing heavier cloud and rain showers, and then often torrential rain, by which time all sight of any nearby island has vanished. Then comes a break, the wind changes direction, and blue skies return. Finally, it all calms down, and the high reasserts itself. This drama might sometimes be over within a few hours and, if you are on land with a good vantage point, it can be fun to watch the rain squalls skating across the ocean. Winds come from the west, travelling eastwards, and this is reflected in the higher rainfall of the Western Group. In early summer, winds are mainly from the southwest and by July and August are predominantly northeasterly, gentle and with frequent calms. By September they return to the southwest and become gradually stronger. Occasionally bad storms hit the islands, but mostly they follow a narrow path. As you drive round the islands from time to time you will see cryptomeria trees snapped off like broken toothpicks.

Another major climatic influence on the Azores is the ocean currents, especially those originating from the Gulf Stream. This is a movement of warm water of equatorial and tropical origin into the colder northern waters of the Atlantic. West of the Azores, the Gulf Stream splits into two main branches: the North Atlantic Current that passes north of the islands, and the Azores Current passing to the south. This Gulf Stream gives the Azores their warm temperate climate. A further complication is the North Atlantic Oscillation (NAO), a northern equivalent of El Niño, which concerns atmospheric circulation.

credibility, when the next surveyors arrived, there was no trace of the island; in just four months the sea had washed it away and all that remains now is a bank 40m below sea level. Most recently, in 1957, an eruption began just off the west coast of Faial that added a further 2km² of land to that island.

More information about the volcanoes and how the islands were formed is given in the chapters on the individual islands. See also www.azoresgeopark.com, the website of the Azores Geopark Association, a non-profit association established in 2010 and based in Horta with wide objectives concerning the environment, socio-economic, cultural and sustainable balanced development of the Azores. A geopark is a defined area with an exceptional geological heritage that is a base promoting the population's wellbeing at the same time as respecting the environment. There is a network of Geosites on the nine islands and surrounding sea floor representing the geodiversity of the archipelago, and the website lists the principal sites together with various tourist routes (these are yet to be fully developed).

**COLONISATION** Oceanic islands such as the Azores differ from continental islands in that they are usually basaltic volcanoes, distant from the mainland and surrounded by vast oceans. They have to gain their flora and fauna by invasion, unlike continental islands that are close to geologically diverse landmasses to which they were once attached. The flora and fauna of an oceanic island is therefore distinct because it is made up of those organisms that can cross oceans. This barrier filters out many potential colonists so that the Azores lack certain groups, such as mammals (excluding bats), that are important on the mainland.

Not only has half the Atlantic Ocean to be crossed to reach the Azores from the nearest land, but on arrival landfall is extremely tough, on a new, raw, volcanic island presenting hardened flows of lava or desert-like ash. How tough a challenge it is to colonise new ash deposits can be seen at Capelinhos on Faial. This area was engulfed and enlarged by an eruption in 1957. When you stand by the remains of the old lighthouse and the wind drives sharp volcanic sand into your face with stinging force, look at the few plants that are establishing. There is *Arundo donax*, planted and artificially aided by humans, and the human-sponsored evening primrose. Left entirely to nature, colonisation takes a long time.

Winds and sea brought life to the Azores. Ocean currents transported marine organisms and shoreline animals to scavenge and survive upon what the sea washed ashore, along with others such as land crabs that have a marine larval stage. Travelling on prevailing winds and also the jet stream came spores of ferns, algae, fungi, lichens and mosses, seeds and microscopic animals, even spiders and other insects. All lightweight and adapted to wind dispersal, they landed in the Azores, even falling to earth in raindrops. Ground-nesting seabirds deposited their guano, providing further food for scavenging invertebrates and micro-organisms while rain slowly washed out minerals from the lava, all helping to create a very fertile soil. Currents, prevailing winds and distance from landmasses all influence which organisms will become established on an island, and where they, or their ancestors, came from. Land birds that have wandered or been blown off course by storms will bring seeds, either in their stomachs or attached to their bodies. For the early colonists, survival would have been a harsh process, but it needed only some to succeed.

Slowly these first organisms changed the bare habitat by contributing organic matter to form soil. By retaining moisture, and modifying light, temperature and exposure, they enabled later arrivals to establish, thus slowly creating a more hospitable environment which in turn would allow further colonists to establish. They had to be adaptable, able to adjust to climatic variations and different food sources, and to survive both competition from other species and many other challenges in a new habitat. Variation in some species may have allowed them to adapt better to the conditions, thus leading over time to new species and subspecies. Today, there are 60 endemic plant species in the Azores, unique to the islands and found nowhere else in the world.

The Azores, along with the other archipelagos of Madeira, the Savage Islands, the Canaries and the Cape Verdes, comprise the region known as Macaronesia. The most characteristic vegetation is the dense evergreen forest, or laurisilva. It is a representative relic of the evergreen forests that grew in late Tertiary times (around 2.75 million years ago) in what is now southern Europe and northwest Africa. Possibly because of the Azores' oceanic climate, these forests escaped the extremes of climatic changes and thus survived while elsewhere they became extinct.

Colonisation and evolution never cease. New plants will arrive – see *Two bullies*, pages 10–11 and others will be eliminated by changing circumstances. Islands are living laboratories where the processes of dispersal, immigration, establishment, adaptation and extinction can all be studied. These are just some of the reasons why areas need to be protected from human depredation so that they may be there for future generations of students and provide an account of the changes going on around us.

**THE VEGETATION** The dense evergreen forest that once covered much of the islands has long been cleared for agriculture and settlement. Visually the quite extensive plantations of the exotic conifer *Cryptomeria japonica* now add considerably to the aesthetics of the Azorean landscape since tree cover within the lifetime of elderly islanders has been very considerably less than it is today. Planted to reduce erosion, lessen water loss, provide shelter for cattle and produce timber, these plantations are a substantial if sometimes controversial plus. Emigration has left many previously cultivated areas abandoned, to be invaded by a mix of native *Myrica faya*, *Erica azorica* and introduced and subsequently naturalised *Pittosporum undulatum* and, encouragingly, some other **native species** such as the endemic *Picconia azorica*. There is a tremendous battle raging, because *Myrica faya* is light-demanding, and must fight with the pittosporum for survival.

The native vegetation remains in a number of isolated areas. Evergreen forest is found as remnant forest or as individual species surviving in hedgerows above the 500m contour. The quite different coastal region of steep cliffs, of lava flows, agricultural land and seashore have their own mix of native, endemic and introduced exotic species.

The Azores archipelago has a total of 850 or more **plant species**, most of which have been introduced by humans. Of the total, some 300 are native, and of these possibly 60 species are endemic, found nowhere else in the world. Of the 11 species of native trees, eight are endemic to the Azores, and two others are found elsewhere only in Madeira. Dominant species of the forest include holly (*Ilex perado* ssp. *azorica*), juniper (*Juniperus brevifolia*), tree heather (*Erica azorica*) and laurel (*Laurus azorica*). Growing in the mountains at altitudes where the hillsides are often embraced by cloud, such vegetation is called **cloudforest**; often the trunks and branches are adorned with epiphytic ferns, while bryophytes (mosses and liverworts) can be exuberant, sometimes even thriving on the leaves as epiphylls.

The largest area remaining of undisturbed forest is on Terceira, on the Caldeira de Santa Bárbara and a small area between Juncal, Pico Alto and Serra do Labaçal, not the easiest to access. The forests of the Caldeira de Santa Bárbara, at over 800m, are often cloud-covered and are largely dominated by juniper (*Juniperus brevifolia*), although all of the Azorean tree species can be found in gullies and other places. Areas of natural grassland are to be seen inside the caldera and endemic grasses such as fescue (*Festuca jubata*) and soft-grass *Holcus rigidus* are to be found growing with endemic herbaceous species such as *Tolpis azorica*. However, the caldera is a reserved area and to visit one should contact the Mountaineering Society in Angra do Heroísmo (page 148) and book a local guide as there are no trails and the weather can suddenly close in within 20 minutes.

São Miguel's only remaining area of natural forest can at least be easily seen! It is to be found at the eastern end of the island, and covers about 600ha on Pico da Vara.

Pico island has the most accessible of all native forest, although little remains and that in small patches, often where the ground is badly tumbled with small boulder-sized lava and has therefore escaped the predations of farmer and cattle. There are patches of *Viburnum tinus* ssp. *subcordatum*, *Euphorbia stygiana*, *Ilex perado*, *Vaccinium cylindraceum*, *Frangula azorica*, *Hedera helix* ssp. *canariensis*, *Juniperus brevifolia* and its green-branched parasite *Arceuthobium azoricum* and occasionally, in the loose gravel at the edge of the asphalt road, *Thymus caespititius*.

The coastal flora has been badly disturbed by numerous developments and in places by the escape and spread of garden ornamentals such as the several members of the succulent Aizoaceae. However, while some of the species are endangered, none is on the verge of extinction and all are to be found, often in places where one least expects them, and in the most inhospitable sites. All the islands have suitable habitats. Characteristic species include the endemic grass *Festuca petraea* and the rush *Juncus acutus*. Widely located but found in small concentrations by the coast is

*Gerby Michielsen*

At one time given little attention as a birdwatching destination, the Azores are now seen as an excellent choice for the observation of avian species. For keen birdwatchers, the starting point in the archipelago are two of Europe's rarest birds, the Azorean bullfinch (*Pyrrhula murina*), endemic to a small area of São Miguel island (page 109), and the Monteiro's storm petrel (*Oceanodroma monteiroi*), which breeds only on two tiny islets lying off the south of Graciosa. May and the end of August/beginning of September are the best times to join a pelagic tour to search for this elusive storm petrel, with opportunities to sight other seabirds like the Macaronesian shearwater (*Puffinus baroli*), band-rumped storm petrel (*Oceanodroma castro*), Bulwer's petrel (*Bulweria bulwerii*), Zino's petrel (*Pterodroma madeira*), and Fea's petrel (*Pterodroma feae*). Pelagic tours can also be organised on São Miguel (page 110).

Other species that are well worth a trip to the archipelago to see are the Atlantic canary (*Serinus canaria*), an exclusive species from Macaronesia, as well as several subspecies such as the common chaffinch (*Fringilla coelebs moreletti*), three different subspecies of goldcrest, the Azores woodpigeon (*Columba palumbus azorica*), and the common buzzard (*Buteo buteo rothschildi*).

Currently, the Azores hold the world's largest colony of Cory's shearwater (*Calonectris diomedea borealis*), a somewhat enigmatic bird whose strange call can often be heard at nightfall, when it returns to land to feed its chicks. Here also is one of the largest colonies of roseate tern (*Sterna dougallii*) worldwide. Altogether, the archipelago has over 30 bird species which nest, and due to the islands' central position in the Atlantic you may also observe a large number of migratory birds coming from America and Eurasia.

The total number of species recorded in the islands is over 400, including a few which are extremely rare and some which have been newly sighted in the western Palearctic.

Rare 'vagrants' from both the Americas and Eurasia, often blown in on strong Atlantic storm systems, can be seen all year and on all islands but the chances of seeing American birds are higher in the Western island group during October. (As are recordings, consequently, of birdwatchers on sleepy Corvo and its neighbour, Flores.)

Hotspots for birdwatchers on other islands are Fajã dos Cubres on São Jorge, Cabo da Praia and Paul da Praia on Terceira, Pico island's Lajes do Pico, the lakes of Sete Cidades and the northwestern tip of Mosteiros on São Miguel. The small ponds around the airport of Santa Maria can also bring rewards. To increase your chances and save time, a local specialised wildlife guide can steer you towards the avian highlights that might coincide with your visit.

one of the most handsome of all Azorean endemics, the perennial, slightly shrubby *Azorina vidalii*.

(See also *Appendix 2, Flora*, for an aid to identifying plants you are likely to see, and the website www.horta.uac.pt/species/plantae.)

**Two bullies** Amid all the excitement of introducing new plants into the show gardens of São Miguel came two very gardenworthy species which have more than outlived their mid 19th-century patrons. From the middle altitudes of the Himalaya came the **Kahili ginger**, *Hedychium gardnerianum*, a handsome plant about 1.5m tall with beautiful, sweetly scented, terminal spikes of orange-yellow spidery flowers. Away from its native habitat it found itself in the Azores in a permanently moist climate, with nothing to limit its growth. It has become a superbly aggressive invader: it can adapt to various Azorean habitats; it is a strongly competitive plant; cut it down and it can quickly recover; it produces abundant efficiently dispersed seeds; can easily reproduce vegetatively; and once established it dominates the site for many years. As a consequence it has smothered areas of native vegetation, prevents the re-establishment of desirable species and has invaded large areas of cryptomeria forest – a real pest, and very difficult to eradicate. The second garden delight is **Gunnera tinctoria**, one of the 'giant rhubarbs' from South America. You will see this invading parts of the Furnas Valley and especially the pastures high above; also Lake Fogo, a protected area for flora, and Sete Cidades. Deeply rooted and with a strong constitution, it covers hectares of pastures; the occasional container-load taken to Holland for sale to garden centres makes little impact.

**WHALES AND OTHER CETACEANS** Cetaceans, from the Greek meaning 'sea monster', are members of the order Cetaceae, commonly known as whales and dolphins. Altogether there are a little over 80 species worldwide, and some 27 species have been sighted off the Azores: the islands are now recognised as being one of the world's best whale-watching destinations. Cetaceans are mammals, have lungs and nostrils (blowholes), suckle their young and have front flippers evolved from forelegs. Within the Cetaceae are two subgroups: the toothed whales and the baleen whales. The former have teeth and a single blowhole while the latter have, instead of teeth, a horny baleen or plate descending from the upper jaw and paired blowholes. This difference is important when feeding; the toothed whales eat larger prey such as cephalopods and fish and the baleen whales use their comb-like plates to filter very small fish and the shrimp-like krill. Many of these filter-feeding whales often undertake long migrations because they need warm waters for the growth and development of their young, but they also need the food resources that concentrate in colder waters.

The mid-Atlantic location of the steep-sided volcanic islands of the Azores causes great upswellings of coldwater currents from the ocean depths which meet the warm waters of the Gulf Stream, producing nutrient-rich waters. The species most readily identified with the Azores is the sperm whale or cachalote (*Physeter macrocephalus*), the largest of all toothed whales. Other toothed whales frequently seen during the main season are Cuvier's beaked whale (*Ziphius caviostris*), northern bottlenose whale (*Hyperodon ampullatus*), short-finned pilot whale (*Globicephala macrorhynchus*) and Sowerby's beaked whale (*Mesoplodon bidens*).

Dolphins seen regularly are common Atlantic (*Delphinus delphis*), bottlenose (*Tursiops truncates*), Risso's (*Grampus griseus*), Atlantic spotted (*Stenella frontalis*) and striped (*Stenella coeruleoalba*). Since 2001, observations of baleen or great whales have increased, during early April to late June. Species include fin (*Balaenoptera physalus*), sei (*Balaenoptera borealis*), humpback (*Megeptera novaeangliae*) and the blue whale (*Balaenoptera musculus*), thought to be the largest animal ever to have lived on Earth.

**CONSERVATION** The Azores Regional Government has committed to a policy focused on the environment and national heritage – sites of high botanical, fauna, ecological, landscape and geological interest – and the surrounding marine environment. The Azores have one of the richest marine ecosystems in the world, including some eight hydrothermal vents of the Mid-Atlantic Ridge.

*David Sayers*

Although organised commercial whaling was first carried out by the Basques in the Bay of Biscay, as early as the 10th century, whaling reached the Azores only in the 18th century and thus its history is short. For the Basques, the hunt was for the northern right whale (*Eubaleana glacialis*) and they pursued it to near-extinction, first in the Bay of Biscay, then much later across the Atlantic on the eastern seaboard of Newfoundland.

In the Azores, only the resident sperm whales (*Physeter macrocephalus*) were hunted, starting around 1765 when American colonists arrived in the archipelago. At 20m the sperm whale is the largest of the toothed whales, and their odourless oil fuelled lamps and made candle wax. Later it provided watch oil, lubricants for delicate instruments, cosmetics, textiles (preventing fibres from unravelling when twisted into threads), soap, jute, varnish, explosives and paint, and went into margarine until the 1960s, when it was replaced with vegetable oils. Despite the attacks of privateers and pirates, the Americans found the Azorean waters to be profitable, recruiting locals as crew and exploiting their expert seamanship.

By the 1800s, American whalers were regularly calling at Horta for victuals and water, and also to tranship barrels of oil. This golden age of American whaling, when New Bedford was known as 'the city that lit the world', continued until the 1850s, but by then whale oil was becoming unaffordable and was being replaced by kerosene, a product of the embryonic petroleum industry. Additionally, whaling ships were destroyed by Confederacy ships in the American Civil War, and the golden age was drawing to a close.

But in the Azores, the demise of ship-based whaling encouraged the growth of shore-based whaling in Faial. In Pico, whaling provided welcome compensation for the simultaneous collapse of its wine industry and the island established several whaling companies, then obtained concessions from other islands to whale. By 1908,

Designating areas to be protected began in 1972 with the Faial caldera and two years later Lagoa do Fogo on São Miguel. In the next decades there followed forest nature reserves with a wider remit, and the first marine reserves. Today, visitors see onsite noticeboards declaring protected areas, often followed by a run of acronyms.

The European Union's Natura 2000 (*http://ec.europa.eu/environment/nature/natura2000/index_en.htm*) is a network of sites in a European-wide partnership at the heart of which are two Directives. The 1979 Birds Directive seeks the establishment of Special Protection Areas (SPAs) for birds, aiming to protect and manage areas important for rare and vulnerable species because they use them for breeding, feeding, wintering or migration; the 1992 Habitats Directive requires Special Areas of Conservation (SACs) to be designated to provide increased protection and management for rare and vulnerable animals, plants and habitats. These Natura 2000 sites now cover about 20% of the European territory and, as their website says, most European citizens will not live far from a Natura 2000 site. There are further acronyms, including Site of Community Importance (SCI), which contributes to the maintenance or restoration of a natural habitat or species or biological diversity, and also contributes significantly to Natura 2000. The rich geological and volcanic heritage is recognised by selected locations under Regional Natural Monuments (RNMs). Most recently, to better administer and manage the protected areas the regional government established three management units: Island Nature Parks – on all nine islands; Marine Parks; and Local Protected Areas, there were whaleboats in Terceira, Graciosa and Faial. Flores and São Miguel began whaling a couple of decades after Pico, the latter with its whale station and try-works at Capelas, which benefited from the greater number of whales that passed its shores than those of the Central and Western groups. Corvo, with its dangerous coastline, caught few whales and these were mostly taken to Flores for processing (working-up). There was also whaling at Santa Maria, but it lapsed in the 20th century, only to be revived just before World War II, with the highest catch per boat of all the islands, while São Jorge became as active as Faial during the first 40 years of the 20th century.

The commercial success of whaling suffered market vicissitudes beyond the control of the islanders. New substitute products, prices, and in the late 1940s the big Antarctic sperm whale catches, impacted upon Azorean sales, but markets during the two world wars and the Korean War saw high demand. In 1935, as many as 99 sperm whales were taken, and in 1969, the catch was 263. In terms of overall totals, the Azorean catches made little impact: annual worldwide catches in the 1930s exceeded 40,000 whales, and some species were driven almost to extinction. The Washington Convention of 1946 was an attempt to regulate whaling and as the century continued the numbers allowed to be caught were reduced substantially. Economics, declining stocks, falling prices and the ready availability of substitutes caused nations to abandon whaling. By 1954, Azorean whaling was seen as a relic industry. The factory on São Miguel closed in 1972, and whaling ceased in the Eastern Group of islands. The International Whaling Commission in 1982 agreed zero commercial quotas, but Norway and Japan, and now Iceland, continue. Whale hunting in the Azores became a very minor affair, and had ceased altogether by the mid-1980s. I remember standing on the quay at Lajes on Pico watching in the shallows a huge jawbone slowly being grazed by sea creatures; it must have belonged to one of the very last whales to be caught.

created by local municipalities to safeguard local parks, gardens, lookouts and the Recreational Forest Reserves.

At the same time the OSPAR Convention for the Protection of the Marine Environment of the northeast Atlantic (*www.ospar.org*) is creating in conjunction with Natura 2000 a network of Marine Protected Areas (MPAs) that are both ecologically coherent and well managed. The northeast Atlantic has been divided into five regions. In the wider Atlantic region six MPAs have been established, four in collaboration with Portugal, covering a total area of 285,000km$^2$, protecting a series of seamounts and sections of the Mid-Atlantic Ridge and hosting a range of vulnerable deep-sea habitats and species. This is of special significance for the Azores since their maritime area is greater than their terrestrial. Member states are expected to pay for the management of their sites, but there are various community funds that can assist.

The presence of onsite wardens, rangers, professional naturalists and voluntary workers is still in its infancy throughout the Azores. Exceptions are the Capelinhos eruption site of 1958, the base supervising access to Pico mountain, lava caves on Terceira, Pico and Graciosa, the whaling centres of Lajes on Pico and Horta on Faial, and the Priolo Environmental Centre on São Miguel.

The islands of Corvo, Flores and Graciosa are recognised by UNESCO as Biosphere Reserves; these are protected areas intended to demonstrate an equilibrium between man and nature, conservation and sustainable development.

*David Sayers/Murray Stewart*

Whether through whale hunting or whale watching, these largest of sea creatures have impacted across the Azorean archipelago and its economy for over 250 years, and continue to do so today.

In the heyday of ship-based whaling, carried out by visiting American whalers, the Azoreans, so long accustomed to seafaring from childhood, excelled in jobs as lookouts, oarsmen and harpooners in the small boats lowered from ships to hunt and kill the whales. A hard life, often with poor food and conditions, low pay, and increasingly long voyages nevertheless offered an escape from compulsory military service. For some, it provided a new life in New England and the chance to send money home to dependants in the islands.

Portugal itself never established a deep-sea industry. Attempts to fit out whale ships in the Azores failed due to the lack of capital available in the islands and the increasing success of shore-based whaling.

Shore-based whaling relied on lookouts onshore spotting passing whales. On sighting a blow, a rocket was fired from the *vigia* (lookout tower) to let the whalemen know to launch their boats, and a white flag was raised. If a kill was made, the flag was flown at half-mast to warn the try-works to get ready for processing. The boats would sail or row out, and in later years were towed out by motor launch, guided by large sheets laid out on the cliffs or by radio telephone. Once the whale felt the harpoon it fled or dived, rapidly taking out line; friction could set it on fire, so water was poured over it. Sails and mast had to be lowered, and the crew had to avoid the running line to avoid the loss of a leg or worse. Once several hundred feet of line had been taken out and the pace began to slacken, the line would be fixed to the loggerhead, a post at the back of the boat. With the line fixed, the whale would feel the drag and take off again to tow the whalers at around 25–30km/h, often called the 'Nantucket sleigh ride', which was another dangerous period because the whale could capsize the boat. When the whale tired, rope was taken in, but let out if the whale surged again. Since a whale in one breath can exchange 85–90% of air, an objective was to break the animal's breathing pattern to prevent it from diving deeply. Eventually the whale tired sufficiently for the boat to close, when lances were used for the kill.

More recently, in March 2016, the *fãjas* (page 174) of São Jorge island were also given UNESCO Biosphere Reserve status. With the islands' increasing emphasis on renewable sources of energy, conservation strategies and environmental management, it is hoped that the Azores could in time become a model for future sustainability.

## HISTORY

**DISCOVERY** The islands were pristine until the 15th century; there were no indigenous peoples, and no-one had ever settled there. They were known to exist, for in the *Medici Atlas* of 1351 the seven islands of the Central and Eastern groups are shown. Less than a century later the **Portuguese 'Age of Discoveries'** began and Portuguese explorers made the first recorded landfalls on Madeira

The most important modern innovation was the gradual introduction from 1909 of motorised tow-boats, enabling several boats to be rapidly towed to the whale regardless of unfavourable winds once it was sighted by the lookouts; this greatly extended their range. The engine noise would have scared off the whales, so the last mile was covered by sail, oars and finally by paddle to within harpooning range. Tow-boats enabled longer chases and offered support in case of a whaleboat being smashed by the whale; they also allowed the towing of dead whales back to shore, a backbreaking task when done by the whaling boat under oars. Although harpoon guns and exploding lances were used to hunt whales, the Azorean whalemen used the hand harpoon and lance. Similarly, processing or *saving* of the dead whale changed little; first the whale was *cut in*, meaning the blubber was cut up or *flensed* with the animal either beached, or tied alongside a jetty using cutting-spades, ropes and at most a hand capstan. With the blubber and spermaceti removed, these were then *tried out*, by being placed into try-pots or iron cauldrons to melt and reduce over a basalt oven to make sperm oil and 'head oil'. The carcass, with its meat and bone, was simply towed back out to sea and abandoned. It was not until 1934 that sufficient capital became available to invest in modern processing equipment using powered winches and pressure cookers when the whole animal was utilised. Just after World War II radio-telephones were first used for communication between the lookouts and the motor tow-boats, purchased from the US military, who sold off the stock very cheaply.

Nowadays, many examples of the old *vigia* can still be spotted all around the islands, some restored, most of them redundant. But not all, as the many companies engaged in whale watching still spot their 'prey' from a few of these coastal towers, communicating with the boat captains by radio. As well as enjoying the wonders of whale watching, visitors to the Azores can choose to visit one or more of several museums dedicated to the era of whalehunting, understanding the rigours of a life at sea and the intricacies of catching and processing whales.

The annual whalemen's festival, Festa dos baleeiros, continues to be held on the first Sunday in August in the tiny church on Monte da Guia, above Porto Pim in Horta. In Lajes do Pico there is also a whalers' festival, and still some of the old whaling villages beautifully maintain old *canoas* (whaling boats) and sometimes even commission new ones, now used for sailing races and offering opportunities for visitors to take to sea and experience the sensations of past days.

(c1419), the Azores (c1427), Cape Verde (1456–60), Saint Helena and Ascension (1501–02) and Tristan da Cunha (c1506). Bartolomeu Dias rounded the Cape of Good Hope in 1488 and thus opened access to the Indian Ocean, and Pedro Álvares Cabral landed in Brazil in 1500, to say nothing of the numerous inland expeditions in Africa and elsewhere. It is not known for certain who discovered the islands for the Portuguese, nor the exact dates; numerous stories abound from which to take your choice. One which caps the debate is that a caravel came upon them by chance when sailing homewards from the west coast of Africa using the trade winds. Another is that the Infante Dom Henrique (Prince Henry 'the Navigator') ordered one Gonçalo Velho Cabral to sail westwards to find the islands he thought must exist. Cabral found only the Formigas rocks ('The Ants'), and went back home, getting a low mark from the Sagres Management School. Sent out again the following year, and sailing 15 miles distant from the

From their initial settlement in the 15th century, the Azores have played a pivotal role in the history of the Atlantic. On Terceira, the Bay of Angra (Angra meaning 'Anchorage') provided protection and was soon defended, later by the great fortress of São Filipe and smaller São Sebastião. By the early 1500s, it was an obligatory port of call for the fleets serving Africa and the East and West Indies and for 300 years was a link between Europe and the New World.

When Spain overran Portugal, the 'Reprisal Pirates' of England sought to capture their treasure ships, and to protect them the Spanish in 1555 formed the first convoy system, with merchant ships defended by armed escorts.

Powerful nations must have long coveted the Azores for their strategic location. However, one enthusiast in the early 1800s proposed that Britain should acquire the archipelago, not only for use as a base between Africa and America and as a staging post in the transportation of troops to the Cape of Good Hope and the East Indies, but also because at the time the British Empire had no colony that produced wine(!), and that São Miguel and Terceira would make excellent penal colonies with transportation costs much less than the long voyage to Australia.

In November 1914, Portugal declared war on Germany, co-operating closely with the Allies, thus giving them access to the ports in Horta and Ponta Delgada for anti-submarine warfare and a safe harbour for repairs and refuelling convoys – convoys being a repeat of the Spanish strategy centuries earlier. In World War II, agreement to the use of the facilities in the Azores came much later as President Salazar was very reluctant to give Nazi Germany cause to invade mainland Portugal. Churchill famously called upon the Treaty of Eternal Friendship of 1373, or Treaty of Windsor; this was between England's King Edward III and King D João I of Portugal and had been further sealed a year later when King João married Philippa of Lancaster, daughter of John of Gaunt. Reinforced from time to time through the following centuries, the treaty is still in force today after more than 600 years, and is the oldest alliance between any two countries. Negotiations were time-consuming, but eventually Britain was allowed by August 1943 to develop

Formigas, a much better prospect came into view. Since it was 15 August, the Feast of the Assumption, he called the island he reached first Santa Maria and was later appointed governor. São Miguel was supposedly discovered when an escaped slave clambered up a hill and saw a much larger island in the distance; this was settled around 1444. By chance some unknown mariners spotted a third island, and with a stroke of originality called it Terceira, 'Third Island'. Another version is that Prince Henry sent out caravels, date unknown, to find the islands and they discovered five, later named Santa Maria, São Miguel, Terceira, Faial and Pico. Most popular accounts give the Portuguese explorer Diogo de Silves the credit for finding the first island, Santa Maria, in 1427. In 1439, Alfonso V sanctioned Henry to settle seven islands, so they must have been discovered before that year. Flores and Corvo were certainly added last.

**SETTLEMENT** Colonisation of the islands was undertaken in a typically medieval way. King Alfonso V granted them to his nephew, the Infante Dom Henrique (Henry the Navigator) as Master of the Military Order of Avis, of Crusades origin. It was this Order of Avis that financially supported the discoveries of the 15th century and for reward was given the new lands to explore and populate. The Infante in an airstrip at Lajes on Terceira. Known as *aerovaca*, these simple airstrips were on several of the islands and regularly grazed by cattle. This time the farmers on Terceira were not only losing pasture, but to greater consternation there was also an *aguardente* (firewater) factory in the middle of the site. Marsden matting, an interlocking perforated metal sheet, was used initially to make a 6,000ft runway. Soon afterwards, the United States military were also allowed to use Lajes and they later made it a permanent airfield for heavy transports as the eventual liberation of Europe drew closer. A second airbase was needed and the US was given permission under cover of Pan American Airways to construct one on Santa Maria, so that it would seem Portugal was building it for post-war communications. Work began towards the end of 1944 and three A-shaped runways were built. Access to the Azores proved vital to the Allies in protecting the Atlantic convoys from German U-boats. There was a north Atlantic route which had protection from bases in Newfoundland and Iceland, and a southern route, but these left the mid-Atlantic as an undefended black hole; significantly, it was also the shortest crossing, saving time and vital fuel. Enemy U-boats prowled the seas around the Azores and Allied shipping losses were appalling. With the Lajes base the odds were turned, U-boats were sunk and shipping losses dramatically dropped and eventually the wolf packs were called off. Had Hitler built more U-boats as his admirals wanted, and implemented the Nazi plan to invade the Azores, how different might the outcome have been.

By 1947, all military operations had been transferred to Lajes, leaving Santa Maria as an important stop for commercial transatlantic flights until the 1970s, when newer aircraft could cross non-stop. The only airstrip in the Azores long enough, it even hosted an occasional visit from Concorde. In 1948/49, Lajes was used in the Berlin airlift to counter the Soviet blockade, and this experience influenced the decision to negotiate long-term use by the American military for a base. It also continues as a Portuguese airbase. Portugal was one of the founding members of NATO, and in Ponta Delgada there is a NATO naval fuel depot and terminal.

turn delegated control over administration, defence, justice and land grants to the Captain Donatário (donatory or lord proprietor, the Portuguese equivalent of a colonial governor), together with the revenue from certain taxes, and the monopoly control over mills, salt and the ovens for baking bread. The king retained oversight of customs, control of selected taxes and of the death penalty.

The usual practice was followed when discovering islands; cattle, goats and pigs were landed to provide future food, and also very likely to begin the tremendous task of penetrating the dense vegetation. The first islands to be populated were Santa Maria and São Miguel, followed by Terceira in about 1450. Settlers came from mainland Portugal, particularly the Algarve and Alentejo, and from Madeira. Portugal's population was only 1.5 million, so Henry encouraged **immigration from Flanders**, and in 1466 Faial and Pico were settled by Flemings, under the Captain Donatário Josse Van der Huertere, and a few years later Flores by Willem Van der Hagen; for a time, these islands became known in northern Europe as the Flemish Islands because so many settled there, refugees from the scourges of the Hundred Years' War.

The first settlers faced an enormous task and probably used fire to begin to clear the vegetation, though cattle also played their part. On some of the islands

In the 15th century, when the islands were first settled, one of the first things that was done was to introduce many Portuguese domestic animals. Of these the cow was extremely important because she not only provided milk and meat but was also a hardworking animal around the farm, for ploughing, carting, etc. Some of the distinct cattle breeds that were imported from Portugal include Alentejana, Mirandesa, Minhota and Algarvia. There is also historical suggestion that some cows were imported from Flanders but there is no information on specific breeds. Importation would have continued until the numbers reached a reproductive level that was self-sustaining, and then probably stopped. The following five centuries of cross-breeding between the original breeds imported from Portugal and Flanders evolved into a distinct breed known today as Ramo Grande. This Ramo Grande breed dominated on most of the islands. Then, in the 1950s, Friesians were imported from England and later on from the USA and soon after that an artificial insemination programme was set up on Terceira and São Miguel. By the 1980s, there were quite a few importations of dairy heifers (Holsteins) and beef breeds (Limousin, Charolais and Fleckview) from Germany, England, Holland, France and Canada. A small number of Jersey heifers have since been added, plus Jersey embryo transfers. Consequently, and in a very short time, the Azorean breed became almost extinct.

Fortunately, in the area of Ramo Grande on Terceira, a group of farmers continued to maintain small herds of these animals. Today there is increasing interest in the conservation of this Azorean genetic heritage, and in its potential for producing beef; its specific characteristics have been defined and all individuals are now registered. At present, the genetic line in the Azores is mostly Holsteins for dairy and Limousin and Charolais for beef. From a study of various dairy breeds, the Azores University, through its Agricultural Sciences Department, concluded that Jerseys would be the most suitable for the region. Hopefully, the Azorean Ramo Grande will survive the effects of globalisation and someday might even contribute its distinctive characters to future breeding.

this would have revealed a very stony soil, and especially on Pico it must have been heartbreaking. Huge neatly piled stacks of stones metres square and 2m tall remain testimony to this tenacity and determination, as do the numerous stone walls; their creation had nothing to do with marking territorial boundaries. With such an inhospitable coastline, wherever it was possible to land must have dictated the location of those first settlements. Looking at them today, some still appear daunting, often at the foot of steep cliffs or ravines. Farming slowly spread across the islands as the vegetation was cleared and by the next century there was a surplus of production for export: wheat for the Portuguese garrison in North Africa, sugar and woad for dyeing to Flanders. Each island grew more of the crops that best suited its climate and terrain. However, by the end of the 17th century, the peasants were eating the introduced American corn (maize) and yams, so freeing the wheat crop for export for townspeople and cash export.

During the middle of the 16th century, vessels returning from India using the westerly trade winds passed through the Azores, but it was at the beginning of the Portuguese colonisation of Brazil and the discovery of America when the islands

For me, and I suspect for many, the name woad brings to mind school lessons telling of Boadicea and her warriors painted blue doing battle with the Roman invaders. Knowledge of the dye goes back to the Ancients, and the Greeks and Romans used it medicinally – it is a good astringent. In the cabbage family, *Isatis tinctoria* is a greyish, medium-tall biennial herb native to eastern Europe and western Asia; cultivated in Europe since the 10th century, it may now be found naturalised as a relict of former cultivation. First the leaves and stems were washed and dried, then ground in a mill; the powder thus obtained was again wetted and again sun-dried. The resultant concentrated black and granular extract was then formed into cakes and large balls called pastel. By the 13th century, French Languedoc became a main area of woad cultivation, centred on Toulouse, making the city very wealthy. It was from here the plant was introduced into the Azores at the end of the 15th century, where it was grown for almost 200 years, but only 100 of these were economically important. Woad's success was linked to the fortunes of the European textile industry, and the Azores and the English textile towns, especially Exeter, enjoyed a mutually profitable trade and more than a dozen English merchants lived in Ponta Delgada. At its peak, it is thought that woad was grown on more than 30% of São Miguel's arable land. Unfortunately, the dye constituent indigotin in woad is the same as in a dye plant in the pea family, *Indigofera*, or indigo, and being chemically inert they can both dye the same textiles; indigo also is much less vulnerable to fading, and was thus ideal for military uniforms. Limited supplies had come from India, but when the Portuguese discovered the sea route to India, imports rose. The woad lobby was considerable, imports were banned and in England indigo dye was prohibited for over 100 years, until 1685. Because it was so valuable, the French began its cultivation on their Caribbean islands; the climate was ideal, and the crop demanded slaves. Britain followed in Jamaica and South Carolina, and by the middle of the 17th century, cheap imports and heavy taxes imposed by Lisbon had killed the Azorean pastel trade, and the resident English merchants slowly dwindled.

Orchil or archil, *urzela* in Portuguese, is the source of a dye prepared from certain lichens of several genera. The Cape Verde Islands were a major producer, using it to dye their cotton trade cloth, but the discovery of abundant supplies in the early 19th century in Angola and Mozambique killed their market. In the Azores the lichen *Roccella tinctoria* is found on maritime rocks and when processed with stale urine (or ammonia) and dried it was sold in powder form, later known as cudbear, or as a paste, which gives a purple-red colour. Lichen dyes change colour in reaction to acids or bases – red to acid and blue to alkaline – and are used in litmus paper, while Orcein from *Roccella tinctoria* is used to make a purple stain for studying chromosomes. Never as significant in the Azores as pastel, its export was short-lived; indeed, one commentator claimed the revenue went as pin money to the queen!

began their great development, mainly in the coastal village of Angra on Terceira because it offered sheltered anchorage. It became a principal port for exporting Azorean produce, and significantly an assembly port for ships returning from Brazil laden with valuable cargoes. Here they would form convoys for the journey to Lisbon, protected by warships against the marauding pirates.

In 1580, Spanish Castile annexed Portugal and the Azores supported Dom António, the next in line to the throne, who, with French help, held out on Terceira, becoming the last Portuguese resistance to Castilian power. The Spaniards defeated the French fleet off Terceira in July 1582 and the following year overran the islands. In 1591, the Spanish were attacked by the English, giving rise to the famous Tennyson poem *The Revenge* (page 233). Liberated in 1640, the islands became an important staging post for British trade and for British naval strategy, until the opening of the Suez Canal over 200 years later.

Although so distant from the Portuguese mainland, the Azores nevertheless have often played an important part in Portuguese history. They contributed to the conquest, defence and supply of the Portuguese strongholds on the north African coast, caravels stopped in the Azores on their return from India, they supported the ships sailing to the Americas, and they strongly resisted Spanish domination between 1580 and 1640. Two centuries later the islands featured in the Liberals' struggle with the Absolutists; two presidents in the First Republic came from the Azores and, most recently, the islands provided important bases for the Allies in the two world wars, and in the Gulf War.

## GOVERNMENT AND POLITICS   *with Albano Cymbron*

Initially, except for a period during the Spanish occupation, the Azores had no central government, and it was not until 1766 that a governor and captain-general for the whole group were appointed by the **Marquis of Pombal**. He was very much a man of the 18th-century Enlightenment, and had lived for several years in the main capitals of Europe, so was well aware how backward Portugal had become. He became Prime Minister of Portugal in 1750 and implemented economic and educational reforms, abolished slavery, revised the tax system and introduced commercial regulation. He implemented a new administrative system throughout the kingdom, creating districts or provinces. The Azores became a single province, governed by the captain-general (*capitão-general*), with Angra on Terceira – the archipelago's capital – doing away with the semi-feudal privileges of the various donatories and the islands losing their autonomous captaincies. While this may have been logical in Lisbon, it went against the vigorous individualism of the islands and greatly displeased the people of São Miguel, for theirs was the largest and richest island and they were accustomed to resolving their problems directly with the central government. Under the new arrangement, each island was totally independent of the others, and for approximately 60 years this regime prevailed; it was a time of struggle and indiscipline between the governor in Terceira and the other islands, mainly São Miguel.

In 1807, Napoleon's forces invaded Portugal; Napoleon wanted to stop **Anglo-Portuguese trade** and demanded Portugal blockade the ports, but the Portuguese refused to comply, so beginning the **Peninsular War**. The Portuguese royal family, their court and important citizens fled to Brazil and made Rio de Janeiro the capital of Portugal, leaving Portugal to a military junta with orders not to resist. In 1808, British and Portuguese troops under Sir Arthur Wellesley (the later Duke of Wellington) gained control over Lisbon and a treaty allowed the French to withdraw. In the meantime Napoleon forced the Spanish King Charles IV to abdicate and replaced him with his brother, Joseph Bonaparte. Also in 1808, the French invaded a second time, and again Wellesley repelled them, forcing them to retreat to Galicia. Their third and last invasion in 1810 ended with their defeat at the Battle of Busacco, near Coimbra and they were eventually forced to retreat to Spain, from where they were finally evicted in 1814. The consequences were considerable, with the Azores playing a valiant part, but it would take many long years for Portugal to recover from the ravages of the war.

Liberal ideas resulting from the French Revolution spread to Portugal with the French invasion and found fertile ground in a country that was in a deplorable state, its king and government in Brazil, and in their absence Lisbon ruled by the English Marshal Beresford and British commercial interests. The economy was in crisis, previously being dependent on a trade monopoly with Brazil and now, with the king residing there, this commerce had been opened to all friendly countries with the English benefiting most. Lisbon felt it was a colony of Brazil.

A **Liberal revolution** quickly spread from its beginnings in Oporto, demanding the return of the royal court, a constitutional monarchy and that Brazil revert to its old status of colony trading exclusively with Portugal. Beresford was replaced by a junta and in 1821, a Constituent Assembly was elected in Lisbon, the same year as the publication of the first Liberal constitution. A few months later the king, João VI, returned to Lisbon leaving his son, Dom Pedro, Regent of Brazil. In September, the assembly voted to abolish the Kingdom of Brazil and so bring it under direct control of Lisbon; the following year Brazil declared its independence, and Dom Pedro its first emperor.

Under the new constitution, adopted in 1822, deputies were elected by the people (landowners and merchants) and the king had no powers, not even to dissolve parliament. This was strongly opposed by João VI's queen, Carlota-Joaquina, who, together with her son Dom Miguel, prompted a countrywide insurgency against it in the name of Absolutism and a call for the king to abdicate. It was a very troubled time, as is common with any change of regime, with revolts against revolts with either the Traditionalists (Absolutists) or the Liberals in power. João VI died in 1826 and eventually in 1828, the youngest brother of Dom Miguel was declared king absolute, totally against the constitution only recently accepted by the crown. Liberals dissatisfied with or persecuted by the absolutist regime withdrew to Terceira, which remained loyal to the Liberal cause against the central government.

Meanwhile, in Brazil, following a political crisis King Pedro abdicated in favour of his son, Pedro II in 1831, and crossed to Europe to oppose his brother Dom Miguel. Going first to England where there were many exiled Portuguese Liberals, he moved in 1832 to Terceira, which he used as his base for the coming invasion of Portugal, and formed an interim **government-in-exile**. In July, he led a military force including the French and English, and took Oporto in the north, with the Duke of Terceira capturing Lisbon. Final victory came in 1834.

Reforms followed, and a new administration for the Azores was created by making the islands a province of Portugal, with Angra the capital. São Miguel strongly opposed the consequent dominance of Terceira and this was eventually resolved by first creating two districts, and then three. São Miguel and Santa Maria came under Ponta Delgada District, while Angra administered the islands of Terceira, Graciosa and São Jorge. Horta District presided over Faial, Pico, Flores and Corvo. Each district was independent of the others and managed its affairs directly with the central government in Lisbon. The provincial governor was appointed by Lisbon. So began the process of territorial division which later led to the creation of further autonomous districts that lasted until 1974. Interestingly, it was resentment over taxes that prompted the first ideas that the islands should have autonomy. This first occurred in 1869 with the **'Dízimo' tax** that obliged people to pay 10% of their earnings to the Church. Later came a tax on the alcohol produced in the Azores, introduced to protect the same industry on the mainland.

Prime Minister, and later President, Salazar led the authoritarian right-wing government which controlled Portugal from 1932 to 1974. He established public order which was previously lacking, and the political and financial stability for economic growth. A basic education was provided for everyone, and a substantial investment made in infrastructure. Many of the often very attractive schools in the Azores owe their origins to this period. His dictatorship followed a strict Catholic social doctrine opposed to class struggle and economic dominance, with a secret police to counter opposition. On his death a leftish military coup slowly changed the regime to a democracy leading to free elections and in 1976, the first constitutional government.

In 1976, the Azores became an autonomous region with its own government of Regional Assembly and Executive. The Executive or Regional Government is responsible politically to the Regional Legislative Assembly. The region elects five deputies to the national parliament in Lisbon. The Regional Government has 51 deputies elected every four years and meets in Horta. The President of the Azores, whose official residence is in Ponta Delgada, is the leader of the party with the greatest number of elected deputies. There are nine regional secretaries, each in charge of a department, eg: Finance and Planning, Tourism and Environment. The secretariats, or ministries, are based in Ponta Delgada, Angra do Heroísmo and Horta. Each island is divided into district councils, from six on São Miguel to just one on each of the smallest islands, which are in turn divided into parishes. The islands' autonomy includes responsibility for their economy, education and health, while the army, police and judiciary are controlled directly by the national government in Lisbon. The Portuguese government is represented by the Minister of the Republic who maintains residency in Angra do Heroísmo, Terceira. The Azores are represented in Europe by two MEPs.

## ECONOMY

During the 30 years before the 2008 economic crisis in Europe, island infrastructure was given priority, and new airports, harbours and telecommunication systems were completed. The Azores, or at least Ponta Delgada, have changed hugely in the past few years with new industrial/commercial estates on the outskirts and many new shops in the town. Everywhere in the islands one frequently saw (and still sees) the European Union flag on a hoarding announcing funds for some new development, from further new port facilities to a tiny family enterprise for rural tourism. While some of the road building may be questioned, such as the recently finished highway to Nordeste on São Miguel and the asphalt surfacing of many of the minor farm tracks throughout the islands that once were easy and enjoyable walking trails, the airfields, new port facilities for cruise liners and tourism will pay dividends. But with the economic crisis came austerity measures, with substantial increases in personal and corporate taxation, VAT rises and cuts in government budgets. Portugal was quick to try to reduce its budget deficit, and to meet the conditions of its EU bail out, but with forecasts of continuing reduced growth times are lean. However, the Azores, while affected, are faring better than the mainland and Madeira due to lower debts and a strong family structure, although there have been many job losses in the construction industry. Apart from the public sector, the greatest contribution to GDP has been and remains the export of cattle and dairy products. Then there are minor crops of pineapples, potatoes, wine, tobacco and tea; all labour intensive. Tourism has long been gaining in importance, and 2015 was a record year for visitors, with a 40% increase from Britain, 25% from Germany and 17% from the USA. Although proportionately small, Azorean fishing is also artisanal, providing a relatively large number of jobs per tonne of fish landed.

|  | Length (km) | Breadth (km) | Surface Area (km²) | Population |
|---|---|---|---|---|
| São Miguel | 65 | 14 | 746 | 137,800 |
| Pico | 42 | 15 | 447 | 14,100 |
| Terceira | 29 | 17.5 | 382 | 56,400 |
| São Jorge | 56 | 8 | 246 | 9,100 |
| Faial | 21 | 14 | 173 | 15,000 |
| Flores | 17 | 12.5 | 143 | 3,800 |
| Santa Maria | 17 | 9.5 | 97 | 5,500 |
| Graciosa | 12.5 | 8.5 | 61 | 4,400 |
| Corvo | 6.5 | 4 | 17 | 430 |

Given their different characters, it is not surprising economic activities have different relevance for individual islands. Dairy and beef are more relevant for Graciosa and São Jorge, fishing is more important to Faial and Pico, tourism for São Miguel, Pico, Faial and Flores, and other exports on the more diversified São Miguel. Transfer payments (money from central government) are important to Corvo because of its small size, to Terceira for its military airbase (although this has changed as the USA has now reduced its presence to only 10% of its previous strength), and to Santa Maria, which hosts the air control of the north Atlantic.

**ENERGY** The Azores have been dependent upon imported oil to generate electricity but are now increasingly seeking and exploiting energy from geothermal, wind and solar sources. The first hydro-electric plant was built on São Miguel in 1899 and ran until 1950.

In 1975, the Institute of Geosciences of the Azores was founded and in the following year began drilling wells down to 1,500m on São Miguel. The first pilot geothermal plant generating 3MW opened in 1980 and this success led to the exploration of the Ribeira Grande field. Now some 44% of São Miguel's electricity is from geothermal sources, with lesser contributions made by all the other islands except for Santa Maria.

Nine separate islands in the archipelago means nine isolated energy grids, each with specific characteristics and possible solutions for renewable energy. Flores generates almost 50% from renewables (33% hydro), São Miguel 55% (mostly geothermal), and Terceira 8.5% from wind, the island's Serra do Cume wind farm setting a then world record for generation in 2010. On Graciosa, a project by German company Younicos is designed to harness a combination of wind and solar power to produce carbon-free electricity for the island. Short-term power fluctuations will be balanced by a photovoltaic power plant and lithium batteries. The project has been delayed but commissioning is now scheduled for late 2016.

São Jorge gets 15% of its energy from wind. Tiny Corvo has fitted solar panels to most of its houses and combined with heat pumps, which has reduced imports of liquefied petroleum gas. By 2018, the Azores aims to generate 75% of its electricity from renewables, though this may be optimistic.

## POPULATION

The total population of the Azores is just over 246,000 (2011 census), an increase of 1.79% over the previous decade. Movement within the islands varies, with some islands or towns losing populations while others increase.

For centuries emigration has played a major part in the life of the islands. Overpopulation and economic hardship have been the underlying causes. Since the early days numerous initiatives were tried to find crops that could be exported to give a cash income to the islands. Many succeeded, only to be dashed by changing world markets, war in Europe or America, or pest and disease, leaving thriving communities destitute. Other natural disasters like earthquakes and eruptions drove islanders away after their homes and fields had been destroyed, even as recently as the 1980s. As a result there are large populations of Azoreans in Canada, the US, Brazil and elsewhere, still preserving their culture and heritage and returning regularly to the archipelago, particularly at festival times. Mass emigration largely ceased with the entry of Portugal to the EEC.

**EMIGRATION** Emigration has deeply impacted upon the psychology and economics of the Azores over the centuries and is integral to the culture of the islands.

Following the decline in commerce with India, exploration of Brazil was encouraged, and sugar plantations were established in the northeast. In 1746, King João V announced a package of incentives to promote settlement in the south: land, tools, seeds, two cows and a mare. As a result some 6,000 Azorean peasant farmers and fishermen settled in a period of six years, mainly in the state of Santa Catarina.

Throughout Azorean history poverty and lack of opportunity have been the main driving forces underlying the need to emigrate. Fundamental to this was overpopulation, eased by a wave of emigration, the population then only to increase again. By the 19th century, the land was the only source of income for the islanders, but land tenure did not offer opportunities for individuals to better themselves, and landowners were conservative and not open to innovation, so crop yields were low.

For a young man living in a close-knit community on a small island in a vast sea, with no big-city experience or that of a faster way of life, and speaking only Portuguese, emigration must have been a daunting prospect.

Around 1800, the Portuguese government introduced compulsory military conscription for 14 year olds. Pay was poor, advantages few, and this, coupled with the trap of peasant land tenure, spurred many to emigrate. At the same time American ships increasingly visited the Azores, including whalers, and very many young males escaped by joining the crew and eventually landing often years later in America via the east-coast whaling ports. Then disease and pests struck the grape vines, and later came the collapse of the orange crop, disasters that led to huge further exoduses from the archipelago.

With Brazil less inviting after gaining its independence, America offered better jobs and opportunities, and many Azoreans had already settled there from the whaling ships. By 1920, there were over 100,000 Azoreans in the United States, those from São Miguel having settled mostly on the east coast and Rhode Island, while people from the Central Group of islands made for California.

Immigration then virtually ceased due to new US immigration laws. In 1957, Capelinhos volcano erupted on Faial, destroying villages and farmland. The US, under President Kennedy, passed refugee laws for Azoreans, and Canada also opened its doors. The emigrants were not only refugees from the volcano, but many were also economic migrants since the Azorean population was at its highest ever, at around 350,000 and 100,000 more than it is today. At the same time many middle-class people emigrated to join their families, because whole family groups had gone, leaving many individuals alone.

Between 1878 and 1888, 17 ships carried 11,057 immigrants from the Azores and Madeira halfway round the world, including rounding Cape Horn, to Hawaii for work in the cane fields. Unlike to other destinations, this was the only mass immigration and contact was lost with the Azores. Only in the 1980s was the connection resumed by the Azorean regional authorities, although the community had kept alive their Portuguese names and traditions such as the Holy Ghost celebrations.

Bermuda, another warm-temperate archipelago with geological origins linked to the Mid-Atlantic Ridge, was from the second half of the 19th century a popular destination of choice for Azoreans, especially from São Miguel, peaking in the 1960s and 1970s. Permanent residence was never permitted, and a contract of employment was essential to obtaining a visa. Most worked in Hamilton, either in tourism or gardening.

Repeatedly through history, some Azorean migrants have returned to their home island, with material goods and money to build a new house or maybe refurbish an old family holding. Both hardy and hardworking, the Azoreans' work reputation has a long pedigree and their labour has always been welcomed. But the generations that have been born abroad, while recognising their ancestral links with the islands, often visit now as American tourists along with their American culture, sadly a price that perhaps has to be paid. On the other hand, some are returning permanently, preferring to raise their young children in the Azores. This quality of life in the islands, where few are wealthy, but rich in a traditional way, where there is little crime and the landscape beautiful, is ironically now attracting foreign nationals seeking tranquil retirement.

## LANGUAGE

Portuguese is both the national and native language, but there are strong regional dialects and vocabulary that often mother-tongue Portuguese-speakers from the mainland find difficult to understand. Natives of each island can be quickly recognised by fellow Azoreans, and even from which part of an island they come. Try learning some Portuguese before you travel; it is gesture that will be welcomed, though English is widely and willingly spoken on the bigger islands, especially by the young. It is mostly in smaller cafés that it is useful to speak Portuguese, and in villages to ask the way. Some taxi drivers are fluent in English; many know enough to get by, but many others speak only Portuguese. In the towns very many people speak English, it is a standard subject in school, and there are numerous Azoreans who have worked abroad and even more who watch Hollywood films! There are English-language television channels as well: CNN, BBC World and Sky News. Some French is spoken in Faial and Flores. Worldwide, Portuguese is the third-most widely spoken European language. (See *Appendix 1*, pages 263–7, for a list of useful phrases.)

## RELIGION

The Azores have been Catholic from their first settlement. The rare Protestant churches were built much later, for example in Ponta Delgada on São Miguel in the 19th century, primarily in response to the mainly English merchants who came to live on the islands to manage the orange trade. Although very much a minority, there was also a strong Jewish presence from the early days, with some Jews originating from North Africa. The Catholic parish priests were very influential, and the religious orders, especially the Franciscans, built many convents and churches and organised the first schools. In modern times it is the older parishioners who mostly make up church congregations, although young people still make up the numbers on festival days and religion is noticeably stronger here than in many European mainland regions.

**ARCHITECTURE AND ART** *With thanks to Dr Isabel Soares de Albergaria*

**Secular architecture** Architecture in the Azores is an offshoot of the designs known in continental Portugal, sharing the simplicity of form common to the Mediterranean. It does, however, have its own characteristics. The most obvious are the easy integration of the buildings in the landscape and the structure of the settlements, in which streets tend to converge in small irregular squares where stand the most imposing buildings, the church and town hall. Until very recently most houses were modest in size and appearance and had distinctive features: they were built of stone, with a characteristic contrast between whitewash and black basalt.

Vernacular architecture, less affected by variations in style and the dictates of fashion, perhaps best reflects the Azoreans' relationship with their island environment. Their isolation, the simple agrarian way of life and the use of naturally available materials have led to very simple, almost rudimentary, designs for both houses and utilitarian buildings such as barns, cowsheds and mills. These, together with the small shrines and chapels have, through the centuries, gradually developed their own style and form, leading to regional styles.

As you go around the different islands variations emerge: Santa Maria has white houses with coloured bars marking the shapes and windows and Algarve-style prismatic chimneys, while on Pico, houses are black with no plaster on the walls and balconies running along the upper floors are accessed via outside staircases. On Terceira a long house is common, with its row of windows and doors with the kitchen at one end indicated by the presence of the broad chimneys called *de mãos postas* ('with joined hands'). On São Miguel low window–door–window-style houses are more frequent, similar to those in the Alentejo or, in some areas, houses with their gable end directly on the street. Variations can also be seen in the generally very simple decorative elements, focused around the windows and doors: mouldings of curved lines; the *aventais* (aprons) of the windows outlined in black; the characteristic staircase eye-windows decorated with geometric motifs, possibly Arabic in influence; or the windows with wrought-iron balconies, with a more cultivated influence. Another very common element, especially in the islands of the Central Group, is the bands of basalt that cut vertically and horizontally across the façades, as a form of proof against earthquakes.

It is not possible to talk about popular Azorean architecture without mentioning one of the most peculiar and unique aspects of its heritage: the *impérios* (small chapels) of the Holy Spirit. Linked to an age-old religion, which existed in the Azores from the times of their earliest settlement, the *impérios* are fundamental to the ritual practices of this extraordinary cult that on the mainland disappeared long ago. Here again variations can be seen between the various islands, but the most famous are the *impérios* on Terceira, immediately recognisable for their festive appearance, bright colours and designs, and triangular pediment.

**Religious architecture** On approaching any Azorean village from the sea, the most prominent feature is always the more or less imposing façade of a church. The most notable in this respect is the view of Horta on Faial, with the façades of the parish church, the Convent of São Francisco and the beautiful façade of the Carmelite monastery dominating the group of houses and 'gazing out to sea'. Hills near the villages are often topped by little pilgrimage chapels; of the many that are to be found scattered through the islands is the group of chapels and pilgrimage houses of Nossa Senhora da Ajuda above the small town of Santa Cruz da Graciosa,

From the writings of early travellers to the Azores it appears that at least until the end of the 16th century only watermills, *moinhos de água*, were present in the islands, and that the windmills were a later innovation. Old long-disused watermills are still abundant and often now hidden beneath the vigorous growth of ginger lilies that also like the humid stream beds. The mills were built either over streams or below specially constructed dams, or were even seasonal, relying upon the heavier winter rains to drive them.

Like so many aspects of the archipelago, individual islands developed their own style of windmills, and there were at least eight different versions, of which four are still extant.

**SÃO MIGUEL TYPE** These are similar to the so-called 'Dutch' type and are found mainly on São Miguel, Santa Maria and Graciosa, with small differences between those on each island. They have a conical stone-built base with a wooden semi-ovoid rotating roof, and have four cloth-covered sails.

**FAIAL TYPE** This has a truncated cone-shaped stone base with a substantial timber upper structure called a *casota*, or 'little house'. Access is by a staircase which also acts as a central tail to the *casota*. Originally it should have had a long mast with a pointed tip and eight crossed poles tied by guides and wire fasteners for triangular cloth sails, without bars. Today it is almost always of the square type, or is even replaced by rotors of two or four vanes. This type is to be seen on Faial and Pico.

**SÃO JORGE TYPE** São Jorge has two types of windmill: the mechanical mill now most commonly seen is a modified form of an earlier mill. This earlier version had four triangular sails made of cloth without lattice work. The later, adapted version has a stone-built conical base upon which is a narrow vertical mill providing an elevated support for the rotor of either two or four blades. This small mill can either rotate or be fixed, in which case only the dome rotates. The narrow tail leads either from the body of the mill or its dome, reaching to the ground.

**CORVO TYPE** Corvo's distinctive type has a low stone base and a squat conical tower, almost always rendered and whitewashed. The tower is built well inside the edges of the base so there is a wide ledge all round. The mast is long and pointed, leans upwards at a low angle and has eight sail poles with guides and fasteners for triangular cloth sails. Internal access is through a door in the tower reached by an external stone stairway rising from the ledge.

Background Information CULTURE

1

27

among which is also what is perhaps the best example of a fortified church with huge buttresses, decorative battlements and ribbed vaults inside.

In spite of limited resources, religious art in the Azores always had the benefit of fine talents and this enabled the islands to keep up with the artistic developments of mainland Portugal. The initial period, characterised by Gothic-Manueline architecture which lasted until the mid 16th century, is represented by almost all the surviving early parish churches of the main towns; for example the parish churches of São Sebastião in Ponta Delgada and of São Sebastião on Terceira. Then followed a long period of Portuguese classicism, known as *estilo chão* (plain architecture) because of its bare, austere and purely functional style exemplified by the Cathedral of Angra, and the Parish Church of Santa Cruz on Graciosa. The majority of monastic buildings in the Azores belong to this group, in spite of the decorative alterations many of them underwent during the Baroque period, of which examples include Nossa Senhora da Graça in Ponta Delgada and São Boaventura in Santa Cruz on Flores.

The religious way of life, with its ritual of offerings, processions and pilgrimages, had its origins in the mendicant orders established in the early Middle Ages in continental Europe. Monks came to the Azores during the early phase of settlement (15th century), the Franciscans being the most prominent; their monasteries soon sprang up in every town and city. Later on the Jesuits joined them. Soon after receiving papal approval, in 1540, the Company of Jesus promoted the building of great and elaborate colleges for the whole Portuguese Empire, including the islands. By royal initiative, the Colégio da Ascenção in Angra (the present Palácio dos Capitães-Generais) was founded in 1570, then the Colégio de Ponta Delgada, dedicated to All Saints (1591) and only much later, in 1680, the Colégio de São Francisco Xavier in Horta (today the seat of the parish church, municipal hall, treasury and museum). The present churches of Angra and Ponta Delgada are not, however, the original ones, there being various reconstructions and additions in later years.

Baroque architecture is well represented in the islands, particularly on São Miguel. It was dominant throughout the 18th and early 19th centuries, and is characterised by exuberant sculptural and decorative forms. Monastery churches entirely rebuilt or substantially altered (for example the Monastery dos Frades in Lagoa, São Miguel; Santo André, c1744; Esperança, 1740–86 and Conceição (Carmo), c1754, Ponta Delgada; São Gonçalo, Angra, 1730–50) use black basalt in capricious curves, highly indented mouldings, twisted columns, garlands and medallions, which form the new decorative language. The reconstruction of the Parish Church of São Pedro de Ponta Delgada (1737–42) was developed on an octagonal plan, original for the period, and the idea was repeated in the Parish Church of Fajã de Baixo. The Church of Santo Espírito, on the island of Santa Maria (18th century), is another example of originality, this time with the application of a dense and compact decoration, which is reminiscent of South American Baroque. Private chapels were often associated with the construction of Baroque manor houses such as Santa Catarina in Ponta Delgada; also of the 18th century were extravagant Baroque *misericórdias*, institutions for the poor offering medical care, food and other charitable benefits.

**Military architecture** Because of their strategic location between Europe and the New World the Azores were important for shipping, especially the returning treasure ships, but the islands were constantly threatened by corsairs. During the reigns of Dom João III and Dom Sebastião in the mid 16th century, a series of fortifications were begun 3km apart around the coast, with São Miguel, Terceira and Flores the most fortified. Construction was inspired by Renaissance technology and supervised by Italian military engineers and examples are São Brás in Ponta Delgada and Santa Cruz in Horta. In Angra on Terceira the castle of São Filipe, later renamed São João Baptista, was built during Philippine sovereignty (1580–1640), again as part of a general defence plan; construction was supervised by the Portuguese military engineer João de Vilhena and the Italian fortification specialist Tiburzio Spanochi, and was only completed after the Restoration. Practically impregnable, the castle benefited from the natural situation of Monte Brasil and included, on the landward side of the isthmus, a defensive platform with bulwarks and powerful curtain walls with deep moats. By this device the forces loyal to the Spanish crown were able to resist for long months after the King of Portugal took power.

Surprisingly few vestiges of this vast military effort are left to us. This is probably due to two factors. First, the quality of the constructions varied since often, with an attack imminent, the work was organised by the town hall and executed by the population using the materials and technology immediately to hand. Second, advances in warfare made many buildings obsolete, so that they were abandoned and left to the mercy of the elements and vandalism. Only more recently has the historical and architectural value of this heritage been recognised and efforts are slowly being made to save it from total ruin.

**PAINTING AND DECORATIVE ARTS**  Most paintings, carvings, glazed tiles, furniture and gold artefacts in the Azores come from studios abroad following commissions made in a religious context. Only in a few cases is the artist or school, those who commissioned the item and the iconographic association known to us. On the whole, however, the quality of the work is comparable to the rest of Portugal, with the obvious exception of the royal court.

As with the architecture, genuinely Gothic artefacts are extremely rare. One of them is the triptych of the Virgin Mary in the Church of Dos Anjos (on Santa Maria), a portable altarpiece that according to tradition belonged to Christopher Columbus, on which Gothic designs can be distinguished. Another example is the murals of the Church of São Sebastião on Terceira.

Later 16th-century **Flemish art** is much more visible in the archipelago, both in works imported from the workshops of Antwerp, Brussels and Mechelen, and in works of local artists who succumbed to a veritable passion for the Flemish style. This fashion spread throughout the Portuguese territory, largely because of the privileged relationship Iberia had with this northern European region in the 15th and 16th centuries. In the Azores the Flemish influence was exercised directly by Flemish settlers and through a significant trade in woad and urzela, two dye plants used in the textile industry.

Imported Flemish art includes numerous small sculptures such as the *Virgin and Child* (Horta Museum), *St Sebastian tied to a dry tree trunk* (Ponta Delgada Museum), or the larger sculpture *Our Lady of the Miracles* in the Church of Vila do Corvo, all from Mechelen. More elaborate and emotionally charged is the *Crucifixion and Saint Mary Magdalen* (Horta Museum), a delicate work that must have come from the hands of a Brussels artist around 1520. Another theatrical composition is the *Christ being taken down from the Cross*, probably also from the 15th century, now exhibited in the Church of the Altares on Terceira. A moving group presents the scene of *Our Lady, St John and the Holy Women*, with Roman soldiers and citizens; at the bottom you can see skulls, the bones of Adam and some souls from purgatory. Probably also of Flemish influence, but from the first half of

1

the 17th century, is the magnificent sculpture of *Our Lady of the Tears* (Church of São Pedro, Ponta Delgada), a powerfully modelled work of great expressiveness.

Among paintings, the triptych of *Saint Andrew* (Church of Nossa Senhora da Estrela, Ribeira Grande), which came from the chapel of the same name, is a 16th-century work whose Flemish affiliation is obvious in the drawing and sculptural appearance of the figures, the warm colours and delicate play of light on the background landscape, made in perspective. Although more archaic, the Flemish influence is visible also in the magnificent triptych of the *Adoration of the Magi* (Angra Museum) and in the painting of *Saint Ursula and the Eleven Thousand Virgins*, commissioned by the Jesuits of Angra perhaps in the late 16th century, in which a Mannerist style is already evident.

The 16th-century purely Portuguese painting also achieved very high standards. Some exceptionally good works of this period can be seen in the Azores, including the polyptych in the Church of Santa Cruz da Graciosa depicting scenes from the Passion of Christ and the *Legend of Vera Cruz*, and showing all the signs of the late-Renaissance pathos that characterises this work. In the Carlos Machado Museum in Ponta Delgada (currently closed), there are two paintings from the Coimbra studio of Manuel Vicente and Vicente Gil, with Gothic-style features, as well as the polyptych of the *Holy Martyrs of Lisbon*, by an anonymous artist but from a major Lisbon studio, closer to the Italian Renaissance style.

The **Counter-Reformation** movement, the setting up of the Inquisition in Portugal (1547) and Catholic orthodoxy dictated by the Council of Trent (1545–63) dealt a serious blow to artistic expression; painting became increasingly conventional. Altarpieces developed a tendency for compositional repetition and the command of anatomical detail became somewhat precarious. In spite of that there were still some worthwhile works of art, linked to the Italian or Spanish school. These include *Our Lady with Angel Musicians*, commissioned by Ponta Delgada Jesuits from Vasco Pereira for the Church of Ponta Delgada (now in the Carlos Machado Museum) and produced in Seville in 1604, and a set of Mannerist paintings by Francisco Álvares in the sacristy of the Church of São Pedro (Ponta Delgada). Outstanding is the group of eight paintings representing the infancy of Christ, painted by an anonymous artist for the Church of São Gonçalo in Angra; it is already linked to the early Baroque and shows a clear Italian influence. Simultaneously with the imposition of artistic conventionality ran the taste for luxury and ostentation in religious rituals; this led to churches being covered in gilded carvings, panels of glazed tiles and altars adorned with gold, silver and marble.

Sailing ships arriving from the **Orient** brought into the Azores new riches; marble figurines of the Good Shepherd in the meditative pose of the Buddha or Virgins in Glory with oriental features and a hieratic pose of which a collection can be seen in the Carlos Machado Museum. Others include Indo-Portuguese counters with inlays of marble and mother-of-pearl (examples in Angra Museum and the Palácio de Sant'Ana in Ponta Delgada) and bookcases designed to hold the plainsong books (Ponta Delgada parish church, Angra Cathedral). In the same way Chinese porcelain – pots, vases, plates and platters – sent by the Companhia das Índias from the 17th to the 19th centuries was also imported, as were Hindu tapestries which greatly influenced the designs of glazed tiles. Worthy of special mention in the context of Hindu–Portuguese art originating from the Malabar coast (Goa) and Sri Lanka are the two paintings in the Church of Santa Cruz da Graciosa, depicting St Francisco Xavier and Saint Inácio de Loyola dressed in long robes with golden adornments, brought in during the 17th century.

## WOMEN IN BLACK   *David Sayers*

On São Jorge, the island of black lava rocks, many women were always seen in black. Religious custom demanded that any widow had to dress in black for the rest of her life. Apart from black clothes, a widow had to wear a black-fringed square shawl and have her head covered by a triangular woollen scarf. After a loss of a parent, black was obligatory for two or three years; the loss of a brother meant black clothes for a year.

Many women therefore spent most of their life in black. The rule was less strict for the men: mourning was expressed by a simple black band on the upper arm, except for Sundays when they all took out their black suits; this was usually the suit made for the wedding and used until the last journey to the cemetery. In the last 20 years, young people have adopted the colour black as a fashion statement, and under the American influence, the widows are changing slowly to wearing grey and even some colours, but in the countryside the traditional black persists.

Portuguese art makes great use of the **glazed tiles** that bring colour and brightness to architectural space and can be used to depict natural scenes, tell stories in narrative sequences or extend architectural patterns by illusion. There was no local production in the Azores, so the existing tiles are the product of commissions from the mainland where they have been made for centuries. After the phase of Hispano-Arabic glazed tiles, some 16th-century examples of which are in various Azorean chapels (the most complete comes from Seville and is now in the Museu Municipal (formerly Casa da Cultura) at Ribeira Grande), Portuguese glazed tile-making expanded, patterns diversified and new techniques developed. There are polychrome altar fronts with a symmetrical composition and plant motifs, directly inspired by oriental textiles, which were in former Azorean shrines and chapels. Good examples are to be seen in the Carlos Machado Museum, once it eventually reopens, though this could be some years; the sets are full of peacocks, vases of flowers and friezes of exotic animals. There is also the pediment of the private chapel of the Chaves, now in the Palácio de Sant'Ana in Ponta Delgada; another is from the chapel of Anjos, on the island of Santa Maria, dating from 1679. Equally abundant are the wall coverings with blue, white and yellow glazed tiles, called *padronagem de tapete*; they repeat stylised plant motifs, applied inside decorative borders. A fine example of these is the 17th- and 18th-century glazed tiles that completely line the beautiful chapel of the Monastery of Caloura (São Miguel). Entirely Mannerist are the tiles from the sacristy of the Church of São José de Ponta Delgada, Church of São Roque (São Miguel), chapel of the Almas of the Church of São Francisco de Vila do Porto (Santa Maria), and Church of Conceição de Angra (Terceira).

In the **Baroque** period glazed tiles reached their zenith in terms of figurative, narrative compositions in blue and white. There are many examples. Among the finest are the panels in the lower choir of the Church of Esperança (Ponta Delgada) by António de Oliveira Bernardes, dated 1712 and relating scenes from the Passion of Christ; and the tiling of the main chapel in the Church of São José (Ponta Delgada) and in the Church of São Francisco in Horta: both illustrate the life of St Francis of Assisi and date from the same period. Also in Horta and worthy of special mention is the set from the parish church (former church of the Jesuit monastery) with scenes relating the life of Saint Inácio de Loyola. In Angra the glazed tiles which line the Church of São Roque (c1725) are worth seeing; in Livramento there is a fine picture depicting the Sermon of St Anthony to the Fishes; and the chapel of the Santíssimo Sacramento in the Church of Nossa Senhora do Monte do Carmo, with an excellent allegorical composition on the Eucharist, is one of the finest works in the archipelago, made in Lisbon around 1740.

The **Rococo** period is represented in the Azores by some top-quality pieces. The return of polychromy, the spread of borders, bands, garlands, shells and other forms of decorative framing of great linear elegance, make the aesthetics of this Baroque period easily identifiable. The little Church of Santa Bárbara das Manadas on the island of São Jorge has one of the finest sets of polychrome glazed tiles with *rocaille* (shell) motifs, as well as a set of locally made carvings and paintings, which make this church a precious example of the alliance between cultivated and naïve art. Other examples of Rococo glazed tiles are in São Pedro de Alcântara at Lajes do Pico and in the Church of Santa Cruz da Graciosa. In the Piedade chapel in the Church of São José (Ponta Delgada), the Rococo glazed tiles are combined with mouldings consisting of gilded carvings on white backgrounds.

Azorean Baroque is not expressed just in richly decorated glazed tiles; the entire church interior is usually full of gilded carvings, paintings and painted wood. The history of carving also goes back a long way but again it peaked in the Baroque period, especially during the reign of King John (Dom João V), when many shipments of gold came from Brazil, enabling the carvings to be gilded. The Renaissance retables (carved and sometimes painted panels behind the altar) are replaced by the Baroque-style ornamentation with twisted columns, fluttering angels, birds pecking at grapes and drawn-back curtains. Examples can be found in almost every church; particularly rich are the carvings in the Church of São Gonçalo, Angra; in the main chapel of the Church of Esperança, Ponta Delgada, which covers the whole vault; in the Parish Church of Horta; and the most imposing of all the Azorean retables, the one in the main chapel of the Church of the Jesuits in Ponta Delgada, already in transition to Rococo style.

The range of **devotional sculptures** is impressive, if not always of great quality. In addition to the gallery of Catholic saints and tutelary figures, the Virgins in Glory are a favourite theme; Horta parish church contains one of the most spectacular examples. Other subjects include the Holy Family, scenes dedicated to the cycle of Christ's Passion, including *pietàs*, and nativities such as in the churches of São Miguel in Vila Franca do Campo and Angústias in Horta.

Throughout this period in which religious art dominated, gold work was associated with liturgical ritual. A vast range of ornaments and precious objects including chalices, salvers, monstrances, incense boats, censers, chandeliers, candlesticks, crucifixes, processional crosses, etc, today fill the church treasuries and are still used in worship. Only a few genuinely old pieces have survived the centuries of constant plundering by pirates, for whom churches and monasteries were a particularly rewarding target. The processional cross of the Church das Altares on Terceira is a late Gothic rarity, Flemish-made; also unique is the altar front in wrought silver in the chapel of the Sacramento in Angra Cathedral (17th century), probably Spanish in origin. Much more common, yet having enormous symbolic significance for the Azoreans, are the Crowns of the Holy Spirit in wrought silver, some dating back to the 17th century. In material riches and artistic value, however, nothing surpasses the treasury of Senhor Santo Cristo (Santuário da Esperança, Ponta Delgada). Consisting essentially of five pieces (*Glory, Crown, Sceptre, Cords* and *Reliquary*) that accompany the figure of Ecce Homo, originally designed and made in the 18th century during the reign of João V, it was later enriched with new gifts from the faithful. The *Glory* stands out, a fabulous piece weighing 4.85kg; it is made of gold-plated platinum and contains 6,842 precious stones, among them four extremely rare topazes from Brazil. Made in Lisbon by the finest goldsmiths of João V, the *Glory* presents a complete lesson in theology, containing the symbols of the Trinity, Redemption and the Passion of Christ, all executed with wonderful precision and detail.

Progressively moving away from the religious context, the 19th and 20th centuries finally began to place art in the service of a bourgeois public with secular ideas. The initially timid decorative schemes that the Azorean nobility used in their manor houses and town houses (an unusual example dating from the 1940s is the glazed tile panels alluding to the loss of independence and restoration of Portugal, in the Palácio Bettencourt in Angra) gradually expanded and diversified. The new urban and Liberal bourgeoisie, grown rich on the orange trade, contracted artists to paint their portraits and indulged in luxurious furniture, porcelain and textiles bought in England or France. Ambitious artists went to Paris to receive a proper academic training; such was the case with Marciano Henriques da Silva (1831–73) and Duarte Maia (1867–1922), the first a romantic, the second a naturalist, with work in the Carlos Machado Museum, Ponta Delgada.

The **20th century** began with a new generation of artists who gathered in Paris, the city of light, along with many others seeking inspiration from the artistic avant-garde. Two Azoreans stand out: **Domingos Rebelo** (1891–1975) and **Ernesto Canto da Maia** (1890–1981). Rebelo, a painter, caricaturist and ceramicist, followed a path that diverged from the vanguard, focusing all his attention on local reality, on the landscapes, appearances and attitudes of the simple and common people that he perceived as the most authentic aspect of this landscape, and capturing them with the detail of an ethnographer. His most famous work, *Os Emigrantes* (*The Emigrants*), portrays with contained feeling the drama experienced by thousands of Azoreans obliged to leave the islands in search of a better future (his paintings may be seen in the Palácio da Conceição, Museu Carlos Machado, Arte Contemporânea in Lisbon, Viseu, Caldas da Rainha, The Gulbenkian Foundation for Modern Art and in countless private collections).

Sculptor Canto da Maia embraced Parisian life with enthusiasm, showing in his synthetic and graphic style traces of the symbolism and stylised decorativeness of the 1920s and 1930s. Even so, his work reflects the deeper quest of a probing mind, meditating upon the themes of life, death and love. (Examples of his works are to be found in the Núcleo de Santa Bárbara in Ponta Delgada (page 83), The Gulbenkian Foundation, Musée des Années 30, Boulogne, and the Musée Jeu de Paume, Paris, as well as in various public spaces.)

In 1901, Carlos and Amélia, the Portuguese royal couple, officially visited the Azores. Their temporary residence was to be the Palácio de Sant'Ana in Ponta Delgada, and the occasion was a perfect excuse for the most complete decorative renovation that had ever been carried out in a non-religious context. From 1915 to the late 1930s, painters, sculptors, decorators and carvers, both Azorean and from the continent, worked at Sant'Ana. Worth examining are the enormous paintings in the vestibule by Ernesto Condeixa, referring to the royal visit; the frieze in the former armoury; a bas-relief in gilded plaster of Paris by Canto da Maia; and the dining room lined with magnificent carved panelling and furniture entirely made by local artists. There are also extensive glazed-tile pictures made by the painter Jorge Colaço.

In the second half of the 20th century, particularly in the last two decades, Azorean arts blossomed. Art exhibitions and galleries of fine arts were supported and new art programmes initiated. Throughout its history, Azorean art has mirrored movements in Europe, and developed its own style affected by local conditions

1

The Festival of the Holy Ghost differs a little from island to island and from village to village and São Jorge celebrates the festival in its own way. Every village that has a church also has a small chapel called an *império*. The festival extends beyond its religious role; it is also a good excuse to have a great time.

The old traditions can still be enjoyed in the village of Rosais; they are centred on the *Carro das bandeiras* – an oxcart carrying a boat constructed from bamboo canes and green leaves and decorated on all sides with paper flowers, with colourful flags waving from long canes on the top. The carts are not just decorative, they have an important role: to bring to the *império* wine, sweet bread, cheese and lupin seeds. The lupin seeds have to be soaked in seawater for three tides, after which they are boiled. The festive food is then served free to all visitors during Saturday. Usually there are two carts and much rivalry exists between the two competing teams of villagers. The ornaments with which the horns of the oxen are decorated are kept strictly secret until the festive day and can never be repeated.

Independent of the religious festival is Mordomia, in which anyone in the village can participate, after joining one of many local groups. Donations of corn and other products are made, usually the previous year, and sold, and the proceeds are used to help with the preparation of the festival. The remaining expenses are divided between the members of individual organising groups. Mordomias are organised by most villages on São Jorge, so don't be surprised if you see cars stopped in the middle of the street to be offered some wine and sweet bread. These celebrations take place on the Saturday before the Festival of the Holy Ghost.

The organiser of the religious festival is called the *imperador* and is usually someone who has undertaken the work voluntarily. These types of festivals are increasingly expensive to organise because in some villages, like Beira and Topo, there is a tradition to invite anyone who passes through to eat for free. In the

and materials. In the 21st century, the internet adds to the external influences, while artists and photographers pursue contemporary Azorean themes and concerns.

**FESTIVALS** These are many, both religious and secular, and take place on all the islands, mostly during the summer months. They are listed in each island's chapter; some festivals are common to all the islands, while others are island-specific. Some dates are fixed, others change each year, and you should check with the tourist information office. Visitors during the summer months will be very unlucky not to chance upon one during their stay; they are often joyful occasions and the kindness and generosity given to strangers make for happy memories.

The most important festival that is celebrated throughout the archipelago is that of the Holy Ghost (Espírito Santo), held six weeks after Easter on the seventh Sunday. It can also be repeated on the following Sunday if enough people have made promises to make the festival, and if emigrants come back to visit in the summer it can again be celebrated. Of 13th-century medieval origin imported from the mainland, it is one of the most traditional, although each island and each village has its own variation. On the chosen day, offerings of bread, meat and wine are distributed among the needy, followed by a procession through the town or village. You may notice small, pretty chapels called *impérios* in most of the villages at road junctions or on prominent corners. These are a source of great pride and they form past people did not have cars to get about and only local people came for the meal. Now the feast can attract many people from the entire island and it can be crowded. The village of Manadas has its festivities at lunchtime on the Thursday before the Holy Ghost day. Food is served on long tables, sometimes outside in the street. There is a special Holy Spirit soup, wine, *alcatra* sweet bread and sweet rice for dessert.

In Rosais you can also see the *foliões*: two or three men, one or two playing the drums and the other one singing in front of the *império* and walking up and down the square. The singing is improvised, sometimes repeated; it can be about God and the kindness of the Holy Ghost, or it can praise the organisation. The musicians are accompanied by the *cavaleiro*, a young man with two helpers. The *cavaleiro* carries a flag and the helpers bring two huge loaves of bread, called the castles, usually quite hard because they are so big (100cm x 50cm). On Sunday afternoon after the mass and the procession, the *foliões* and the *cavaleiro* perform a traditional dance with the bread, to the accompaniment of the drums and the singing. After that there is a merry game for all. The *cavaleiro* comes out of the *império* with a cake or dolls made of sweet bread in his hands, and attempts a dance, to be accosted suddenly by someone trying to steal the cake and run away with it. The helpers must then run behind and try to touch the thief with a rod. If they succeed, the thief has to return the cake; if he escapes, the cake is his. The more people take part, the more fun there is to be had.

In Norte Grande, each evening of that week a big dog-whelk shell is used to call everyone to the *imperador's* house. The sound carries round the entire village. The *imperador* then invites the guests to sing the rosary at his house, where he keeps an altar made especially for this event. It is decorated with candles and flowers and at the top is the crown of the Holy Ghost. The rosary is sung in a way unique to this event. After the rosary, the *imperador* offers sweets and drinks to all comers.

the centrepoint of the **Espírito Santo Festival**. This festival is under the direction of a local group of men, a brotherhood, who undertake the care of the *impérios* and the giving of food to the poor, an important feature of Espírito Santo. Above the doors of most *impérios* you will find symbols: the crown, the sceptre, the dove and a red banner. The symbols are also to be found on the silver crowns which are worn by the *imperador*, the member of the brotherhood in charge of that day's festivities. Several *imperadores* may be crowned in each village during the festival season and each has the honour of guarding the crown and sceptre on a throne in his home until the next procession. Some of these precious village crowns and sceptres are many hundreds of years old. Fireworks signal the end of the opening church service and the start of a procession from the church to the *império* led by the crowned *imperador*. Music is provided by the local brass marching band, or *filarmonica*. These bands are a major part of village life in the Azores, where there are more such groups than in all of Portugal. After the procession a beef-based broth, called *sopas do Espírito Santo*, is served along with another Azorean food with a strong tradition: *massa sovada*, a slightly sweet bread made in homes by groups of women taking turns during hours of hand-kneading. This festival, brought by the first settlers to the islands in the early 1400s, is seldom seen in Europe today, but is celebrated by communities of Azorean ancestry around the world, especially in the US, including Hawaii, and in Canada.

Other festivals are for saints' days or for vows made long ago to God. The most colourful is the Festival of Corpus Christi, and the preparation is as interesting as the procession. This takes place in June. Early in the morning many baskets of various small colourful flowers and finely chopped soft branch tips of the conifer *Cryptomeria japonica* are brought in and laid out in geometrical patterns upon the roadway using wooden templates, the colours all kept in separate shapes. The flowers and petals are frequently sprayed with water to keep them fresh and to stop the wind from disturbing the patterns or blowing them away. Sometimes dyed woodshavings are also used. Summer flowers in baskets and pots adorn balconies, and bright bedcovers hanging from windows add further colour. The procession is led by the priest under a pallium escorted by his followers and many small children dressed as angels. Much less formal is the June Festival of São João, marked with picnics at the many barbecue sites throughout the islands. The secular festivals get bigger every year and are celebrated by music, dance, arts, local culture, food stalls and sporting events. Music includes not only folk, but also pop groups from the mainland and Brazil, something not always viewed with enthusiasm by everyone.

**Tourada à corda – bullfights on a rope** In the Portuguese version of bullfighting, the bulls are not killed and the only blood spilt is that of overconfident humans! Terceira is especially noted for its *tourada à corda*, but other islands also participate.

The organisers have introduced regulations and planned a classification system for the bulls. No more than four bulls are allowed at any one event. Each must be at least three years old, and can appear only once for no more than 30 minutes. Cloaks and similar items are allowed, but anything that could cause injury to the bulls is banned. Action can only take place during daylight, and in the late afternoon/early evening. In practice, they mostly start around 18.00, beginning on 1 May until 15 October, almost daily during July and August, with some 50 runs in the latter month.

The bull is at the end of a long rope that is held by several men to try to keep him under some control. The fun comes in approaching the bull as close as one dares and then outmanoeuvring him while keeping clear of his horns. One year, the bull really got up speed and chased five boys the length of the quay. Having nowhere else to go, they leapt off the end into the harbour and the bull had so much momentum he could not stop and went in on top of them to a tremendous cheer from the crowd and creating a huge tidal wave. The bull appeared to rather enjoy it, a nice cooling swim to the slipway at the end of a warm afternoon! Terceira and Graciosa both have bullrings, but here the bull is let loose without a rope.

These events have become very popular, with over 200 meetings each year. Dating back to the 16th century, in the past it was not only an entertainment but also an excuse for people from different villages to meet, both socially and for business. Animals could be bought and sold, goods traded or exchanged, youths could demonstrate to the girls their dash and courage with the bulls, there would be refreshment stalls and it was all huge fun. It still is.

# 2

# Practical Information

These mid-Atlantic islands are nothing if not green. This means the weather is variable, and while at any time there can be a week or more of continuous glorious sunshine and blue skies, it can also be fickle.

You will be welcomed everywhere and find that English is widely spoken in the main towns, but when you enter a café away from the main centres or seek directions out in the country you might have fun trying to communicate. You should also be very safe, for there is little crime or street violence. Although drugs and alcohol are problems locally, they are no more so than elsewhere in western Europe.

Ferry services and domestic flights keep reasonably well to the timetables except for understandable delays through bad weather – in the case of aircraft this can just be wind affecting certain of the airports. Communications are excellent, the islands and their public facilities are very clean, and standards are high.

The cost of many items is greater than in mainland Portugal but compared with northern Europe prices for the visitor are reasonable, and the well-informed budget traveller can certainly get by. In winter it gets dark about 18.30, in summer about 21.00, and time is Greenwich Mean Time −1.

## WHEN TO VISIT

There are small variations between the individual islands, with Santa Maria seen as the sunniest, while the western islands are the wettest. July and August are the warmest months and should have the most stable weather. November to January are the wettest. April and September normally tend to be the most changeable, but all the old patterns are changing, like everywhere else in the world. Every month is a delight in the Azores and even in January it can be possible to enjoy the ritual walker's lunch of local cheese, fresh bread and a bottle of wine, sitting in a field in bright sunshine without jackets or jerseys.

The time to go depends upon what you want to do. If it is to do with the sea – inter-island ferry travel, whale watching, sailing or fishing – then you need to go in the summer months between mid-April and early October. People swim throughout the year, but the popular times for the beaches are again the summer months and into October, but remember the Azores are not beach destinations. Regarding flowers, there will always be something of interest but for the beautiful and spectacular hedgerows you should consider June and July to see them at their best, and for native species May to September is the best time. For walking, the whole year is good, but the rain in winter is usually colder than in summer! In winter you will also have to take extra care in the mountains. In summer there are more accommodation and eating places open, and the latter keep longer daytime opening hours. During the high season of July and August hotels throughout the islands are usually fully booked and the casual traveller may have difficulty in getting accommodation. The same goes for car rental. In summer it is impossible to rent a car on arrival and advance reservation is essential; similarly for bicycles. Increasingly this is becoming the situation for June and September, as the increasing visitor numbers cause a lengthening of the high season. In addition to inbound tourists, many Azoreans who emigrated to North America come back to see relatives, particularly at festival times, while second and third generations return to discover their roots. March and April, still officially low season, are beautiful months because spring is usually early in the Azores and by now nature is wide awake; autumn is a much longer season than in northern Europe and October and November have lovely warm days while the golden hues of falling leaves prevail into December. And December is the Christmas festival season, when every town is festooned with lights and decorations in a very Azorean way that is so charming and does not hint of commercialism.

## HIGHLIGHTS

The greatest attraction for many is the tranquillity and the lack of pollution: the quiet rural scenes of small houses, the pastures, the grazing cows on a stage of lush green grass and the backdrop of a deep blue sea, farmers on horseback with milk churns hanging from their saddles, the little pony cart clattering along the cobbles with more milk churns, the cattle dogs perched on top. The scenery is the true star of the Azores: ever-changing, from sea to coast and often spectacular cliffs, to pastures or stony vineyards, up into forest and hills of often conical shape until culminating in a volcano's caldera and other heights lost in cloud. Blue hydrangeas and the Azores may have become a cliché but to see an island seeming as if a fisherman's net with extra-large holes had been thrown over it creating a pattern of blue lines and enclosures remains, all the same, a remarkable sight.

Even the largest towns, including relatively busy Ponta Delgada, have an irresistible allure that urges the visitor to explore them. Many ordinary street buildings have an elegant simplicity with lovely adornments of wrought-iron balconies or perhaps some ornamented basalt carving while grander places may show a more ornate Manueline influence. Small retailers are modest and sometimes do not even bother to advertise their presence while often the stock is held in the shop's dark recess so that it is difficult to even decipher what it is they are selling. Frustrating? No – simply refreshing. The narrow cobbled backstreets have constricted pavements while bigger thoroughfares have grander ones; whatever their size they are made of small squares of black basalt and imported white granite that is used to make designs appropriate to the place: caravels, whaling boats, whales, fish, figures dressed in the no-longer-worn *capote* or cloak, windmills, sheaves of corn – there is no end to the *pavior*'s enterprise. For the foot-weary there are street cafés to enjoy while watching island life pass by, or many a quiet church for deeper contemplation.

Certain islands are perfect for exploring by car, and endless hours can be spent discovering rural roads or following up those that do not appear on maps. There are so many tempting places to park the car and just lean on a fence post and enjoy a view or listen to the birds. Should you tire of rural scenery, then comes the satisfying contrast of dropping down to the coast and into a little village; maybe at its centre is the main church, a tiny public garden with its bandstand, and a café, or perhaps you have chanced upon a fishing village with a harbour and nearby natural swimming pools for an ocean swim and a fish restaurant to follow.

Whale watching has become tremendously popular since it first began on Pico years ago and still uses the old expertise of the lookouts in hilltop towers to spy the cetaceans. It is a truly world-class cetacean hotspot and a single three-hour trip might reveal two or three whale species and almost certainly some playful dolphins. Numerous enterprises now offer the experience. Diving affords a range of unique opportunities, from wrecks to sea cliffs and extraordinary underwater lava formations, and several companies on many islands offer their services. Many small fishing boats can be seen, either drawn up on the harbour quays or gently bobbing a short distance offshore, and if you feel tempted there are fishermen registered to take you out to fish for your supper. At the other end of the spectrum, the Azores are renowned internationally for sport- or big-game fishing, especially for blue marlin, and many world-record catches have been made, although of course these are for putting back and not for eating.

Going hand in hand with the tranquillity and clean environment are walking and cycling, the finest ways to acquire a real feel for the islands. Several companies offer organised cycling tours, and it is often possible to borrow or hire bicycles from hotels or guesthouses. There are short walks and long walks, in the mountains, along the coast, sometimes on narrow trails, at other times on seldom-used farm roads. The views are always changing, and relics of the past are everywhere, from wheel-worn donkey paths hidden beneath the summer's flush of vegetation to abandoned farmhouses and crumbling watermills. Hiking routes have been waymarked and documented and are kept reasonably well up to date. Some published walks are short and many are linear rather than circular; the narrative descriptions can be vague and maps weak, but the waymarking itself is good and the whole trails programme is under constant review. Winter storms cause landslides, and vegetation is so lush that in a very few weeks freshly cleared paths are concealed. For all walks it is best to check with the local tourist information office or your Azorean travel agent that the walk is clear before setting out; also the official trails website (*www.trails-azores.com*). One gets the impression some routes are devised by office-based bureaucrats, and not by a practical ranger or forester on the ground. However, if you are prepared to risk some possible frustration and the need to fall back upon your own sense of direction, you will enjoy many a memorable walk. For those who prefer, guides are available, as listed in the island chapters or through the local travel agencies (page 41).

The golf course at Furnas (page 111) on São Miguel must be one of the world's most intimate and exquisitely beautiful courses, given its mountain setting with sheltering forests and numerous elegant tree ferns. It is little known, but for any golfer who values the environment and surroundings in which he or she plays, this course cannot fail to impress. However, it is not without hidden challenges, for its luxuriant vegetation reflects its relationship with the clouds, and it can be quite entertaining to drive off into a white mist that has suddenly descended and might well instantly clear to give advantage to your opponent. There are two other equally green courses to play, both at much lower altitudes, at Batalha (also on São Miguel) and one on Terceira; see pages 111 and 146.

## PLANNING AN ITINERARY: WHICH ISLANDS?

The pace of the Azores is slow, and slowly is how one should discover them. There are nine islands and if you were to attempt to see them all in one visit to the archipelago you would need several weeks to do them all justice. Should you try to visit too many islands in a short period you will end up spending a disproportionate amount of time waiting in airports or for ferries. If you have just a week, then you might be well advised to concentrate on the largest and most diverse island, São Miguel, which is also the aviation hub. If you have more time, maybe combine São Miguel with Faial, and Pico with perhaps Terceira as well for your first visit (these islands will easily take up two weeks) and then see other islands on return visits. Various islands suit different means of touring. Plan your trip carefully and consider hiring a car for just *some* rather than *all* of your stay on each island.

If you like to hire a car and take your time exploring then São Miguel, Santa Maria, Terceira, Pico, São Jorge and Flores would make the best choices.

If you prefer to tour with someone else driving, then much of São Miguel can be accessed by bus. Graciosa is small, there are buses, but distances are so short taxi fares are reasonable. Terceira largely means the city of Angra, for which you do not need a car, and adjacent Monte Brasil can also be explored on foot. A half-day taxi tour would provide a glimpse of many of the other highlights. Faial offers Horta and nearby attractions, and a half-day taxi tour will take in the island's main features. Pico can be visited in a day from Horta, with a half-day tour seeing the western sector, but do stay a night or two there, especially if you intend to conquer the summit.

For walkers, São Jorge, São Miguel, Faial and Flores are all excellent, and there is Pico if you want to climb Portugal's highest mountain. In truth, there are now walks on every island. For cycling, São Miguel is the most developed, with activity companies to guide you, though bikes are easy to rent on Pico and Santa Maria, too. São Miguel is best for gardens and Pico has the most accessible native flora. Birdwatchers should give priority to São Miguel, São Jorge, Pico and especially Flores and Corvo in the autumn, although the old quarry at Praia on Terceira is also excellent for rare waders at this time, and the airport area of Santa Maria attracts many species as well.

## TOUR OPERATORS

The Azores are very popular with the Germans, after which come visitors from the USA, the Dutch, Spanish and then the British (with around 14,000 visitors in 2015 – a year-on-year increase from 2014 of 40%). Of course there is a very heavy Portuguese tourist traffic from the mainland, making up around 55% of the total visitors. For years it has been mostly small companies that have offered this destination, but now bigger tour operators are also doing so. Tour operators in their brochures sell the Azores for their tranquillity, landscapes and the islands' way of life, and their retailers should know these qualities. Earlier, the average high-street travel agent knew little about the Azores, and the poor inbound agents in the islands found themselves at the receiving end of irate complaints from clients who had just arrived to realise that there was no constantly blazing sun and endless sandy beaches; this is changing, but still some visitors arrive ill-informed. For those who wish to travel out of the main season or go to different islands from those offered in the standard package, some of the operators will be able to make a bespoke tour programme for you. There are over 20 UK tour operators offering the Azores, including the following:

### UK

**Archipelago Choice** 1b Museum Sq, Keswick, Cumbria CA12 5DZ; \01768 721020; e info@ azoreschoice.com; www.azoreschoice.com, www. archipelagochoice.com. Well-established UK operator, offering tailor-made holidays & with a great reputation on the islands. See also ad in 3rd colour section.

**Biosphere Expeditions** The Henderson Centre, Ivy Lane, Norwich NR5 8BF; \0870 446 0801; e uk@biosphere-expeditions.org; www. biosphere-expeditions.org. Arranges hands-on conservation projects collecting data on whales, dolphins & turtles.

**Explore Worldwide** Nelson Hse, 55 Victoria Rd, Farnborough, Hampshire GU14 7PA; \01252 883681; e sales@explore.co.uk; www.explore. co.uk. Spring/summer island-hopping tours.

**Naturetrek** Mingledown Barn, Wolf's Lane, Hampshire GU34 3HJ; \01962 733051; e info@ naturetrek.co.uk; www.naturetrek.co.uk. Whale- & dolphin-watching holidays.

**Ramblers Worldwide Holidays** Lemsford Mill, Lemsford, Welwyn Garden City, Hertfordshire AL8

7TR; 01707 331133; e info@ramblersholidays. co.uk; www.ramblersholidays.co.uk. Walking holidays.

**Regent Holidays** 6th Floor, Colston Tower, Colston St, Bristol BS1 4XE; 0203 131 0715; e regent@ regentholidays.co.uk; www.regent-holidays.co.uk. A well-established tour operator which includes the archipelago amongst its worldwide holiday destinations. See also ad on inside front cover.

**Saga Holidays** The Saga Bldg, Enbrook Park, Folkestone, Kent CT20 3SE; 0800 096 0074; www. saga.co.uk. Island hopping & cruises for the over 50s.

**Sunvil** Sunvil Hse, Upper Sq, Old Isleworth, Middlesex TW7 7BJ; 020 8758 4722; e discovery@sunvil.co.uk; www.sunvil.co.uk. One of the leading promoters of responsible tourism, offering the Azores since 1990. See also ad in 3rd colour section.

**Wexas Travel** 45–49 Brompton Rd, London SW3 1DE; 020 7590 0610; e europe@wexas.com; www.wexas.com. Tailor-made holidays.

## CANADA

**Karavaniers Voyages d'Aventures** 4035 Rue St-Ambroise, Local # 220 N, Montreal, Quebec, H4C 3EI; +1 514 281 0799; e expeditions@ karavaniers.com; www.karavaniers.com

**Sunmed Holidays** 2055 Dundas St E, Mississauga, Ontario, L4X 2V9; +1 800 263 0858; e info@sunmedholiday.com; www. sunmedholidays.com

## DENMARK

**Svante Rejser Acacietorvet** 2A, 1 sal, 3520 Forum; +45 3315 2525; e info@svante.dk; www.svante.dk

## NETHERLANDS

**Girassol Vakanties** Helderseweg 14, 1815 AB Alkmaar; +31 20 428 0555; e info@ girassolvakanties.nl; www.girassolvakanties.nl

**SNP** Molukkenstraat 7, Nijmegen; +31 24 327 7000; e info@snp.nl; www.snp.nl

## US

**Tour Azores** 176, Columbia St, Fall River, MA 02721; +1 888 678 9093; e eduardodemelo@ tourazores.com; www.tourazores.com

**LOCAL TRAVEL AGENTS** There are several travel agents based in the Azores, offering the usual services of car hire, hotel reservations, airport transfers, etc; these offer certain other activities.

**Geo-fun** Centro Solmar Av, Av Infante D Henrique 71, Ponta Delgada; 296 092 670; e info@geo-fun.com; www.geo-fun.com. A small company focused on active tourism with a special interest in geology, birds & flowers, offering day excursions with a naturalist leader.

**Melo Agência de Viagens** Rua de Sta Luzia 7–11, Ponta Delgada, São Miguel; 296 205 385; e catarina@melotravel.com; www.melotravel. com. Established in 1971 & the first company to offer walking holidays in the Azores. Tailor-made holidays are a speciality & they have self-guided programmes for nature lovers. They also pioneered cycling holidays & offer an 8-day package. For whale watching, daily departures in season are offered from São Miguel, Faial & Pico, & a 7-night package on Pico. Again for individual travellers, 3-, 4- & 5-island tours are available.

**Teles Agência de Viagens** Rua da Sé 138, Angra do Heroísmo, Terceira; 295 213 236; e angra@ telestravel.com; www.telestravel.com. Offers a variety of packages from 2 to 10 nights to various islands, an 8-night golf package to Terceira & São Miguel, a week whale watching on Pico, & various anti-stress, recuperation & revitalisation health programmes at the Hotel do Caracol on Terceira.

**Whale Watch Azores** c/o Norberto Diver, Marina da Horta, Horta, Faial 292 293 891; e info@ whalewatchazores.com; www.whalewatchazores. com. Week-long cetacean-watching tours.

## TOURIST INFORMATION

**AZORES TOURISM AUTHORITY** The tourist board has branch information offices on all the islands (contact details are given in each island chapter) and publishes informative brochures on each island illustrated with excellent photographs, together with various other publications. Compiled each year are lists of approved hotels, *residenciais* and rural accommodation, available via its excellent, comprehensive website (*www.visitazores.com*).

Confusingly, as well as the tourist offices, there are also a string of tourist kiosks labelled *Quiosque*, which can often be found within spitting distance of the official offices. Why? Politics. Either version of tourist office will have maps and basic information, though the *quiosques* earn some of their revenues from commissions on selling tours and during the research for this update, some of the *quiosque* staff were not able to speak English.

## RED TAPE

As the Azores are part of Portugal – a full member of the European Union – nationals of other EU countries do not require a visa. Given the United Kingdom's decision in 2016 to exit the EU, the situation for UK citizens could change during the lifetime of this edition.

Should you need consular assistance during your stay, these are the contact numbers of those consulates represented in the Azores. Largely these responsibilities are undertaken by private individuals in an honorary capacity without official premises. They can issue emergency passports and contact relatives.

**❸ UK** [78 A5] Rua Domingos Rebelo 43a, Ponta Delgada; 296 628 175; e amgm@net.sapo.pt; www.ukinportugal.fco.gov.uk

**❸ USA** [78 C4] Av Príncipe do Mónaco 6-2-F, Ponta Delgada; 296 308 330; e ConsPontaDelgada@state.gov

**❸ Canada** [78 D4] Rua Carvalho Araújo 94, Ponta Delgada; 296 281 488; e canadapdl@mail. telepac.pt

**❸ Denmark** [79 H1] Praceta Gonçalo Velho Cabral 8–1°, Ponta Delgada; 296 284 291; e info@cmjrieff.pt

**❸ Finland** [79 G1] Rua Machado dos Santos 63, Ponta Delgada; 296 281 251; e fredericopascoa-77a@adv.oa.pt

**❸ Netherlands** [78 C4] Rua da Pranchincha 92, Ponta Delgada; 296 201 580; e nlgovazores@ financor.pt

**❸ Norway** [79 F1] Largo da Matriz 61, Ponta Delgada; 296 205 030; e jloazevedo@mail. telepac.pt

**❸ Sweden** [78 C5] 47 Rua Dr Gil Mont' Alverne Sequeira 8, Ponta Delgada; 296 281 161; e ambassaden.lissabon@gov.se

## GETTING THERE AND AWAY

**BY AIR** From the UK there are direct flights with Azores Airlines, formerly SATA Internacional (*www.azoresairlines.pt*), from Gatwick to Ponta Delgada (São Miguel) every Saturday between April and October, with a flying time of four hours. (See also ad in 2nd colour section.) Ryanair (*www.ryanair.com*) currently offers once-weekly flights on a Saturday direct from Stansted to Ponta Delgada. TAP Air Portugal (*www. flytap.com*) has departures throughout the year from Heathrow or Gatwick to Ponta Delgada, changing planes in Lisbon, and with less frequency from Lisbon to Horta (on Faial), Lajes (Terceira), Santa Maria and Pico. Ryanair is due to fly from Lisbon and Porto directly to Terceira by the end of 2016. Flying via Lisbon or Porto allows you to then fly with Azores Airlines directly to Santa Maria, Pico and Faial; you could also break your return journey and spend some nights in Lisbon. Flights take approximately two hours from the UK to Lisbon and another two hours from Lisbon to the Azores.

From the rest of Europe there are direct flights from Gran Canaria and connections from Frankfurt, Munich, Amsterdam, Copenhagen and Paris; from Portugal there are direct flights from Faro, Lisbon, Porto and Funchal (Madeira).

The standard way of getting to the Azorean islands from the UK is increasingly to book a direct flight from London to your chosen island with Azores Airlines, which will involve a plane-change or stopover in Ponta Delgada. If booking with a budget airline from London, you will have to book a separate inter-island flight with Azores Airlines from Ponta Delgada to your chosen island. However, it *could* be more economical to do things a bit differently. If you are flying to Ponta Delgada, Faial, Pico or Santa Maria **from either Lisbon or Porto**, then Azores Airlines includes the price of an additional free onward flight to any other island from any of those four 'gateways' (inter-island flights are actually operated by SATA Air Azores, but they are part of the same group). Even if you arrive in the Azores on another airline from Lisbon or Porto, Azores Airlines will provide you with an onward flight to your chosen island, at no extra cost. However, a stipulation is that you cannot stay more than 24 hours in the 'gateway' on your way through, and this is strictly enforced. For foreign visitors, this is how you work it:

- Either on the Azores Airlines website or via their call centre, first check the timing and availability of seats on your intended onward flight from the 'gateway' to your chosen Azorean island.
- If seats are available, then book your flight from your starting destination (London, Amsterdam, Paris, etc) to Lisbon/Porto. Also book your flight from Lisbon/Porto to the 'gateway'.
- Contact Azores Airlines immediately, telling them what flight you want from your 'gateway' to your chosen island, and that you have a flight already booked from Lisbon/Porto to the 'gateway'. You'll have to prove it, and ensure that you have less then 24 hours in Ponta Delgada, but your onward inter-island flight should be provided free.

Why would you bother with all this? Well, going via mainland Portugal *might* work out cheaper than flying directly into Ponta Delgada from your home, and then buying a flight from there to your chosen Azorean island. Also, flights from London, etc, do not service the Azores daily, so might not suit your own schedule. For your journey back, the same restriction applies: no more than 24 hours in the Azorean gateway on your way through! You should also consider simply booking an Azores Airlines ticket from your starting point (eg: London) to your final Azorean destination, as this is cheaper than separately booking two flights (eg: starting point to Ponta Delgada, then Ponta Delgada to final destination).

From the US and Canada there are direct Azores Airlines flights throughout the year from Boston and Toronto to Ponta Delgada, and now a weekly flight from Boston to Terceira. A new weekly summer flight from Providence was announced for 2016. Flights generally increase in summer, and there are codeshare flights via various cities to/from other US and Canadian cities.

## BY SEA
**By cruise ship** Increasing numbers of cruise ships are calling in at the Azores, particularly at Horta and Ponta Delgada, and this is an important part of Azorean

tourism. Ponta Delgada receives the most cruise visitors and with a single ship carrying up to 5,000 passengers, the impact on the town's cafés and restaurants can be almost overwhelming. Small-ship cruises also operate, visiting all nine islands using onboard Zodiac craft for some excursions. It was in 1867 that the first scheduled cruise ship put in at Horta, steaming from New York on a five-month cruise to the Mediterranean.

**Ponta Delgada (São Miguel)** The largest town in the Azores has a bespoke terminal complex – *Portas do Mar* or 'Gateways of the Sea', opened in 2008. From the pier into town is just a 200m walk. A separate tourist information office is on the pier, and around the promenade are shops, a bank and pharmacy, bars and restaurants. Various onshore tours are available, going to some of the places described in the São Miguel chapter, and there are plenty of guides waiting for the cruise-ship passengers as they disembark.

**Horta (Faial)** The cruise-ship quay is located about a 1km walk along the harbourfront. Tourist information is available on the quayside. Bus excursions take in Capelinhos, site of the last volcano eruption and its excellent new visitor centre.

**Praia da Vitória (Terceira)** Cruise ships dock 4km from the town (usually covered by bus excursions!). Tourist information is available in town, and excursions to Angra do Heroísmo and other highlights start from the quay.

**By yacht** Facilities are concentrated in the four principal ports, the most popular of which for transatlantic yachts is Horta on Faial. Opened in 1986, and having held the European Blue Flag since 1987, it can take 300 vessels and claims to be the fourth-most-visited ocean marina. Second-most popular is Ponta Delgada on São Miguel, with a new marina taking 470 yachts, followed by Praia da Vitória on Terceira. All three provide fuel, water, waste handling and repair services. There are also small marinas opened in recent years at Velas on São Jorge, Madalena on Pico, Lajes on Flores, Vila do Porto on Santa Maria and Vila Franca do Campo on São Miguel. The website www.noonsite.com/Countries/Azores gives latest information on facilities, immigration, etc, and anchorages on the other islands.

# HEALTH *with Dr Felicity Nicholson*

All EU nationals visiting the Azores are entitled to the reciprocal arrangements covering medical care and expenses but will need the appropriate documentation. Dental treatment will mostly have to be paid for. British nationals should have their European Health Insurance Card (EHIC), obtainable by phone (✆ *0845 606 2030*), online (*www.dh.gov.uk/travellers*), or from the post office and some travel clinics. The validity of this card for British nationals may be in doubt, once the UK exits from the EU. You should in any case have additional private travel insurance. Pregnant women, travellers with pre-existing illnesses and those travelling with children or going to remote areas should identify healthcare facilities prior to departure. However, larger hotels and tour company representatives are usually able to provide addresses for local services. The Foreign and Commonwealth Office (*www.fco.gov.uk*) can provide details of the nearest relevant embassy or consulate for emergencies.

Hospitals in the Azores are modern and equivalent to normal European standards. They are located on São Miguel, Terceira and Faial. On certain islands where there are limited services emergency medical cases have to be flown either to Faial or Terceira. Health centres (*centros médicos*) provide non-hospital treatment.

Pharmacies are widespread, but you should always take a sufficient supply of prescription drugs to more than last the length of your holiday. When travelling, do not pack them all in your suitcase; always make sure you have enough tablets and any medical equipment you use regularly in your hand luggage. The pharmacies in larger towns will have a rota for out-of-business-hours opening; if you need anything, ask at your hotel or a police station to see which one is open.

Tap water in the hotels is generally safe to drink; on some islands it tastes better than some bottled waters. However, if you are in any doubt then drink bottled or treated water (boiled or with chlorine drops/tablets). Mineral water is widely sold by the bottle, imported mostly from the mainland, but also sourced locally, and is inexpensive.

It is wise to be up to date with routine vaccinations, including MMR and diphtheria, tetanus and polio. Occasionally hepatitis A and hepatitis B may also be recommended, which will depend more on lifestyle and/or occupation.

A few cases of leishmaniasis from sand flies and west Nile fever from mosquitoes have been reported from the Azores. The only way these diseases can be avoided is by using a good DEET-based insect repellent – ideally containing 50–55% DEET (eg: the Repel range).

Rabies is not considered a risk in the Azores in terrestrial animals, but all bites from animals should be assessed carefully. Rabies vaccine is only recommended for travellers involved in activities that could bring them into direct contact with bats. These travellers include wildlife professionals, researchers, veterinarians, or adventure travellers visiting areas where bats are commonly found.

**TRAVEL CLINICS AND HEALTH INFORMATION** A full list of current travel clinic websites worldwide is available on www.istm.org. For other journey preparation information, see http://travelhealthpro.org.uk (UK) or http://wwwnc.cdc.gov/travel/ (US). Information about various medications may be found on www.netdoctor.co.uk/travel. All advice found online should be used in conjunction with expert advice received prior to or during travel.

## WOMEN TRAVELLERS

With the usual common-sense approach, women travelling to the Azores on their own should not expect any difficulties or unwanted attention from local males. Foreign females now residing in the archipelago report that it is a safe and unthreatening place to live.

## GAY AND LESBIAN TRAVELLERS

Despite the Azorean culture being a relatively conservative one, and one in which the Church is still strong compared with many parts of the European mainland, it is also very tolerant. As a result, it would be highly unusual for gay and lesbian visitors to experience any discrimination; bars are generally relaxed places in which everyone is welcome. Hotels are also tolerant. As in many places, intense displays of public affection – by visitors of any sexual orientation – are found by some locals to be distasteful.

## TRAVELLERS WITH A DISABILITY

The Azores are not geared towards travellers with mobility problems, since narrow cobbled streets and a lack of ramped kerbs don't create a wheelchair-friendly environment. However, latest developments do recognise the difficulties, and some hotels have facilities and adapted rooms. Airports have wheelchairs for use on site. New museums are adapted, with some offering information in Braille.

## SAFETY

The Azores are considered to be one of the safest places in the world and crime is, on the whole, limited to minor thievery. However, you should sensibly take the same precautions as you would at home. A few beggars operate in Ponta Delgada, but are not aggressive; they seem to be non-existent in other towns.

## WHAT TO TAKE

The clothes you take need to correspond with the quickly changing weather so always remember you are in the mid-Atlantic! In summer generally the temperatures are very comfortable and at sea level it is doubtful if you will need a jersey. In winter, there will be days when you also do not need a jersey, but then for many days at sea level there will be times when you are very pleased to have one, as well as a windproof jacket. At all times you will need to be prepared for weather changes, so a raincoat is recommended, although in summer you may find it too warm and prefer to have an umbrella. It can also be very humid. If travelling in winter, early spring or late autumn, some warm nightclothes or thermal underwear are a good idea, as some accommodation does not have heating.

Many of the streets are cobbled, so wear sensible shoes; you will be handicapped in high heels or fashion shoes. Generally, townspeople dress smartly casual, and cotton items are popular. In the evening, men will wear ties and jackets in the more expensive hotels and restaurants. Away from the coast you should always take a windproof and waterproof jacket for the mountains, warmer ones in winter. The same applies if you are making any ferry journeys and like to stay on deck. Walkers will need to bring their own equipment, including their favoured walking shoes or boots, as outdoor shops are few and far between. Waterproofs in the mountains are fine, but at low altitudes many find them too warm and a poncho style may be more comfortable. Always ensure you have sufficient warm clothing if you are going into the mountains. Always take water with you. You might find a whistle useful to keep in touch with straying companions should the clouds descend and kill visibility. A mobile phone can be an asset.

Hotel laundry services are very good, but for same-day service a 50% surcharge is usually levied, and beware of weekends and public holidays. Finding a self-service laundry is virtually impossible, though service washes can be sourced in Ponta Delgada, Horta and Madalena. Tourist offices will advise of their location and the cost is by weight, usually around €3.50/kg, which works out quite expensive. Increasingly, hairdryers are provided in hotel bedrooms, but this should certainly not be relied upon, and in the cheaper hotels there is not always a shaver socket. The electricity supply is 220V, the standard in western Europe, and the plugs are the usual continental European two-pin.

Budget travellers should take a towel as those provided in cheaper accommodation are often thin and very small, and a universal basin plug.

Photographers using a digital SLR camera could usefully take a standard UV filter to minimise glare off the sea – and protect the lens at the same time. In winter the light is wonderfully clear and sharp and there are some dramatic results to be had.

Portugal is a member of the European Monetary Union and the currency is the euro. Most banks in the main centres have plentiful multi-lingual ATMs and this is certainly the fastest way to obtain cash. Acquiring a pre-paid currency card in advance is a good way of avoiding transaction charges while abroad. Credit cards, especially Visa, are accepted in hotels and some shops but not in all rural accommodation, restaurants or the smaller cafés/bars, nor in some petrol stations.

Banks are generally open between 08.30 and 14.30 Monday to Friday, but are closed on Saturday and Sunday and public holidays.

**TIPPING** In the Azores it is not normal to leave a 10% tip, but certainly not more. A small tip can be left on the table, one or two euros, but it does depend on the category of the restaurant. If you do wish to give a tip, consider a euro to hotel porters, but tipping taxi drivers or guides is not a common or 'must-do' thing.

## BUDGETING

Many overseas visitors come to the Azores on a pre-purchased package bought from their travel agent so they know roughly what their main costs are going to be. UK prices start at around £850 for a seven-night stay in São Miguel on a bed-and-breakfast basis including flights and transfers. Cycling, walking, whale and dolphin watching, and fly-drive tours are available.

The Azores are now reached by budget airlines, making it in theory a cheap-flight destination if you book at the right time. Having arrived, you will find a wide range of accommodation, from one- to five-star hotels and apartment hotels, to small *residencias* and camping sites. There are also youth hostels, open to all ages. The most visited islands, São Miguel, Terceira, Faial and Pico, are a bit more expensive than the others. Using ferries to travel between the islands is cheaper and more fun than flying (though see box, page 43), but you do need to be prepared for changes in the timetables and these can be complicated. Using buses will be considerably cheaper than taxis, but they can be logistically challenging, as they cater mainly to local people going to and from work, and children going to school.

Hiring general guides is expensive if you are on your own and in the busy summer months they are often already occupied with pre-booked clients and tour groups. If you need a guide, then you can pre-book, using the contact details in the individual island chapters that follow. An alternative is to contact the local travel agencies, who may be able to assemble individual clients to make a small tour group (see page 41 for local travel agencies).

Often there is not a huge difference between the prices various restaurants charge, and those that are a bit more expensive are indicated in this book. Eating in smaller bars/cafés will be cheaper than the tourist restaurants and

### ADMISSION CHARGES

Although there is the odd exception, admission to museums throughout the Azores is very modest or sometimes free, usually around €2, with discounts for students, seniors, adolescents and teachers. Children under 12 are nearly always free. It's worth asking about family tickets, too. Some museums are free on Sundays.

hotels, and lunches can be either a cheap and filling *prato do dia* (dish of the day) in a modest restaurant or even a delicious picnic with island products from the local supermarket or market. In fact, restaurant portions are so generous that a light picnic for one meal is often preferable.

A budget traveller can expect to spend around €65 per day in the high season. This roughly breaks down into: accommodation (based on camping or dorm bed in a youth hostel) €20; supermarket lunch/*prato do dia* €8 per person; dinner including wine €20 per person; bus fares, occasional taxi, museum entrance, coffee, say a daily average of €17 per person. Any inter-island travel or car hire are excluded.

For the traveller who likes accommodation with some more comfort and privacy, and who enjoys spending time over dinner, then allow around €100 per day, to include: €45 per person for accommodation (based on sharing with your partner/friend); a light lunch with wine €10 per person; dinner €25 per person; bus fares, occasional taxi, museum entrance, coffee, etc, a daily average of €20 per person, excluding inter-island travel or any car hire.

Beyond that, you can spend more by staying in a four- or five-star hotel, hiring cars or private guides, though spending a lot of money on eating out is difficult. There are no really top-end restaurants.

## GETTING AROUND

**INTER-ISLAND TRAVEL** Most visitors coming by air from Europe or North America arrive in Ponta Delgada on São Miguel or Lajes on Terceira, much less often Horta on Faial.

**By air** Azores Airlines (formerly SATA) is the only inter-island airline and its website (*www.azoresairlines.pt; see also ad in 2nd colour section*) contains all the information you require to plan your trip.

Flights are inevitably subject to the weather, and can be delayed or cancelled. When it happens, it is bad luck and you simply have to be philosophical about it and make sure there is a good book to hand.

Getting between the islands is not always straightforward, especially in winter, but more flights are being introduced every year, and independent travellers should spend time studying the Azores Airlines website. Most non-stop flights between each island take about 30 minutes, except São Miguel to Flores, which takes 80 minutes. For travellers with an international Azores Airlines air ticket, the airline offers some advanced purchase reductions; again see the website and also the box on page 43.

Not all flights are non-stop: some will stop at one or two islands *en route*, and others will involve a layover of a few hours and a change of plane; not all flights operate every day, with islands such as Graciosa and particularly tiny Corvo being served less than daily.

Careful planning is required, but the airline is reliable and most islands can be reached on most days of the week. One-way flight prices are from €30 for the 15-minute hop between Flores and Corvo, to around €90 for longer inter-island trips. Note that on many inter-island journeys there is no allocated seating, so getting to the front of the queue to bag a window seat can be advantageous.

**By ferry**  Taking a boat is great fun if you have the time; there are always seabirds to look out for, and if you are lucky there is a chance of seeing dolphins or maybe even a whale. Tickets can be purchased at the quayside office a few days in advance, or via travel agents. On some islands, you buy the tickets at the RIAC (Citizens' Support Office) – see individual island chapters. With a credit card and after a registration process, you can now also reserve online and print off your confirmation, which must then be exchanged at the ticket office for your ticket.

Not all services operate year-round; some are summer-only and some see an increased schedule in the warmer months.

Throughout the year there are several sailings daily between Horta (Faial) and Madalena (Pico), a 30-minute crossing, costing around €3.60. Between Flores and Corvo, there is a year-round passenger service (*45mins, €10*), though weather can disrupt this in winter.

In summer (*Jun–Sep*), there is a twice-daily Horta–Velas (São Jorge) service (*around 2hrs 20mins, €15.50*), sometimes via Pico (Madalena and some sailings also via São Roque). This means that, in summer at least, it is quite possible to make day excursions to São Jorge from Faial or Pico, and vice versa.

Thrice-weekly in summer there is a ferry service between Horta and Angra do Heroísmo (*6hrs, €32*) calling into São Jorge at both Calheta (*3hrs 10mins, €27.50*) and Velas (*4hrs 20mins, €32*). Again in summer, you can get between Santa Maria and São Miguel (*2hrs 35mins, €30*) up to three-times weekly, and from Graciosa to both Velas on São Jorge (*2hrs 15mins, €32*) and Praia da Vitória on Terceira (*3hrs 15mins, €27.50*). From Praia da Vitória to Velas (*6hrs, €32*), there is a summer service with a stop-off in Graciosa. An infrequent summer service also runs between Ponta Delgada on São Miguel and Praia da Vitória on Terceira (*4hrs 5mins, €50*).

For up-to-date details of current ferry services, route-map, prices and reservations, check the website www.atlanticoline.pt, which has an English-language option.

**By car**  As in Portugal, driving is on the right. The Azorean pace of life is relaxed and generally this is reflected in a fairly modest average driving speed. Azoreans are respectful and patient, certainly not crazy drivers and the best advice for visitors is to show similar patience, too. If a local wants to stop his pick-up truck in the middle of the road to chat to his neighbour … well, so be it. Very refreshing is that pedestrian crossings are universally respected by drivers, so make sure you do the same. At crossroads vehicles approaching from the right have priority. Seat belts have to be worn at all times, including the rear passengers, though on some islands the rule is ignored by drivers.

The new main roads are good but the small country roads can be pot-holed and narrow. One thing to be very careful about when driving in fog or low cloud and poor visibility is the Azorean black-and-white cow wandering on the road, either singly or in a scattered herd; in such conditions they are superbly camouflaged! Vehicles are often parked on the main road, however narrow it may be, so careful driving is required. Many of the minor roads are not signposted. Diversions for roadworks are signposted, but if the sign disappears after a few days it is seldom replaced because by then it is assumed everyone knows the way!

For UK drivers, a full driving licence is required and those aged under 25 years should check minimum requirements for hiring a car at the time of making a booking. They may have to pay a premium. Citizens from non-European countries similarly require a driving licence, along with a passport or other form of official identification. Normally there is no upper age limit but again this should be checked at the time of booking. In peak summer season there is a shortage of hire cars, and reservations should be made well in advance. A daily rate for a small car in high season would be around €50, dropping in low season to €30.

There are many car-hire companies in the Azores, and some are very small. Two well-established firms with their main offices in Ponta Delgada and coverage across the islands are:

🚗 **Autatlantis** ☎ 296 205 340 (reservations); e info@autatlantis.com; www.autatlantis.com. See also ad in 3rd colour section.

🚗 **Ilha Verde** ☎ 296 304 891 (reservations); e reserve@ilhaverde.com; www.ilhaverde.com

Prices can differ between islands. Rates do not include any extra insurances, such as CDW (collision damage waiver). Diesel cars, where available, cost substantially more. It should be noted that car-hire companies do not allow their vehicles to be taken on board the ferries.

Several islands have scooter hire, but this is not for the faint-hearted or inexperienced. However, it is a cheap way to get around and rental starts from around €20 per day. A full driving licence is again required and helmets are supplied and must be worn. Bicycles are also available, and some companies renting these are detailed in the individual island chapters. Otherwise, check with the tourist office for latest rental companies.

**By bus**  Some islands are better served than others. On São Miguel you can see a lot of the island by public bus. You can make a circuit on the islands of Faial and Pico, and some trips by bus on Terceira and São Jorge. For details see the *Getting around* section for the individual island. For the other four islands, bus services are not very frequent. Most tourist offices have bus timetables to hand out.

 ## ACCOMMODATION

This varies hugely, from the comfort of large conventional hotels, apartment hotels, to simple family hotels, smart guesthouses/B&Bs, delightful old manor houses with character, converted forts, youth hostels and camping. There is a five-star hotel on Terceira, plus one on São Miguel, where there is another due to open in late 2016. In addition to serviced accommodation, there are also self-catering apartments and cottages to rent. Apart from the self-catering options, breakfast is usually included in the price quoted.

Accommodation has hugely improved and expanded over the past few years and will likely continue to do so. São Miguel has seen the biggest increase in new hotels, mostly around Ponta Delgada. Angra on Terceira and Horta on Faial have also seen a substantial increase in the number of new places to stay.

There is also new accommodation on all the other islands. All this building has greatly eased the acute shortage of beds in the peak season, but of course it creates a surplus in the winter months – another reason to come off-season, when deals can be done! One word of caution: the Azorean weather means constant painting and maintenance for accommodation owners, and sometimes they will close suddenly

## HOTEL PRICE CODES

Based on a double/twin room per night, for two guests, breakfast included:

| | |
|---|---|
| €€€€€€ | > €150 |
| €€€€€ | €125–149 |
| €€€€ | €100–124 |
| €€€ | €75–99 |
| €€ | €50–74 |
| € | < €50 |

in winter when the weather allows for a bit of decoration: booking in advance will ensure you get a bed.

Hotels are graded according to the price of a double or twin room in high season. Low-season rates can fall by up to 50%. The highest season is generally July and August, but prices in May/June/September will be somewhat higher than in midwinter. Single-room rates are generally only a little below the double-room rate. Many hotels offer special deals; check their websites for the latest offers.

For self-caterers, check the website www.casasacorianas.com, which lists dozens of quality-checked rural houses rentable usually by the week or longer. The site has photographs and details of all the houses, many with online reservation available.

All islands have official campsites, most with basic amenities and nominal charges, and some are very attractive, though sometimes lacking in shade or shelter. Details are given under the respective islands. The sites are very popular with the local people – it's just nice to get away from home for a couple of days or so, read a book, go fishing, find a good restaurant or eat outside at the barbecues provided. They are also very popular with teenagers in the school holidays.

For youth hostels, which can currently be found on São Miguel, Santa Maria, Terceira, Pico and São Jorge, see the website www.pousadasjuvacores.com. You don't have to be a youth or a member, and most have a limited number of private rooms as well as dormitory accommodation.

 ## EATING AND DRINKING

**EATING** Eating out in the Azores can be a very variable experience. The true positive is the quality of the meat and the fish, which are first-class. Usually, these are simply prepared, and a rich accompanying sauce would be a rare find. Sometimes you can strike it lucky in the more expensive eateries and be given a sophisticated and well-presented dish, depending on who is cooking that night. Many Azoreans admit that there is often a focus on quantity rather than quality and you will surely never be underfed here. Most islands have one or two stand-out restaurants (though not really 'top-end' by European standards), raising the standard or doing something a bit inventive or different, and these are highlighted by this guidebook. Azoreans have fairly conservative tastes, which results in the appearance of boiled potatoes or chips with many meals. Often, meals will be served with potatoes *and* rice, plus a huge basket of bread to accompany it: for many, far too much carbohydrate. Vegetarians will have to look hard for variety, though Ponta Delgada has one excellent meat-free restaurant. Larger hotels usually have some vegetarian options, too.

Sadly it cannot truthfully be claimed that the islands are a gastronomic delight, but this is changing, albeit slowly. The lower- and mid-priced restaurants often

The Azorean kitchen has more or less maintained the flavours of the Portuguese kitchen from the time of the Discoveries. There does not seem to be any influence from the early Breton or Flemish population. History tells us that they kept their language only for a generation and the same seems to be true about their food. One of the reasons may be that the Portuguese have always kept in touch with their continental homeland while other settlers perhaps did not.

The Azorean staple is soup. In the old times the main meal of poor rural inhabitants was often simply a thick vegetable soup with *chouriço* and bread. People are now better off but soup is still served as a starter twice a day, the thicker the better. There is a variety of vegetable soups, one of the most famous being *caldo verde*, a potato soup with finely shredded cabbage leaves cooked in it. Chicken broth is also popular and sometimes fish soup. Until the 1950s, the rural social structure was very archaic and the limited economic possibilities of the population meant that fish was the basic component of daily meals, meat being a luxury served only on festive days, where tradition decreed three dishes of chicken, pork and beef, some boiled, others roasted, should be served.

Interestingly, on the island of São Miguel all dishes are flavoured with hot pepper (*pimenta*) in different forms: powdered, salted or as a paste.

Cod is one of the main raw materials in the islands. According to Portuguese tradition, there are 365 different recipes for cod, one for each day of the year. Even at formal dinners, it is usual to prepare a codfish dish. There is *bacalhau à Brás* (fried potatoes, small pieces of boiled cod mixed with scrambled eggs), *bacalhau com natas* (fried potatoes, small pieces of codfish, olive oil-based béchamel sauce and cream on top), or *bacalhau na chapa* (a thick piece of codfish baked in the oven with olive oil, onion, garlic and red pepper).

There is a large variety of local fish. Small fish, *chicharros*, were regarded in former times as food of the poor since they were very cheap and eaten fried almost daily for lunch, on their own or with a garlic and lemon sauce or a hot pepper sauce, or parsley, olive oil and onions (green sauce). Recently the price rose astronomically – no-one could explain why the fish almost completely disappeared, only to return. Many medium-sized fish appear on restaurant menus, fried, grilled, steamed, sometimes filleted. They include *abrotea*, white hake, and *cherne*, 'wreck fish'. These are considered the best of the white fish. They are huge, so they appear mostly filleted. In summer one can find fresh tuna which is sliced as steaks and served fried. Swordfish (*espadarte*) is also a dark-flesh fish that is usually served fried.

As for seafood (*marisqueira*), octopus cooked in the regional wine, *vinho de cheiro*, is very popular, as is barbecued European squid. There are *cracas* (a type of barnacle), a seafood typical of the Azores but increasingly rare, now found only in restaurants specialising in seafood. They are eaten as an appetiser, the tiny morsels retrieved with a special hooked tool from the shell that clings to a piece of rock. *Lapas* (limpets) are another shellfish eaten in various ways, most commonly baked with garlic and lemon juice. Rice with *lapas* is also popular, or *lapas de molho Afonso* spicy sauce. There is *cavaco*, an endemic kind of crab, and *lagosta* (spiny lobster), and shrimps that are mostly imported.

seem to share the same menu so that after a week you are beginning to look for novelties. To find these is easier in Angra, Ponta Delgada and Horta, where there are more restaurants to choose from. With such a good growing climate there should

For meat, pork, beef and chicken are all on the menu. Typical dishes here are *cozido à portuguesa* – pork, beef and chicken mixed mostly with cabbage, root vegetables and potatoes, all cooked together. Many restaurants serve this dish once a week as the dish of the day. In Furnas, *cozido* is a speciality but here it is cooked slowly in volcanic heat in the ground and called *cozido nas caldeiras*. Terceira has *alcatra*, a special meat dish cooked in wine and spices.

A meal in an Azorean restaurant is often preceded with cheese, bread and pepper sauce offered while waiting for the meal. A local cheese is usually given: on Faial and Pico the cheese will be *São João do Pico*; on São Jorge it is *São Jorge*, a strong sharp-flavoured cheese, considered to be the best in the Azores. On Terceira the *Castelinhos* cheese and on São Miguel the *Agua Retorta* cheese or a fresh white cheese with the ever-present *massa de pimenta* are served.

The most typical appetiser on Faial, Pico and São Jorge is blood sausage with yams, a tropical vegetable cultivated on all the islands, while on São Miguel blood sausage comes with fresh pineapple.

Religious festivals have their own special dishes. During the Holy Spirit Festival, a meat broth with bread is cooked in the islands of the Central Group. During the carnival, *malassados*, a rich dough, like that for doughnuts, is deep-fried and sugared. *Massa sovado*, sweet bread somewhere between bread and cake, is baked year-round.

Formerly, village people ate only home-baked bread, because corn was widely cultivated to feed both humans and animals. Corn bread is a greyish, moist kind of bread that tends to mould rather quickly. Typical local restaurants often serve both corn and wheat bread. White Azorean bread tends to be too dry; the so-called home-baked bread, a big round loaf, is better.

There is a great variety of locally grown fruit in the Azores and many fruits were introduced following the disease that attacked orange trees in the last century. Pineapples were cultivated but it was soon found that the climate was not warm enough for outdoor growing, so greenhouses were built to obtain a reasonable crop. The Azores are now the only place in the world where pineapples are grown commercially in greenhouses. Economically they cannot compete with pineapples imported from Africa and South America and are heavily subsidised. They are generally sweet and juicy but can be acidic in winter. Again, the Azorean climate is a little too cool for bananas, which are generally smaller and sometimes brownish, but compensate by being sweet.

Other tropical fruits such as avocado, guava, mango, papaya, annona, *maracujá* (passion fruit) and *diospyros* (persimmon) are also grown. Citrus fruits including oranges, mandarins, clementines and lemons are still grown in quantity. While bananas and pineapples are ripening all the year round, the others are mostly winter fruit starting in October and available until May or June. Typical summer fruits such as apples, pears, plums and peaches do not grow too well in the islands. A lack of a definite cold period means poor flowering; thus cherries do not crop at all, although insects are abundant in summer, since insecticides are not generally used. Only in the higher altitudes such as the Furnas Valley can one get a reasonable crop.

be a wonderful range of vegetables on offer but it seems most townspeople prefer simply to buy from the supermarket rather than grow much for themselves, and the supermarkets are not very adventurous. This is then reflected in the restaurants,

Generally, most restaurants open for both lunch and dinner and the usual hours are noon–15.00 and 19.00–23.00. Depending on the town or island, they are closed all day either Sunday (especially Ponta Delgada) or Monday, but there is always somewhere open.

Prices range from €8 to €12 per main dish for lunch and €10 to €17 for dinner and it is rare that you will pay any more than this. Desserts are around €2–3. A bowl of soup is usually a bargain €2, sometimes less. Some places have special lunchtime offers for around €7, including coffee. There are some restaurants that offer buffet meals only which often include a selection of regional dishes for €7 to €12 per person, excluding dessert and drinks.

Many large hotels offer a buffet meal from around €20 per person, excluding drinks, plus an à-la-carte menu.

Prices given in the *Where to eat* listings in this book are an average cost of a main course, without drinks.

which is no excuse, however, for serving rice and chips in combination, together with tinned diced mixed vegetables. Salads are mostly lettuce, some tomato, sliced onion, maybe grated carrot and if you are lucky, some cucumber, rarely all together; dressing is usually left to you, from a bottle of olive oil and vinegar. Hotels often offer more variety, and can be very good, but even the best can include some of the routine ingredients cooked unimaginatively. Portions are generally huge, sometimes overpoweringly so, especially meat. Fish including seafood is usually excellent, best eaten plain grilled or else as a local version of *bouillabaisse*; the *alcatra* on Terceira is an excellent example, though often this is made with meat instead. *Bacalhau* (dried cod), the traditional village dishes and Azorean sausages can be very good indeed, as can the spicy *chouriço* (smoked sausage) and the black blood sausage, *morcelas*, with pineapple, but not too often in the same week!

Mercifully Azorean cheeses are excellent and quality mainland Portuguese wines have been unsung for far too long, leaving the diner feeling very content with the world. Some chocolate desserts can be gorgeous.

## DRINKING
**Wine** The settlers in the Azores had their priorities well ordered because wine has been produced since the very early days. On Pico grape varieties brought by the first settlers from mainland Portugal failed to acclimatise. The Verdelho grape was imported around 1500, possibly from Sicily, or maybe from Madeira, or perhaps by a Jesuit from Italy.

Vines were first planted on a large scale in the 16th century by the Catholic orders of Franciscans and Carmelites and by Jesuits in the following century. On Pico the vines were brought to Silveira, but here the surrounding land was too good for grapes and needed for essential foods such as wheat. Instead they went to the geologically youngest area of the island where the ground was very poor and stony, around the west coast. It is so heavily lava-strewn that it was only with great labour and difficulty that sufficient stones were cleared, using them to make what became the characteristic walls, or *currais*, of small enclosures that provide such wonderful shelter from salty winds and at the same time extra heat. Surplus stone was neatly stacked into rectangular piles called *richeiros*. This was done mainly along the western edge of the island and now, almost half a millennium later, it is a protected zone because of its history. Other interesting features

An aspect of Azorean restaurant dining that can cause confusion is the 'unwanted cover charge'. Having ordered your meal, or perhaps even before doing so, your waiter may present you with a basket of bread, sometimes accompanied by a plate of cheese or even some olives. Tuck in if you feel like it, but don't be surprised when it's added to your bill, as it invariably will be. Some visitors may think that there has been an attempt to dupe them, but the bringing of these items is simply an Azorean custom. If you don't want them, simply tell the waiter politely that this is the case and he will remove them, without complaint and without charge.

of this extraordinary memorial to the energy and persistence of the islanders include the *decansadouros*, the resting places for those carrying full baskets of grapes; made of stone, they are in two levels, one for those carrying on their heads and one for those carrying baskets on their shoulders. At the height of production some 30,000 barrels or 15 million litres were produced annually. Among the countries it was exported to were Britain and famously to the Russian tsars, apparently by a German trading family. Quite what this wine was is not known as there were very few written records kept about how it was produced. However, Edward Boid, visiting in 1832, wrote that the merchants in Horta took the Pico wine and mixed it with wine from São Jorge and added brandy. It was then heated to between 110°F and 130°F for four to six months, during which time any evaporation from the casks was topped up with more wine and brandy. It seems that different blends were produced for different markets.

Because of the rocky terrain, transport of the barrels was difficult, and to get them onto the waiting ships, wooden boards were laid over rocks that had previously been cut and roughly levelled. You might see old stone slipways or *rola-pipas* used to get the barrels into the sea, where they were then towed out to the waiting ship. The best Pico wine was said to be 'so good it should be drunk in the middle of a prayer'.

When disease struck in the mid 1800s the first vines were replaced with the hardy Isabella grape whose strong aroma gave rise to the *vinho de cheiro* – fragrant wine. This is widely made throughout the islands for village consumption, and many a walker has staggered onward under the influence of spontaneous hospitality.

Twenty years or so ago small-scale experiments were conducted with new continental varieties, and some old stone enclosures replaced by long, straight rows supported by wires that always looked impressively immaculate in their level fields of cinders. However, it is the traditional method with its long history that is the remarkable showpiece and has most recently been rejuvenated in a number of ways, firstly by recognising various areas of vine growing and production – the Zonas Vitivinícolas – and secondly by the establishment of a Regional Commission based in Madalena to guarantee quality and production methods, and certification. Named quality wines produced in a demarcated area are designated VLQPRD (*vinhos licorosos de qualidade produzidos em região determinada*), which covers *vinhos licorosos* or fortified sweetened wines recommended as an *aperitivo*, and includes the white table wine Pedras Brancas from Graciosa, now happily much reduced in price from a few years ago. The VLQPRD include the Brum wine from Biscoitos on Terceira and Pico's Lajido. Also from Pico is a more versatile red wine from Verdelho and Arinto grapes called Czar. Finally there are the certified Azores Regional Wines (Vinho Regional Açores): the whites Viosinho and Gouveio, Frei Gigante, Terras de Lava and

Maresia from Pico, Moledo from Terceira and the red from Pico, simply labelled Cabernet Sauvignon and Merlot.

On Pico the Cooperativa Vitivinicola da Ilha do Pico now has some 250 small growers. Wine production is far from conventional, not just because of the lava habitat but also because complications affecting acidity, sugar content, maturation and other aspects are created by the extremes of cold air falling from Pico mountain and the sun on the rocks and the salt in the air.

Terceira's first true vineyard was planted more than 400 years ago. A certain Pero Anes do Canto was in charge of the Portuguese navy and owned land at Biscoitos and it was he who introduced a Verdelho grape from Sicily. Production took off and records for 1693 show that taverns in Angra sold over 1,000 barrels of 500 litres each of Verdelho wine. It seems the same quantity was also sold to the island's eight convents! This may have been a translation error, but wine was certainly exported to the Portuguese colonies. Subsequent introduction of the Baco variety helped make the vineyards more resistant to disease.

Legislation ensures urban development is limited in the Biscoitos region to protect the vine-growing area. In 1993, the Biscoitos Society of Verdelho Wines was founded with the objective of promoting the Verdelho wines of Biscoitos as well as all of the quality wines of the Azores. Members are founders, honorary members, brothers and novices and wear a blue cape with a gold trim, blue representing the colour of the Azorean flag and gold the colour of the Verdelho. The society's coat of arms in addition to the Azores arms includes a *tambolhadeira*, a drinking cup resembling the traditional clay *taladeira* used in Terceira to taste the new wine, a ritual that takes place on St Martin's Day. The Brum family wine museum at Biscoitos is open to visitors (page 144).

Graciosa quietly produces wine from its one remaining winery, the Adega Cooperativa da Ilha Graciosa, which started in 1960 with an initial production of 200,000 litres of dry white wine. By the 1980s, this had languished and production ceased for a time but now with government support the situation is reversed, and its white table wine Pedras Brancas has certified status.

Several liqueur wines are also made, especially São Miguel's well-known *Maracujá* liqueur (passion fruit). This, mixed half and half with *aguardente* – fire and passion – is a great ending to a typical feast of traditional Azorean dishes! Others are made from local fruit such as Japanese plum (*Eriobotrya japonica*, the loquat), figs and blackberries. This last, called *Amora*, is less sweet than the others, and imbibed not in moderation has the kick of an island donkey.

**BEER** Beer-drinkers can try the São Miguel brew, Especial, which is a pleasant if unexceptional drink on a hot day. Many locals prefer the imports, mainly Super Bock and Sagres from the Portuguese mainland. When ordering beer, you can choose a *fino* (very small, in a straight glass), *tulipa* (small, in a tulip-shaped glass) or *caneca* (half litre). Prices are very reasonable when compared with elsewhere in Europe.

## PUBLIC HOLIDAYS AND FESTIVALS

The main public holidays are 1 January; 25 April (marking the Revolution of 1974); Good Friday and Easter Sunday; 1 May (Labour Day); 24 May (Autonomy Day); end of May/beginning June, second Thursday after Whitsun (Corpus Christi); 10 June (National Day of Portugal); 15 August (Feast of the Assumption); 5 October (Proclamation of the Republic); 1 November (All Saints' Day); 1 December (Restoration of Independence); 8 December (Feast of the Immaculate Conception); and 25 December (Christmas Day). There are also municipal holidays, each municipality taking them on different dates so that there are some 18 of these during the summer, but they should not significantly affect the visitor.

**New Year's Eve** is celebrated throughout the islands and in Ponta Delgada there are fireworks and brass bands, and sometimes a rock band. More modest celebrations are also held in Angra do Heroísmo and Horta and smaller towns.

**Carnival** is another islands-wide celebration, in Ponta Delgada marked by a grand ball and a masked ball during the third week of February. Visitors are welcome, but tickets need to be pre-booked. On the last day of this five-day festival the carnival ends with a water battle at the marina.

Portugal's second-largest religious festival takes place in Ponta Delgada on the fifth Sunday after Easter, the **Festas de Santo Cristo dos Milagres** (Christ of the Miracles). There are many festivals in August throughout the islands and two of the most important are the **Sea Week** with music and sailing regattas based on Horta between the first and second Sundays in August, and **Whaler's Week** on Pico during the last week of that month. The **Angra Jazz Festival** (*www.angrajazz.com*) is held every year in early October when performers come from both Europe and America to play for several days.

There are festivals throughout the year, and the principal ones are detailed in the chapters for the individual islands. You can also use the useful calendar on the www.visitazores.com website.

## SHOPPING

In addition to the handicrafts (page 58), cheeses from the islands are always a popular purchase. Homemade jams are as good as or better than grandmother's, while tea from the two tea estates on São Miguel is a very original gift and easiest of all to carry home. Somewhat heavier are one or two fresh pineapples in a presentation box, and island wine, *aperitivos*, liqueurs and *aguardentes*. For food gifts try the supermarkets, and at the airports on São Miguel and Faial there is at least one shop selling Azorean products, and new outlets are appearing all the time. Also, check out the main markets in Ponta Delgada and Horta. Azorean tea can also be purchased directly from the estates (pages 104–5). Please note that some shops close from 13.00 on Saturday until Monday morning.

2

Scrimshaw is an art born of boredom and loneliness on the whaling ships of the 19th century and links the Azores to many countries. Ships' crews would while away their time engraving on whales' teeth, and then rubbing lamp black into the lines to bring up the design. In the Azores this tradition continued, using the teeth taken from whales killed off the islands and brought ashore for processing. It has all but disappeared because time passes and also the supply of teeth is diminishing. Fifteen years ago divers could still find them on the seabed near old whaling stations on Pico and on Madeira, but now such finds are rare.

Modern artists sand down the tooth ridges, then use car polish to coat the tooth. A layer of Indian ink is applied to blacken the surface to be engraved. Machine-powered needles are used to engrave through the ink, the polish, and into the tooth. The engraved lines appear white and Indian ink is then applied a second time and this time it enters the unwaxed lines that form the design. The first coat of black is then removed.

**HANDICRAFTS – *ARTESANATO*** There are many items common to all or most of the islands, with their own variations, while some handicrafts are specific to one island or village. All use natural raw materials; you cannot fail to see charming corn dollies or *escravela japonesa*, folk figures made from maize husks, wickerwork baskets, ceramics, various items from cut basalt, embroidery, delicate flowers made from fish scales or fig pith, simple rugs made from maize or rags, and superb woven bedspreads made on São Jorge. Look for products bearing the *Cores* label, as this is a guarantee of their Azorean origin. There are also models of whales and items to do with whaling, and some scrimshaw (products made from whale teeth; see box above). Shops do offer whalebone items, but please be aware it is illegal to take these products out of Portugal and their purchase encourages this trade. Several shops now sell items made from environmentally friendly alternative materials. Something new is very attractive local jewellery made from basalt, ladies' earrings, brooches and necklaces, but only a few jewellers stock them.

## ARTS AND ENTERTAINMENT

Entertainment is very modest, but the number of places to go out in the evening is increasing, although their names are not emblazoned across the night sky and they are still relatively few in number. In larger towns on summer evenings there will often be rock, jazz and folk bands playing in the public squares or by the harbour. There are a handful of pubs, again scattered widely. A lively nightlife thrives, but is much more private than commercial and has a quite different meaning from that in the big city. There can be evening dress balls and other social events associated with the many organisations that thrive in the islands, of which the casual visitor remains unaware. As you travel around the islands you will see many barbecue sites at *miradouros* and in sylvan roadside glades. In summer these are busy after office hours when family and friends meet for an alfresco supper and evening together. At weekends and holidays they will again all be occupied, as will the woodland picnic sites laid out in so many lovely places by the forestry services. Summer is for outdoor living, which is also when the festivals and folklore gatherings mostly take place. Very noticeably over the past few years cafés and bars have put out tables and chairs on the pavement, especially around the new marinas and quaysides and pedestrianised squares, so that now friends and families stay out late quietly enjoying a beer, bottle of wine or coffee. On a balmy summer evening the visitor can enjoy a promenade around the main harbours with their pretty lights reflecting on the water, or sit in a garden square and nibble a snack from a street stall or watch the world go by from a pavement café. During your stay in Ponta Delgada check whether there is anything on at the recently restored **Teatro Micaelense** (*www. teatromicaelense.pt*); this offers a wide range of cultural events throughout the year, from ballet, musicals, *fado*, jazz and chamber recitals to fully staged operas, the programmes often linked with the Coliseums in Lisbon and Oporto. In Horta, on Faial, the *teatro* near the main square has also been restored and offers a mix of Hollywood and art cinema together with occasional orchestral and jazz music.

## ACTIVITIES

**WALKING** Walking in the mid-Atlantic is a most wonderful experience. Whether you are high in the mountains, following a coastal walk, or merely strolling along a country lane, there is a purity in the air, an exhilaration in the light, and ever-changing cloud patterns. In places trails lie dark and dank between 2m-tall embankments, with hedges of cryptomeria, pittosporum and endemic shrubs, while the banks themselves are moss-covered or draped with soft green curtains of selaginella, a primitive fern ally. At other times when high up in the mountains the scene is more akin to moorland, with low-growing grasses, rushes and mossy flushes in the wetter areas, and elsewhere a knee-high scrub of heather, and often a view of the distant sea. Perhaps best of all is to file along a narrow path contouring a steep sea cliff, when the views are spectacular, very special and pure Azores. However, gentler walks along farm roads through patchworks of pastures with the sight of healthy, contented cows out to grass all year, and past farm buildings with ever-changing rural scenes, are equally as satisfying in their different way. A survey of visitors from the UK a few years ago showed that 80% came principally for walking, though this may have diminished with the arrival of budget flights and the increased popularity of other land- and sea-based activities.

Buried beneath the vigorous alien vegetation of the islands lie many old cobbled trails, used long ago by the islanders to travel between the villages by donkey, oxcart and horse. Before the advent of roads these trails were the economic and social lifelines for the villages, for the fishermen carrying basketloads of fish to inland villages, for the workers walking to their fields, to the vineyards, their fruit and orange orchards, and for religious pilgrimages. The history and stories they could tell are as lost to the visitor as is the dustiest archive in the deepest cellar. Maybe one day local historians will make all this tangible and readily accessible, but meanwhile all we have are brief glimpses of this earlier age. If old trails happen to lead to pastures or to vineyards then their weathered surfaces can still be seen, perhaps for just a few metres, maybe for 100m or more. They are there for the observant traveller to find, and then to let the imagination fill in the stories. Certainly if these hidden paths could be rediscovered they would make wonderful walks and stories for our time and century. And if time and tide have in part destroyed them, then maybe new routes could be found to link them.

Walks are being lost, but 'new' ones are being spruced up, waymarked and presented to visitors. For years unsurfaced farm tracks were given asphalt surfaces with the help of EU funding; great for the farmer, but bad news for the walking tourist. Seismic tremors and flash floods cause human tragedies, and also send favourite walks permanently into memory, their imprint on the landscape forever destroyed by nature. Whether the pioneering efforts and appeals over the years have influenced the authorities one does not know, but recently waymarking and maintenance of walking routes has at last been taken seriously and there are now over 70 official walks covering all the islands; 21 on São Miguel, 14 on Pico and between two and eight on each of the others. This is tremendous news, and hopefully they will now go from strength to strength. These trails vary in length from 2km to 78km. Some are circular; others follow some of the old inter-village paths. Unfortunately cows like to use the marker poles as scratching posts and pushed sideways they do not always point in the right direction, while walls with paint marks get knocked down, so one still needs to keep a good sense of direction! There are descriptive brochures for each trail available from the local tourist offices, and all can be downloaded from the website www.trails-azores.com which is an excellent service, because should any walks be made impassable by storms, etc, then updates are regularly posted. At present the texts are not as detailed as they should be, the maps are a bit sketchy and how one accesses the walks or gets home afterwards is often frustratingly vague.

While all the islands now have attractive walks, the best are on São Jorge, São Miguel and Flores, and new trails on Pico and Faial are rightly proving very popular. Pico also offers the ascent of Pico mountain, the highest in Portugal. Some of these walks are described in the relevant island chapters.

Remember always to take with you sensible kit – layers for warmth, a waterproof/windproof outer jacket, and sun protection. Always take adequate water, and for some of the walks where the route takes you across lava or the few arid areas, take double the normal quantity. A most useful item to have with you in the Azores is a mobile phone to call a taxi at the end of a walk – and the number of the taxi firm!

**CYCLING** Next to walking, this is the finest way to get to know the islands, following quiet rural lanes and passing through pretty villages for frequent pit-stops. Autatlantis (*www.autatlantis.com*) offers cycle hire at €12 per day or €6 per day in conjunction with its car hire, and €10 or €6 respectively per day for three to eight days' hire from some of their outlets. Some travel agencies in the Azores offer fully supported eight-day packages with two-centred accommodation and daily transfers for around £850 excluding flights, while UK and other tour operators offer all-inclusive cycling holidays.

**WHALE AND DOLPHIN WATCHING** Whale and dolphin watching has become a major focus of ecotourism and the increase in its popularity is phenomenal; it's the fastest-growing tourist activity worldwide. Beginning as a commercial enterprise in 1955 on the southern California coast, it is claimed whale watching is now organised in about 120 countries with 13 million participants – 2008 figures; its popularity continues. For some economies, it has become an industry in its own right; divide the number of whales viewed into the cash generated, and each whale must be worth a small fortune. Good news in support of the conservation argument for, in this role, whales are more valuable than if they were hunted and killed. Another important plus is that in many places commercial whale watching has become a recognised tool for education, and is supporting research by the observations and recordings made during whale-watching trips and other inputs. All the more extraordinary that, with government subsidy, Norway, Iceland and Japan continue to hunt and kill around 2,000 whales commercially each year ... and at the same time offer whale-watching trips.

It is essential that these 'subjects' of our recreational curiosity are viewed with the respect they deserve. In the Azores, whale and dolphin watching has become a much-advertised and popular activity and there are now many operators offering whale-watching trips; some have more than one boat. This brings into question what effect this has on the cetaceans; they are sensitive animals surviving in a very tough environment doing the things we do, finding food, rearing young and socialising. They have highly sensitive hearing and are distressed when their communication is interfered with, when speedboats tear around them, gunning their engines. Bothering them by too close a contact and in other ways can alter their migration patterns, separate groups and interfere with their reproduction. What the stress thresholds are is not known and more research is needed, so given our ignorance the best policy is: don't do it unless you know it is harmless. Swimming with cetaceans is controversial and is banned in several countries.

A 2011 estimate revealed that some 48,000 people went whale watching in the Azores that year, supporting 53 boats and 195 jobs. This is but a small window into the situation worldwide, and it is pleasing to note that the Azorean government has passed regulations controlling the number of boats allowed, passenger safety, and visitor behaviour when near the animals. The regulations also aim to encourage the companies involved to work more closely together, reduce competition and limit the number of boats around any one pod.

If you are going to visit them, there is an accepted etiquette to follow (see box, page 62). Rather than book a trip at random, study the notes about what you should know before you go out to sea, and how your boat crew should handle the situation. When you have absorbed these, check out the operators, ask the right questions, and when you find one that suits you, go ahead. Check whether they have an experienced biologist on board at all times; ask how many people they take as a maximum, if there is shade from the sun, a lavatory, and if drinking water is supplied. You can also ask if you are contributing to scientific research by choosing their boat.

For those who do not like the idea of venturing into the mid-Atlantic in a small rigid inflatable boat and enduring three hours banging into the waves as you speed along, there are now larger, more comfortable vessels that have cabins and decks where you can move around. You are no less likely to see whales and dolphins this way and your view from the raised decks of these vessels is much better. Seeing whales and dolphins out at sea is a memorable and special experience; to really get the most out of your boat trip, do your homework first, read up about the creatures, be informed; only then should you intrude upon them and with a clearer conscience.

Because of the weather, the main season is from April to October, although cetaceans may be seen throughout the year and you may find there are opportunities in winter. Winter trips are more prone to cancellations, caused by rough seas or bad weather. With 27 species now recorded in Azorean waters out of a total of some 83 species of whales, dolphins and porpoises, this makes the Azores one of the world's top places to observe them. In January 2009, the first northern right whale for 110 years was recorded in the Azores, five miles south of Faial. The islands most geared up for organised excursions are Pico, Faial and São Miguel.

Typically there are two departures each day, around 09.00 and 14.00, each lasting about three hours. Thirty minutes before departure there is usually a pre-trip briefing. The cost varies, but is generally around €40–65 per person. A seven-night whale-watching programme staying on Pico or Faial costs from around £700 excluding flights. Typically this would be: arrive and briefing on day 1; further briefing and talks on the history of whaling, etc, and afternoon whale-watching boat trip on day 2; then days 3–6 morning boat trip with afternoons free for optional land-based activities or

## WHALE- AND DOLPHIN-WATCHING ETIQUETTE

Legislation has been passed in the Azores to regulate the increasing demand for whale and dolphin watching but supervising behaviour out at sea and out of sight is not easy. You, the client whale watcher, can do this by reporting back any malpractice you encounter or posting it on the ubiquitous review sites. The new economic significance of whale watching and the widening concern and support from those who participate is likely to do more than anything else to help protect these animals on the world stage and change political opinions.

- Cetaceans should not be chased.
- Boats should approach by maintaining direction parallel and slightly to the rear of the cetaceans, keeping an open field of 180° to the front of them.
- When approaching, boats should avoid changes in direction, keep to slow speeds of under 10 knots and when 400m from the area reduce to 4 knots.
- A maximum of only two boats are permitted inside a radius of 400m around an individual whale or group of whales.
- It is prohibited to approach cetaceans closer than 50m; when they are resting they may not be approached at all.
- Only one boat at a time is permitted to approach to the minimum distance of 50m from the whales, and the engine should be kept on low revs.
- Boats should not come between animals in groups thereby separating them, especially the young.
- Whales with small calves should not be approached closer than 100m.
- Movements of all boats must always be on the same side, parallel to and a little to the rear of the animals.
- The maximum time to be spent in the area observing is 30 minutes near the animal.
- After observation, boats must depart from the area to the rear of the animals, and maintain a slow speed within 400m of them.
- No swimming is allowed with cetaceans.
- Skippers must explain to clients the dangers of swimming with dolphins and that they do this at their own risk (there is no insurance available).
- When swimming with dolphins, one extra crew member, apart from the skipper, must be allocated for surveillance of swimmers at all times and be equipped for swimming.
- Only two swimmers with dolphins should be allowed in the water at the same time and they should be equipped with snorkels; they must remain quietly on the surface and not touch the dolphins.
- Swimming time with dolphins is limited to 15 minutes maximum.
- The boat's motor must be in neutral at all times when swimmers are in the water.

at leisure; and final day flexible, allowing for any replacement boat trips if earlier bad weather caused cancellations. Several tour operators offer whale-watching packages including international flights and various extras on São Miguel, Faial and Pico.

Should you like more information, then Whale and Dolphin Conservation (WDC), the world's most active charity dedicated to the conservation and welfare of all whales, dolphins and porpoises, has an excellent website (*http://uk.whales.org*).

**SWIMMING** The steep rocky sea coasts mean that swimming opportunities are mostly focused on small beaches, little bays and a combination of natural and manmade rock pools. The more popular locations often have changing facilities, toilets and sometimes lifeguards, while amenities are improving rapidly all the time. As of 2016, the coveted European Blue Flags signifying the beaches or swimming areas that meet stringent standards have now been awarded to 34 sites in the Azores. Few of the natural swimming places are really suitable for non-swimmers There are various adverse conditions and dangerous currents unknown to the visitor and swimming should be enjoyed only in clearly designated areas. Please be very aware of the coded flags flying according to prevailing conditions on designated swimming beaches:

| | |
|---|---|
| **Green** | Safe to swim |
| **Yellow** | Be careful, no swimming |
| **Red** | Danger, keep out of the water |
| **Chequered** | Beach temporarily without a lifeguard |

Many larger hotels and even rural accommodations have conventional swimming pools and recent investment has created attractive public pools near some of the main population centres, while local municipalities have created simpler facilities, often modifying rocky sea-washed locations – many with natural built-in wave machines! Seldom, however, around any of the sites is shade provided from the sun. But the sheer diversity of opportunities to swim is remarkable, from the sea and rock pools, formal and indoor pools, volcanic lakes, to a naturally warm geothermal pool.

**DIVING** For a long time few people thought of the Azores as a diving destination, but this has changed, with operators in most of the islands taking advantage of a unique underwater environment and excellent marine life. The seabed, being of volcanic origin, offers large areas of lava and various volcanic debris, tunnels, arches, vertical cliffs, small caves and rock needles while the Gulf Stream brings together both Atlantic and tropical fish. Large schools may often be seen – barracuda, mackerel, trigger fish – and very large sting rays as well as occasional giant mantas, curious octopus and a diversity of other marine organisms. Giant whale sharks have also been spotted. With a visibility range of up to 20m, the great joy of diving off the Azores is that you never know what you are going to see.

Because the weather is unpredictable dives usually take place in the mornings when the sea is most likely to be at its calmest. June to November are the best months, but diving can be enjoyed in any month.

There are now specialist companies listed on all the islands except Corvo, offering shore dives with easy access to the water, and boat dives. Experienced divers are catered for as well as those less experienced, and instruction is available for beginners and refreshers. Night diving is also offered. Single dives start from around €45 and ten dives from €330 plus hire of dive gear. For those who prefer to snorkel, both instruction and tours are available. Up-to-date details of all Azores-based diving companies can be found at www.azoresweb.com/diving_azores.html.

**COASTAL FISHING** Open-boat fishing with a guide is available out of Faial, São Miguel, and from other islands offering bottom-fishing, jigging, trawling live bait and sea fly fishing. Species include mackerel, barracuda, bonito, scabbard fish, sea bream and more, depending on the depth. The cost is around €250 for a maximum of three persons for a half day's (four–five hours) boat hire.

**SPORT OR GAME FISHING** The Azores marine environment attracts large fish including 'granders', a fishing term for blue marlin weighing 1,000lb or more, and many world records have been caught in these waters. The season usually runs from early July to mid-October when the water temperature is above 20°C and the weather is generally warm and calm. Apart from the Atlantic blue marlin, various tuna species, several different sharks and numerous white marlin, there are also small game fish. With an instructor and skipper prices are around in excess of €1,000 per day for a group of up to four, with São Miguel and Horta on Faial being the principal centres. Operators are listed in the individual island chapters.

**CAR RALLIES** Several rallies are held annually in the islands and those wishing to attend should make sure they have their hotel accommodation booked well in advance. Anyone coming to the Azores for a quiet holiday should plan their itinerary accordingly! Dates vary each year and should be checked with your tour operator or the Azores Directorate of Tourism. Some of the major ones are:

| | |
|---|---|
| **São Miguel** | June: Azores Airlines Rallye |
| **Santa Maria** | First or second weekend of August, usually one week before the big religious festivities of 15 August: Rali de Santa Maria |
| **Terceira** | Around 20–21 April: Rali Sical |
| | Around 14–15 September: Rali Ilha Lilás |
| **Graciosa** | Mid-July: car rally |
| **Faial** | May: Rali Ilha Azul |
| | November: Rali do Faial Além Mar |
| **Pico** | October: Rali Ilha do Pico Além Mar |

**SAILING** Skippered boat charter is available on São Miguel. With a minimum of four people, maximum six, prices are around €85 per person with a minimum charge of €425 for a full day sailing along the south coast of São Miguel; to Santa Maria for the weekend €1,400. Other trips are possible, too: for further information, see the website www.azoressailing.com.

Inclusive sailing holidays from the UK, including international flights, sailing between and around São Miguel and Terceira with an option to extend to Santa Maria, start from around £1,200; around the three central islands of Faial, Pico and São Jorge from around £1,000.

These notes are made for the land visitor: sailors have their own cruising guides! Apparently the first American pleasure yacht to cross the Atlantic called in at Horta on its way to the Mediterranean in 1867, and in 1895 Joshua Slocum put into Horta while making the first single-handed circumnavigation of the world. Since then small boat arrivals have increased and with the construction of marinas and onshore facilities the number of yachts now visiting Horta is around 1,400 annually. Many are doing the milk-run, bringing boats over from Bermuda or the West Indies to the Mediterranean or similar for the summer, allowing their owners who do not like real sailing to fly across later. The Azores are also a major focus for several famous international races, and there are also local yachting events. The calendar is something like this:

| | |
|---|---|
| **Last Saturday in April** | Competitors windsurf from Velas to Cais do Pico and then cycle via the coast road to Madalena and then kayak to Horta. |
| **First week** | Faial yacht club organises a race for cruising yachts from |

| in July | Horta to Velas on São Jorge and back, including an overnight party in Velas! |
| End of July | Atlantis Cup: a big date in the calendar; the route varies from year to year, ending in Horta. |
| Beginning first Sunday in August | Semana do Mar or Sea Week, with events connected with the sea as well as other cultural events. In Horta. |
| Every four years | The famous Azores and Back race organised by the Royal Cornwall Yacht Club every four years since 1975, binding Falmouth with Ponta Delgada. For further details, see www.azab.co.uk. Next due in 2019. |
| Every two years | Race from Brittany to Horta and back is organised by Société Nautique. |
| Further events | Include the Yachting World ARC Europe rally from the Canaries to the West Indies; Canaries–Bermuda–Horta–Ponta Delgada to either Plymouth or the Algarve; Rotterdam–Horta and back by Dutch Sports Planning International; rally by Ocean Cruising Club of England. |

**GARDENS** Portuguese gardeners took their inspiration from the Romans and Moors, as well as the Italians and French, and later the romantic English style of the 19th century, and made their own landscape style. Combined with the unchanging skills and methods of Azorean gardeners, the historic gardens in the Azores offer a special charm. Around the mid 1850s there was a veritable outbreak of garden development and of these one garden on Terceira and five gardens on São Miguel are open to visitors. The owners of three gardens in Ponta Delgada vied with each other to have the latest introductions and the rarest plants, importing plants from famous nurseries in Belgium, France and England, and from mainland Portugal and Brazil. Architects and gardeners were invited from overseas to superintend the landscaping, including from Britain David Mocatta, who studied under Sir John Soane and designed several of the stations for the London to Brighton railway; Peter Wallace, a gardener to the Duke of Devonshire at Chatsworth and who later died in Ceylon; Jean-Pierre Barillet-Deschamps, a leading French horticulturist who worked with Haussmann and transformed Paris, creating the Jardin du Luxembourg and Parc Monceau among many others; Georges Aumont, designer of the Barbieux Park in Lille; and Francisco Gabriel, who came from the famous Makoy nursery in Liege and introduced to the Terceira garden (page 151) many plants from Parisian and Belgian nurseries.

**RECREATIONAL FOREST RESERVES** These areas have been designated for public recreation and are found on all islands except Corvo. Dominated by *Cryptomeria japonica* forest often along with oaks, chestnut and other deciduous species, often there are camellias or azaleas too and more recently native species have been introduced as part of a broader educational and conservation programme. These mature habitats offer peaceful places for a relaxed and tranquil walk or a picnic, and often a loo. Those listed in this guide have special merit for the overseas visitor. They are generally open 08.00–19.00 Monday–Friday and 10.00–20.00 Saturday and Sunday in summer, 08.00–16.00 Monday–Friday in winter.

**OTHER ACTIVITIES** These include kayaking, canyoning, coasteering and other physical pursuits. Specialist companies are listed in the relevant island chapters. If you want to design an action-packed holiday involving these activities before you leave home – advisable in high season – then one of the tour operators listed on pages 40–1 should be able to help.

**Canyoning** This is walking in streams, rappelling down waterfalls and generally getting wet in a diversity of geological settings. Because this is usually the only way to experience some of these places, there is often undisturbed native vegetation and rare plants plus birds as a bonus. Barely heard of just a few years ago, this activity has now burgeoned and has an enthusiastic local following as well as organised expeditions for visitors. There are at least 50 bolted routes of various difficulty levels and three islands are especially good; on São Miguel the challenges are less steep, Flores has the greatest diversity, and São Jorge offers the hardest routes as most are accessible only by boat.

**Kayaking and canoeing** This is largely done on the caldera lakes of Sete Cidades and Furnas on São Miguel, and on the open sea exploring small islets, visiting caves and watching seabirds off the islands of Terceira and Flores. On Flores there is a spectacular coastline and waterfalls to enjoy and, by contrast, Terceira offers the bay of Praia and along the southeast coast with its many sandy shallow bays and is emerging as one of the best locations. Organised trips are either half day or full day, with experienced guides.

**Horseriding** There are programmes available throughout the year for both beginners and experienced riders, with excellent centres on São Miguel, Faial and Pico, as well as opportunities on some of the other islands. Contact details are given in the relevant island chapters.

**Family holidays** With so many different things to see and do, the Azores are a perfect family destination for those with children who enjoy the outdoors and an active downtime. Swimming has to be approached with caution, but the novelties of bathing in natural rock pools or carefully crafted manmade alternatives will surely excite most youngsters. Biking and hiking are abundantly available, and the more adventurous still can try kayaking, canyoning and coasteering. The islands will also suit inquisitive youngsters, with educational opportunities provided by the volcanic landscapes, geothermal activities, whale watching and nature at its finest.

## MEDIA AND COMMUNICATIONS

**POST** Postal services are efficient and reliable. Expect cards and letters to take around three to five days from Ponta Delgada or Lajes on Terceira, possibly longer from the other islands. You can recognise a post office by the sign *Correio*, or *CTT* and they open Monday to Friday only, though they often have stamp dispensers outside. There are two levels of service, and outside post offices you will see two post boxes, one for ordinary mail and one for express blue mail, which costs three times the price.

The ordinary rates for mailing abroad are: up to 20g, Europe €0.75; to rest of the world €0.80.

**TELEPHONE** The telephone service is excellent. The international code for the Azores (Portugal) is 351. The islands also have codes: 296 for São Miguel and Santa Maria; 295 for Terceira, São Jorge and Graciosa; 292 for Faial, Pico, Flores and Corvo. You need to dial the whole nine-figure number no matter where you are.

Off-peak (economic) time is from 21.00 to 09.00. The cheapest way to make a call is to buy a telephone chargecard and use a public callbox. Many public phone boxes also accept debit or credit cards and, once inserted, there is a button with a flag to press until your chosen instruction language appears.

Mobile reception is generally very good, though the mountains do create blank spots.

**NEWSPAPERS AND BROADCASTING** The main daily newspapers are *Açoreano Oriental, Diário dos Açores* and the *Correio dos Açores,* all in Portuguese. *Azores News* is an English-language free newspaper published occasionally in Horta offering always interesting snippets of news about the islands and which can usually be found in hotel lobbies.

Portuguese state-owned RTP (Rádio e Televisão de Portugal) provides local radio and television in the Azores. Most medium and large hotels have at least one English-speaking television news service, usually CNN, BBC World or Sky News, and sometimes all three.

**INTERNET** It was once said that Portugal had the best internet coverage in Europe. Whether this is (or ever was) true is difficult to prove, but certainly all Azorean towns of any size have free municipal Wi-Fi, as do all the island airports and many of the marinas. Additionally, nearly all accommodations now provide this service and you never have to look hard to find a café with free Wi-Fi. On the other hand, internet cafés are now almost non-existent now. The larger hotels offer internet services, or if you are stuck then it's worth trying the local library.

## BUYING A PROPERTY

Just a few nationals from northern Europe have bought houses and are living permanently in the Azores. Some have holiday homes and there appear not to be any eccentric barriers to ownership. Until recently there was little evidence of estate agents, but they are now appearing, along with rental and property management services. Just put 'Azores property' into your search engine. The best way is: first, decide which island, and then get to know it and ask around.

## CULTURAL ETIQUETTE

Through the ages the Azoreans have had plenty of contact with the outside world, from pirates to tourists, and from their own travels for work abroad, family members in mainland Portugal, business, higher education and so on. For all this, the communities remain tight-knit, especially in rural areas. It is also a country with strong Catholic traditions. Simple courtesy and respect remain refreshingly important and the visitor will find these greatly contribute to first impressions. Boorish behaviour is not appreciated and will not go unremarked. Neither will topless sunbathing, or changing on the beach – use the cabins provided.

**PHOTOGRAPHY** If you are taking photographs of people, then do ask first; your smile will in most cases be returned and permission granted.

## TRAVELLING POSITIVELY

If you have enjoyed your visit and the islands' hospitality, you may have the feeling you would like to say thank you, and give something back.

The **Portuguese Society for the Study of Birds (Sociedade Portuguesa para o Estudo das Aves) (SPEA)** (*SPEA – Açores, Apartado 14, 9630 Nordeste, São Miguel;*

\ *296 488 455;* m *915 836 123;* e *acores@spea.pt; www.spea.pt*) is a not-for-profit organisation promoting the study and conservation of birds in Portugal. They are very active in the Azores and need all the support and help they can get since there is much to do to protect and regenerate wildlife habitats in the islands.

Early farmers killed the once locally abundant endemic Azorean bullfinch or *priolo, Pyrrhula murina,* to save their crops, especially oranges, from its attacks. However, from the 1920s, forest clearance and general habitat destruction, together with the invasion of alien plant species destroying its food plants plus probable predation by rats and feral cats, made this small bird increasingly rare. It is now confined to about 6km$^2$ of native forest on Pico da Vara and Serra da Tronqueira in the east of São Miguel. Long thought to be down to between only 200 and 300 individuals, in 2008 the first full census was made and the estimate revised to 775 individuals. Under the 2009 IUCN Red List, the *priolo* was officially categorised as 'Critically Endangered', because of its small population and limited distribution.

The area where it survives is designated a Special Protection Area under the EU Wild Birds Directive and is included in the São Miguel Natural Island Park. Since 2003, SPEA, along with governmental agencies and municipalities, have undertaken conservation work in the *priolo*'s main distribution area; they have recovered its habitat, the Azores laurel forest or laurisilva, by controlling invasive plant species and planting native species to increase its desperately needed food supplies. This is a long-term commitment. This work allowed the *priolo*'s population to increase from a low of 120 birds up to its present-day 1,000 individuals, allowing it to be downgraded to only 'Endangered' by the IUCN. SPEA's work has also contributed to sustainable development of the territory by restoring peatland areas in the Planalto dos Graminhais and promoting sustainable tourism in the territory. In 2012, the 'Lands of Priolo' (Nordeste and Povoação municipalities) were awarded the European Charter of Sustainable Tourism.

The society's first ever visitor/interpretative centre is located within the protected area, in the Cancela do Cinzeiro Forest Recreational Reserve. The **Priolo Environmental Centre** (m *918 536 123;* e *centropriolo@spea.pt;* ⊕ *May–Sep 10.00–18.00 Tue–Sun; Feb–Apr & Oct–Nov noon–17.00 Sat & Sun; other times available by appointment*) offers information about the flora and fauna of the Serra da Tronqueira and Pico da Vara and especially about the *priolo*, with temporary exhibitions, a nearby small garden of native plant species, and facilities for its education programme for schools and the local population. In addition, there is a shop with merchandising.

Visitors are made very welcome, and the centre may be reached via the unsurfaced road off the main Povoação to Nordeste road, either just beyond Povoação, or from above the village of Lomba da Pedreira, or from Nordeste (ten minutes). You can find more information about the centre and its activities at the website http://centropriolo. spea.pt. Membership is available to families or individuals. Members receive the society's magazine three times a year and news of regular field trips (free to members).

Your financial donation and/or your participation in voluntary work (educational activities, fieldwork activities, professional or academic visits) are fundamental for the success of the project and for the conservation of the *priolo* and its habitat.

# Part Two

## EASTERN GROUP

38°

*São Miguel*

✈■ **Ponta Delgada**

46nmi

*Ilhéus das Formigas*

*Santa Maria*
✈

Vila do Porto

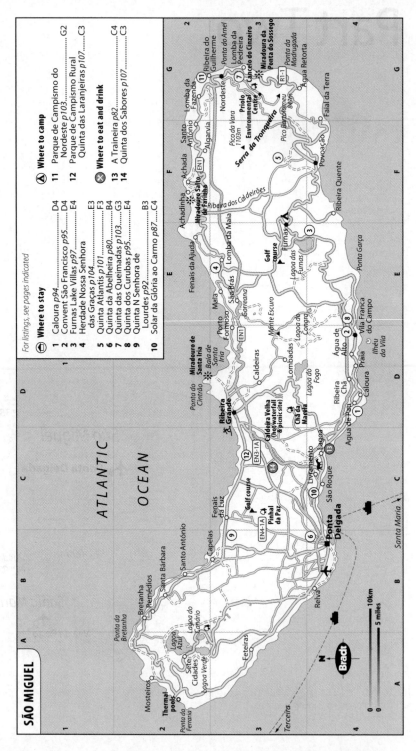

A   B   C   D

ATLANTIC

OCEAN

Ponta da
Bretanha

Lagoa
Azul

Sete
Cidades

Lagoa Verde

Ponta do
Ferraria

Thermal
pools

Mosteiros

Bretanha
Remédios

Santa Bárbara

Lagoa do
Canário

Feteiras

Santo António

Capelas

Fenais
da Luz

Golf course

Pinhal
da Paz

EN4-1A

9

Ponta
Delgada

Relva

Santa Maria

Terceira

Bradt

N

0        10km
0    5 miles

Ponta do
Cintrão

Ribeira
Grande

Miradouro de
Santa Iria

Baía de
Santa
Iria

Caldeira Velha
(hot waterfall
& picnic site)

Caldeiras

Lombadas

Chã da
Maceira

Lagoa do
Fogo

Ribeira
Chã

Porto
Formoso

Gorreana

Mata

EN1

Fenais da Ajuda

Achadinha

Miradouro Salto
do Cavalo

Ribeira dos Caldeirões

Lomba da Maia

São Brás

Monte Escuro

Lagoa do
Congro

Lagoa das
Furnas

Golf
course

Furnas

Lagoa de
Congro

Água de
Alto

Praia

Ribeira Quente

Ponta Garça

Faial da Terra

Água Retorta

Ponta da
Madrugada

Ponta do
Arnel

Ribeira do
Guilherme

Lomba da
Fazenda

Santo
António

Algarvia

Pico da Vara
1103m

Serra da Tronqueira

Pico Bartolomeu
847m

Priolo
Environmental
Centre

Cancelo do Cinzeiro

Miradoura da
Ponta do Sossego

Lomba da
Pedreira

Nordeste

Povoação

R1-1

EN1

Achada

For listings, see pages indicated

**Where to stay**

1   Caloura p94................................D4
2   Convent São Francisco p95.....D4
3   Furnas Lake Villas p97.............E4
4   Herdade Nossa Senhora
      das Graças p104....................E3
5   Quinta Atlantis p101...............F3
6   Quinta da Abelheira p80........B4
7   Quinta das Queimadas p103..G3
8   Quinta dos Curubas p95.........E4
9   Quinta N Senhora de
      Lourdes p92.........................B3
10  Solar da Glória ao Carmo p87...C4

**Where to camp**

11  Parque de Campismo do
      Nordeste p103....................G2
12  Parque de Campismo Rural
      Quinta das Laranjeiras p107...C3

**Where to eat and drink**

13  A Traineira p82........................C4
14  Quinta dos Sabores p107........C3

# 3

# São Miguel

With photographs of the lakes of Sete Cidades appearing in so many travel brochures and promotions, São Miguel has become the best-known island of the archipelago; it is also the biggest in terms of area and population, has the greatest diversity of interests, the best choice of accommodations and restaurants, and the most operators of outdoor activities. It also has the largest town and busiest harbour in the Azores, Ponta Delgada. Although all the islands are green, São Miguel is known as the *Ilha Verde*, the 'Green Island', after the highly productive central area that has very good soil. There is an area of true mountain wilderness with endemic plants around its highest point, Pico da Vara (1,103m), and a varied coastline with small black-sand bays and precipitous sea cliffs. Ponta Delgada is large only by Azorean standards and charms its visitors with its gentle Portuguese architecture, pedestrianised streets, cafés, shops and long esplanade that wraps itself around the ferry terminal, marinas, commercial port area and fishing harbour.

More cosmopolitan than the other islands, São Miguel has in recent years become increasingly sophisticated and is now the focus for the archipelago. Ponta Delgada's airport, towards the island's southwest, receives most of the international air traffic. Yet, in spite of new marinas, new hotels, a second golf course, numerous restaurants, out-of-town supermarkets and so on, considerable rural charm is still to be found: even on the western edges of Ponta Delgada, cows graze peacefully in fields up close to adjacent industrial units.

Most famous of the island's attractions are the two lakes of Sete Cidades, one blue, the other green, steeped in mythology and nestled in the caldera that dominates the western topography. Ribeira Grande has a charming town centre that, heading east, you pass through to reach the only tea estates in Europe, at Gorreana and Porto Formoso, midway along the north coast. In the southeast the small spa of Furnas, which physically has changed little over the years, is a must. Here, bubbling hot springs and fumaroles, together with the smell of sulphur, remind you that you are on a volcano in spite of the verdant surroundings; in fact you are in the centre of another large crater. Twenty-two mineral waters, all with different tastes, spout out of the ground; some have elaborate manmade ornamental surrounds, while others just flow from between the native heather bushes. The 30-acre garden of Furnas's Terra Nostra Garden Hotel, mostly dating from well over 150 years ago but with beginnings in the late 18th century, with its naturally warm thermal swimming pool and meandering walks beneath some 2,000 trees, is contact with the genteel life of earlier times. In the far northeast is Nordeste, a region not often visited by tourists, with a spectacularly beautiful coast which can be enjoyed from several splendid viewpoints and picnic sites. Vila Franca do Campo in the middle of the south coast was São Miguel's first capital, and is still a thriving and pretty town; the town square and the nearby harbour should be seen before taking a coffee and trying the local *queijadas* or Vila Franca cake. Pineapples are still grown under glass on the island, and there are a number of nurseries that can be visited near Ponta Delgada.

If you have a full week to spend exploring São Miguel, you will depart still leaving unseen places for your next visit. If you have the time and are entering and leaving the Azores through Ponta Delgada, it is a good idea to spend the first two or three nights of your holiday in Furnas, and then the last two or maybe three nights in Ponta Delgada itself. This way you can get a real feel for the island and its diversity, and Furnas is an ideal 'inland resort' to begin to relax, unwind and get into a holiday mood. São Miguel has changed, and is changing, faster than the other islands. But for the moment, its charms are still plentiful.

## BACKGROUND

**GEOLOGY** Now the biggest island of the Azorean archipelago, São Miguel was at one time two islands as evidenced by the two large volcanic massifs, one at each end, and the low central area that emerged later from the sea following further eruptions. About four million years ago, the first island appeared, from an eruption on the seabed 2,000m below sea level. Erosion has given us today a broad upland of thick basaltic flows, probably originating as a shield volcano (one gently sloping and built of lava from many closely spaced vents and fissures) with frequent eruptions, with Pico da Vara the highest point. Towards the edge of this upland the

### THE ORANGE TRADE

Even today there is evidence of the great orange-growing industry that dominated several of the islands in the 19th century; look in the numerous small gardens with their tall enclosing hedges of banksias and pittosporum. Grand town houses also reflect the wealth this crop generated, and the development of the countryside by land purchased for rural estates is significant history.

Far less known are the implications all these oranges had for transportation between the Azores and England, the major export customer. Citrus was a luxury fruit, available in season from November to May only, and its peak of desirability for the Victorians was Christmas, when oranges and lemons were the fruit to have displayed on the table. And most of these came from the Azores.

'Buy my fresh St Michael's' was a common streetseller's cry, although it is doubtful that, like today, many customers would have known where 'St Michael's' was. Oranges were grown in the Azores already by the 16th century, brought in from Lisbon, in turn introduced by Portugal's Indian viceroys. From 1600 to 1800, the citrus trade steadily increased, with most oranges coming from Valencia and lemons from Sicily, but it was the ending of the Napoleonic Wars that accelerated exports from the Azores so that by the mid 1800s, several hundred ships and several thousand seamen were employed in the trade. The topsail schooner was the favoured ship, one that could travel fast, for oranges are a quickly perishable cargo. The ships were of small tonnage since a larger vessel would have been no advantage; the boxes of oranges could not be stacked high otherwise those at the bottom would have spoilt, and the boats were loaded in the open roadsteads, so speed was essential. Also, should a large consignment have arrived in one ship, the quantity would have swamped the market and reduced the price. In 1854, 60 million oranges and 15 million lemons were exported to London alone, using at least 70 vessels.

stratovolcano (a steep-sided cone of layered lava flows and other ˎ of Povoação developed about three million years ago, and the calde. have occurred in two stages about 820,000 and 700,000 years ago, but ˎ wall is lost.

Approximately one million years ago, a stratovolcano from the sea addeˎ land. About 18,000 years ago its caldera collapsed, and later – some 13,500 yˎ ago – further collapsed to form an inner caldera; it may be that there was a thirˎ, even later, collapse. There were three lakes. A series of explosive eruptions followed, with the largest throwing out a huge volume of pumice from a vent in a flat area which today gives us one of the most loved places of the entire archipelago – Furnas. In 1630, a violent eruption lasting just a few days sent a pyroclastic flow, a fiery avalanche of hot gases, rocks, pumice and ash down the gorge to Ribeira Quente into the sea to form a small delta, and distributed pumice and ash over a wide area. Two of the lakes disappeared and the surviving lake was probably dammed, resulting in Lake Furnas now being almost 100m above Furnas village. It is thought the average interval between eruptions over the past almost 3,000 years is just 362 years.

Around 290,000 years ago, two stratovolcanoes began to form on the ocean floor, one to form the separate Sete Cidades volcano to the west and Água de Pau volcano to add to the already extant island to the east. Água de Pau, more or less in the middle of São Miguel, is known for its much-visited Lagoa do Fogo ('Lake of Fire') 250m below the caldera rim. With more than 200,000 years of eruptive

At first English merchants came out to the Azores at the start of the season to supervise purchase and loading, but by the mid 19th century many, along with their families, lived permanently on São Miguel in their large houses. Each fruit was picked as it turned from green to yellow and was wrapped in a dry sheathing leaf of the Indian corn cob. Loading was done with small boats from the shore taking the boxes out to the waiting ships. Speed in loading was vital, for should bad weather suddenly blow in, the vessel would have to stand out to sea only part-loaded, and several days might pass before loading could be completed. Typically a crew of not more than six under a master ran the ship, and it was tough sailing during winter in the north Atlantic. The average sailing time was 10–14 days, but it could sometimes be done in seven days. An added anxiety for the voyage home was to inspect the boxes daily for rotten fruit, since a clean cargo meant a bonus for the master. Today such an event would have been spun to equal the fame of the tea clippers, but there was a race each year to deliver the first oranges of the season. It is recorded that the first ship home sold all its cargo within six hours at three guineas a box (£3.15). When others arrived, 47 ships within 40 hours, the price fell to 4/6d (22½p).

These schooners flourished until about 1860; steam was already transporting lemons from Sicily by the early 1850s, but there was no harbour suitable in Ponta Delgada for steam ships, a real problem in bad weather if they had to stand off burning coal, with no bunkering facilities onshore. About ten years later, harbour construction began and the schooners' days were numbered, with an ever-decreasing number being chartered up until about 1870. Then, in the 1880s, disease struck the orange trees and harvests plummeted, by which time supplies from other countries, including California and Florida, became available, from orchards established with parent trees taken from the Azores.

...story, its most vigorous period of growth was between 100,000 and 40,000 years ago, with the caldera enclosing a lake formed some 15,000 years ago. It has a history of violent eruptions followed by long periods of dormancy. Plinian eruptions, explosions of gas, steam and ash followed by pyroclastic flows, occurred over the following millennia. The most recent happened in 1563, over a period of six days, burying crops and houses in ash and lapilli, small volcanic stones, together with further destruction from the associated earthquakes. Four days after this eruption began, another started to the northwest in Pico Queimado, of Hawaiian type, with lava fountains and scorieae or cinders, which flowed down to engulf the village of Ribeira Seca, just west of Ribeira Grande. There you can see the fountain and the surrounding lava.

Sete Cidades volcano is now 14km across at sea level. The early eruptions of dark basalt were slowly followed by pale-grey trachyte, only later to be succeeded by violent explosions that can be seen in the abundant layers of pumice. The caldera collapsed about 22,000 years ago, and remained quiet for 17,000 years although there was activity around its flanks. Some 5,000 years ago, eruptions again began in the caldera, creating a number of broad cones including those containing the crater lakes of Lagoa Rasa and Lagoa de Santiago; these craters together with other sites within Sete Cidades erupted again at later periods, as did numerous satellite vents on the outer lower slopes. The last eruption on Sete Cidades was around the middle of the 15th century, with more recent 19th-century eruptions out to sea northwest from the Ponta da Ferraria. At Ferraria you can see an example of a littoral cone, a secondary cone caused by steam trapped under lava which has flowed into the sea.

The middle region, the Região dos Picos or Complexo dos Picos, which unites the two islands by joining Sete Cidades to Água de Pau, began to form about 50,000 years ago. In contrast with the stratovolcano and their collapsed calderas of São Miguel's two extremities, volcanism here is fissural, and produced about 250 cinder cones and domes, and ash-covered lava flows that are now cultivated. These fissures, or cracks so deep they allow magma to reach the surface, are in places close enough that some of the cinder cones are joined together while smaller, separate cones are as high as 200m. These cones lie in a broad band parallel with the south coast and some 5km inland, and are a most conspicuous landscape feature when seen from an aeroplane coming in to land at Ponta Delgada airport, or from the ferry arriving from Santa Maria. The dominant cone, distinguished by its double hump, erupted about 4,400 years ago. During the past 3,000 years, more than 18 eruptions have occurred. This bridging fissure zone, together with the volcanoes of Sete Cidades, Fogo and Furnas, are all potentially active zones, and only the very far eastern end of the island is considered inactive.

**HISTORY** São Miguel's first settlers came from the Estremadura, Alentejo and Algarve provinces of Portugal, and there were also Madeirans, Jews, Moors and French. The first capital was Vila Franca do Campo, but in 1522 a severe earthquake and mudslide that killed most of the 5,000 inhabitants was so destructive that the island's principal port, Ponta Delgada, which was also sited on the more geologically stable area of the island, took precedence and became the capital in 1546. Already there were some wealthy merchants, trading with mainland Portugal, Madeira, the Canaries, Flanders and elsewhere; some 25 English merchant ships are recorded as having visited in one year. Early crops included wheat, woad and sugarcane, and there were also dairy products. The port area was fortified during the 16th and 17th centuries against the frequent attacks by pirates and corsairs. Terceira was the key island in maritime trade and journeys, but with the restoration of Portuguese independence in 1640, São Miguel became the commercial centre although there were many economic difficulties. During the 18th and early 19th centuries, the island prospered, much of the time through the development of the new export crop, oranges, and many substantial homes and churches were built. In 1831–32, resistance to the Absolutist regime was organised from the island and it was from Ponta Delgada that the Liberal expedition with some 3,500 Azoreans sailed to northern Portugal.

Around 1860, oranges began to lose their share of the British market, partly to cheaper sources of supply from mainland Portugal and Spain, and partly because the orange trees succumbed to disease. This eventually caused an economic crisis and resulted in emigration to the Americas. New crops such as tea, pineapples, chicory, sugarbeet and tobacco then began to be introduced, together with livestock and, later, the development of fishing. Work began in 1861 to improve the port in Ponta Delgada which later stimulated industrial development, but it was after World War II in 1947 that it was greatly expanded. The basalt city gateway was removed to its present position in the nearby square (pages 87–90), and the new Avenida do Infante D Henrique and the colonnaded buildings along the seafront transformed the town's appearance: truly a piece of excellent town planning much enjoyed today by townspeople and visitors alike.

## GETTING THERE AND AWAY

For information on getting to and from São Miguel island, see pages 42–4 and 48–9. By any international measure, São Miguel's airport is small; by Azorean standards, it's large. It has all the facilities of a larger one and it acts as the main hub for the archipelago. For those without a car, there is a bus to town, the **Aerobus** (*Office in the airport; ☎ 296 306 777; www.utcazores.com; €5 return*), which stops and picks up at the major hotels (listed on its website) and the tourist information office. Times are scheduled to coincide with the incoming and outgoing flights.

There is a tourist information kiosk at the airport (🕘 *06.30–midnight daily*), post office, ATMs, bank branch, money exchange, cafeteria, car hire, airline offices (Azores Airlines, TAP and Ryanair), and free Wi-Fi.

**Azores Airlines** [79 H1] Av Infante Dom Henrique; ☎ 296 209 720

**TAP Air Portugal** Airport; ☎ 296 205 233

**Airport information** João Paulo II; ☎ 296 205 400; www.ana.pt

## GETTING AROUND

**BY CAR/TAXI** Usually starting in Ponta Delgada, island tours by taxi generally fall into two separate programmes. One covers Sete Cidades in the west, often a half-day tour, while the second is a full day going to Ribeira Grande and the tea estates on the north coast, followed by Furnas and Vila Franca on the south coast, combined with some viewpoints in the mountains on the way, depending upon the route taken. Another option is to take a guided tour, guaranteeing that you will get some insight into what you are seeing (see page 76 for tour guide details). Visitors with a rented car can also advantageously divide their touring of São Miguel into three sectors, depending on available time: the western part including Sete Cidades and the northern coast to Capelas; the central area of Ribeira Grande, Lagoa do Fogo and Vila Franca; and the eastern part embracing Nordeste, Povoação and

Furnas. Alternatively, do the western section in a day, then spend two or three days exploring the east and centre with an overnight stay in Furnas or elsewhere. Taxis (📞 296 282 000) can be found in either the Praça Vasco da Gama or Praça Goncalo Velho Cabral (map, pages 78–9). Call m 938 346 759 for a wheelchair-adaptable cab. A taxi to the airport is around €7/9 without/with luggage. Prices for island tours are displayed on signboards at the above two locations.

**BY BUS** São Miguel has a good bus service, with services running along both the north and south coasts. With an early start in Ponta Delgada, it is possible to enjoy a full day in Nordeste, Furnas, Povoação, Ribeira Grande, Sete Cidades and Capelas. The timetable changes little from year to year, but to be safe and to use the buses most effectively, get a current timetable from the tourist office or, when closed, study the posters displayed just west of the office, or visit the transport website (*www.smigueltransportes.com*). The schedules may not always be very convenient for tourists – they are set up to suit workers, students and schoolchildren – but they work well in combination with taxis, perhaps taking a bus for the outward journey and a taxi for the return.

All buses from Ponta Delgada leave from the esplanade – Avenida Infante Dom Henrique – by the tourist office. Bus stops for Capelas and Sete Cidades are on the north side; the others are on the south (harbour) side nearer the fort.

## TOURIST INFORMATION

Being the most visited island, São Miguel is best set-up in terms of tourist information services. As well as offices at the airport and Ponta Delgada, there are others dotted around the island and their details are given throughout the chapter. Most staff manning the offices are multi-lingual.

### ISLAND TOURS
**Harmony Trail** m 910 591 678; e harmonytrailazores@gmail.com; www. harmonytrailazores.com. Hiking, biking & guided tours, by a personable & knowledgeable young Azorean-Canadian.

**Rui Medeiros** m 914 616 240/962 758 186; e rm@vivazores.com; www.azoresprivatetours. com. A reliable & reputable local guide, speaking perfect English, Rui has both a saloon car (max 3 passengers) & a 7-seater vehicle for larger groups, but the tour is always private. €150/75 full/half day (car); €180/100 full/half day (7 seater).

## PONTA DELGADA

With a population of around 35,000 – and double that in the wider parish – this is the largest town in the Azores, serving as an administrative capital and commercial and transport hub. It's also home to a university, established as recently as 1975. Natives of other islands view Ponta Delgada and São Miguel with ambivalence, perhaps envious of how the availability of budget flights has swiftly accelerated its number of visitors, yet at the same time worried at how this influx has changed the town and island.

The laziest and fastest way to get to know Ponta Delgada is to take the Lagarta Trolley (a miniature train, page 77), but in a town this pretty, following the walking trail (detailed on pages 87–90) allows for a more leisurely and deeper appreciation of its charms.

The fairly nondescript, utilitarian apartment blocks that characterise the outskirts of town should not diminish the appreciation of Ponta Delgada's attractive core. No visitor, surely, can fail to be smitten by the patterned cobbles of the old town's narrow streets and pavements, the shuttered or balconied houses – alternately with peeling paintwork or adorned with new, bold colours – and the well-manicured gardens, often dedicated to poets or Azorean luminaries, that manifest themselves on a stroll around the compact centre. A few funky murals add a dose of alternative ambience to this easy-on-the-eye, delightful town.

**GETTING AROUND** For most visitors to Ponta Delgada, walking around the compact centre will be both the most convenient and most rewarding way to savour the joys of the town. For anyone who doesn't fancy it, there is a frequent service of half-sized buses (the PDLs) which tootle around the narrow streets, with three lines servicing most places of interest in and near the centre. These run from 07.30 to 19.30 and the routes are marked on the bus stops, with a single fare costing a nominal €0.50.

**Town tour by train** [78 D5] (*Av Infante Dom Henrique;* ✆ *296 629 446; www. lagarta.net;* ⏱ *ticket office: 09.00–18.30, later in summer*) The Lagarta ticket office and stop are at the western end of Avenida Infante Dom Henrique, opposite the Forte de São Brás. Between May and October five different themed circuits are offered at different times: heritage, historical, beach, gardens and outskirts. In winter, the schedule reduces, sometimes only running when a cruise ship is ready to discharge its hordes, and the choice is down to three routes. A commentary is given in English, and – depending on the route – the fare is between €5 and €7.50, free for under 11s.

**TOURIST INFORMATION OFFICE** [79 G2] (*Av Infante Dom Henrique;* ✆ *296 308 621/625;* ⏱ *09.00–19.00 daily*) Multi-lingual staff dispense various brochures, bus timetables and maps, all available free of charge. The tourism department sells its own picture books to each of the islands, illustrated with splendid photographs.

 **WHERE TO STAY** The principal hotels in Ponta Delgada are grouped into: those in the west, the centre and the east of the town. All are within 10–15 minutes' walk of the town centre, but those in the west are more convenient for the public buses and those in the east for the marina and swimming pools.

### In the west

🏠 **Royal Garden** [78 B5] (193 rooms) Rua de Lisboa; ✆ 296 307 300; e royalgardenhotel@ investacor.com; www.investacor.com. An extra couple of minutes' walk to town over the following establishment, but a well-designed, oriental-themed, 1970s building with lots of light & feeling of space, built round an attractive inner enclosed garden planted with bamboos & cloud trees. Good-sized indoor, outdoor & children's pools (all heated), tennis court (extra charge), sauna, Turkish bath, jacuzzi & gymnasium, off-street free parking & free Wi-Fi. Copious buffet b/fast. €€€€€

🏠 **Hotel Vila Nova** [78 C6] (102 rooms) Rua João Francisco Cabral 1–3 ; ✆ 296 301 600; e book.vilanova@platanohotels.com; www. hotelsplatano.com. Family owned & run, a comfortable, modern hotel suited for both holiday &

business use. Buffet restaurant, gymnasium, outdoor heated pool, free Wi-Fi, parking (€2.50 per day). Rates inc b/fast. €€€

### In the centre

🏠 **Hotel Casa Hintze Ribeiro** [79 G1] (22 rooms) Rua Hintze Ribeiro 62; ✆ 296 304 340; e reservas@casahintzeribeiro.com; www. hintzeribeiro.com. Ultra-chic & dripping with style, a welcome addition in 2015 to the town's accommodation choices. Innovative touches, free Wi-Fi, some rooms with balconies, all with s/c option (extra charge). Adults' & children's rooftop pools, sunloungers, spa (sauna, steam room, jacuzzi), small gym. B/fast not inc. €€€€€€€

🏠 **São Miguel Park Hotel** [78 C3] (163 rooms) Rua Manuel Augusto Amaral; ✆ 296 306 000; e smgparkhotel.reservas@bensaude.pt; www. bensaude.pt. Situated towards the rear of the town

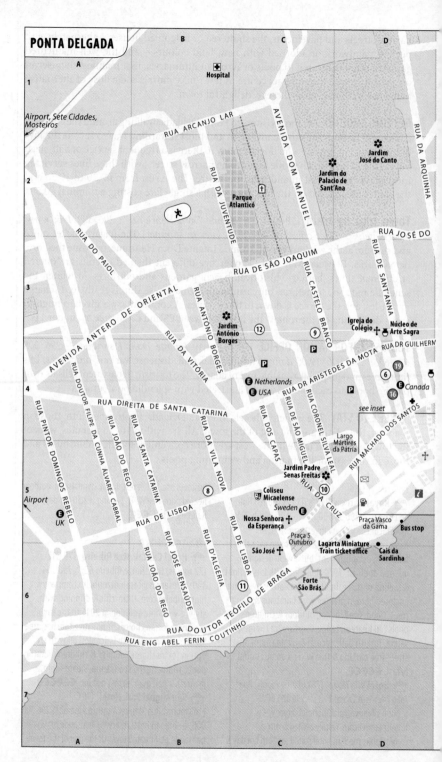

# PONTA DELGADA

Airport, Sete Cidades, Mosteiros

Hospital

RUA ARCANJO LAR

AVENIDA DOM MANUEL I

RUA DA JUVENTUDE

Parque Atlanticó

Jardim José do Canto

Jardim do Palacio de Sant'Ana

RUA DA ARQUINHA

RUA JOSÉ DO

RUA DE SÃO JOAQUIM

RUA DE SANTANNA

RUA DO PAIOL

AVENIDA ANTERO DE ORIENTAL

RUA ANTÓNIO BORGES

RUA CASTELO BRANCO

Igreja do Colégio

Núcleo de Arte Sagra

Jardim António Borges

12

9

RUA DR GUILHERM

6

19

RUA DA VITÓRIA

P

P

RUA DR ARISTEDES DA MOTA

E Netherlands
E USA

E Canada

16

RUA DOUTOR FILIPE DA CUNHA ALVARES CABRAL

RUA DIREITA DE SANTA CATARINA

RUA DOS CAPAS

RUA DE SÃO MIGUEL

RUA CORONEL SILVA LEAL

P

see inset

RUA MACHADO DOS SANTOS

RUA JOÃO DO REGO

RUA DA VILA NOVA

Largo Mártires da Pátria

RUA PINTOR DOMINGOS REBELO

RUA DE SANTA CATARINA

Jardim Padre Senas Freitas

Airport

UK

8

Coliseu Micaelense

Sweden

10

RUA DE LISBOA

RUA D'ALGERIA

Nossa Senhora da Esperança

Praça Vasco da Gama

Bus stop

RUA DE LISBOA

RUA JOSÉ BENSAÚDE

RUA JOÃO DO REGO

São José

Praça 5 Outubro

Lagarta Miniature Train ticket office

Cais da Sardinha

11

RUA DA CRUZ

Forte São Brás

RUA DOUTOR TEÓFILO DE BRAGA

RUA ENG ABEL FERIN COUTINHO

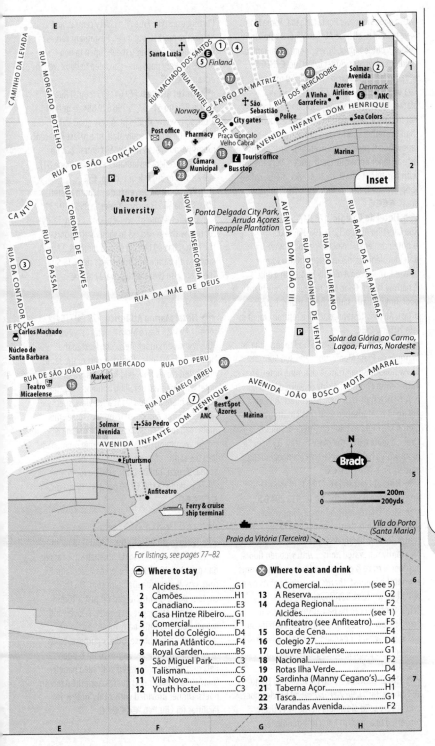

**Inset**

Santa Luzia
Finland
Norway
Post office
Pharmacy
Praça Gonçalo Velho Cabral
City gates
São Sebastião
Police
Câmara Municipal
Bus stop
Tourist office
RUA MACHADO DOS SANTOS
RUA MANUEL DA PORTE
LARGO DA MATRIZ
RUA DOS MERCADORES
AVENIDA INFANTE DOM HENRIQUE
A Vinha Garrafeira
Azores Airlines
Solmar Avenida
Denmark
ANC
Sea Colors
Marina

CAMINHO DA LEVADA
RUA MORGADO BOTELHO
RUA DE SÃO GONÇALO
RUA CORONEL DE CHAVES
RUA DO PASSAL
RUA DA CONTADOR
CANTO
CA NTO
Azores University
NOVA DA MISERICÓRDIA
RUA DA MÃE DE DEUS
Ponta Delgada City Park, Arruda Açores Pineapple Plantation
AVENIDA DOM JOÃO III
RUA DO MOINHO DE VENTO
RUA DO LAUREANO
RUA BARÃO DAS LARANJEIRAS

DE POÇAS
Carlos Machado
Núcleo de Santa Barbara
RUA DE SÃO JOÃO
RUA DO MERCADO
RUA DO PERU
Market
Teatro Micaelense
RUA JOÃO MELO ABREU
AVENIDA JOÃO BOSCO MOTA AMARAL
Solar da Glória ao Carmo, Lagoa, Furnas, Nordeste
Solmar Avenida
São Pedro
AVENIDA INFANTE DOM HENRIQUE
Best Spot Azores
ANC
Marina
Futurismo
Anfiteatro
Ferry & cruise ship terminal
Vila do Porto (Santa Maria)
Praia da Vitória (Terceira)

N
**Bradt**

0 — 200m
0 — 200yds

For listings, see pages 77–82

**⌂ Where to stay**

| | | |
|---|---|---|
| 1 | Alcides | G1 |
| 2 | Camões | H1 |
| 3 | Canadiano | E3 |
| 4 | Casa Hintze Ribeiro | G1 |
| 5 | Comercial | F1 |
| 6 | Hotel do Colégio | D4 |
| 7 | Marina Atlântico | F4 |
| 8 | Royal Garden | B5 |
| 9 | São Miguel Park | C3 |
| 10 | Talisman | C5 |
| 11 | Vila Nova | C6 |
| 12 | Youth hostel | C3 |

**✕ Where to eat and drink**

| | | |
|---|---|---|
| | A Comercial | (see 5) |
| 13 | A Reserva | G2 |
| 14 | Adega Regional | F2 |
| | Alcides | (see 1) |
| | Anfiteatro (see Anfiteatro) | F5 |
| 15 | Boca de Cena | E4 |
| 16 | Colegio 27 | D4 |
| 17 | Louvre Micaelense | G1 |
| 18 | Nacional | F2 |
| 19 | Rotas Ilha Verde | D4 |
| 20 | Sardinha (Manny Cegano's) | G4 |
| 21 | Taberna Açor | H1 |
| 22 | Tasca | G1 |
| 23 | Varandas Avenida | F2 |

with a good view over Ponta Delgada. Some rooms have balconies, all have AC, free Wi-Fi & satellite TV. Indoor & outdoor pool, fitness room, restaurant, bar, children's playroom. Buffet b/fast inc. €€€€€

🏠 **Hotel Canadiano** [79 E3] (50 rooms) Rua do Contador; ☎ 296 287 421; e geral@ platanohotels.com; www.platanohotels.com. Rooms are all very spacious, & more modern than the rather spartan reception area (a renovation is promised & overdue). Most rooms face an inner open courtyard garden. Very friendly, with bar, buffet b/fast, room service menu, coffee shop, lounge & free parking. Free Wi-Fi in public areas. €€€€

🏠 **Hotel do Colégio** [78 D4] (55 rooms) Rua Carvalho Araújo 39; ☎ 296 306 600; e hoteldocolegio@mail.telepac.pt; www. hoteldocolegio.com. Converted from a former convent, this is conveniently located in a quiet & narrow street. Good bar, restaurant, courtyard pool, Turkish bath, sauna, free parking. Rate inc b/fast. Already tasteful, due for a refurbishment in late 2016. €€€€

🏠 **Hotel Talisman** [78 C5] (53 rooms) Rua Marquês da Praia Monforte; ☎ 296 308 500; www.hoteltalisman.com. A charming hotel, an 18th-century house stylishly converted in 1992 in Art-Deco style by a French architect, & later enlarged & refurbished with small rooftop pool, gym & lift. Right in town on a pedestrianised street, a quite delightful place to stay. Try to get a room with a balcony, preferably overlooking the garden. Free Wi-Fi. €€€€

🏠 **Hostel Comercial** [79 F1] (8 rooms) Rua Machado dos Santos 73; m 919 294 000; e residencialacomercial@gmail.com; www. commercialazoreshostel.com. Right in the centre, 'hostel' barely does justice to this small, pleasantly renovated house, with wooden floors, outdoor terrace & communal lounge area. Rooms are not the biggest, there's no parking of its own, but all rooms have bathroom, free Wi-Fi. B/fast (not inc) can be had at the restaurant down below (page 81). Good value, even if you factor in paying for parking. Phone in advance, as there's no permanent English-speaking receptionist. €€€

🏠 **Hotel Camões** [79 H1] (36 rooms) Largo de Camões 38; ☎ 296 209 580; www.hotelcamoes. com. A very solid old manor house inventively converted to a modern hotel in a traditional

Portuguese style. Free Wi-Fi. Very central, just below the market, but quiet. Restaurant serves light lunches & evening meals; open to non-residents. Very popular – you need to book well in advance. €€€

🏠 **Hotel Alcides** [79 G1] (15 rooms) Rua Hintze Ribeiro 61–67; ☎ 296 629 884; e geral@ alcides.pt; www.alcides.pt. A very good-value 2-star hotel with friendly staff, fine b/fast & decent rooms with TV, AC & free Wi-Fi. Central, but no parking. Excellent restaurant next door (page 81). See also ad in 3rd colour section. €€

🏠 **Pousada da Juventude** (Youth Hostel) [78 C3] Rua São Francisco Xavier; ☎ 296 629 431; e pja.acores@sapo.pt; www.pjazores.com. Fairly central, with easy access to shops & transport. The hostel has 90 beds in shared rooms & 2 family rooms with bathroom. Dorm beds cost €18.50. There are also twins with private bath. €

## In the east

🏠 **Hotel Marina Atlântico** [79 F4] (184 rooms) Av João Basco Mota Amaral 1; ☎ 296 307 900; www.bensaudehotels.com. Next to the Hotel Açores Atlântico (which is part of the same group, but closes Nov–end Mar) this is a smart hotel with external detailing influenced by the adjacent marina. If you want a sea view, specify when booking. A pedestrian bridge crosses the main road to give easy access to the marina & public swimming pools, & it's a 10min promenade into the centre of town. Indoor pool, health club, sauna, jacuzzi, Turkish bath, reading room, free Wi-Fi, parking (a stiff €7.50 per day). B/fast inc. €€€€€€

## Around Ponta Delgada

🏠 **Quinta da Abelheira** [70 B4] (8 rooms, family room, 1 apt) Pico da Abelheira 17, Fajã de Baixo; ☎ 296 383 903; e reservas@azoreanbliss. com; www.quintadaabelheira.com. On the eastern side of Ponta Delgada & just a 10min drive to the centre, yet very quiet. A lovely old manor house, traditionally furnished, some rooms within the house, others purpose-built in an adjacent annexe. Games room & pool. Relaxing garden, decorated with tiled panels from 1932 & illustrated quotes from the Azorean poets. Dinner provided with 24hrs' notice. No facilities for children. €€€€€€

**Solar da Glória ao Carmo** [70 C4] (3 rooms, 2 apts) Rua da Glória ao Carmo 5; 296 629 847; e info@gloriaaocarmo.com; www.gloriaaocarmo.com. A few km east of town, a rather austere building conceals a beautifully restored interior with period furniture, plus modern s/c apts. The suite is sumptuous, if your budget can stretch. Heating, no AC or TV in rooms, but a roof terrace, free Wi-Fi & a truly excellent b/fast. Evening meals available on request. €€€

**WHERE TO EAT AND DRINK** São Miguel now has many, many restaurants, and you can even find Chinese, Japanese, Mexican or Italian cuisine in Ponta Delgada if you need a change from the local fare. In town, you can easily encounter cheap eats (lunchtime main courses from around €6) in the backstreets, though price largely reflects the quality. Popular, though verging on fast food, are the relatively new places along the promenade next to Ponta Delgada's marina near the ferry terminal. The restaurants listed below are recommended, though of course the scene changes all the time.

## Ponta Delgada

**A Comercial** [79 F1] Rua Machado dos Santos 75; ⏰ 08.00–20.00 Mon–Fri, 08.00–13.00 Sat. A good cheaper option, join the queue of office workers waiting for excellent lunch fare. Served canteen-style, but the food is good, especially if you're hungry & on a budget. €6

**Adega Regional** [79 F2] Rua do Melo 70; 296 284 740; ⏰ noon–15.00 & 18.00–22.00 Tue–Sun. Well-priced regional specialities, without any fancy touches but a good choice of fish dishes. €11

**Alcides** [79 G1] Rua Hintze Ribeiro 61–77; 296 281 290/296 282 677; ⏰ noon–15.00 & 19.00–22.00 daily. Has a well-deserved reputation for its steak, renowned by locals as possibly the island's finest. Part of the hotel next door, but with the feel of a separate establishment. €13

**Anfiteatro Restaurant & Lounge** [79 F5] Pavilão do Mar; 296 206 155; www.efth. com.pt; ⏰ lounge: noon–15.00 & 18.30–22.00 Mon–Fri, noon–22.00 Sat, Sun & hols; fine-dining: 12.30–14.30 & 18.30–22.00 daily. With a lounge & a fine-dining restaurant to choose from, this establishment also trains culinary students & tries hard to do something different. It is hidden beneath the can't-miss amphitheatre on the waterfront. The lounge/café/bar on the ground floor serves a wide choice of cocktails & gins, salads, sandwiches, etc, – not much of a nod to Azorean traditions, but a pleasant change; the dining room is on the 1st floor & is focused on tasting menus. Upstairs is not cheap: somewhere for a special occasion, perhaps. €10 (lounge), €25 (fine-dining, 3 courses)

**A Reserva** [79 G2] Travessa do Aterro 1; m 910 543 159; ⏰ 18.00–22.30 Mon–Sat. Nothing Azorean about this highly rated place: food & wines are all from the Portuguese mainland. Tapas are heavily orientated towards sausage, tinned fish & a variety of tasty cheeses. You can 'mix & match' & order as many as you want. Wine list is huge, with bottles starting around €7. Not expensive, but order wisely, as your bill can spiral quickly upwards. Tapas start from €3 per dish. €14

**Boca de Cena** [79 E4] Largo Sao João 4; m 963 132 857; ⏰ noon–14.30 & 19.30–23.00 Mon–Fri, 19.30–23.30 Sat. Highly rated & characterful chef producing hugely popular dishes. Surroundings are a bit spartan, but ambience perks up in the evening, with a more extensive menu. €12

**Colegio 27 Grill & Jazz Club** [78 D4] Rua Carvalho de Araujo 27; m 910 441 214; ⏰ Easter–end Oct 18.30–midnight Tue–Sun. A dinner-music club, with a relaxed ambience, a bit of an Azorean rarity. Live music 3 times per week, varying from jazz to *bossa nova*. You can perch at the bar, if there's room & just sip a glass of wine, or book a table for dinner (reservations advisable, essential in summer). The short menu is more expensive than most, but is well received by customers. €16

**Restaurante Nacional** [79 F2] Rua Açoreana Oriental; 296 629 949; ⏰ noon–15.00 & 18.00–22.00 Mon–Fri, 18.00–22.00 Sat. Established in 1947 & some of the smart, friendly waiters have been here nearly as long! Traditional fare, served in a quaint, semi formal dining room. Portions are generous, prices reasonable. €11

**✕ Restaurante Rotas Ilha Verde** [78 D4] Rua Pedro Homem 49; ✆ 296 628 560; www.rotasilha. blogspot.com; ⏱ noon–15.00 & 19.00–23.00 Mon–Fri, 19.00–23.00 Sat. A rare vegetarian restaurant, with a creative & extensive range. Cheap *pratos do dia*. Vegans catered for, on request. Specials might inc pear soup or aubergine strudel. Small & usually packed, so booking advisable. *€11*

**✕ Sardinha ('Manny Cigano's')** [79 G4] Rua Engenheiro Jose Cordeiro 1; ✆ 296 285 765; ⏱ noon–15.00 Mon–Fri. Cheap lunchtime eats, with horse mackerel the speciality. Served in a cramped dining room, at tables shared with locals. Manny still cooks, at the ripe age of 79, & his family serve the tables. It's rough & ready, you won't be encouraged to linger, but Manny's is a Ponta Delgada institution – & it's cheap. *€6*

**✕ Taberna Açor** [79 H1] Rua dos Mercadores 41; ✆ 296 629 084; ⏱ noon–15.00 & 18.00–22.00 Tue–Sun. With a tempting selection of tapas-style dishes, you can graze at your own pace & eat as much as you like, served by an energetic young team of servers. You can wise-up on your knowledge of Azorean cheeses here. *€10*

**✕ Tasca** [79 G1] Rua do Aljube 16; ✆ 296 288 880; ⏱ noon–15.00 & 18.00–22.00 Tue–Sun. Firmly established as one of the town's top tables, justifiably popular with visitors, but with an excellent ambience. Check out the daily changing dishes, or order from an extensive & inexpensive menu. Good wine list, too. *€11*

**⌨ Louvre Micaelense** [79 G1] Rua Antonio Jose Almeida 8; ⏱ 10.00–20.00 Sun–Fri, 10.00–23.00 Sat. Selling a variety of island tea, wines, & good coffee in a refurbished haberdasher's shop which retains some tasteful original features. A good place to buy Azorean edibles & gifts, some of which are imported from Portuguese mainland. Free Wi-Fi. *€5*

**⌨ Varandas Avenida** [79 F2] Rua de Santa Luzia 28 (corner of Praca Vasco da Gama); ⏱ 07.00–20.00 Mon–Sat (summer to 23.30). With a great selection of pastries & an early opening, this is a good b/fast location. Popular with locals heading to work, José & crew will do you bacon & eggs, if you ask. Lunchtime *prato do dia* is good value. Outside tables, too. *€6*

## Around Ponta Delgada

**✕ A Traineira** [70 C4] Rua Dr Jose Pereira Botelho 55, Rosario, Lagoa; ✆ 296 965 249; ⏱ noon–23.00 daily. Characterful owner will collect you in his car from Ponta Delgada (& deliver you home again). A great place for fish, with 3 or 4 fresh choices every day. Popular, advance booking essential in high season. *€13*

**NIGHTLIFE** Although Ponta Delgada is by far the most important and busiest town in the Azores, nightlife remains mostly quiet and traditional. Many simply enjoy an evening promenade by the harbour after a good dinner, though in summer things can get quite lively, with popular music events in the city's squares and by the marina. **Teatro Micaelense** [79 E4] (*www.teatromicaelense.pt*) offers a wide range of cultural events throughout the year, from ballet, musicals, *fado*, jazz and chamber recitals to fully staged operas, the programmes often linked with the Coliseums in Lisbon and Porto. **Coliseu Micaelense** [78 C5] (*Rua de Lisboa;* ✆ *296 209 500;* e *geral@coliseumicaelense.pt; www.coliseumicaelense.pt*) has a similar variety of performances as the Teatro. The Coliseu is a beautiful, Old-World venue with 76 numbered, private boxes which will transport you straight back to 1917, the year of its opening. Fully restored in 2002, it's worth poking your head into the auditorium to admire the architecture and period décor. Temporary exhibitions are sometimes held upstairs, with a small admission charge.

Even if you're not dining at **Colegio 27 Grill & Jazz Club** *(page 81;* ⏱ *Easter–end Oct)*, it's a cool hangout with live music three times per week. No cover charge for non-diners, though bar stools are at a premium – it's small!

**SHOPPING** Pottering around the quaint streets of Ponta Delgada will bring you in contact with a few souvenir shops, especially around the Praça Goncalo Velho Cabral [79 G2]. As well as the slightly tired **Solmar Avenida Center** [79 H1], which does contain a good bookshop, the **Livraria Solmar** (✆ *296 629 720;*

*www.livrariasolmar.pt*), there is another (and huge) mall – the **Parque Atlanticó** – at the north edge of town [78 C2]. It has no Azorean character, but could let you pass a wet afternoon if you like shopping.

**A Vinha Garrafeira** [79 H1] Av Infante Dom Henrique 49; ☎ 296 205 358; ⏰ 11.00–19.00 Mon–Fri, 10.00–14.00 Sat. A wine shop on the main promenade, with a good selection of Azorean wines & liquors. Very popular with cruise-ship escapees. Magma is a renowned brand of white wine from Terceira, & from Pico Frei Gigante is also reputable, while the Tinto Atlanticó is a good-option red from the same island. Atlantis is semi-sweet & fortified. Excellent mainland wines are also sold here.

## OTHER PRACTICALITIES
**Emergency** ☎ 112
**Police** [79 G1] ☎ 296 282 022
✚ **Hospital** [78 B1] Av Dom Manuel I; ☎ 296 203 000. Northwest of the town centre.
✉ **Post office** [79 F2] Praça Vasco da Gama; ⏰ 08.30–18.00 Mon–Sat.

**Laundry Wash Now** [79 H1] Solmar Avenida Center; ☎ 296 283 427; ⏰ 10.00–17.00 Mon–Fri. Not self-service, nor very cheap, but cheaper than your hotel's service.

**WHAT TO SEE AND DO** For individual activity listings, see *Activities*, pages 109–13.

**Museums** [70 C4] Ponta Delgada's main museum, the Museu Carlos Machado, has been under restoration for years, with no concrete news on a reopening date. Around the island, small museums seem to be opening all the time and they are all most charmingly staged, often in picturesque settings.

*Museu Carlos Machado* [79 E4] (*Rua João Moreira, Ponta Delgada*) Founded in 1876, this important museum is in the former convent of Santo André, named after the first patron saint of Ponta Delgada. Intended to house Clarissa nuns in the late 16th century, it has undergone several structural changes and its present appearance dates from the first half of the 19th century. The museum is named after its founder, Carlos Machado. An imposing building, sadly it has been closed for several years and reopening is still uncertain. The tourist office can update on any developments. Meanwhile there are two associated museums which house some of the collection, the Santa Barbara Centre and the Museum of Sacred Art (see below for further details).

*Núcleo de Santa Bárbara (Santa Barbara Centre)* [78 D4] (*Rua Dr Carlos Machado, adjacent to the Museu Carlos Machado, Ponta Delgada;* ☎ *296 202 930; museucarlosmachado.azores.gov.pt;* ⏰ *10.00–18.00 Tue–Sun; €2/1/free adults/under 25s & seniors/under 15s, admission free Sun*) Mainly temporary exhibitions, plus a permanent display of sculptures by Ernesto Canto da Maia (1890–1981), one of the Azores' greatest artists, revered also in mainland Portugal. A visit to the adjoining church is included. English-speaking staff will help with information.

*Igreja do Colégio (Museum of Sacred Art)* [78 D3] (*By the Antero de Quental memorial garden, Ponta Delgada;* ⏰ *09.30–12.30 & 14.30–18.00 Tue–Sun; €2/1/free adults/under 25s & seniors/under 15s, admission free Sun*) The church has the two most important examples of 18th-century Portuguese art: the magnificent carved cedarwood altarpiece is the greatest wooden monument in Portugal, begun after 1737 and

One of the most important festivals is that of **Senhor Santo Cristo dos Milagres** (literally Lord Holy Christ of Miracles), to whom intense devotion was given during the 17th century when the island was racked by frequent earthquakes and tremors, and whose celebration has strengthened through the centuries. In Ponta Delgada, the monastery and nearby Praça 5 Outubro (Square of 5th of October) are illuminated and the street decorated with flowers and at the end of the week, on the fifth Sunday after Easter, a large procession passes round the town with the crown of golden thorns at the front. Behind come men in religious clothes, some barefoot, some carrying large, very heavy candles to declare their thanks for a blessing received during a period of affliction. These are followed by youth organisations with their brightly coloured banners, children, some dressed as angels, priests, then the figure of Senhor Santo Cristo dos Milagres carried under a dossel of velvet and gold decorated with 18th-century woven flowers. Temporary bars are set up around and about.

A much less conspicuous celebration, but one that perhaps makes a greater impression upon the visitor by its gravity and simplicity, is that of the **Lenten pilgrims**. During the seven weeks of Lent, groups of men led by a 'master' walk right round the island (*romarios*) and pray at the churches and chapels dedicated to Our Lady. As they walk they say the Ave Maria; you can ask them to say one for you, but in return you must say as many yourself as there are men walking in the group. Flyers are issued, warning you of their presence on the roads!

Of great significance in the religious calendar is the **Holy Ghost Festival** that climaxes on the seventh Sunday after Easter. It is a festival with German origins when an Imperial Brotherhood was set up to help people in times of calamity; it spread widely in Christian Europe including Portugal. On São Miguel its importance grew after the tragic consequences of the earthquake that virtually destroyed Vila Franca do Campo in 1522. The **Procession of Bom Jesus da Pedra** is one of the oldest religious festivals and attracts many emigrants from around the world.

**Cantar às Estrelas**, Our Lady of the Stars, is celebrated by singing at night in the streets in thanks for the star that guided the Three Kings to Bethlehem.

In May is the festival of **São Miguel Arcanjo**, which has been celebrated for more than 400 years. Its secular content involves a procession of different professional

left partially gilded in 1760 when the Jesuits were banished; the tiled panels are 5m high and depict Eucharistic allegories framed by Baroque ornamentation. For these two works alone it is well worth visiting, but there are also temporary exhibitions which focus on aspects of island culture. Audio guides are available in English, for €2 extra, but only cover the old Jesuit church, which was reopened in 2004 after restoration.

***Museu Militar dos Açores*** [78 C6] (*Forte de São Brás, at the western end of the harbour, Ponta Delgada;* ✆ *296 304 920; www.exercito.pt;* ⊕ *10.00–17.30 Tue–Fri, 10.00–12.30 & 13.30–17.30 Sat & Sun; €3/1 adult/student or senior*) The Military Museum of the Azores has displays of uniforms, World War II guns used to defend the harbour, various historical armaments going back 200 years, military communications, field equipment and medical services. Opened to the public in 2006, the museum, while modest, affords fascinating access to the fort itself which makes it well worth the visit. The fort was built in the 16th century to defend the port and still serves as a regional command centre for the Portuguese military.

groups – fishermen, potters, shoemakers, barbers and farmers, etc. The **Festival of São João** on 24 June is also Vila Franca's municipal holiday; celebrations continue for a week with marching bands, dances, bonfires and barbecues.

**Cantar às Estrelas** Ribeira Grande; beginning of Feb

**Festa de São José** Ponta Delgada; procession 3rd week of Mar

**Easter** Mar/Apr

**Festa Sr dos Enfermos** Furnas; weekend after Easter. *The streets are covered with azaleas & other flowers for the procession.*

**Festa de São Pedro Gonçalves – Festa do Irró** Vila Franca; end of Apr. *The fishermen process down to the harbour.*

**Festa do Sr Santo Cristo dos Milagres** Ponta Delgada; 5th Sunday after Easter

**Festa da Flor** Ribeira Grande; May. *Flower festival.*

**Festas do Espírito Santo** May to Sep; intermittent

**Festas de São João da Vila** Vila Franca; middle of Jun. *With popular singing groups & food stalls, dancing, bonfires & barbecues.*

**Império da Trindade** Ponta Delgada; 3rd week of Jun. *Ending of the Holy Ghost Festival.*

**Festa do Corpo de Deus** Povoação; last week of Jun

**Cavalhadas de São Pedro** Ribeira Grande; last week of Jun. *Horsemen pay tribute to St Peter in traditional song asking protection for the island's governor.*

**Semana do Chicharro** Ribeira Quente; middle of Jul. *Fishing festival.*

**Festa de N Sra de Lourdes** Capelas; end of Jul

**Festa de Santana** Furnas; end of Jul

**Festa de São Nicolau** Sete Cidades; middle of Aug

**Festa de N Sra dos Anjos** Água de Pau/Fajã de Baixo; middle of Aug

**Festa de N Sra da Conceição** Mosteiros; 3rd week of Aug

**Semana da Cultura** Povoação; last week of Aug. *Handicrafts & other activities.*

**Festa de Bom Jesus da Pedra** Vila Franca; last week of Aug. *One of the oldest religious festivals, attracting many emigrants from around the world.*

**Festival de Bandas** Povoação; 1st week of Oct. *Road show.*

**Dia das Montras** Ponta Delgada; 2nd week of Dec. *Shop windows are dressed for Christmas & prizes awarded for the best.*

## Gardens

**Gardens** During the middle years of the 19th century, at least three great gardens were developed in Ponta Delgada, and their owners vied with each other to have the latest introductions and the rarest plants. They are within walking distance of the town centre.

*Jardim António Borges* [78 B3] (*entrance from Av Antero de Quental or Rua António Borges, Ponta Delgada;* ⊕ *winter 09.00–18.00, summer to 20.30; admission free*) Begun in 1858 by the affluent landowner António Borges, this 3ha garden remains by far the most ornate, or rather fanciful, of the gardens. Now a public garden managed by the municipality, there remain a great fern ravine with its romantic bridge, as well as small lakes and watercourses. Boating and garden parties here must have been huge fun in bygone days. Most of the original planting has long gone but a great buttress-rooted *Ficus macrophylla*, and a huge *Albizia* spp are worth seeing. Although kept clean, the garden has seen better times – it's now a popular hangout for schoolchildren.

**Jardim José do Canto** [78 D2] (*Rua José do Canto, Ponta Delgada;* \ *296 650 310;* *www.josedocanto.com;* ⊕ *Apr–Sep 09.00–19.00, Oct–Mar 09.00–17.00, daily; €3.50/ free adult/child*) José do Canto was probably the most knowledgeable gardener of his time and, from the mid 1800s, began to build a plant collection that over the next 50 years would total several thousand species. Not only did he compile lists of the species he wanted to acquire, he even kept a long list of the plants he did not want to grow! The garden of more than 5ha was considered one of the finest private botanical gardens in Europe. Much of the design and planting was supervised by English gardeners. The garden remains in private ownership, is next door to the Sant'Ana Palace (see below), and is now the grounds of the **Pensão Casa do Jardim** (\ *296 650 310; www.residencialcasadojardim.com*), if you want to stay overnight. Without doubt the finest specimen trees in the Azores are to be found here, in maturity a noble memorial to the man who worked so hard to introduce them. Look especially for Australian Moreton Bay figs (*Ficus macrophylla*), honeymyrtle (*Melaleuca decora*) and Kauri pine (*Agathis robusta*), *Araucaria columnaris* from New Caledonia, the Japanese Kusamaki tree (*Podocarpus macrophyllus*), and Chinese camphorwood (*Cinnamomum camphora*). If you follow the cobbles to the top of the hill, you won't get much of a view, but you will meet a magnificent 160-year-old rubber tree.

**The Presidential Palace or Sant'Ana Palace** [78 C2] (Rua Jacome Correia, *Ponta Delgada;* \ *296 301 100;* e *presidencia.palacios@azores.gov.pt;* ⊕ *(garden only) Apr–Sep 10.00–16.00, Tue–Fri 13.00–17.00; Oct–Mar 13.00–17.00 Sat only; €2, max 30 visitors at any time, guided tours can be booked*) Now the office of the President of the Autonomous Region of the Azores, it is (unsurprisingly) one of the best maintained gardens in the Azores. The house was once a family home of the Correia family who commissioned the English architect David Mocatta to build it in 1846. With three wings, it is in a neoclassical style with sculpture and statuary on the front elevation. Inside, in the main entrance and stairway, there are paintings by the Lisbon artist Ernesto Ferreira Condeixa commemorating the royal visit of King Don Carlos and Queen Dona Amélia in 1901. In the first-floor dining room an *azulejo* panel depicts the 1831 Liberal victory over the Absolutists at Ladeira da Velha, on the north coast east of Ribeira Grande. The 7.5ha garden is principally attributed to the work of two gardeners: Peter Wallace from Chatsworth for the general design; and, later, the Belgian François Gabriel who notably introduced many camellia cultivars. With the original layout little changed, it is a good example of 19th-century Victorian garden design. There are a number of mature trees, an attempt at a garden of native Azorean plants, and an impressive long *allée* of box trees. For the sharp-eyed, there are interesting shrubs to discover.

**Ponta Delgada City Park** [79 G2] (*Located to the north of the city's historic centre, off the road to Capelas, the Caminho da Lavada, entrance near the park's club house;* ⊕ *08.00–22.00; admission free*) This public park of 18ha was begun in 2007 and completed in 2011 with the construction of a club house with bar and restaurant next to a golf driving range. Soil contouring has been added, to reduce traffic noise from the busy radial road and create a sense of privacy. The defining pathways and their secondary paths, the traditional stone walls creating enclosed walkways like the rural *canadas* separating farm fields, the long pergola of granite pillars, expansive grass areas with groups of endemic and indigenous plants, others of ornamental shrubs, and of course many trees promise a most inviting future.

***Arruda Açores pineapple plantation*** [79 G2] (*Rua Dr Augusto Arruda, Fajã de Baixo;* \ *296 384 438;* ⊕ *May–Sep 09.00–20.00; Oct–Apr 09.00–18.00*) Admission is free to see the greenhouses and includes tasting of pineapple liqueur and delicious pineapple boiled sweets. There are pineapple fruits for sale, loose and in presentation boxes, plus various handicrafts. This was an orange farm in the 19th century, when the garden was first planted. With the demise of the orange trade towards the end of the century, the farm adapted and went over to pineapple production under glass, and remarkably set out at the same time to be a tourist attraction. There is a belvedere which was used as a lookout for the arrival of the orange boats.

## Walking trail around town *The town trail on the following pages should take about 2 hours, excluding any time spent in cafés or museums.*

The tour begins at the tourist information office on the main promenade [79 G2], the Avenida Infante Dom Henrique.

With your back to the office door, turn left and left again around the corner into the square, the **Praça Gonçalo Velho Cabral,** where you will find the three ornate and distinctive arches of the original (1783) **gates to the city** [79 G2], which once stood by the old harbour wall. The modern statue commemorates the man after whom the square is named, supposedly the discoverer of the islands of São Miguel and Santa Maria.

Ponta Delgada had become important as a trading port, and in the 18th and early 19th centuries it was especially significant for the export of oranges. On several of the houses you will see square attic-like structures on the roof; here a servant would be stationed to watch for and give early warning of the approach of an orange schooner. This gave the grower or merchant valuable extra hours to harvest the fruit as it had to be picked fresh to travel well. Ships had to moor

### PINEAPPLES

Pineapples were introduced as a replacement crop for oranges around 1850, and became so successful that after ten years they were being exported to northern Europe, including England where they featured in royal banquets. The Azores are not warm enough for their outdoor cultivation, and there were some 3,000 glasshouses producing yearly about 2,000 tonnes of fruit. With the high capital costs of new greenhouses, it is doubtful if this crop will continue when existing houses need to be replaced, though at present the fruit is readily available. The main growing area is in Fajã de Baixo on the edge of Ponta Delgada, also in Lagoa and Vila Franca do Campo. It takes two years to produce a ripe fruit with an average weight of 1.5–2kg. Earlier, heather, ferns and moss were taken from the mountains and made into a thick growing bed but nowadays, to protect the mountain vegetation, leafy branches of pittosporum and other shrubs are used. As these decay they give off heat, and in a closed or carefully ventilated glasshouse this is sufficient for the plants to thrive. Old stems are used for propagation, which take six months to produce young plants. These are planted out to grow on for another 12 months, at which stage ivy and other vegetation is burned in old oil drums to create a dense smoke. This triggers the plants to flower all at the same time, and in six months they are ready for harvesting. Without 'smoking', flowering would occur intermittently and it would take much longer before the crop could be cleared and the cycle begun again.

offshore and lighters (transportation barges) conveyed passengers and cargo from shore to ship. The harbour in those days was very small, and in fact was situated in the very square in which you are now standing. The bank on the east side and the adjacent buildings all have many internal arches which once fronted the sea. Land reclamation work pushed the sea back, allowing the new bank and other buildings, as well as the main promenade road, to be built in 1947.

Cross the square diagonally, and stand with your back to the **Parish Church of São Sebastião** [79 G1]. You are now facing the back of a run of buildings that once fronted on to the sea. The city gates originally joined on to these. On your left, facing the side of the Church of São Sebastião, is a tiny entrance to the **Café Mascote** (previously known as the Café Chesterfield); go into the old part, No 66, and see the arched roof while sipping a coffee. This was once part of the original colonnade at the harbour's edge. Tiled murals in the café give a good indication of how things looked in times gone by.

Now exit the café and turn right and then right again down a small side street. At the end on the left is the police station, formerly the customs house. Take the little turning on the right about halfway along to go to the rear of the Café Mascote. Again you will see some arches in the outside wall, part of the colonnade at the edge of the harbour, also with decorative tiling.

Return the same way as you came, to the **Church of São Sebastião**. This began as a very small chapel built to fulfil a vow made during the plague of 1523–31; in the 18th century, it was greatly added to in the Baroque style and the interior was decorated with ornate woodcarving. The exotic timbers used, especially jacaranda, reflect imports from the Brazilian colonies. (Some additional information about the church, in English, is given by a panel by the entrance.)

Retrace your steps towards the city gates and turn right, to see the **Câmara Municipal** [79 F2] or town hall. Originally it was the residence of one of the town's wealthy families and was converted only at the beginning of the 20th century. The bell tower dates from 1724 and houses the oldest bell (16th century) in the Azores. Look in at the ground-floor entrance between the steps; here there is often a temporary exhibition of local interest. The statue in front of the building is of São Miguel Arcanjo (St Michael), patron saint of the island.

Continue past the town hall taking the road on your left, **Rua de Santa Luzia**. At the end, on the left, the large, handsome building is the old post office. Cross the square, the Praça Vasco da Gama, diagonally and continue westwards along the main promenade towards the **Forte de São Brás** at the end of the present-day harbour. Behind you is a pleasing homogeneity of architecture along the waterfront. Try to ignore the one blemish, the intrusive tower block at the far eastern end of town.

Well before reaching the fort, opposite the **Praça Vasco da Gama** square, note the floating deck at the harbour edge with its café tables; this is the **Cais da Sardinha**, and was where sardines were once landed. Continue along the *avenida*, past the present-day customs house, and see a white corner building with a circular tower, the local headquarters of the Ministry of Defence. In the harbour opposite, there may be activity around the colourful chunky fishing boats, landing their catch. The 16th-century Forte de São Brás was built to defend the village against corsairs and pirates, including some from England. Enlarged in the 19th century, it is now the army headquarters and military museum (page 84).

Opposite the fort is the square of **Praça 5 Outubro** (aka the Campo de São Francisco), a large space which is the traditional site for festivals. Dwarfing the many pollarded trees around the square is a massive tree (*Metrosiderus tomentosa*), an Australasian import over 140 years old. On one side, the square is overlooked by the fine, green-washed, former Franciscan monastery. On the far, northern side of the square, parallel with the seafront, is the **Convento da Nossa Senhora da Esperança** (Our Lady of Hope) [78 C5], completed in 1541 and occupied by the nuns of the Order of St Francis. The chapel is decorated with magnificent 18th-century tiles and gilding and is associated with the worship of the Christ of the Miracles. There is also an image of Ecce Homo, a statue that came to the Azores in the 16th century. The sculptor is unknown, but it came from Paris to the convent that existed at that time in Caloura. To protect the statue against frequent pirate attacks, the nuns left the coastal convent and took it with them to the newly built Nossa Senhora da Esperança. Some 150 years later a young girl called Teresa da Anunciada (1658–1738), from a rich family in Ribeira Grande, devoted herself to the nunnery and especially to the worship of this image. News of her devotion and fame of the miracles granted carried to all the islands and even as far as mainland Portugal. Subsequent emigration spread the worship of the Christ of the Miracles, and now pilgrims come from Azorean communities overseas to join the annual festival, the second-biggest religious festival in the whole of Portugal. The image may be seen from closer up, between 17.30 and 18.30 every evening when a nun opens the internal gates (around the corner from the square) to allow visitors in to see it, as well as the vestments and treasures. There is also a splendid ceiling and Baroque ornamentation. On the fifth Sunday after Easter, at the Santo Cristo Festival, the image is taken on procession through the city, passing along the narrow roads carpeted with fresh flowers in geometrical designs.

Outside, in front of the chapel, there is a statue to Madre Teresa da Anunciada. Behind, at the first seat, the poet and political activist Antero de Quental shot himself in 1891, aged 49. The church to the left of the convent, **Igreja São José** [78 C6], was part of the Lady of Conception convent and in the 16th century took 60 years to build. The façade is 18th century. Inside, it has a fine ceiling and much 18th-century decorative art. It is the major church of the old village and parish of São José.

From the square and by the convent, the cobbled, semi-pedestrianised road leading off is officially signed as the Rua Dr Gil Mont Alverne but has always been called the central road or **Rua Direita**, although today it is not so central. Pass along the convent buildings and you come to green metal gates. Here you will find the side entrance to view the Ecce Homo.

Continue along the Rua Direita which becomes the Rua Marques da Praia e Monfort, where even now traditional shops can still be found. On the right, directly opposite the Hotel Talisman, you will come to the former house of the Marquis de Praia, now a government building and with a square observation tower on the roof. Next to the hotel, note the attractive garden, the **Jardim Padre Senas Freitas** [78 C5], named after a writer, orator and polemicist. (The eye-catching, blue-painted building at the park's southern end is an administrative building.) It was the Marquis de Praia who in 1843 purchased the land in Furnas and began the great expansion of the renowned Terra Nostra garden (page 96). Continue in the same direction, then take the next road on the left, up the **Rua Comandante Jaime de Sousa**. Shortly you come to **Largo Mártires da Pátria** (Martyrs' Square) [78 D5], at the far side of which is a secondary school, originally the grand home of the wealthy 'Fonte Bela', so nicknamed because of his many water installations on the island. He was one of the first and most important of the orange growers and the largest landowner. The blue-and-white building on the left, to the west, is the old government or **Parliament House** of the autonomous region. Note the church with its ornate Manueline façade.

Take the **Travessa de Conceição** and then turn left into the Rua Machado dos Santos. A very small chapel at the top of a short flight of basalt steps is the **Chapel of Santa Luzia** [79 F1], dated 1584. Luzia was the daughter of a rich family and was losing her sight; she promised that if she could keep her sight she would build a chapel in gratitude.

Turn left into the **Rua Carvalho Araújo**; your attention is immediately grabbed by the splendidly ornate early 17th-century Baroque **Igreja do Colégio** [78 D3], which dominates the far end of the street. Following the expulsion of the Jesuits the church remained open for worship, but after a tenuous period in the early 19th century was first used for storage and then eventually abandoned. Acquired by the regional government, they began renovations in 1993 and in 2004 it opened as a museum, now housing the Carlos Machado Museum's collection of sacred art (**Núcleo de Arte Sagra**). By the early 18th century in Ponta Delgada there were three religious communities (Franciscans, Augustinians and Jesuits), four nunneries, three sanctuaries for lay females and 28 churches. There were over 650 people in religious orders plus others totalling about 1,200 – one in eight adults of the Ponta Delgada population, with probably about a third of the population benefiting economically from the religious foundations. Enjoy the many wrought-iron balconies as you walk up this street. Next to the convent is the memorial garden to the São Miguel-born poet Antero de Quental (1842–91), with its elegant Art-Deco sculpture, *Emotion and Reason*.

From the convent go eastwards along Rua Dr Aristides da Mota and Rua Dr Guilherme Pocas and keep going until the narrow road opens out and you see a large building to the right surrounded by a tall whitewashed wall enclosing a garden. This is the **Carlos Machado Museum** [79 E4] (page 83), which has been closed for years; turn right and follow the wall round to the entrance. If you have time, once the museum is restored, do make a visit; meanwhile the **Núcleo de Santa Bárbara** (page 83) is just across the road.

Take the Rua Santa Barbara downhill and turn left on to the Rua de São João to soon reach the tall **Teatro Micaelense** [79 E4]. Ugly from the rear, elegantly modern from the front, this was originally the site of a military fortress, destroyed by fire in the early 1900s. The theatre was opened in May 1917, and is modelled on the Coliseum in Lisbon. It has been restored and seats 1,500. If you want to visit the **market** [79 E4], selling fresh fruit, vegetables, flowers, meat, fish, cheese and some handicrafts, continue along on to the Rua Mercado for about 100m and you'll find it on the right-hand side. On Saturday mornings and festival times, it generates a certain buzz. (Next door is an excellent cheese shop.) There are also public lavatories, and a snack bar.

Afterwards, retrace your steps to the theatre. Walk down the hill and turn left into the **Rua da Misericórdia** and you will come to a **library** on your left with the red gates at the top of the steps. Take the right fork along past the former **Hotel São Pedro** [79 E4]; this was once the residence of Thomas Hickling, built 1799–1812, in Georgian style. Hickling was the wealthy Bostonian who built a summer house at Furnas and began what later became the Terra Nostra Park. Opposite on elevated ground is a church, the main **Church of the Parish of São Pedro**. Climb the steps for a good view out over the ferry terminal, the marina and out to sea. Ponta Delgada has over the years absorbed the surrounding villages and today has three parishes, two of which we have now met, and the central parish of São Sebastião.

From here walk down to the seafront and continue right along the promenade to return to the tourist office.

**THE WESTERN PART OF THE ISLAND** For individual activity listings, see *Activities*, pages 109–13.

**Lagoa do Canário** On the way to Sete Cidades from Ponta Delgada you will notice a forestry services sign to this lake on your right after you have passed a lovely old stone aqueduct. An unsurfaced narrow road lined with azaleas leads down to a car park, where there are picnic tables and barbecues. There are several things to see here. As you drove in you will have passed a small lake on your left down among the trees. Not only is this a lovely spot; around the lake is a very healthy community of royal fern, *Osmunda regalis*. From the car park another wide road leads you further on between the cryptomeria forest; it is a 15-minute walk to one of the finest *miradouros* (viewpoints) in all the Azores, a truly stunning view of the Sete Cidades lakes and village. As you return to the car park, on your left is a small track leading down; this takes you to a deep, very narrow ravine filled with a gurgling stream, tree ferns, several endemic plants and many ornamental azaleas. It is cool and moist, and wonderful for ferns and mosses.

**Sete Cidades** Mythology provides a romantic history. Once long ago in the kingdom of the Seven Cities, there was a king. He had a very pretty daughter who loved the countryside and happily roamed the fields, the little valleys and the surrounding hills. One day she came across a handsome shepherd boy tending his animals, and they shyly spoke. As the days went by she saw him again, and then again, and slowly romance blossomed and they fell deeply in love. Unfortunately, her father came to hear of this romance and was furious, because he intended his daughter to marry a neighbouring prince who was heir to a large kingdom. He forbade his daughter ever to see her shepherd boy again, but she pleaded so well that he agreed they could meet for one last time. At the final parting, they both cried so much two lakes were formed, one blue from the princess's eyes, the other green from those of the shepherd boy, and although they were parted forever, their tears have remained united.

Inevitably you will stop at the main viewpoint, the **Vista do Rei**, named from King Carlos's visit in 1901, where you can see both lakes of tears. The circumference of the caldera is roughly 12km.

The raffish traveller Thomas Ashe, describing his travels on São Miguel in 1813, wrote that the banks were planted with hemp or flax, which was cured in the lakes. There were only half-a-dozen houses in the valley where the hemp growers lived, and manufacturing was done by the village of Bretanha and neighbouring villages; some 50,000 yards was used domestically and more for export. The surrounding hillsides with their trees in little groves and bowers and the long winding valleys 'made them pre-eminently beautiful, and particularly favourable for romantic leisure and tender passions'. See pages 115–16 for a guided walk around Sete Cidades.

**The northwest coast along to Capelas** Out beyond the airport the whole of this coastline is very pretty, and there are some especially lovely stretches of road running beneath tall, elegant plane trees with grass banks solid with blue agapanthus and topped with blue hydrangeas. At **Ponta da Ferraria** you can view the *fajã* from the road at the top of the cliff. In the rocky parts by the sea there are the **Termas da Ferraria** (signposted, page 92), thermally heated natural pools. The level track leading from the sea was used by horse-drawn water carts to carry water to the bath house, used by patrons who could not afford to travel to Furnas. If the wind is up, the crash of Atlantic Ocean on volcanic rock here, and the height to which the spray is projected, is truly humbling. There is a restaurant, too. **Bretanha** is a pretty area originally settled by the French from Brittany; in the village is a restored windmill and a spectacular cliff walk starts from near here (pages 116–17). Pass through **Remédios** and come to **Santa Bárbara**. The **Miradouro Santo António viewpoint** overlooks small fields, the village and the sea beyond. Finally you come to the large village of **Capelas**, which once was an important whaling centre with a factory for processing the animals. Don't forget the **Museu M J Melo** (see below).

## 🏠 Where to stay

🏠 **Quinta N Senhora de Lourdes** [70 B3] (2 apts, 1 room) Rua da Igreja, S. Vicente Ferreira, Capelas; 📞 296 919 626; m 914 954 509; e qnsl@ yahoo.com; www.quintalourdes.com. On the left, just before Capelas as you approach on the main road from the east. Look for the pink building on the corner. Quirky place, set in a pleasant garden which adjoins a house built by a priest. Some interesting artefacts, inc whaling harpoons. 2 of the units (1 of which is a family apt) are s/c. Wine cellar (they make their own), snooker table, sun terrace. Gym, small pool & children's pool. Free Wi-Fi. €€

## What to see and do

*Termas da Ferraria (Thermal pools)* [70 A2] (*At Ponta da Ferraria, signposted;* 📞 *296 295 669; www.termasferraria.com;* ⏰ *11.00–19.00 Tue–Sun, closed first 3 weeks in Jan; €6/3 adult/child. Spa costs from €29 for 4hrs; note that under 6s are not allowed in any of the pools or spa.*) Thermally heated natural pools. The old bath house is where a doctor would visit twice a week, descending by donkey along a little trail where now the road winds down. Now, it houses a plush spa downstairs, with sauna, jacuzzi and so forth, and you can indulge yourself for a few hours. If the tide is right, the seawater mixes with hot thermal outflow to produce a hot ocean bath!

*Oficina-Museu M J Melo (Museum)* (*Rua do Loural 56, Capelas;* 📞 *296 298 202; www.oficinamuseu.net;* ⏰ *09.00–noon & 13.00–17.00 Mon–Sat; €2/free adults/under 10s. Guided tours may be available – ask on arrival.*) Signposted from Capelas town centre, this is a most remarkable and extensive display of recreated bygone retail and artisan shops in the style of a street, all the work of a retired Capelas schoolteacher. From the modest entrance door, you would never guess what's about to be revealed. Not only has Senhor Melo made the museum, he has also financed it, without any grant-aid. It is in part of his house, and he may well be there to greet you himself. Well worth visiting, as it will surely rekindle some childhood memories. Traditional Azorean music is available from the gift shop. Recommended.

## THE EASTERN PART OF THE ISLAND: THE SOUTH COAST FROM PONTA DELGADA TO FURNAS For individual activity listings, see *Activities*, pages 109–13.

Once you're heading east out of Ponta Delgada, particularly if you divert where possible from the dual carriageway, you'll realise how sophisticated the island's biggest town can seem when set against the gentle rural life outside its boundaries. While you may be heading for Furnas with its unique setting and ambience, it is far more pleasant to take your time, potter along and visit some of the towns on the way and perhaps include an overnight stay or two. To complete an anticlockwise loop, visiting Furnas, Nordeste and Ribeira Grande and ending at the Lagõa do Fogo would best be done over two or three days, taking in the sights and places described in the *From Furnas to the east and north coasts* section, page 100. Alternatively, you could make a series of day trips if you're staying in Ponta Delgada.

Just east of Ponta Delgada, from the road you can see the high stone walls which once protected the orange trees. On a hilltop there is also one of the remaining 'orange towers', once used to spy approaching ships coming from England to trade. The places below are listed from west to east, starting in Ponta Delgada.

**Lagoa** Lagoa has long been the centre of São Miguel's pottery industry, which began in the 19th century. Crockery, pots, bowls, vases and other items in traditional designs and colours are made here and visitors are welcome to tour the factory, showrooms and museum of Cerâmica Vieira, founded in 1862 (see below). The old town's harbour was once busy with exports of woad and wheat.

### What to see and do
**Observatorio Vulcanológico e Geotérmico dos Açores (Volcanoes House)** (*Av Vulcanológico 95, Lagoa;* m *965 353 694; ovga.centrosciencia.azores.gov.pt;* ⏰ *14.30, 15.30 & 16.30 Mon–Fri (by guided visit only, with English-speakers); €1.50/free adult/under 12s*) On the west side of Lagoa, signposted right as you enter town from Ponta Delgada, is a combination of permanent and temporary exhibitions explaining the geological and vulcanological history of São Miguel and the other islands.

**Expolab** (*Av da Ciencia, Lagoa;* ✎ *296 960 520; centrosciencia.azores.gov.pt;* ⏰ *10.00–17.00 Tue–Fri, 14.00–18.00 Sat; €2*) A fairly modest science museum, with a few interactive displays for children, at whom the centre is largely aimed. They can also carry out their own laboratory experiments(!) with some instructions in English, or play with robots. There are also exhibitions on insects, forests and temporary displays.

**Ceramica Viera** (*Rua das Alminhas, Lagoa;* ✎ *296 912 116;* ⏰ *08.00–noon & 13.00–17.00 Mon–Fri, 09.00–12.45 Sat; admission free*) A chance to buy some of the distinctive pottery from one of the island's last remaining manufacturers. Poking around the factory, you will come across some of the workers finishing the pieces by hand. A family business, in its fifth generation.

**Caloura** This is a pretty area with a tiny fishing harbour and a natural swimming pool at the end of the breakwater, surrounded by old vineyards, each with its own stone wall. In the past few years substantial new homes have been built and it is now obviously a very desirable place to live; for the property-curious, it is interesting to see how a severe, stony landscape can be transformed. Seek out the **Castelo Centro Cultural** (*Canada do Castelo, Caloura;* ✎ *296 913 300; www.cccaloura. com;* ⏰ *10.30–12.30 & 13.30–17.30 Mon–Sat; €2/0.50/free adult/student/under 12s*), an art gallery with a private collection featuring Portuguese artists, including Azoreans Canto do Maio and Domingos Rebelo. The centre also has a 10-minute video (in English) introducing the islands and you should wander outside into the surrounding garden, full of fruit trees sheltered by high stone walls.

By the harbour is a good fish restaurant and café, the **Caloura Bar** (*Largo do Barrracao 1;* ✎ *296 913 283*), where reservations are advisable in summer; a tourist information office in the harbour may (or may not!) be open daily in high season, closed on Mondays in low season. There is also a charming little convent with a beautiful tiled façade, dating from the 16th century, now privately owned.

In the adjacent village of **Água de Pau**, do visit the **Casa do Pescador** (*Rua dos Ferreiros 26, Água de Pau;* ⏰ *09.00–noon & 13.00–15.00 Mon–Fri*), a small museum created by and dedicated to the local fishermen. If you rejoin the highway by Água de Pau, note the tobacco-drying sheds with metal roofs. Tobacco grown on the islands is nowadays used in making cigars.

## 🏠 Where to stay

🏠 **Caloura Hotel Resort** [70 D4] (80 rooms & suites) Rua do Jubileu, Água de Pau; 📞 296 960 900; e info@calourahotel.com; www.calourahotel.com. An oceanfront resort 17km from Ponta Delgada offering double rooms inc junior suites for 4 people, most with private terrace; panoramic restaurant, bar, swimming pool, fitness room, sauna, scuba-diving base & tennis. The location is stunning, & you can walk the narrow roads round to Caloura's pretty harbour with its fishing boats & simple swimming facilities. Formerly an area of tiny vineyards, these have largely been removed in favour of pasture & housing. A sheltered sun trap, it is ideal for a winter holiday, but you will need a car if you want to explore the island. Free Wi-Fi, b/fast inc. **€€€€€**

### What to see and do nearby

**Ribeira Chã Museums** (⊕ 09.00–noon & 13.00–17.00 Mon–Sat; *visit the religious festival museum first, to get access to the others – if you're lucky, there may be someone who speaks English; €3 for all 3 museums*) This charming south-coast hilltop village between Lagoa and Vila Franca has three small places of interest, plus the modern church in the village centre. To the right of the church, a small museum displays exhibits related to the various **religious festivals** held in the village, including the Cavalhadas de S Pedro, a horseback procession held on 29 June. Exhibited also is a replication of the way the *imperador* displays the crown and sceptre as part of the Espírito Santo Festival (page 35). The museum was the idea and initiative of a long-serving parish priest whose statue is outside the church, and includes many photographs and items such as wedding dresses and old school textbooks donated by the parishioners, and the priest's own collection of coins.

Close by is the **Casa Museu Maria dos Anjos Melo**, once the home of a lady (1909–92) who as a child emigrated to the US and returned when 17 years old and taught English in the village, marrying a local stonemason. She bequeathed her house to the parish on her death and the priest had the idea of making it a museum. The house has not been changed, and reveals the very simple bygone way of living typical of the Azores.

A short downhill walk takes you to the **agricultural museum,** another excellent local initiative. Cultivated in the garden are yams, woad, oranges, flax and other early crops together with traditional medicinal herbs and endemic species. In the farm building is a series of model nativities cleverly made by schoolchildren from corn cob husks, pine cones, tiles or wire wool. There are gourds once used as swimming aids, wine barrel cleaners, and a nice section on Dragon's Blood (from the dragoeira tree, not a fire-breathing monster!); it was grown in Flores for export as a dye to Germany, and it seems Azoreans diluted it with *aguardente* and egg yolk for treating back pain, and the girls used the pure sap to paint their nails. Another interesting exhibit is the manufacture of pastel balls for export to Flanders, the *goma e rezinhas*, a mix of pastel and beeswax; during the 16th and 17th centuries, Ribeira Chã had 700 people working on pastel. Another small storeroom has wine-making equipment. In the grounds are several wooden buildings with fitted artefacts: a typical bar, shop, shoemaker, barber, a weaving shed, carpenter's shop, and homemade toys, among others.

## Vila Franca do Campo
Located on a fertile plain or 'campo', Vila Franca was once a duty-free zone whose residents were exempt from paying taxes. It was also the island's first capital. There is good swimming and a large programme of

tourist development is happening, including an aquarium theme park, a marina near Vinha d'Areia, health centre and Clube Naval expansion. There is a harbour with small fishing boats and there are fish restaurants – try the **Praia Café** (*Lugar da Vinha d'Areia;* ⊕ *noon–15.00 & 19.00–22.00 Tue–Sun*) – and good local cakes called *Queijadas da Vila*. Among many buildings of historical architectural merit is the **Matriz**, the Church of São Miguel Arcanjo or St Michael the Archangel. Completed in 1537, it has an impressive façade built completely of basalt, with a carving of Christ on the Cross. On the edge of the town by a pretty little public garden is the old church and convent of São Francisco, dating from 1525; it is now a hotel. Don't forget the museum (see below). On the way into town you will pass the tourist office.

Just off the beach is the **Ilhéu da Vila**, the remains of an old volcano where the sea has breached the crater wall creating a protected swimming area. Extremely popular with local people, it is accessed by a regular boat service between June and September. The island is also a nature reserve: there is a conflict of interest between conservation and recreation, and a daily quota of visitors has been set.

If you have time, it is well worth driving up to the **Chapel of Nossa Senhora da Paz**, which can be seen from Vila Franca high on the hillside behind the town. From here there is a splendid panorama of Vila Franca and its surrounding pineapple glasshouses, and of the green landscape spreading down to and along the coast.

### Where to stay

**Quinta dos Curubas** [70 E4] (5 houses) Estrada Regional, Ribeira Seca, Vila Franca do Campo; m 961 739 880/962 515 189; e geral@ quintadoscurubas.com; www.quintadoscurubas. com. Just east of Vila Franca, s/c timber chalets, set in a large garden property on a hillside overlooking Vila Franca & its bay. Very comfortable with all eco credentials, mod-cons, plus a popular colony of resident ducks. Free use of 3 bicycles, free access to the produce from the owner's vegetable garden, & a welcome pack of basic foodstuffs inc, & there are special deals for 7-night stays. Some chalets have connecting doors, ideal for families. €€€€€€

**Hotel Convent São Francisco** [70 D4] (13 rooms) Av da Liberdade, Vila Franca do Campo; 217 803 470; e info@arteh-hotels.com; www. conventodesaofrancisco.arteh-hotels.com. On the west side of town, before you reach the tourist office, a restored convent with an air of serenity befitting its former purpose. All heavy stone polished wood & impressive furniture, large rooms with free Wi-Fi. There is a communal lounge for TV-watchers. Buffet b/fast served, but no other meals. Some rooms have views to the sea. Next door is a well-kept garden, accessible at any time. €€€€

**What to see and do** Note that the town's little harbour offers whale-watching trips, an alternative to the operators in Ponta Delgada (page 113).

**Museu Etnográfica de Vila Franca do Campo** (*Rua Visconde Botelho, Vila Franca do Campo;* 296 539 118; ⊕ *09.00–12.30 & 14.00–17.30 Tue–Fri, 14.00–17.00 Sat & Sun*) An excellent museum in the renovated 19th-century house of an orange merchant, and, in 1900, the first house to have electric light.

## Furnas
Furnas enjoys a hint of the ambience you might find in an English spa town, with the addition of boisterous geothermal activity that adds a tinge of exoticism. If you approach from the north along the main road, get yourself some aerial perspective by taking the turning off to your right, signposted **Pico do Ferro**. This is a fine viewpoint over the Furnas lake and valley, helping you to get your bearings once you're finally down below. There is also a circular walk starting from here, as well as a shorter one down to the lake. Along with the view of Sete Cidades,

*David Sayers*

In 1770, the noted orange farmer Thomas Hickling built a simple summer house on the high mound overlooking what is now the thermal swimming pool at Furnas. It was surrounded by trees which would have sheltered fashionable summer parties and music; of those trees, I believe the old pollarded English oak in the corner by the pool is the only one that remains, and is therefore probably the oldest tree in the garden, though its days are numbered. Hickling died in 1834, and it was not until 1848 that the Visconde da Praia purchased the property and on the mound built the present house. The Viscondessa was a keen gardener, and over the years they enlarged the estate and laid out the garden in a grand style with water, dark groves of trees and parterres of flowers. After the Visconde's death in 1872, his son enhanced the house and laid out the garden more or less as it is today with its serpentine canal and grottoes, and walks. New tree species were introduced from around the world so many of these now-mature trees are at most 140 years old.

The newly refurbished Terra Nostra Garden Hotel (page 97) opened in 1935, and soon after, Vasco Bensaúde, who was a very keen gardener, purchased the by now-neglected garden; the family's company still owns it today. With a head gardener from Scotland and a veritable army of workmen, he totally refurbished the house and restored the garden within two years. World War II came and ended the fashionable life of Furnas based on the hotel, casino, spa and gardens, and the place continued to slumber for years afterwards until tourism once more asserted itself.

In 1990, restoration began once again, this time with English gardeners, and a team of tree surgeons climbed the equivalent of Mount Everest from sea level working on the 2,500 trees while local engineers refurbished the canals. Many new trees were planted, a garden of Azorean native species begun and, significantly, a collection of Malesian rhododendrons was planted. This is the only garden in Europe that can grow, out of doors without protection, these tender rhododendrons native to tropical mountains; they flower intermittently all year and come in spectacular colours and some are perfumed. The head gardener, Fernando Costa, together with his daughter Carina and a team of around a dozen workers, continues with new developments. In recent times these have included a fern garden, a formal flower garden, a garden devoted to cycads and most recently an ever-expanding collection of camellias which in 2016 numbered around 800.

this village in its huge caldera is among the best-known images of the Azores, certainly of São Miguel. Two places from this area appear in all the brochures: the **hot springs** with their bubbling water and burping mud, and the beautiful **Terra Nostra garden**. Popular as a spa in the 19th century, Furnas attracted patients from as far away as England. The spa building, which dates from the mid 19th century, has now been turned into a plush hotel. The municipal garden in front of what is now the Furnas Boutique Hotel (page 97) was laid out in 1940.

The largest, noisiest and perhaps most fearful of the many fumaroles (gaps in the earth's crust) in town is named *Pêro Botelho*, a 16th-century nickname for the devil. Around the calderas area some 22 different mineral waters emerge from the ground, the best-tasting from fountains, the lesser ones out of simple plumbers' pipes. The local large flat soft rolls called *bolos levedos* are made in Furnas and are delicious, especially in the spartan surroundings of the **Café Atlântida**, near the Terra Nostra Garden Hotel, when filled with cheese and ham and toasted.

There are several large summer homes built by grandees in the 19th century, some with once lovely gardens. Terra Nostra garden (see box, page 96), belonging to the Terra Nostra Garden Hotel, has a long history; it is open to non-residents, for whom there is an entrance charge (page 98). Another most charming 19th-century garden is the **Beatriz do Canto Park** on the Rua de Santana that was earlier called Myrtle Park, from the Ribeira das Murtas stream that flowed nearby. It was created as a public park to further beautify Furnas.

## Where to stay

**Furnas Lake Villas** [70 E4] (10 timber chalets sleeping 2+2 or 4+2) Estrada Regional do Sul, Lagoa das Furnas; ☎292 584 107; e reservas@ furnaslakevillas.pt; www.furnaslakevillas.pt. At the southern end of Furnas lake, a comfortable, well-fitted s/c option on a quiet, spacious site with a pool, surrounded by mountains. Chalets have TV, internet & a wood-burning stove. Canoe & cycle rental. Special packages offered. New restaurant opened in 2015, available to non-residents with advance booking. Price reduces if you stay more than 1 night. B/fast available, but not inc. €€€€€€

**Terra Nostra Garden Hotel** (86 rooms) Rua Padre José Jacinto Botelho 5; ☎296 549 090; e recepcao.htnl@bensaude.pt; www.bensaude. pt. The hotel dates back to the 1930s & has a very strong period atmosphere. There is a newer wing with large balconied rooms looking into the garden. Most rooms in the original part of the hotel overlook the road with a view across it to the handsome former casino & its little formal garden. The hotel was completely refurbished in winter 2012/13, but the Art-Deco styling has been retained. There is a restaurant, bar, comfortable residents' lounge, children's play area, indoor pool, spa, gym, jacuzzi, massages (extra charge) & outdoor thermally heated pool. Free Wi-Fi. Residents have free access to the famous garden at all times. €€€€€€

**Quinta da mó** (3 separate 1-bed houses & restored watermill with 3 bedrooms) Rua das Águas Quentes 66; m 917 800 281; e reservas@

quintadamo.com; www.quintadamo.com. Secluded accommodation with full catering facilities & bicycles within a luxuriant & very different garden crossed by a briskly flowing stream in Furnas village. Outdoor jacuzzi, free Wi-Fi. €€€€€ (2 persons), €€€€€€ (6 persons)

**Furnas Boutique Hotel** (54 rooms); Av Dr Manuel de Arriaga; ☎296 249 200; e reservas@furnasboutiquehotel.com; www. furnasboutiquehotel.com. Just outside the centre, a 2015 newcomer that will find favour with lovers of modernity. Indoor & outdoor pools, restaurant, bar, gift shop, & an ultra-chic designer interior. €€€€€

**Hotel Vale Verde** (10 rooms) Rua das Caldeiras 3; ☎296 549 010; e geral@ hotelvaleverde.com; www.hotelvaleverde.com. Right in the centre, 200m from the tourist office, a no-frills, pleasant hotel with polished floors, spacious rooms, foreign-channel TV, free Wi-Fi & most rooms with balconies. Downstairs bar & (in summer) a restaurant. Buffet b/fast inc. Staff are helpful. €€

### Camping

**Parque de Campismo das Queimadas** ☎296 584 307; e parquecampismovaledasfurnas@ gmail.com; ⊕ all year. In a lovely position overlooking the fumaroles, but a rather confused site with hideously built facilities, tennis court, children's play area, small snack bar & large surfaced car park. €

## Where to eat and drink
If you want to try a *cozido nas caldeiras* (page 99), then advance booking is advisable – after all, it takes a few hours to cook!

**Caldeiras e Vulcões** Rua das Caldeiras 36; ☎296 584 312; ⊕ 11.45–15.00 & 18.30–21.30 Wed–Mon in winter; daily in summer. Furnas is not blessed with gastronomic diversity, though

this place is making efforts to provide something different in its stylish dining room. Yes, you can still get your *cozido* here, but the chicken breast with honey & mustard sauce provides a lighter experience. Vegetarian & children's options, too. Recommended by many locals. €12

**✗ Summer Breeze** Rua das Caldeiras 18; 📞 296 588 204; ⏰ noon–16.00 & 18.00–22.00 Thu–Tue. Ideal for something less than a full meal, at prices that are a step down from elsewhere in town. Simple fare, no fancy frills. €10

**✗ Terra Nostra Garden Hotel Restaurant** See *Where to stay*, page 97; 📞 298 549 090. Probably the town's top choice, a formal setting inside the posh hotel. Their *cozido* is lighter on the stomach than other places, though their idea of a vegetarian version lacks any punch. Otherwise, good quality & the plush setting is reflected in the price. Service is efficient but friendly. €16

**What to see and do**  After visiting the gardens and fumaroles of Furnas, you can head out of town to walk around the **Lagoa das Furnas** (pages 118–20) or visit its sights. Canoes are available for rent from the garden ticket office (see below). On the return journey to Furnas, take the sign marked Lagoa Seca and head up to the viewpoint (Lombo dos Milhos) for a view over the town and the crater in which it sits. A steep descent takes you back to Furnas.

### In Furnas town

*Terra Nostra Garden*  (*www.parqueterranostra.com*; ⏰ *Apr–Oct 10.00–19.00; Oct–Jan 10.00–17.00; Feb & Mar 10.00–17.30; admission €6*) Admission is for the whole day, and includes use of the outdoor thermal pools and jacuzzi – a real bargain. See box, page 96.

*Beatriz do Canto Park*  (⏰ *09.00–18.00 daily, Aug only*) Once known as Myrtle Park because it lies on the banks of the Ribeira das Myrtas that flows through the village. Begun in the mid 19th century and funded by a group of property owners from Ponta Delgada who spent their summers in the valley, the English gardener George Brown dammed the stream to create a lake, and created lawns and walkways. Completed around 1862, it was also intended to include five summer residences for the members of the partnership, but this collapsed and only Ernesto do Canto built his chalet. Designed by the French architect A Hugé in 1866, it is a most charming building with ornate embellishments and balconies, its pink-washed walls fitting enticingly into the mature garden. Privately owned, it has been a long tradition to open the garden during August, but it is closed the rest of the year.

*Poca da Dona Beija (Thermal Pools)*  (📞 *296 584 256; www.pocadadonabeija.com; ⏰ 07.00–23.00 daily; €3/2.50 adults/under 6s*)  With changing rooms, showers, towel hire and even a shop selling swimming costumes, this group of five smallish thermal pools is all geared up to let you take a hot dip. *Very* hot, actually, with average temperatures of 39°C. Very popular; in high season they turn people away due to lack of space. Café and parking on site.

*Recinto das Caldeiras (Hot Springs Area)*  At the extreme east end of town, just off the road to Ribeira Quente, you can wander around, free of charge and unhindered, this area of hot springs and pools as they bubble menacingly below you. A pleasant garden has been crafted in amongst the sulphurous fumaroles. Keep your balance.

*Observatório Microbiano dos Açores (Microbe Observatory of the Azores)*  (*Antigo Chalé de Misturas;* 📞 *296 584 765; omic.centrosciencia.azores.gov.pt; ⏰ Jul & Aug 10.00– 17.00 Wed–Fri, 14.30–18.00 Sat & Sun; Sep–Jun 10.00–17.00 Tue–Fri, 14.30–18.00 Sun; €1/0.75/0.50 adult/students & seniors/children. Pre-booked guided tours are* available (min 4 people, €10 pp) which also include lunch, tour of the geothermal area & entrance to the Terra Nostra garden.) An observatory in a heritage building promoting the importance of microbial life on earth, with an emphasis on the microbial diversity in the Azores thermal springs. Exhibits explain what micro-organisms look like, where they live and what size they are, whether there is life inside the fumaroles and many other related topics and visitor activities. Adds a fascinating dimension to fumarole watching.

## Around Furnas lake

*Caldeiras* ( ⊕ *06.00–20.00; entry to car park €0.50 pp, €3 extra if you bring your own food to have it cooked underground*) Down by the north side of the Furnas lake, south of town, amidst an area of geothermal activity, are the *caldeiras*, where for generations people have come to cook the famous *cozido nas caldeiras*. Holes are made about 1m deep in the hot earth into which a container is lowered filled with different meats, sausage and some vegetables, mostly kale, cabbage and potatoes. It is all left to cook gently for around seven hours. You can see the mounds of earth marking where the cooking is happening, with the restaurant names on signs showing whose is whose. If you bring your own food, assistance is on hand. Cooked slowly, and so evenly, all the flavours and delicious juices are retained, although those with timid appetites can find it a little daunting. Up to 1,000 visitors per day make their way here in high summer, to marvel at this traditional cooking method and walk the wooden walkway amongst the bubbling hot pools. A colony of ducks and a few stray cats add to a rather strange scene. Toilets and picnic tables on site.

If you fancy a walk around to the lake's southern side, there are other attractions to see. If arriving by car, continue south of the *caldeiras* area to find the car park on your left at the lake's southern edge. Modest parking charges apply. Park up, cross the road, go through the barrier, and follow the lakeside path to find the church, garden and finally the interpretation centre, all detailed below, It's a ten-minute walk. On the way, look out on the tree trunks for a few 'bat-boxes', helping to preserve the only endemic Azorean mammal, the Azorean bat (*Nyctalus azoreum*).

*Capella Nossa Senhora das Vitorias (Chapel)* (*Ask at the garden ticket office for a guided visit*) This pseudo-Gothic chapel dedicated to Our Lady of Victories was built by José do Canto, one of the Azores' great gardeners, who vowed in 1854 to build a chapel if his wife – who was ill – recovered. She did recover, but died shortly after it was inaugurated in 1886. It is a family vault and do Canto and his wife are now buried there.

*Mata-Jardim José do Canto (Jose do Canto Garden)* (*www.matajosedocanto.com; ⊕ winter 10.00–17.00; summer 10.00–18.00; €3/1.25/free adults/juniors & seniors/children, includes entrance to the church*) Now open to the public, you can stroll around the 10ha of the garden, created in the mid 19th century, and discover the waterfall, 'Valley of Ferns' and enjoy the 1,000 or so camellias, which are in bloom from December to March. The ticket office, on your left opposite one of the lakeside houses, sells locally made handicrafts, and an information leaflet/map in English is included in the ticket price.

*Centro de Monitorizaçao e Investigaçao das Furnas (Furnas Monitoring and Research Centre)* ( ↖ *296 584 436; ⊕ 15 Jun–15 Sep 10.00–18.00 daily; 16 Sep–14 Jun 09.30–16.30 Tue–Sun; €3/1.25/free adult/seniors & juniors/children under 12, guided tours available*

At the end of December 1839, Joseph and Henry Bullar spent a winter in the Azores and later published in London a detailed account of their travels. Here is their description of a thermal bath at Furnas, or the 'Baden-Baden of St Michael' as they named it.

After looking at the calderas, we took our bath, and it was certainly never my good fortune before to bathe in an invigorating warm bath. It produced a feeling of strength instead of lassitude, and the skin seemed not alone to have been cleansed and rendered most agreeably smooth, but to have been actually renewed.

While bathing, our man cooked eggs for us in one of the small boiling springs, and we afterwards went to the iron-spring for a draught [of mineral water]. This flows from a stone spout into a hollow stone basin, and trickles down a bank into a stream below: it has a strong but not disagreeable iron flavour, effervesces slightly, and is extremely grateful and refreshing. The bath and the spring seemed the two things best suited to the outside and inside of man, on first rising from his bed; natural luxuries when in health, natural remedies when sick – luxuries without after-pain, remedies without misery in taking them – both which evils seem to be inseparable from the luxuries and the remedies of our own invention. Most invalids feel that before-breakfast existence is burdensome; but this bath and draught of liquid iron were as breakfast in producing serenity and happiness, and were more of a breakfast in giving warmth and briskness, and a feeling of health, as of the flowing of younger blood through the veins ...

at 11.00, 13.00 & 15.00 Tue–Sun, lasting 30mins) Next stop on your lakeside walk is this newish centre, ten minutes' walk in from the main road. Opened in 2011 and attracting much press comment and praise, this very modern building was designed by the Portuguese architects Aires Mateus and Associates; inspired by the landscape, it uses building materials traditional to the island and blends in harmoniously. Owing to the extensive conversion of woodland to pasture for cows and the subsequent fertilisers applied, the nitrogen run-off into the lake has caused eutrophication, an algae and phytoplankton bloom causing the death of animal life from oxygen starvation. The research centre is monitoring the various actions taken to recover the quality of the lake, by the removal of grazing animals, converting old pastures to productive legumes, establishing native flora on watersheds and other projects. Much is being learned about the life histories and requirements of individual plant species from the process of propagation and establishment of new native forest (laurisilva), and trials are still underway to select from the native blueberry, *Vaccinium cylindraceum*, one that produces improved fruit for possible commercial use. There is a café and small gift shop.

## THE EASTERN PART OF THE ISLAND: FROM FURNAS TO THE EAST AND NORTH COASTS
For individual activity listings, see *Activities*, pages 109–13.

Leaving eastwards from Furnas, you can decide to take a diversion directly south down a phenomenally lush valley to the coast at Ribeira Quente, a busy fishing port with a car park by its beach, its size indicating its summer popularity. If you choose this option, you have to come back to rejoin the road to c ontinue east, as there is no connecting coast road from Ribeira Quente. From Furnas to Povoação, you will be confronted with a landscape of green, cows grazing peacefully while seemingly oblivious to the improbably steep inclines, villages clinging to narrow ridges above

*above*     Capelhinos on Faial was the site of the 1957–58 eruption and now hosts a widely acclaimed visitor centre
(SS) page 207

*right*     The bubbling hot springs and mud pools of Furnas draw many visitors to taste some of the 22 different mineral waters
(PO/D) pages 95–9

*below*     The famous crater lakes on the west of São Miguel, timeless, and glorious to explore
(AMA/S) page 91

*above*   The elegant sweep of Ponta Delgada's waterfront invites the visitor to take a stroll (SS) pages 87–90

*left*    The 19th-century Nossa Senhora da Conceição at Santa Cruz das Flores is one of the most substantial buildings in the town (SS) page 250

*below*   Horta is an important stopover for many yachts crossing the Atlantic (AC/AWL) pages 202–6

*above*    Small and intimate, Santa Cruz de Graciosa is centred around the old harbour (MdA/DRT/APVA) pages 168–9

*right*    A traditional house on Santa Maria – architecture varies from island to island (TA/APVA) page 26

*below*    São Mateus on Terceira is one of the most important fishing harbours on the islands (SS) page 153

*above* Involved patterns of carefully laid flowers, chopped conifers and coloured wood shavings prepare the way for the Nossa Senhora de Piedade procession at Ponta Garça, São Miguel (SS) pages 84–5

*left* Introduced in the 18th century, tea is still produced commercially on São Miguel and is much sought by connoisseurs (SS) pages 104–5

*below* *Cozido nas caldeiras* is a delicious stew, prepared using vegetables and several different meats and gently cooked in the ground for about seven hours (SS) page 99

| above left | The *tourada à corda* is the Portuguese version of bullfighting, but the bull is not harmed (MA/AWL) page 36 |
| above right | Bread is distributed to the poor during the festival of Espírito Santo (JD/D) pages 34–5 |
| right | For a different swimming experience try the iron-rich warm-water pool at Terra Nostra garden (SS) page 96 |
| below | Religious festivals take place in many villages and towns throughout the islands and draw large crowds (SS) pages 34–6 |

*above* Because of their isolation, the islands of the Azores have a number of endemic plant species, including *Viburnum treleasei* (left) and *Prunus azorica* (right) (both CC) pages 268–77

*left* Steep sea cliffs are important nesting sites for Cory's shearwater (SS) page 10

*below* The rare *priolo*, or Azorean bullfinch, can be found only in one small part of São Miguel island (GM) page 68

above left     On São Miguel, Terra Nostra is one of the archipelago's finest gardens (MS) page 96

above right    There are no native land mammals on the archipelago, but cattle were introduced in the 15th century
               (SS) page 18

below          The sperm whale is the largest of all toothed whales: males can measure up to 20m (SS) pages 11–15

azores airlines

# GET READY FOR ADVENTURE!

We've booked the best seat, just for you!
Take a look out of the window, get a taste of what awaits you on our
beautiful islands. Breathtaking scenery, here in the mid-Atlantic.
Dream your dream. Then climb on-board and we'll make it a reality.
You and Azores Airlines: together, let's get ready for adventure.

www.azoresairlines.pt

Photo by Paulo Melo

deep-cut *ribeiras* as they plunge down to the sea. Beyond Povoação, the road is prone to winter washouts and landslips, so it's wise to check before setting out that the route is open. Assuming that all is well, you can take the signposted gravel track up to the left to the Serra da Tronqueira, or continue along the tarmacked coastal route. The gravel track runs for around 17km, and can be badly affected by heavy rain at any time of the year. However, should it have been recently graded and in good condition it is a wonderful drive on a clear day. If the clouds are low, however, you will not see anything, so do not waste your time.

If you choose the coastal road, at Água Retorta, a signpost on the main road informs you that you are 2,500km from London, 4,500km from Toronto and 7,500km from Rio do Janeiro. 'Coastal' is possibly a misleading adjective, as the steep cliffs prevent you from getting very near the sea at all, though the route is still exhilarating.

Following Água Retorta, the surface of the coastal road to Nordeste was being redone in 2016 to repair damage caused by bad weather. Note that while there are several viewpoints along this road, with toilets and manicured gardens, there is really nothing much else by way of facilities until you reach Nordeste itself. The coast between Faial da Terra and Ponta do Arnel is a Special Protected Area; it is an important nesting site for shearwater and common tern, and there are some endemic plants and invertebrates.

**Ribeira Quente** The valley down which you approach the village from the Furnas–Povoação road is particularly verdant and on the way you will pass beneath two tunnels where there is a waterfall. The town has a long, well-developed seafront, protected by sea defences, and a beach reachable by following the 'Zona Balnear' signs. Maybe one of the locals will tell you where the thermal area is; here, at low tide, the sea is very warm. At the east end of the promenade is the busy fishing harbour. Between beach and harbour are several restaurants, popular in summer for their seafood. The village is divided naturally by the watercourse bringing its fresh load down the *ribeira* to discharge into the ocean: tiny, colourful houses line the banks. In the eastern side of town, a large area is set aside for disentangling and mending the fishing nets.

**Povoação** This was the first settlement on São Miguel, and now has a pretty little town square and old streets leading down to the harbour, where a sculpture pays homage to the early arrivers. The harbour is big and bolstered against the waves, yet there is virtually no fishing fleet here, compared with Ribeira Quente. The church of **Nossa Senhora do Rosário**, built in the 15th century but restored in the 19th century and again recently, is thought to have been the first building of worship on the island. Don't forget to visit the Wheat Museum, a couple of kilometres out of town (see below).

###  Where to stay

 **Quinta Atlantis** [70 F3] (5 rooms) Lomba da Botão 87; m 916 256 055; e info@ quintaatlantis.com; www.quintaatlantis.com. Tucked up high on a ridge, a few km inland from Povoação, Atlantis has tasteful themed rooms, some with shared, some with private bath. Free Wi-Fi, communal TV, lots of books, DVDs available. Prices inc b/fast, which focuses on local products. Would suit those who (genuinely) want to get away from it all. Owners will send detailed directions when you book! €€€

### What to see and do

**Museu de Trigo (Wheat Museum)** (*Located by the Ribeira dos Bispos, between the ridges of Lomba do Loução & Lomba do Alcaide; www.cm-povoacao.pt;* ⏱ *11.00–17.00 Mon–Fri, 11.00–16.00 Sat & Sun; admission free*) Signposted left off the main

There are several *miradouros* and picnic sites along this road, and they are constantly being improved and added to. The Nordeste Municipality has always taken a great pride in these, and deservedly so. You should take advantage of them, to absorb the sheer isolation of this region, and to slow your journey.

**Ponta da Madrugada** is a favourite stop, with toilets, a pleasant garden area, picnic tables and barbecue facilities ideal for family lunches. Good views up and down the coast.

**Ponta do Sossego**, the 'Place of Quietude', is a beautifully gardened belvedere offering splendid views of the steep coastline. The garden is on different levels, with delightful paths amid flowering hydrangeas, hibiscus, azaleas, camellias, palms and summer annuals. Toilets, picnic tables and barbecue facilities.

**Ponta do Arnel** provides a dramatic view down to the lighthouse, the first to be built, in 1876.

road as you leave Povoação on the Nordeste road, this splendid watermill has been skilfully restored in a glorious setting of pastures and hedgerows. Ask the staff and they will open the sluice and set the mill-wheel in motion. It is a triumph of restoration and capture of a past culture, and highly recommended. Although the wall panels are in Portuguese only, translations are promised for the future and staff give explanations in English. Visitors are offered a taste of a local liquor, and there are Azorean-made handicrafts for sale. If you're heading towards Nordeste, staff will advise you of a short cut, avoiding a retracing of your steps.

**Diversion to the Pico Bartolomeu** Starting at the turn-off at Lomba da Pedreira, you can cut inland to visit the Parque Florestal, Centro Ambiental do Priolo (Priolo Environmental Centre) and continue up the road to the heights of the Pico Bartolomeu mountain. The return journey is 16km. Note that this is a dead-end: whatever some maps might tell you, there's no road down the other side of the Pico! If there's low cloud, it's not worth going beyond the Priolo Centre, and if heavy rain is forecast, it is inadvisable. First along this route is the **Parque Florestal** (⊕ *see Priolo Centre, below, guides sometimes on duty*), with a collection of endemic species, then a few metres further up the road is the **Priolo Environmental Centre** (⊕.*15 Feb–30 Apr & 1 Oct–15 Nov, noon–17.00 Sat, Sun & hols; 1 May–30 Sep 10.00–18.00 Tue–Sun*), where you can learn about the *priolo* (Azorean bullfinch), endemic to this part of São Miguel. Once critically endangered, its population has been revitalised by the careful work of conservationists. Shortly after the centre, you take a sharp left and continue upwards with the Pico Bartolomeu as your destination. After a few kilometres of climb, you take a right (signposted), first passing the Miradouro da Tronqueira then crossing along a ridge with drop-offs on both sides before the final ascent to the radio masts of the Pico (847m). The views are great, both inland and along the coast.

**Nordeste** Nordeste is so far from the rest of the island that, hampered by poor roads until the end of the 19th century, boat used to be the preferred means of travel. It has always been a charming, sleepy little place that few tourists ever reached, but now this princess has been kissed by progress and is slowly awakening, with a new restaurant and other small developments, and most recently a fast road connecting it to Ponta Delgada. The town centre is dominated by the 18th-century church, by the left side of which is a small **museum** (see below). The town square is neat, with a central bandstand. There is a **tourist information office** nearby (✆ *296 480 066;* ⊕ *09.30–17.30 Mon–Fri, 10.00–17.00 Sat & Sun*), and a couple of inexpensive but unexceptional restaurants in the area behind the church.

On the northeast side of town, you can turn right off the roundabout to access the town's saltwater swimming pool (*Piscina da Boca da Ribeira*), separated from the raging ocean by a sturdy wall.

## Where to stay nearby

**Quinta das Queimadas** [70 G3] (2 apts, 1 room) ✆ 296 488 578; e queimadas@sapo.pt; www.quintadasqueimadas.com. Open all year, a quirky rural option south of Nordeste, signposted off the main road. Frenchman Pierre has been here for 20 years, his own piece of wilderness. He keeps pigeons & 2 horses, which have gone a bit wild since his daughter went back to France. Free Wi-Fi, b/fast inc, other meals by arrangement. Apts have wood-burning stove – valuable in winter – and own BBQ. Good value & prices reduce for longer stays. €€–€€€

### Camping

**Parque de Campismo do Nordeste** [70 G2] Ribeira do Guilherme; ✆ 296 488 680; e geral@cmnordeste.pt; ⊕ Jun–Sep. Just after Nordeste coming from the south on the main EN1 road, tucked away at the bottom of a river valley, this pretty campsite is beneath trees by a stream with many watermills. Showers & WCs. Semi-natural swimming pool near the sea. €

## Where to eat and drink nearby

**Casa de Pasto O Cardoso** Estrada Regional 19, Lomba da Fazenda; ✆ 296 486 138; ⊕ noon–15.00 & 18.00–21.00 daily. A little north of Nordeste, on the east side of Lomba da Fazenda, a good-quality, well-established restaurant offering daily dishes at favourable prices. Fish are a combination of fresh & frozen, meat portions are generous. Opens early for coffee, English-speaking owner. €7

## What to see and do

**Museu do Nordeste** (*Rua D Maria do Rosário, Nordeste;* ⊕ *09.00–12.30 & 13.30–16.30 Mon–Fri); admission price nominal*) Located down behind the church, this museum features displays of local cultural traditions and skills with old ceramics from Lagoa and Vila Franca, early clothes, weaving and other items pertaining to the area, all housed in an interesting old building.

**Ribeira do Guilherme** Just after you leave Nordeste, look out for the signpost on your right. There is a camping site below, and a picnic site. Also from above, you will see the semi-natural swimming pool by the side of the river where it joins the sea. To see watermills, follow the sign marked *Zone Balnear*. There is also a most charming garden laid out parallel with a stream feeding a watermill.

**Santo António** To see the local handicrafts, including weaving, pop in to the Centro Cultural, on the main road opposite the church.

**Algarvia** The next village to the west, Algarvia has a viewpoint with a beautifully restored whale lookout post (*Miradouro Vigia das Baleias*) with toilets, car park, children's play area, picnic tables, barbecue facilities and garden.

**Ribeira dos Caldeirões** (*Signposted between Achada & Achadinha;* ⊕ *park open at all times; shop 10.30–18.00, summer until 20.30*) Follow the signs from the main road for this charming valley as you drive along the main road, with its lovely tree ferns, working watermill, and in February the heavenly scent of all the pittosporum trees in flower. In 1986, severe floods destroyed most of Nordeste's watermills. More than 100 once existed; now only five remain and only one still works, operated only during the first week of every month (⊕ *08.00–16.00*). (The operator is elderly, apparently, and succession-planning is not in hand, so it may not work for much longer.) Three have been acquired by the municipality to help restore the natural park area of Ribeira dos Caldeirões and to preserve the area's heritage and connect with a past traditional way of life. One mill has been restored as a working museum, and there is a visitor centre, café and one of the most well-stocked gift shops on the island. Opposite is a waterfall, very pretty, though the waters are artificially diverted to ensure your holiday photos look their very best!

**Achadinha** The village 1km east of the **Miradouro Salto do Farinha**, a viewpoint with great coastal vistas to the east and west. Clearly signposted from the road, after heavy rain the 40m waterfall flows briskly and becomes a twin fall. You can walk down the path to the valley bottom and to the sea.

**Fenais da Ajuda** If you have time, drive down to the village and past the main church until you come to a much simpler, smaller, church, which was the first one to be built in the village in the early 19th century. Behind is a cemetery, at the far end of which is a splendid view along the coast to Maia and Ponta do Cintrão in the middle distance, and way beyond to the Ponta da Bretanha, which is the far northwest tip of the island.

**Maia** This is a small fishing village where the large pink building houses a theatre, meeting hall and other community facilities. There is also a tobacco museum.

 *Where to stay nearby*

**Herdade Nossa Senhora das Graças**
[70 E3] (4 rooms & 2 apts) Estaleiro, Lomba da Maia (west of Maia); m 961 127 350; e reservas@ nsgracas.com; www.virtualacores.com/nsgracas. A true agrotourism place, your neighbours are the turkeys, cows & goats. The 1920s house is situated in farmland far off the beaten track, with the s/c apts in a separate building. Lomba da Maia, the nearest village with supermarket & restaurant, is 2km away & can be reached by a farm road in about 30mins' walk. Visitors are given a warm welcome & hospitality standards are high, with splendid evening meals (by arrangement) with authentic Azorean flavours. Peaceful surroundings, you need a car to get here. English & German spoken. €€ room, €€€€ apt

*What to see and do*
**Museu do Tabaco** (*Estrada Regional de S Pedro, Maia;* ✆ *296 442 905;* ⊕ *09.00–13.00 & 14.00–17.00 Mon–Fri, 10.00–16.00 Sat; €2.5/1/free adults/seniors & children/ under 14s*) Especially on São Miguel, until relatively recently one would see large open-sided drying sheds laden with tobacco leaves. Now much rarer, the Azores still produces cigarettes, Coroa and Robusto Estrela cigars and the smaller and thinner Pérolas curubas.

**Gorreana tea estate** (*Plantações de Chá Gorreana, Gorreana;* ✆ *296 442 349; www. azores.net/gorreana;* ⊕ *the estate is open to visitors 08.00–20.00 daily except 25 Dec; there is a small shop & fresh tea is served free. Admission free, guided tours free* *if staff are available; buggy tour through the plantation €10 pp, book in advance.)* The first records of tea growing in the archipelago date from towards the end of the 18th century, although it is thought to have been known before then because of the Portuguese ships passing through on their return from Asia. It was the demise of the production of oranges and their export that stimulated the development of new crops, including tea. The Gorreana estate was founded in 1883 and is now one of the last of several estates that once thrived on São Miguel; 50ha remain, producing some 30 tonnes of tea annually. The first plants were introduced in 1874, grown from seeds brought directly from China. By 1883, these were producing their first crop and the drink proved so popular further varieties were brought from India. To manure the shrubs, lupins, which can fix nitrogen in the soil, were grown around them. Tea plants have thrived so well in the Azores that an especially aromatic variety has developed. The leaves, or rather the young shoot tips, are harvested between April and September by a simple machine operated by three or four men that straddles the rows of bushes; previously they were hand-plucked by women and girls. The leaves are then processed in the usual way in what are now old but beautifully engineered machines, and finally sorted and packed by hand. The distinctive packets are exported to the other islands, continental Portugal, Germany and Azorean communities in North America. In Germany an association has been formed – the Friends of Azorean Tea, and cuttings for propagation have been sent to Tregothnan Estate in Cornwall for their plantation. You can buy the tea, plus other souvenirs. Charming staff speak excellent English, there is a short, subtitled video. Although the estate is open all year, you can see the factory actually processing the tea from Monday to Friday, between April and September.

**Chá Porto Formoso (tea estate)** (On the north side of the EN1, just west of Gorreana; ⏱ *09.00–17.00 Mon–Sat; admission free*) A small tea estate near to the more feted Gorreana, it has a visitor centre, and shows an interesting video of tea production. It also has a charming tea room, shop, panoramic gardens and lovely view. The visit and tea-tasting is free of charge. If you happen to visit on the first Saturday of May, you will find that a big party is taking place, with dozens of locals dressed in traditional costumes, picking the tea by hand. Everyone is welcome – and it's free!

**Porto Formoso and São Brás** You are advised not to visit São Bras village on summer weekends, as it is mobbed and the parking chaotic! Porto Formoso has a fishing fleet and a beach by the port; continuing through and further west takes you to Praia dos Moinhos, with a beach and a watermill converted into a restaurant, the **O Moinho** (↖ *296 442 110*; ⏱ *daily*). It's simple and pleasant … but try the one below, first.

## ✖ Where to eat and drink
✖ **Cantinho do Cais** Estrada Regional de São Brás 1, São Brás; ↖ 296 442 631; ⏱ noon–22.00 Thu–Tue. Well worth a diversion, but only if you like fish. The owner/chef Jorge is a master, & his *molho de peixe* (fish stew, always made with fresh fish) is divine. The fish of the day (usually half-a-dozen choices) is also always fresh; other fish on the menu will be frozen. All served efficiently in a couple of formal dining rooms. No meat, no vegetarian! Menu in English, advanced booking advisable. €12.50

**Miradouro de Santa Iria** Just east of Ribeirinha, this is one of the loveliest viewpoints along the north coast. In summer on a balmy night you can stand here for ages listening to the cry of Cory's shearwaters as they swoop around the cliff below you and, at the same time, become intoxicated by the perfume of the Himalayan ginger lilies. If you have just arrived in the Azores and are transferring to your hotel in Furnas, always ask your driver to stop here; the pressures of the big city fall away and after just 5 minutes of these scents and sounds you already feel at peace and rejuvenated.

**Diversion Inland to Caldeiras and Lombadas Valley** Just east of Ribeira Grande, follow the signs for **Caldeiras**, a 5km drive inland to reach this tiny village of large old houses surrounding a cramped central square where there is a hot spring and a thermal pond (no bathing, though). It must have been delightfully romantic in its social heyday; the **Restaurante Caldeiras** (⊕ *10.00–22.00 Tue–Sun; €10*) offers typical Azorean dishes, with buffeta on Sundays. Behind the restaurant, there is an area set aside for the underground cooking of *cozido* (page 99), though it seems a bit manufactured compared with the lakeside activities of Furnas. Parking here can be impossible. A walk called the *Salto de Cabrito* is well waymarked and begins from here. The road then continues to **Lombadas**, through wild country along a narrow, mainly cobbled road, slippery when wet. At the head of the valley are the remains of buildings where a mineral water spring used to provide most of the bottled mineral water on the island, coming from a length of domestic garden hose whose further end disappeared somewhere under the heather on the adjacent hillside. A landslide several years ago wrecked the operation, but hopefully one day Lombadas water will again go into a bottle. From here you must either return towards Ribeira Grande or take the mountain road over the Cumeira Massif to the south coast.

**Ribeira Grande** The fast-flowing stream that now runs along the side of the very nice-looking town square and past one of the prettiest town halls anywhere originally attracted early settlers to build their watermills here. In 1507, it received its town charter. In France during the second half of the 17th century Colbert, Louis XIV's Minister of Finance, gave considerable support to numerous industries to boost economic development here, but the subsequent religious intolerance made many skilled workers emigrate. With the arrival of French workers, linen and wool weaving brought great prosperity to Ribeira Grande in the 18th and early 19th centuries. Today it is expanding with light industrial development, but still manages to keep tucked away much of its old charm. Visit the main church of **Nossa Senhora da Estrela** to see the sacristy and its paintings of the Flemish School. The *misericórdia* church, the **Church of Espírito Santo**, in the main square, has one of the best Baroque façades in the Azores; curiously it has two doors. There are a few museums to visit and you should certainly drive or walk to the sea, for a grand promenade has been constructed with swimming pool and esplanade. The town has a slightly rough-edged feel to it, compared with Ponta Delgada, but has several points of interest and a couple of good restaurants and guesthouses, if you choose to linger. There is also a **tourist office** (*Rua Luis da Camões;* ⊕ *09.00– 17.00 Mon–Fri*) located just in front of the bus station, with English-speaking staff, which may soon be open at weekends.

 *Where to stay*

🏠 **A Casa de Cascata** [70 D3] (5 rooms) Largo Gaspar Fructuoso 33; m 919 797 183; e vanessasilvaaa@hotmail.com. Very light & spacious, this beautifully renovated house now

contains an excellent guesthouse, with rooms overlooking the square, or towards the sea. Guests have use of an enclosed courtyard, there's a kitchen (no b/fast provided, but there's a café/restaurant across the pretty square). Free Wi-Fi, communal TV lounge. Not all rooms have private bathroom. A pleasant & good-value choice. €

🏠 **Costa Norte** [70 D3] (6 rooms) Rua de Santa Luzia 1; m 914 575 361; e guesthouse@costanorteazores.com; costanorteazores.com. A bit more ramshackle than the Cascata down the road, this place is popular with surfers. Bike

hire, free Wi-Fi, terrace, b/fast inc. Dorm beds available. €

### Camping

🏕 **Parque de Campismo Rural Quinta das Laranjeiras** [70 C3] Canada Roda do Pico 30, Rabo de Peixe; m 962 823 766; www.azorescamp.com; ⏰ all year. €

## ✕ Where to eat and drink

✕ **Alabote Restaurant** Largo East Providence, Ribeira Grande; ✆ 296 473 516; www.alabote.net; ⏰ 10.30–15.00 & 18.00–23.30. Plenty of fish & meat on the menu, plus children's menu & a very limited veggie option in this highly rated town restaurant by the sea. €15

✕ **Monte Verde** Rua da Areia 4; ⏰ noon–16.00 & 19.00–midnight Tue-Sun. In an unpromising part of town, a very promising restaurant. Fresh fish every day, served simply. Excellent fish soup, too. €12

✕ **Quinta dos Sabores** [70 C3] Rua Caminho da Selada 10, Rabo de Peixe (signed off the EN3–1A, south of Rabo da Peixe); ✆ 296 493 700; m 917 003 020; 📘 fb.me/vegidecq. A different kind of experience, this 'farm-restaurant' truly delights with the quality of ingredients, innovation, ambience & personal touch of the family owners. A bit out of (any) town, advance booking is essential, as they are only open for reservations.They will also

discuss the menu with you, in advance. Expect an excellent 6-course feast, but portions are suitably restrained. Vegetables are sourced from their organic farm. No à la carte, just a very good set meal at €30.

✕ **Restaurante da Associaçao Agrícola** Recinta da Feira, Campo de Santana; ✆ 296 490 001; www.restauranteasm.com; ⏰ noon–23.00 daily for dining, 08.00–midnight for bar/coffee service. A few kilometres west of Ribeira Grande (not in the town, as wrongly shown on some inernet maps), follow the first 'Santana' turn-off to the right, if heading west. If the name conjures up a vision of burly farmers discussing the price of milk, forget it. Having shaken off its rustic roots, this is now a huge modern unit, specialising in beef – & a lot of it. Even the waiters admit they are well beaten by the 400g steak which tops the bill. Don't ask for vegetarian. Book in advance at weekends or hols. €15

## What to see and do

**Museu de Emigração** (*On the right-hand side of Rua do Estrela, the main road into Ribeira Grande from Ponta Delgada, next to the market, in a large building with museum flags flying;* ✆ *296 470 770; www.mea.cm-ribeiragrande.pt;* ⏰ *09.00–17.00 Mon–Fri; €1*) Recently reopened after being refreshed, this museum was the result of requests by emigrants to document the movements from the islands over the years, which it does with some interesting photos, artefacts and personal stories from emigrants. Most of the displays have English-language information. The large car park opposite, behind the wall, used to be the cattle market.

**Museu Municipal (Formerly Casa de Cultura)** (*Rua São Vicente, Ribeira Grande;* ✆ *296 470 730;* ⏰ *09.00–17.00 Mon–Fri; €1/0.50/free, adults/seniors & children/ under 6s*) With some excellent working models depicting town life in times gone by and a nativity scene, a visit to this handsome old manor house is recommended, providing a good insight into life as it was in the past. Replicas of an old barber's and a milliner's shop. Also contains a tiny chapel and a display of old tiles. English-language information.

**Casa da Arcano (Museum)** (*Rua João d'Horta, Matriz, Ribeira Grande;* ✆ *296 470 763;* ⏰ *09.00–17.00 Mon–Fri, plus Sat in summer; €2/free, adult/under 6s. You can* *ask for a guided tour, in English, at no extra charge.*) On the road off to the left of the large Chapel of Santa Luzia, the focus of this new museum is an extraordinary assemblage of models made from rice flour, clay, glass, shells, cork and wire, telling the story of the Old and New Testaments. Margarida Isabel Narcisa was the daughter of a wealthy family, and entered a convent. In 1832, the king closed all the convents, so she moved into a house with her sister. In 1835, she began the now-revered construction devoted to São João, only ceasing to add to it in 1858. For years it remained hidden in the Mother Church, but is now on show in the restored house. A video with English subtitles explains more.

**Arquipélago (Contemporary Arts Centre)** (*Rua Adolfo de Madeiros;* ⊕ *10.00–13.00 & 14.30–18.00 Tue–Sun; €3, free on Sun*) Very recently opened, housed in a former tobacco and alcohol factory, and due to showcase both visual and performing arts. For students of architecture, the prize-winning restoration of the building will be of interest; for the casual visitor, it is worth ensuring that there is an exhibition taking place, otherwise the entry fee is arguably not worth it.

**Cerâmica Micaelense** (*Rua do Rosário 42;* ☏ *296 472 600;* ⊕ *09.00–noon & 13.00–18.00 Mon–Fri*) On the road out from town to Furnas is a ceramic workshop making excellent tiles. Numerous original and ambitious designs are displayed in their showrooms and around the workshops, and they will make any design to your order: pictures of your garden, your house, figurative, abstract. More of a shopping trip than a factory tour, though you can watch the tiles being hand-painted.

## Diversion inland to Caldeira Velha and Lagoa da Fogo

*Caldeira Velha* (⊕ *Nov–Feb 09.00–17.00, Mar & Oct 10.00–18.00, Apr–Sep 09.00–20.30, daily; €2/1/free adults/seniors & juniors/under 3s*) On your way up to these now fully developed hot baths, you will pass the geothermal installations in the hillsides behind Ribeira Grande. The complex of silver-painted structures is part of the energy supply to the island. Caldeira Velha itself has been recently turned into what some will see as a little oasis, though its transformation from a rather random place into a slicker operation may dismay others. There is now an interpretation centre, giving out information about subjects such as volcanoes (including the island's previous eruptions, something to ponder as you bathe), biodiversity, etc. There is a small warm-water waterfall which runs into a small artificial pool; there are plenty of iron deposits and sulphurous smells, and it is a popular place to bathe. There are changing facilities and lavatories, and picnic tables beneath the trees. Outside the main entrance is a gift shop and ice-cream van.

*Lagoa do Fogo* Five minutes' drive past the Caldeira Velha and you reach the viewpoint over the Lagoa do Fogo – 'Lake of Fire'. It is a deep caldera with a lake whose waters can display a fascinating range of colours when the light catches them right. Wheeling and arcing over the waters there will be some of the colony of yellow-legged gulls (*Larus michahellis atlantis*). Common terns (*Sterna arundo*) frequent the area between March and September. The caldera walls are steep, but there is a path to the bottom; it is a protected area and several endemic plant species can be seen here. On a day when there are clouds and a strong wind blowing it is good fun to stand at the viewpoint near the edge of the crater and watch the clouds pour in and then get sucked up out again. There is an information panel at the viewpoint car park, from where you can see both the south and north coastlines of the island.

Operators for most, though not all, outdoor activities are based in Ponta Delgada, and will transport their clients to the venue for the chosen activity. Note that while some operators offer a whole multitude of activities on their websites, often in reality they have a few 'core' activities which they carry out themselves while effectively subcontracting the others out. Thus, your whale-watching company might offer canyoning, but is unlikely to actually run the activity themselves. Wherever possible, we list here the companies that actually *do*, rather than simply outsource, the activity.

## CANYONING

**Azores Adventure Islands** m 919 281 220; e info@azoresadventureislands.com; www. azoresadventureislands.com. Enthusiastic & highly rated, will adapt programmes to suit clients. Prices from €60 pp, inc pickup, drop-off, equipment & insurance.

**Azorean Active Blueberry** m 914 822 682; e info@azoreanactiveblueberry.com; www. azoreanactiveblueberry.com. Another experienced canyoning operator who has also pioneered 'coasteering' on the island, giving you the chance to get wet in salt water as well as fresh. Half- & full-day trips available. Prices from €65/95 pp, inc pickup, drop-off, equipment (inc boots) & insurance.

## CYCLING

ර් **Azores Adventure Islands** (see above). Respected operator will take you on MTB tours, with an option of electric bikes, gauging your ability & adapting as you go. Also, straightforward bike hire available.

ර් **ANC Azores Holidays** [79 F4] Dr João Bosco Mota Amaral (in front of the Marina Atlanticó hotel), Ponta Delgada; m 967 309 909; e motorent.anc@gmail.com; www. ancazoresholidays.pt. Cheap bike hire (inc electric options), scooters, quad bikes & buggies. Also guided 4x4 tours in the west side of the island.

ර් **Harmony Trail** See *Island tours*, page 76.

**DIVING** The diving operators more or less all set up shop by the marina, just east of the Portas do Mar in Porta Delgada, below the promenade. Most of these companies will take snorkellers, as well as offering try-dives, single dives, full-day excursions and courses.

✔ **Best Spot Azores** m 963 469 932/912 108 658; e bestspotazores@gmail.com; www. bestspotazores.com. A PADI 5-star centre, with a good reputation. A single dive comes in at €40, while snorkelling costs about €25. Try-dives & PADI courses available.

**EXPLORING NATURE** The most famous rarity of São Miguel is the much-promoted Azorean bullfinch – the *priolo* – found only in the native shrubbery of the **Serra da Tronqueira Nature Reserve** [70 F3].

There are now thought to be upwards of 1,000 individuals and they may be seen from along the unsurfaced road between Povoação and Nordeste. Gardeners will have some sympathy for the early farmers who shot it almost out of existence to protect their crops from its infamous depredations. Here one may also find the Azorean woodpigeon. This mountainous area with its deep ravines and watercourses is densely covered with laurisilva or Macaronesian evergreen forest and the endemic species include holly, juniper, laurel, Portugal laurel and bilberry together with ferns. Make a point of visiting the Priolo Centre and its easy walking trail – see page 102.

São Miguel ACTIVITIES

3

Lagoa do Fogo Nature Reserve [70 D3] provides the most accessible site for endemic plants and even if not tempted by the path descending to the lake through this vegetation, exploration around the viewpoint can be rewarding enough. Juniper, laurel, frangula and erica shelter native hypericum and euphorbia, and a patient search will reveal several more endemics. You cannot fail to hear the Atlantic yellow-legged gulls.

Sete Cidades [70 A2] and its varied sheltered habitats of fields and gardens can be productive for birds, while the lake offers respite for migrant species and in autumn occasional American vagrants (pages 115–16).

The varied habitats around the village of Mosteiros [70 A2] are often rewarding, with migrating passerines in the cultivated areas and, on the lava beach, turnstones, whimbrels, little egret, roseate terns, and less often, sandpipers. Caloura [70 D4] is good for the common and roseate tern which breed here.

## Birdwatching

Gerby Birding  m 967 958 566; e info@ gerbybirding.com; www.gerbybirding.com. Dutchman Gerby speaks excellent English, German & Portuguese too, an expert birder who was also instrumental in documenting many of the walks on the Azores Tourist Board website. Passionate, personable & knowledgeable, he regularly receives birders from many countries. From €65 pp.

## Recreational forest reserves

*Pinhal da Paz* [70 C3] Located midway between Ponta Delgada and Fenais da Luz in the north, from Ponta Delgada take the EN4–1a towards Capelas and turn right at Carreira village and follow the signs. This is a 49ha woodland garden developed on poor land of rocky outcrops and volcanic residues. Used once for grazing goats and sheep, in the mid 1900s it was planted by the grandson of plantsman Jose do Canto with ornamental trees and flowering shrubs including camellias and azaleas. Secured by the Regional Government 30 years ago, in the last few years it has been replanted and small themed gardens added, along with a forest study centre. Quite a few native species occur naturally throughout the reserve. So close to the city, it is a perfect place to spend easy hours walking in delightful woodland, especially in the less frequented northern areas.

*Woodlands of Canário* [70 B2] On the way to Sete Cidades, and a walk of 15 minutes to the Miradouro do Canário, one of the finest views in all the Azores (page 91).

*Chã da Macela* [70 D3] Along the road from Lagoa to Lagoa do Fogo, turn off at the sign to Remédios, and continue as far as Cinco Caminhos, where the forest reserve is signposted. The 28ha range from 350m to 550m and at the reserve's highest point is the Macela *miradouro* from where on a clear day one gets a fine view of the island. Apart from Cryptomerias, there is a fair mix of trees, and away from the play area and other amenities, the reserve has large areas of relative wilderness along with fine scenery.

*Cancelo do Cinzeiro* [70 G3] From the R1–1, take the signposted forest road to Pico Bartolomeu from Lomba da Pedreira. In 10ha of around 550m altitude there are forests and meadows, plus children's and picnic areas and playing fields. Significantly there are pockets of natural native laurel forest and a collection of endemics, along with a resident population of Azores woodpigeons and a breeding population of little shearwaters.

## FISHING

🎣 **Azores Sport Fishing**  m 962 812 982/966 866 826; e zesilvino@gmail.com; www. azoressportfishing.com. Never a cheap activity, a half day begins at €350 per boat (tuna trip) & €500 (blue marlin), inc equipment & insurance.

## GOLF

There are two courses on São Miguel, one at Fenais da Luz just a few kilometres north of Ponta Delgada, the other off the main road northwest of Furnas. Under the same ownership, various three- and five-day packages are available, allowing visitors to play both courses with a worthwhile discount. There is a strict dress code. Shirts must have a collar and sleeves; jeans and tracksuits cannot be worn on the course or in clubhouse facilities. Soft spikes are mandatory, and note that there is no golf-shoe hire available. See also ad in third colour section.

### Prices

Green fee inc trolley 18/9 holes: €65/57
Green fee inc buggy 18/9 holes: €93/65
Set of clubs (18/9 holes): €40/25
Driving range (50 balls): €6

### Tee times

**16 Oct–15 Mar** ⊕ 08.00–18.00 (Furnas 09.00–18.00); 18 holes ⊕ until 14.00, 9 holes until 16.00

**16 Mar–15 Oct** ⊕ 08.00–20.00 (Furnas 09.00–19.00); 18 holes ⊕ until 15.00, 9 holes until 17.00

### Courses

✓ **Golfe da Batalha**  [70 C3] ☎ 296 498 559/560 (clubhouse); e info@azoresgolfislands.com; www. azoresgolfislands. Designed by Cameron Powell Associates & built in 1996 with long fairways, large flowing greens & sinuously contoured bunkers, the course is a combination of links & woodland course with views over the sea. With 27 holes, golfers can mix up the combinations for variety. To play, there is a required maximum handicap: men 28; ladies 36, though they will allow higher handicap players with advance notice. The clubhouse has a restaurant with a stunning view, open to non-players.

✓ **Golfe das Furnas**  [70 E3] ☎ 296 498 559/584 651 (course); e info@azoresgolfislands. com; www.azoresgolfislands.com. Designed by MacKenzie Ross (who also built the Estoril course near Lisbon & restored the Scottish Turnberry courses) & built in 1939 with 9 holes, it was extended in 1990 by Cameron Powell Associates to the full 18-hole course, par 72, & 6,232m long. Required maximum handicap: men 28; ladies 36. It is an intimate course set in a glorious landscape with always verdant grass, forest & tree ferns. At 500m altitude, clouds & mist can often swirl around the course & present a different kind of challenge to the golfer. About 10mins' drive from Furnas or 45mins from Ponta Delgada. Restaurant on site.

## HIKING

For details of organised and guided walking and hiking options on the island, see *Walks*, pages 113–20.

## HORSERIDING

🐎 **Quinta da Terca**  Rua Padre Domingos Silva 221, Livramento (just east of Ponta Delgada); ☎ 296 642 134; m 968 122 398; e reservation@ quintadaterca.com; www.quintadaterca.com. With 40 horses, this excellent establishment based in a 17th-century estate provides a wide variety of half-day & day excursions, plus week-long courses, as well as beginners' courses. They also offer packages with accommodation & excellent food. Half-day trips are around €60.

## SURFING

**Azores Surf Center**  Praia Santa Barbara, just west of Ribeira Grande; m 915 970 726; e info@ azoressurfcenter.com; www.azoressurfcenter. com. Surfing is still fairly rare on the islands, but you can learn from scratch or perfect your skills with Josephine or Ricardo, fully qualified instructors on the north coast. They surf all year, but if the sea is too rough, then it's time to decamp across to the south coast for gentler waters – ideal for beginners. Prices, starting at €30 per lesson (in a group), inc wet suit, board & insurance. English spoken. Will hire equipment to experienced surfers, too.

**SWIMMING** The beaches and pools below are listed in an anticlockwise order, starting from Ponta Delgada. On the north coast swimming can be dangerous as there are many currents and hazards; you will see local people swimming, but they know where the dangers are. Use only obviously developed swimming areas. All beaches are black sand.

## Ponta Delgada [70 B4] At the eastern end of the harbour promenade, harbour swimming and in summer a complex of manmade pools with full services.

## São Roque [70 C4] Here are two beaches: Milicias or Areal Grande, and Areal Pequeno. Supporting facilities are available. Very popular, being only a short drive from Ponta Delgada.

## Lagoa [70 C4] Originally this was a long, popular 150m stretch of irregular coastline, but the old complex was virtually destroyed during the winter storms of 1997. A new complex has been built with greater protection against storm damage with two pools, both heated to 24°C in winter. The largest is a four-lane, 25m pool; the second is for children. There is also an ocean swimming area surrounded on three sides by lava – swimming is dependent on tides and strength of the sea. Sunbathing area, diving boards and slides complete the picture, together with a snack bar.

## Caloura [70 D4] Fishing harbour, natural and artificial pool, no beach, though there are also two small stretches of sand just west of the Caloura Hotel Resort.

## Água de Alto [70 D4] A long stretch of sand between two promontories, by the Hotel Bahia Palace.

## Vila Franca do Campo [70 D4] Two beaches, Praia de Água de Alto and Praia da Francesa, known also as Vinha d'Areia, can be found here. The nearby aquapark is sadly now closed. The Ilhéu da Vila Franca is an offshore collapsed crater with a naturally protected swimming area and is also good for scuba diving and snorkelling. In summer, a boat takes visitors out and back (€5) to let them enjoy this protected nature area: numbers are limited to 400 each day, and in high season the tickets are sometimes all sold by 10.00. This islet is also a venue for cliff-diving championships, which take place in July each year.

## Ribeira Quente [70 F4] A fishing village, at the western end of which beneath steep cliffs is the Praia do Fogo. All facilities are on offer, including showers, café and car park up above, and in summer there are several open-air restaurants. An extremely popular area.

## Ribeira Grande [70 D3] Municipal swimming pools are available on the new esplanade.

## Praia de Santa Barbara, just west of Ribeira Grande [70 D3] Facilities include good parking, toilets with showers, and a restaurant with sea view. Excellent surfing, used for competitions.

**WHALE AND DOLPHIN WATCHING** There are now many operators on São Miguel, mostly in Ponta Delgada but with one in Vila Franca do Campo and one soon to be operating from Rabo de Peixe, where the ocean topography is said to increase the chances of whale sightings to 90%. In Ponta Delgada, many operators have kiosks along the main promenade, but if these are closed, there are offices in the Portas del Mar complex, below the promenade. Lifejackets are provided. Off the south coast of São Miguel was once a profitable area when the islanders used to hunt whales and now, some three generations or so since the last whales were killed, they are again swimming past the former killing shores. For details on whale-watching etiquette, see pages 11–14.

**Futurismo** [79 F5] Marina Pero de Teive, Loja 24–26; Ponta Delgada; 296 628 522; e reservations@futurismo.pt; www.futurismo. pt. The biggest operator, with 7 boats of varying sizes, inc RIBs & a catamaran. Also the longest established, with over 25 years of experience. Each boat is accompanied by a marine biologist. English spoken. Shop & information centre. €55 (whale watching), €70 (swimming with dolphins). See also ad in 1st colour section.

**Sea Colors** [79 H1] Marina Portas do Mar; m 918 529 795/963 766 073; e seacolorsazores@ gmail.com; www.seacolorsazores.com. At the other end of the scale from the big operators, this is a husband & wife owned & run firm, with their boat taking a max of 12 passengers. They carry out research during their trips & data gathered by them on cetaceans is shared with the university, so your patronage helps to support this work. With a passionate concern for the mammals, they do not specifically sell trips that inc swimming with dolphins, believing that some firms that do so then feel obliged to put people in the water even if the dolphins are not 'in the mood' to be swum with. If the mood's right, swimming is possible & no extra charge is made. €55/48pp high/low season. See also ad in 3rd colour section.

**Terra Azul** Marina de Vila Franca do Campo; m 913 453 030; e info@ azoreswhalewatch.com; www.azoreswhalewatch. com. Operate all year round from the former island capital, with 2 trips daily in low season, & an extra 1 in summer. A marine biologist accompanies the boat & speaks English. Swimming with dolphins is another possibility. €57/45 adult/child (whale watching), €85/70 adult/child (swimming with dolphins).

## WALKS

Right from the early years of walking holidays in the Azores, the walks around Sete Cidades have been a highlight. The circuits around the lake of Furnas provide various options and new walks are being gradually added to the island's choices. Recent years have seen an increasing number of companies and individual guides offering their services and two good ones are listed below. For those who prefer to walk without a guide, four walks are described on pages 115–20. In addition to the four walks detailed, another recommended walk is the Faial da Terra–Salto do Prego trail, detailed on the tourist board website (medium difficulty, 4.7km, 1½ hours). This is an excellent, waymarked circular route via the Salto do Prego waterfall and the small, restored settlement of Sanguinho.

The Azores Tourism Authority's website (*www.visitazores.com*) currently details a total of 21 waymarked trails for São Miguel together with their degree of difficulty, distance and time. Always check a trail's status with the tourist office before setting out.

## GUIDED WALKS

**Geo-Fun** [79 H1] Solmar Avenida Center, Av Infante Dom Henrique 71, 1st Floor, Office 123AB, Ponta Delgada; 296 092 670; e info@geo-fun.com; www.geo-fun.com. Very well-established company, with knowledgeable guides who will enhance your experience with insights into the plants, geology,

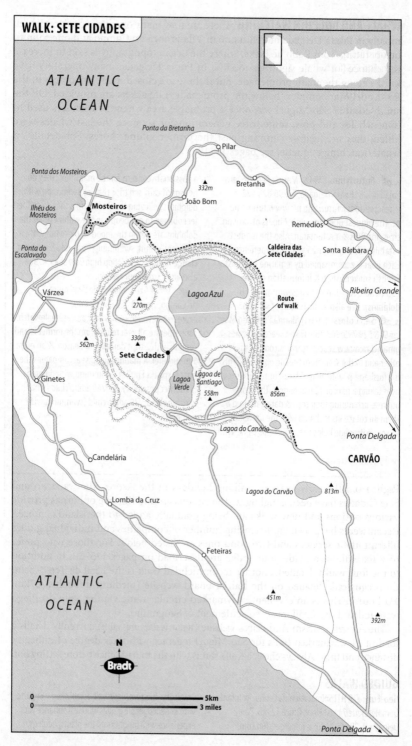

# WALK: SETE CIDADES

ATLANTIC
OCEAN

Ponta da Bretanha

Pilar

Ponta dos Mosteiros

Bretanha

▲ 332m

João Bom

Ilhéu dos
Mosteiros

**Mosteiros**

Remédios

Ponta do
Escalavado

Caldeira das
Sete Cidades

Santa Bárbara

Várzea

Lagoa Azul

Ribeira Grande

▲ 270m

Route
of walk

▲ 562m

330m ▲

**Sete Cidades** ●

Ginetes

Lagoa de
Santiago

Lagoa
Verde

▲ 856m

558m ▲

Lagoa do Canário

Ponta Delgada

Candelária

**CARVÃO**

Lagoa do Carvão

▲ 813m

Lomba da Cruz

Feteiras

ATLANTIC
OCEAN

▲ 451m

▲ 392m

N

Bradt

0 ——————————————— 5km
0 ——————————————— 3 miles

Ponta Delgada

history & culture. Programmed walks every day, of varying distances (6km to 13km) & difficulties. Specialist geology & biology tours available, for specialists. €55 (full day).

**Harmony Trail** (page 76) Hiking with an excellent young Azorean–Canadian guide. €50/30 full/half day.

## SELF-GUIDED WALKS
### Sete Cidades (Mata do Canário) (*Time: about 4½hrs; distance: about 12km; see map, opposite*)
There are numerous choices when it comes to exploring this area for there are several roads going down into the caldera and to the village of Sete Cidades, and there are various roads leading from the caldera rim down to villages along the coast. You will doubtless find various published descriptions of these. The walk described here, known as Mata do Canário, is best, since, in one route, you have the most magnificent caldera views which constantly change as you progress along the rim, and the end of the day offers the contrast of approaching the sea with fine views of Mosteiros and the chance to see what living on a *fajã* is like. Even on a national holiday, at most you will meet a farmer or two attending their cows and maybe another walker.

Footpath conditions are easy, more or less level, with some steep pitches at both the start and finish.

If the weather is very windy it can be very unpleasant, and if there is low cloud, do wait for another day since you will miss all the wonderful views. Half the fun is identifying all the landmarks.

Take a taxi to the area known as Carvão. Approaching from Ponta Delgada go past the Miradouro de Carvão, past the sign on your left to Lagoas dos Empadadas and then take the second asphalt-surfaced turning on your right. This soon curves round in front of an old and rather beautiful stone aqueduct and then into cryptomeria forest. Stop at the first unsurfaced farm track on your left – it is on a bend in the road.

You begin the walk here, slowly ascending through the forest and upon emerging come to a cement road making a very steep ascent up to the caldera, finishing by a building. You may be lucky and have an enthusiastic taxi driver prepared to risk damaging his car; mine had never been there before and insisted on driving all the way to the top where there is a level turning area. He ran to the caldera edge and was dumbstruck by the stupendous view; it is so much more dramatic than from the usual viewing place at Vista do Rei. On a clear day with no wind this has to be the finest view in all the Azores.

From here you simply follow the farm road going anticlockwise around the caldera rim; it soon forks and you bear round to the left. Continue ignoring all roads and tracks leading off from the main road around the caldera. In about two hours you reach a *miradouro* with some picnic tables and a road descending off on your right.

Continue on round the caldera and in about another 30 minutes you see the Ilhéu dos Mosteiros just off the coast, and near here you are above a tunnel that runs from the blue lake out of the caldera above Mosteiros. The track descends a little to come to a junction by a large smooth face of grey tuff with names carved into it. Two roads go down on your right, one either side of the bluff; take the second of these. The road you were following continues on round the caldera.

You now descend, at times between high walls of tuff and, lower down, reeds, to reach an asphalt road after 20 minutes. Cross this and continue down on the track and within two minutes come to a T-junction. Turn left, and the road forks either side of a fountain bearing the sign 'Rua Direita Pico de Mafra'. Take the left fork and follow this steeply down to the houses and continue on quickly to come to a *miradouro* giving a splendid view over Mosteiros, its white houses contrasting with the black lava and blue sea. To go down to Mosteiros take the small concrete road going steeply down on the right, about 50m below the Espírito Santo chapel. From Mosteiros you may get a bus back to Ponta Delgada, or phone for a taxi.

**Bretanha Coastal Walk** (**Atalho dos Vermelhos**) (*Time: about 2½hrs; distance: about 4.5km. Easy, though not suitable if you don't have a head for heights. Not suitable during or shortly after heavy rain.*) This is a pleasant partially coastal walk which affords good views along the spectacular cliffs near Mosteiros. Drinks are available at the shop in Bretanha, where you begin and end your walk.

To reach the start point, look out for the car park next to a picnic area, at the side of the main regional road that passes above João Bom. Park here (or you could take the bus to the same place) and descend on the road down into the village for 80m (Rua do Argentina) to reach a junction where you turn left and pass the mini market (Mini Mercado Pavão), and following the waymarking pass the chapel on your left then turn right into the Rua de Relvinha.

Continue down this road, heading for the sea. The tarmac runs out after a couple of hundred metres, but you continue down this track, lined with bamboo, fern and false tobacco plants, with pasture lands on either side for around 700m. (Occasionally, farmers may put string across the road to deter straying cattle: simply duck underneath and continue.)

Look out for a gate on your left with waymarking at which you turn sharp left to cross a narrow pasture. Head for a gap visible on the other side, go through the gap and follow the path which descends on steps through a small forest. The ocean is soon visible.

Descend down a steep path and cross a stream, before climbing again to follow the clifftop path around and pass some white water reservoirs which perch on a ledge. After the last of these you climb on a wide path, leaving the ocean behind you. The path turns up to the left on a wide ash and grass path.

After a steep climb, the path flattens and you head towards the volcanic, wooded cone of Mafra. Eventually the path takes you around this, leaving it to your left (ignore

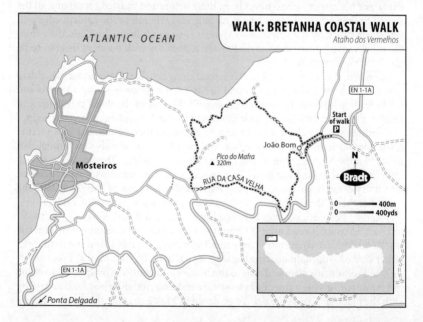

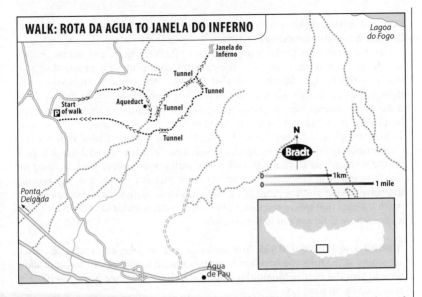

## WALK: ROTA DA AGUA TO JANELA DO INFERNO

Lagoa
do Fogo

Janela do
Inferno

Tunnel

Tunnel

Aqueduct

Start
of walk

Tunnel

Tunnel

N

Bradt

0 ———— 1km
0 ———— 1 mile

Ponta
Delgada

Água
de Pau

a turn-off to your left). After a few hundred metres, you reach a crossroads at the end of the Rua de Pedra Queimada and you turn left down the Rua da Casa Velha. Now follow this unmade-up track before coming to a three-way junction at which you continue straight ahead, downhill. The road continues, then starts to climb and turns into tarmac and returns you into João Bom village where you began.

### Rota da Água/Janela do Inferno (*Time: about 2hrs 45mins; distance: about 7km.* This easy to moderate circular walk includes four tunnels and some crossing of narrow bridges. A torch is advisable, though a mobile phone with flashlight will suffice. Not to be attempted during rain or after heavy rainfall. It is well waymarked. The middle section is beautiful: with lush vegetation, a beautiful waterfall and deep ravines, it has the air of a real 'lost world' and once you exit it back into pastureland, you may scarcely believe that such scenery exists in such a location.)

To reach the start, take the main road east out of Ponta Delgada, then take the turning north on to the ER–6, heading for Remedios and Lagoa da Fogo. After a couple of kilometres, you will reach a triangular junction, where there is a car park, toilets and a signboard for the walk. It starts unpromisingly with a trek up the hill on the tarmac road. Note away to your left the volcanic cones which form the 'middle section' of the island. After around 700m, follow the waymarking off to the right, leaving the tarmac to head downhill on concrete. Note the aqueduct on your right. Soon, follow a dirt track off to your right heading back towards the coast.

After a few hundred metres, turn left down a path with fields on either side. Follow this path, sometimes muddy, downhill until it opens into a pasture, at the end of which you enter a 50m-long, narrow tunnel. Continue for a few hundred metres to reach some abandoned buildings before turning sharp right down some stone steps and cross a stream. The water pipes here once fed a local alcohol factory, but now simply supply the coastal towns with their water.

Ignore a path off to your right. With steep drop-offs to your right, follow the path until you reach a bridge with handrails. Cross and immediately at the end of the bridge follow the signs to your left for Janela do Inferno. After 200m you reach a beautiful vertical rockface with a waterfall gushing from a high-up cave. The pool below is a favourite residence of newts.

Retrace your steps to the bridge and enter the very short and narrow tunnel which takes you to the other side. The path descends gently, then more steeply to reach another bridge (slippery after rain). Cross the bridge and ascend to then turn right through a further tunnel, where a torch or flashlight would be useful. Cross a stream (or stream-bed, in dry weather), then another, then a third and in a few hundred metres look out for tunnel number four. This is the longest one, around 100m in length and down to around 1.40m in height in places (mind your head).

After exiting the tunnel, you reach a wooden gate which you pass through to pick up the waymarking to your left. Follow the path across pasture land, heading for two large grassy mounds. Before reaching them, turn left at a crossroads following the waymarking and continue down the path towards the coast. Eventually you reach a T-junction where you turn right on to a wide, unmade-up road which after a kilometre will return you to the car park.

## Around Lagoa das Furnas
The walks to Furnas lake can easily be varied according to the time you have and how far you want to walk. Don't forget to allow time to visit the Furnas Monitoring and Research Centre – see pages 99–100. See also the map on page 119.

*Option (a)* (*Time: about 2hrs; distance: about 5km*) The easiest option is to take a taxi from Furnas to the chapel of Nossa Senhora das Vitórias at the far side of the lake, and then walk back along the lake edge at the side of the main road to Furnas, downhill all the way, reversing the descriptions below under option (b).

*Options (b), (c) and (d)* The following walks begin at the pretty petrol station with its *azulejos*, near the Teatro das Furnas, just a short distance from the Terra Nostra Garden Hotel. At the garage the main road bears round to the left and a cement road leads off very steeply up the hill. Take the cement road. While the former farm track is now surfaced, there is virtually no traffic and the scenery remains as lovely as ever. Keep to the main route until it bears strongly round to the left with a good track on your right going steeply up into the shade of a belt of trees towards the top of the ridge. From here the road very quickly goes down the other side to the lake. You will smell sulphur and may notice steam coming from fissures in the banks. Now you have a choice of how long a walk you want to make; approximate times are given from the petrol station.

*Option (b)* (*Time: about 3½hrs; distance: about 11km*) To walk around the lake, turn right and pass the cooking area of the famous **Furnas** *cozido* (available in all the town's restaurants) and straight ahead come to a gateway. Simply continue along this track, first along a small stream, following more or less the edge of the lake. You will have noticed an old house by the water on the far side, and a chapel. These once belonged to the family of José do Canto, who created here yet another fine garden. There are many fine old camellias, some magnolias and a fern gully, and the garden is now fully accessible to the public (page 99). Passing the interpretation centre, garden and church, the road continues to join the main south-coast road from Ponta Delgada, which has in some parts been left in its original cobbled state. Turn left on to this road to complete your circuit of the lake, pass the entrance to the *caldeiras*, and about half a kilometre after the road has left the lake on its descent into Furnas you come to a low roadside wall

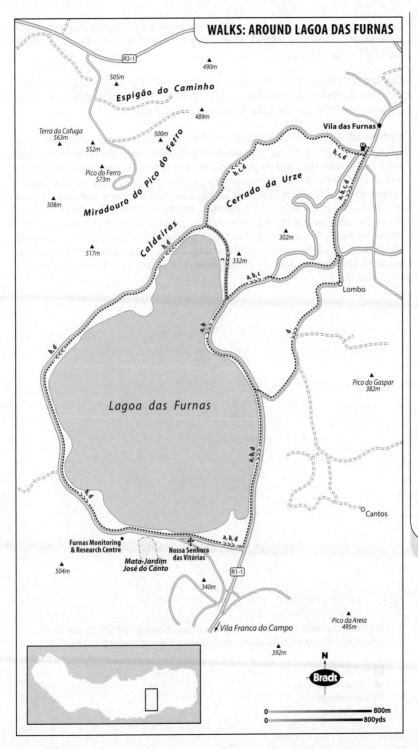

# WALKS: AROUND LAGOA DAS FURNAS

R2-1

490m

505m

*Espigão do Caminho*

489m

*Terra da Cafuga*
563m

500m

**Vila das Furnas**

b, c, d

552m

*Miradouro do Pico do Ferro*

b, c, d

*Pico do Ferro*
573m

a, b, c, d

*Cerrado da Urze*

508m

*Caldeiras*

b, d

302m

517m

c

332m

Lombo

a, b, c

a, b

d

*Pico do Gaspar*
382m

b, d

*Lagoa das Furnas*

a, b, d

b, d

Cantos

**Furnas Monitoring
& Research Centre**

a, b, d

504m

*Mata-Jardim
José do Canto*

✝ *Nossa Senhora
das Vitórias*

340m

R1-1

✓ *Vila Franca do Campo*

*Pico da Areia*
495m

392m

N

**Bradt**

0 ——————— 800m
0 ——————— 800yds

painted white on your right. Where the wall begins there is a wide asphalted track (waymarked in red and yellow), going steeply down. If you take this it is a short cut into Furnas village.

**Option (c)** (*Time: about 2hrs, starting from the Furnas garage; distance: about 5km*) For the fastest return to Furnas, leave the lake in a clockwise direction to join the main road into Furnas. Take the short cut described above.

**Option (d)** (*Time: about 4hrs, starting from the Furnas garage; distance: about 12km*) As for option (b) but after you have turned left on to the main south-coast road, look out for the signs on your right for Lagoa Seca and the Miradour Milhos da Lombo. Follow this to enter a very pretty area around the domed hill, the Pico do Gaspar. Take the road round to your left in a clockwise direction, and take the road for Milhos da Lombo going off on your left, steeply uphill. When you emerge from the cryptomeria trees at the top of the hill, the road turns steeply down to your left. Before following this, just walk ahead for a short distance to the viewpoint, giving an appreciation of Furnas in its crater setting. The steep road down to Furnas takes about 15 minutes, but be very careful because it is very easy to slip. Not for the weak-kneed.

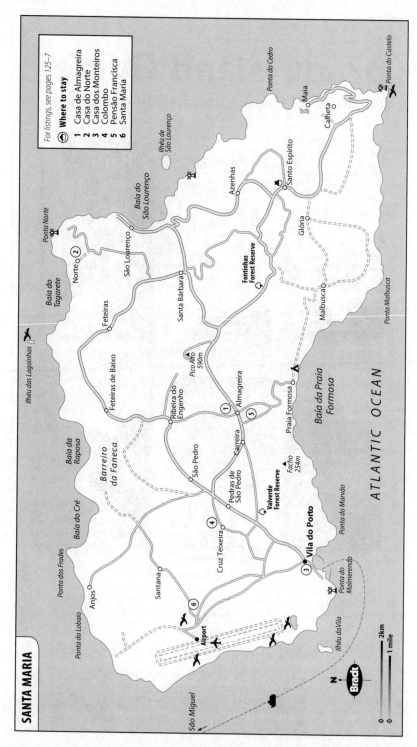

# SANTA MARIA

For listings, see pages 125–7

**Where to stay**
1 Casa de Almagreira
2 Casa do Norte
3 Casa dos Monteiros
4 Colombo
5 Pensão Francisca
6 Santa Maria

ATLANTIC OCEAN

Baía do Tagarete

Baía da Raposa

Baía do Cré

Barreiro da Faneca

Baía do São Lourenço

Baía do São Lourenço

Baía da Praia Formosa

Ilhéu das Lagoinhas

Ilhéu de São Lourenço

Ponta Norte

Ponta do Cedro

Ponta do Castelo

Ponta da Lobaio

Ponta dos Frades

Ponta Malbusca

Ponta do Marvão

Ponta do Molmerendo

Ilhéu da Vila

São Miguel

Norte

São Lourenço

Feteiras

Feteiras de Baixo

Santa Bárbara

Azenhas

Santo Espirito

Maia

Calheta

Glória

Malbusca

Ribeira do Engenho

Pico Alto 590m

Almagreira

Praia Formosa

Fontinhas Forest Reserve

São Pedro

Carreira

Pedras de São Pedro

Valverde Forest Reserve

Facho 254m

Cruz Teixeira

Santana

Anjos

Vila do Porto

Airport

0    2km
0    1 mile

# 4

# Santa Maria

Santa Maria sees itself as the sun island. Its claims that, being a little further south and east than all the other islands, it receives more sunshine and enjoys higher sea temperatures are borne out by statistics. Sheep graze the flatlands around the airport, an area with virtually no trees, but this scenery changes rapidly on the approach to the central peak of Pico Alto, the island's highest point at 590m. Here once again is the typically lush Azorean green forest with cryptomeria trees and pittosporum, mixed in places with native shrubs. Then comes the eastern half and its idyllic, picturesque, tranquil, verdant landscapes of woodland and pastures. These may be sprinkled with glimmering white traditional houses that are either scattered, in little clusters or in small villages. In places there are no buildings at all, or perhaps just a time-weathered basalt shelter tucked away in a corner of a field. There are dramatic coastlines, proud headlands and sheltered bays, and a novelty for the Azores: white sand. This island supplies the potters on São Miguel with some of their clay, and from deposits at Santana and Figueral came the lime to whitewash all the archipelago's houses.

To hire a car and meander along almost empty winding roads through such glorious countryside, stopping for views and parking the car at the end of a farm road and just exploring to the sound of birdsong, makes for a wonderful three or four days' holiday. High sea cliffs provide precipitous views and you can drop down to the coast at Maia and São Lourenço for sea swimming in manmade pools with their own natural wave machine. Between exploring the varied environments you have the white sandy beach at Praia Formosa (though it disappears in the winter waves), and the sea pools at Anjos in which to relax. Other places of interest include the little chapel at Anjos associated with Columbus's first landfall on his return from the Americas and the quite remarkable stone terraced vineyards at Maia, an extraordinary work of such great skill and energy you are left wondering at the effort humankind is prepared to make to produce wine! And then there's the amazing red soils and almost desert landscape of Paul da Serra, not forgetting that, in keeping with its status as the oldest Azore, this is the only island in the archipelago where you can find fossils.

## BACKGROUND

**GEOLOGY** Santa Maria has not suffered any earthquakes during historical times, nor does it have any fumaroles or hot springs; its original volcanic structures are partially eroded or completely destroyed, yet the island nevertheless has features unique in the archipelago.

It has many outcrops of sedimentary rocks including limestones, conglomerates and sandstones, often with abundant and diversified fossil content. It is the only island where several major outcrops of pillow lavas can be seen, sometimes in well-preserved layered sequences. Pillow lava is hot fluid magma that erupts underwater rather like toothpaste coming out of a tube, which then rapidly cools upon contact with the water and forms heaps of pillow or cushion-like structures up to one metre across. Finally, being volcanic in origin as with all the other islands, it offers its own interesting volcanic structures and landscapes. Not only known for its sunnier climate, its beaches are also more like those typically associated with seaside resorts rather than the black gritty volcanic beaches largely found elsewhere in the archipelago. Their light colour is due to the erosion of carbonated rocks, ie: sedimentary limestone.

Santa Maria is the oldest island of the Azores and emerged from the sea around eight to ten million years ago, having been built up from basaltic eruptions from about 2,000m below current sea levels. That some lava flows include layers of sandstones and limestones indicates that at some point the island subsided. Erosion and changes in average sea level have exposed these marine sediments intercalated with volcanic outputs. The oldest basalts are around Vila do Porto – very appropriate, since this town was the first settled in the Azores. Following closely are the lavas from Pico Alto, which is one of a series of peaks that together define a north–south alignment separating a distinct quite flat area in the west which is very dry and poor in vegetation. To the east is a younger mountainous and hilly area very much greener with higher rainfall.

Outcrops of fossil-bearing marine sediments can be seen on the north coast and cliffs of Baía do Cré and Baía da Raposa, just east of Anjos, and most notably along the south coast between Vila do Porto and Baía da Praia Formosa. The Barreiro da Faneca or Red Desert, east of Anjos and Monte Gordo, reminds one of the vast red landscapes of central Australia. It is an arid area of Pliocene (5.2 to 1.64 million years ago) sediments composed of clay minerals on top of a lava flow from the Pico Alto complex. The soils and vegetation, however, developed in a cover of very thin pyroclasts (small fragmentic rocks and ash) coming from the most recent explosive eruptions. The resultant altered clay is red owing to the oxidation of the volcanic products through the alternating warm and humid and contrasting dry periods of the Pliocene. Wind erosion has levelled the areas where there is no vegetation cover. The Barreiro da Malbusca, in the south between Malbusca and Ponta da Malbusca, is an old elevated beach, where nodules of manganese typical of an ocean floor can be found. In parts, it resembles a high-level version of Northern Ireland's Giants' Causeway. Nodule minerals derive from the interaction of hot, upwelling, metal-bearing solutions at a plate boundary with organic sediments and grow very slowly; a centimetre can take well over a million years.

**HISTORY** Santa Maria is generally considered the first island of the archipelago to be discovered by the Portuguese, sometime between 1427 and 1432, and is so named because it was sighted on the Feast of the Assumption of Our Lady. It was also subsequently the first island to be settled. The initial settlement was made in 1439 by people mainly from the Algarve and Alentejo, on the northwest coast at a place named Praia do Lobos, just west of what is now Anjos, by the Ribeira do Capitão. This river is now called Ribeira de Santana. However, between 1460 and 1474, Vila do Porto became the principal administration centre of the island. Exports were woad and urzela for dyeing. In the 16th century, land in the west was developed for wheat. Santa Maria became a commercial satellite of São Miguel and sent to the larger island wheat, orchil, pottery clay and cheese. Needless to say, during the 16th and 17th centuries, French, Turkish and Moorish pirates attacked and destroyed the settlements many times. By the 19th century, demand for Santa Maria's exports had dwindled and emigration increased. It was the American wartime airbase built in 1944 that brought real change, and although military aviation activity moved to Terceira, it later became an international airport for transatlantic flights; in 1977, it received its first visit from Concorde. Currently it is an air-traffic-control centre for the north Atlantic and hosts an important European Space Agency base which processes satellite pictures. The population has dropped considerably owing to emigration: in the 1960s, it had around 14,000 inhabitants; now it is down to some 5,850.

## GETTING THERE AND AWAY

For getting to Santa Maria, see pages 42–3. Santa Maria's former status as an airbase has bestowed it with a long runway. The airport terminal building is modern, with a tourist information office, a few car-hire options (*Autatlantis* ✆ *296 886 530 & Ilha Verde* m *917 369 160*), a cafeteria, ATM and free Wi-Fi. Bus service to town is patchy; better to take a taxi, costing a few euros.

**Azores Airlines** Rua Dr Luís Bettencourt, Vila do Porto; ✆ 296 820 701

**Airport** ✆ 296 820 180

## GETTING AROUND

There is a very limited island bus service on weekdays (even more limited on Saturdays) linking some of the villages, mainly for bringing people into Vila do Porto in the mornings and returning them late afternoon, which is usually of little help to the visitor. Full details are online (*www.transportesdessantamaria.com*), and times are posted on the bus stops, too. Be sure to stick your hand out for the bus, as drivers do not expect tourists as passengers, so if you are alone at a bus stop they could simply drive past without stopping. A very limited service also reaches the airport, so you might be lucky if it coincides with your flight time. For touring, you can use a taxi, (✆ *296 882 199*), which are usually found halfway up the cobbled main street in Vila do Porto, but this is an island best explored with a self-drive car.

### ISLAND TOURS
**Smatur** m 926 468 668; e smatur.37@gmail.com; www.smatur.pt. A young dynamic company offering guided walking, mountain-bike & jeep tours. Has an in-depth knowledge of the unique island geology.

## TOURIST INFORMATION

(*Information office at the airport;* ✆ *296 886 355*) The office opens to meet most incoming flights from Monday to Friday, although times vary month-to-month.

##  WHERE TO STAY

There are now only two large conventional hotels, both outside town, and a new, boutique hotel right in the centre. If you have a car, then the choice is yours, otherwise staying in town might be preferable. There is also some rural accommodation. Given the lack of hosted accommodation on the island, renting a house by the week is also an option. Out of season, shorter stays might be possible at the two houses to rent listed on page 126.

For location of towns, see map page 122.

### HOTELS
 **Hotel Colombo** (87 rooms) Rua Cruz Teixera, Vila do Porto; ✆ 296 820 200; e santamaria@colombo-hotel.com; www. colombo-hotel.com. North of town, facilities inc a restaurant, bar, coffee shop, pool, gym, Turkish bath, jacuzzi, massage & children's room with inflatables, PlayStation, ping-pong, etc. There

is also bicycle hire. Rooms enjoy AC, TV with international channels & free Wi-Fi. The building is an awful intrusion into the landscape, but it is a comfortable hotel. €€€€€€

🏠 **Hotel Casa dos Monteiros** (15 rooms) Rua Teofilo Braga 31, Vila do Porto; 📞 296 882 107; e info@charmingblue.com; www.charmingblue.com. Santa Maria's boutique hotel arrived in 2016, central to town & exuding class in an island with few choices. Rooms are spacious, modernly furnished, with AC, free Wi-Fi & TV (international channels), some with balcony. Outside is a pool & there's a spa with sauna & jacuzzi; there are bikes for hire & a dive centre on-site. A smart restaurant (Mesa d'Oito, see below) is a notch or two up in quality from the standard fare. The island's best choice. €€€€

🏠 **Hotel Santa Maria** (50 rooms) Rua da Horta, Vila do Porto; 📞 296 820 660; e reservas@ hotel-santamaria.pt. Built on the site of the old wartime officers' mess near the airport, the rooms are all on ground-floor level, each a short walk to the pool & with access to a large garden & the tennis courts (extra cost). The bedroom floors are tiled & this strikes cold & uninviting in winter, but could be an advantage in summer as this part of Santa Maria can be hot. Rooms have AC/heating, TV with international channels & free Wi-Fi. Facilities inc a restaurant & bar. €€€

🏠 **Pensão Francisca** (3 rooms, 1 apt) Brejo de Baixo, Almagreira; 📞 296 884 033; e info@ azorean-spirit.com; www.azorean-spirit.com.

A few km north of Vila do Porto, this secluded Austrian/Swiss-owned, eco-conscious B&B serves renowned b/fasts combining local, organic products & Swiss muesli. Free Wi-Fi. Rooms have heating, private bath. €€€

## HOUSES TO RENT

🏠 **Casa de Almagreira** Canada do Outeiro, Almagreira; 📞 282 444 444; m 912 650 006; e azores@nada.pt; www.altoazores.com. A larger house, in the island's centre & sleeping up to 6 adults, plus 2 children. Plenty of outdoor space, BBQ & a peaceful setting. €€€€€€

🏠 **Casa do Norte** Lugar do Norte, Santa Barbara; m 910 649 407; e info@norteazores.com; www.norteazores.com. A beautiful small house, in splendid isolation set in an attractive garden. Ideal for a romantic couple's hideaway. €€€

## YOUTH HOSTEL

🏠 **Pousada de Juventude** Rua Frei Gonçalo Velho, Vila do Porto; 📞 296 883 592; e santamaria@pousadasjuvacores.com; ⏰ closed last 2 weeks of Dec. Fairly new & just 800m from the port, with communal kitchen, outdoor pool, TV rooms, table football & free Wi-Fi. Dorm beds are €17, doubles more. €

## CAMPING

⛏ **Praia Formosa** Open in summer only, near the sea; all facilities; restaurant nearby in village. €

 **WHERE TO EAT AND DRINK**

### VILA DO PORTO

🍴 **Central Pub** Rua Dr Luís Bettencourt; 📞 296 882 513; ⏰ 17.00–02.00 daily. Perhaps the closest thing in the Azores to an Irish pub (though not *that* close), it serves up pizza & all things Italian, as well as the usual fare & some decent grilled squid. Occasional live music at the weekends. *€12*

🍴 **Espaço em Cena** Lugar de Mãe de Deus; m 961 809 446; ⏰ (restaurant) 19.00–22.00 Tue–Sat. At the north end of town, a late, late night weekend hangout for the 30-somethings of Santa Maria. Civilised ambience, with good selection of wines & teas, in a cleverly converted primary school. The food's good, too, with a decent vegetarian meal or two. *€12*

🍴 **Mesa d'Oito** Hotel Casa dos Monteiros; m 917 232 013; ⏰ noon–14.30 & 19.00–22.30 daily. A hotel restaurant, but without feeling like one. Very smart modern interior, elegant surroundings for a short but varied menu. Some vegetarian & Italian specialities, created by an enthusiastic chef, but still at reasonable prices & with a good wine list. *€12*

🍴 **Restaurante Garrouchada** Rua Dr Luís Bettencourt; 📞 296 883 038; ⏰ (kitchen) 09.00–16.00 & 19.00–22.00 Mon–Fri, 11.00–15.00 & 19.00–22.00 Sat & Sun. Usual variety of large snacks, *bifana*, burgers, etc, plus omelettes & fish/meat dishes. *€12*

## ALMAGREIRA

**✕ Snack Bar A Moagem** ↘296 884 133; ⊕ noon–15.00 & 19.00–22.00 daily. A cheap-priced daily dish makes this a good lunchtime stop, just off the main road. More varied menu available, too, & opens as a bar from early to late. *€7*

## ANJOS

**✕ Bar dos Anjos** On Anjos waterfront; m 917 154 859/914 821 230; ⊕ 10.00–midnight. Serving fresh fish, plus a few island specialities such as *caldo de nabos* (turnip soup). *€10*

## SÃO LOURENÇO

**✕ Snack Bar O Ilhéu** ↘296 884 383; ⊕ Apr–Oct until 04.00 daily; winter Sat & Sun only. *€10*

## OTHER PRACTICALITIES

**Emergency** ↘112
**Police** Rua Jose Leandres Chaves, Vila do Porto; ↘296 883 350
**✚ Hospital (Centro de Saude)** ↘296 820 100. With 24hr A&E, though serious cases will be airlifted to São Miguel.

✉**Post office** Rua Teofilio Braga, 38; ⊕ 09.00–12.30 & 14.00–18.00 Mon–Fri
**🖳Internet/Wi-Fi** In most cafés around town, plus in the marina area, free Wi-Fi can be found.

## WHAT TO SEE AND DO

### MUSEUMS

**Dalberto Pombo Environmental Interpretation Centre** (*Rua Teófilo Braga 10–14, Vila do Porto;* ↘ *296 206 790;* ⊕ *15 Jun–15 Sep 10.00–13.00 & 14.00–18.00 daily, other months 14.00–17.30 Tue–Sat; €2.5/1.25/free adult/senior & under 17/ under 13; family tickets available*) Founded on the collections of the naturalist Dalberto Pombo, a Portuguese pioneer in the study of Santa Maria's biological and geological diversity, there are exhibits on butterflies, insects, birds and marine fossils. Information is only in Portuguese, but the helpful staff are English-speaking and will provide an informal guided tour at quiet times.

**Museu de Santa Maria** (*Santo Espírito;* ↘ *296 884 844;* ⊕ *10.00–17.30 Tue– Sun; €1/0.50/free adult/under 25s & seniors/under 15s*) The island's Ethnographic Museum, located behind the church in Santo Espírito, is well worth seeing. Exhibits include early Santa Maria pottery, period household items, costumes and ethnographic items. There are also occasional temporary exhibitions. The information is in Portuguese only, but if you're lucky (or ring ahead), you should

---

### FESTIVALS ON SANTA MARIA

**Festas de Santo António** Santo Espírito; 2nd or 3rd week of Jun
**Festas de São João** Vila do Porto; last week of Jun
**Maja** Folk world music; 1st week of Jul
**Blues Festival** 2nd week of Jul
**Festa do Sagrado** Coração de Jesus Santa Bárbara; 1st week of Aug
**Festa de Nossa** Senhora da Assunção Vila do Porto; middle of Aug
**Festival Maré de Agosto** Praia Formosa; 3rd week of Aug
**Festa das Vindimas** São Lourenço; 1st week of Sep. Grape harvest.
**Festa de Nossa Senhora da Anunciação** Vila do Porto; 3rd week of Sep

4

be able to secure an English-speaking staff member for a guided tour. This can be combined with a visit to the nearby craft co-operative, Cooperativa de Artesanto de Santa Maria, for some of their delicious handmade biscuits (page 132), since both are in the village of Santo Espírito.

## RECREATIONAL FOREST RESERVES
**Fontinhas Forest Reserve** Santo Espírito. This is located in the centre of Santa Maria on the western slope of Pico Alto, and is particularly noted for its tall trees which provide a cool ambience amid beautiful rural scenery. There are pleasant walks between the trees, tree ferns, azaleas and camellias; barbecue facilities and picnic shelters.

**Valverde Forest Reserve** A well-used and much-developed park at the edge of Vila do Porto, its 4ha are dominated by eucalyptus and cupressus trees. There is a deer enclosure.

# ACTIVITIES

## ACTIVITY TOURS
**Smatur** m 926 468 668; e smatur.37@gmail. com; www.smatur.pt. A young dynamic company offering guided walks, mountain-bike & jeep tours, & they also hire bikes out to visitors who prefer to go it alone. They have contacts with local birding experts, too.

**DIVING** Manta rays are the biggest attraction in the nearby waters, with blue sharks and occasional whale sharks also present. Diving is mainly by boat, rather than from the shore. Dive companies are based at the port, but are best contacted in advance. Single dives cost from around €45, but generally the operators need a minimum of four–six people. Snorkelling and boat trips are also available from the following two operators:

*Mantamaria Dive Center* m 917 287 286/ 918 685 447; e info@mantamaria.com; www. mantamaria.com. Well-respected & established operation.

*Paralelo37* m 914 201 281/966 305 838; e paralelo37@sapo.pt; www.paralelo37.pt. PADI centre with 10 years' experience.

## SWIMMING
**Praia Formosa** With its white-sand beach, this place is very popular in summer, but the sands are often invisible beneath the waves in other seasons. There is an area marked off for surfboards and changing facilities with showers, plus seasonal snack bars and ice creams. At the west end, there is an information panel detailing Santa Maria's system of defensive forts.

**Anjos** There are two pools, sunbathing areas, changing rooms and showers.

**Maia** Facilities include a sea swimming pool with changing rooms and showers, and a restaurant and café. O Grota (m *927 296 708*) is the village's open-all-year restaurant while Flor da Maria at the farthest end of the bay is the café.

**São Lourenço** In addition to a sea swimming pool with changing rooms and showers, and a snack bar, there are also small white beaches between the rocks, popular in summer.

**WALKING** There are now six official trails, including one long-distance option that forms a circuit of the entire island. Summaries are given here; maps and route guides can be downloaded from the www.visitazores.com website.

**Pico Alto** Medium difficulty, 6.2km, 2 hours. A super circular walk, enjoying views from the highest point of the island, on forest paths.

**Santo Espírito–Maia** Medium difficulty, 6.8km, 3 hours. Beginning in Santo Espírito, the route takes you through woodland, pastures and vineyards passing several village artefacts and finally down to the sea at the southeast corner of Ponta do Castelo.

**Entre a Serra e o Mar** ('Between the mountains and the sea') Medium difficulty, 9.5km, 2½ hours. A circular walk starting from the parish church in Santa Bárbara past typical houses, rural landscapes and good views.

**Trilha do Costa Sul** (from Vila do Porto to the beach of Praia Formosa) Medium difficulty, 7km, 3 hours. Now waymarked, and fairly straightforward, it follows well-used tracks and offers close-ups of the fossils and terrific views from cliffs high above the sea.

**Trilha da Costa Norte** (northern coastal walk) Medium difficulty, 9km, 4 hours. A linear walk along the northern coast and ending up at Anjos.

**Santa Maria circular** Medium difficulty, 78km, 30 hours' walking, to be spread over 4 days. The first island to have a round-island trail, this ideally should begin and end in Vila do Porto. Plan carefully, remembering that wild camping is prohibited.

## TOURING THE ISLAND

As you travel around the island note the different house chimneys, especially the square-like ones topped with tall slender round chimney pots. Some of the parishes have their house windows and doors trimmed in the 'village colour': Santo Espírito, green; Santa Bárbara, blue; Almagreira, red; São Pedro, yellow; and Vila do Porto, tile coloured.

**VILA DO PORTO** Known originally simply as Porto, it became Vila do Porto in the 16th century when it was given its charter, the first town in the Azores to have this status. What is left of the old town runs uphill from the fort overlooking the harbour, now a modern port. The façades of the old grand houses give an idea of what it must have been like, together with the tiny cottages in the streets behind. All these are protected but sadly many owners of the large houses left for Lisbon in the 1950s and records have been lost, so by default their houses became very run down. They are now being redeveloped. As you walk down from town towards the port (along the Rua Teófilo Braga), look out on your left for the façade of the 15th-century building that supposedly belonged to Governor João Soares de Sousa. It may be recognised by its Gothic windows. Nearby houses have interestingly carved lintels and other details. The **Fort of São Brás** was built in the 17th century and of course provides a good view out to sea; with the cannon in position it is a fertile place in which to imagine early events. A stroll down to the fort after dinner is a pleasant ending to the day. In summer the cooling evening contrasts with the

*Alan Vittery, Santa Maria resident and ornithologist*

Although Santa Maria is by far the oldest island in the Azores archipelago, until recently, it was one of the least studied ornithologically. Intensive field work since 2009 has shown it to be unexpectedly bird-rich, both in terms of the high densities of the resident land birds and the number of migratory terrestrial species attracted by its large plain – a feature unique in the Azores.

In common with all islands far from any mainland land mass, Santa Maria has few resident land birds. The 19 species include two introductions, the house sparrow (*Passer domesticus*) and the goldfinch (*Carduelis carduelis*), neither of which seem to have seriously affected the population of another resident, the Atlantic canary (*Serinus canaria*), which is the commonest breeder with probably more than 5,000 pairs. Also abundant are the robin (*Erithacus rubecula*), the blackbird (*Turdus merula*), the blackcap (*Sylvia atricapilla*), the starling (*Sturnus (vulgaris) granti*), and chaffinch (*Fringilla (coelebs) moreletti*). The last two of these are likely to be soon reclassified as separate species. The distinctive Santa Maria race of the goldcrest (*Regulus regulus sanctae-mariae*) is another candidate for separation. The only resident diurnal bird of prey is the common buzzard (*Buteo buteo rothschildii*), but the long-eared owl (*Asio otus*) is now also known to be present on the island. Grey wagtails (*Motacilla cinerea*) occupy a wider variety of habitats than their mainland brethren.

A resident population of Kentish plover (*Charadrius alexandrines*) has adapted to a life on inland pastures. By far the rarest and most intriguing resident is the newly discovered little button-quail (*Turnix sylvatica*), a mainly tropical species now almost extinct in its only European refuge in southern Iberia, which inhabits scrub-covered grassland at the southern end of the airport.

Summer breeding visitors include large numbers of Cory's shearwater (*Calonectris diomedea*) and common tern (*Sterna hirundo*), an important population of roseate tern (*Sterna dougallii*), and, in most years, a pair of sooty

still-warm stones and makes a different but parallel smell to rain on sun-scorched earth. If you have time, take the old cobbled road down to the port and continue right round to the end of the *mole* (breakwater); there is a splendid view of the fort.

The modern part of the town, which starts roughly around the beginning of the Rua Teófilo Braga, is a linear development which looks as if it will go on growing longer. All the usual small shops are here including several small-scale supermarkets, and a market. The square in front of the town hall might give it some future focus. If the **Câmara Municipal** is open, do step inside for a peep as it is a grand building. It was the first Franciscan monastery to be founded in the islands by the monks who came with the settlers; it grew wealthy, was looted, then rebuilt, then finally converted into a town hall. This is a history repeated throughout the islands, the converted uses also being hospitals and charities.

At the opposite end of the town there is a **forestry park** with a children's play area, picnic tables and washrooms beneath pine trees. A belvedere offers a view of Vila do Porto and the immediate countryside.

**AROUND THE AIRPORT** The area around the airport is limestone country and was once the most productive wheat area. Now the modern civilian airport takes a large percentage of the land, while beyond the boundary remains of the wartime airfield linger in the form of old Nissen huts and concrete slabs. There is also the terns (*Sterna fuscata*) – the only breeding site in the western Palearctic. Small numbers of barolo shearwater (*Puffinus baroli*), Bulwer's petrel (*Bulweria bulwerii*) and Grant's petrel (*Oceanodroma granti*) also breed on Ilhéu da Vila.

Winter specialities on the plain include dotterel (*Charadrius morinellus*), skylark (*Alauda arvensis*) and snow bunting (*Plectrophenax nivalis*), whilst other northern species like fieldfare (*Turdus pilaris*), redwing (*Turdus iliacus*) and song thrush (*Turdus philomelos*) occur in hard winters.

The majority of Santa Maria's 240-plus recorded species are rare or occasional visitors from mainland Europe, North America, the Arctic and northwest Africa. Several desert species, all new to the Azores, have appeared following Saharan storms, finding the island's southern arid plain a suitable temporary habitat. Amazingly, 15 migratory species of birds of prey have reached the island, including no less than five immature Barbary falcons (*Falco pelegrinoides*), a species recorded nowhere else in Europe. North American shorebirds and ducks are regular visitors, mainly in autumn, and a pair of killdeers (*Charadrius vociferous*) stayed on to breed in three successive years from 2010 – a unique series of events in Europe.

Around the perimeter fence of the airport can be found numerous ponds and small wetland areas which can reward the patient birder. Walking or cycling would be the best way to circumnavigate the perimeter, given that the road is prone to rutting after wet weather. Another of the most interesting sites is the small islet of **Ilhéu da Vila** just off Vila do Porto, which can be viewed from the shore or better still a small boat. Other islets good for birds and observable from land include **Lagoinhas** near Tagerete Bay, part of the North Coast Protected Landscape Area.

**Ponta do Costelo** on the southeastern corner and its designated area of 300ha combines a coastal strip of steep cliffs 200m high with an immediate offshore marine area. As well as birds, this is also a passage point for bottlenose dolphin and loggerhead turtle.

big radio station, and much new housing greatly in need of tree planting to soften it. The old officers' mess was the only hotel on Santa Maria until recently; it burned down a few years ago, but was rebuilt. Now the farmland is down to cattle that are thought by the locals to be better eating than those on the higher pastures, and Romney Marsh sheep, farmed for wool, and originally imported from England. If you leave the airport road and take the minor road to Santana you pass through this utterly different countryside; in the height of summer when all is brown and the sun blazes down it can seem quite hostile, but from October/November to May it is green. From Santana the road continues and joins the main road down to Anjos, but before it does you pass through an area of acacia forest which shows a splendid example of wind pruning.

**SÃO PEDRO** This small village near Vila do Porto is noted for its *mata-mouras*, literally 'moor killers'. These are pits in the ground once used to hide grain and other desirables from pillaging pirates.

**ANJOS** Once a tiny fishing village, Anjos then became a centre for tuna; now the factory is closed. The little bay has recently been very nicely developed for swimming. The island of São Miguel, 52 nautical miles away, can sometimes be seen on the horizon. On the roadside above is a picnic site with barbecue facilities.

The village is historically very significant as the first landfall of Christopher Columbus on his return from the Americas. A modern statue commemorates the quincentenary of this event (1493–1993). The **Chapel of Nossa Senhora dos Anjos** is possibly the first place of worship built in the Azores, being 15th century and rebuilt in the 17th century and again restored at the end of the 20th century. The small chapel has a triptych (recently restored) representing the Holy Family, St Cosmas and St Damian which, according to tradition, is from Gonçalo Velho's caravel. The iron rod displayed on the pulpit was a weapon used by pirates. On the outside wall is built a porch dedicated to the Holy Ghost; bread is distributed from here on the feast day.

**SANTA BÁRBARA** This is among the prettiest parishes of the island; in July/August the roadsides are flaming with orange-red montbretias and yellow gingers and there are photo opportunities every 200m. There is wonderful silence apart from the occasional crowing of a cockerel.

**SÃO LOURENÇO BAY** On the northeast coast, the bay is well worth visiting for the spectacular descent by road down the cliff face. On the way down, stop at the signposted **Miradouro do Espigão viewpoint** for a splendid bird's-eye view of the bay and its cliffside vineyards. There are swimming facilities and good beaches.

**SANTO ESPÍRITO** A pretty village surrounded by pastures and green hills. The **Church of Nossa Senhora da Purificação** is well worth visiting and must rate among the best kept of all parish churches. Go inside and be welcomed by the scent of wax-polished floors and pews with a gilt chapel reflecting sunshine from the windows. Originally constructed in the 16th century and beautifully restored in 1966, it is 17th-century Baroque with stone ornamentation on the front façade. It is also noted to be the church linked to the first Holy Ghost festivals in the Azores. The **museum** is located behind the church. For handicrafts, the local **Cooperativa da Artesanato de Santa Maria** (⊕ *08.00–16.00 Mon–Sat*) sells delicious bread and *biscoitos* from its own bakery, and from several looms traditional woven items such as tableware. Weaving takes place in the morning, baking in the afternoon; the dexterity of the half-dozen ladies working here is admirable, as they endeavour to keep alive traditional island skills. Find it about 400m into the village from the church, past the games area and almost opposite the school. There is a snack bar in the village.

**MAIA** Nearly all the houses here are holiday homes, and it is said that only a dozen or so people live here permanently, but between June and September the descendants of emigrants return from North America to take their holidays here and the place comes alive. There is a small port from where fishing boats set sail. It is the stone terracing for grapevines that is truly amazing. Walls enclose areas just a few metres square and these reach up the cliffside almost until it becomes vertical. At intervals there are very narrow stairways between the vine enclosures running in straight lines up the cliff face to provide access. In September, the harvest takes place, with the grapes carried down by hand and the wine (and the local 'firewater') made in several small buildings. A book of photographs of the stones of Maia is for sale at the **Santo Espírito Museum**. The wine, purely for local consumption, is *vinho de cheiro*, plus a very pleasant sweet *aperitivo*. There are swimming facilities, but be sure to drive to the very far end of the village to where the road finishes, especially after rainy times, to see the spectacular waterfall. The access path is stubbornly guarded by a resident colony of ducks.

**PICO ALTO** The side road up to the highest point of the island, at 590m, leaves the main road between Almagreira and Santo Espírito where it forks to Santa Bárbara. Here the landscape is utterly different from anywhere else on Santa Maria, as you ascend through dense cryptomeria plantations to arrive at a tiny summit with fine views and where some native plants can be found. There is a memorial to those who were killed when an Italian passenger jet clipped the summit.

**PRAIA FORMOSA** In a wide bay at the foot of steep cliffs is a very clean, pale sandy beach with rock pools at the eastern end, and it is the best-known swimming beach. Commercial development is really quite limited and the road, with parking, runs along behind the beach. Vineyards tumble down the hillside to meet it. There is a small apartment hotel (open only in summer) and a campsite. In the nearby village there is a restaurant. At the western end are the remains of the 16th–17th-century **Fort of São João Baptista**, which the sea has almost demolished. In summer the cliffs here, normally dark with pittosporum and myrica trees, are marked with 4m-tall yellow flower spikes of agave.

# Part Three

## CENTRAL GROUP

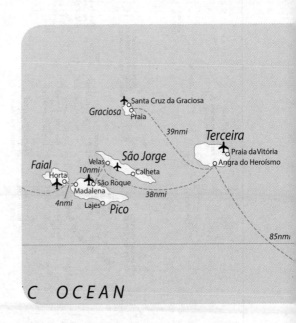

Graciosa — Santa Cruz da Graciosa
Praia
39nmi
Terceira
Praia da Vitória
Angra do Heroísmo
Faial — São Jorge
Velas
10nmi
Calheta
Horta
São Roque
Madalena
38nmi
4nmi
Lajes
Pico
85nmi

C  OCEAN

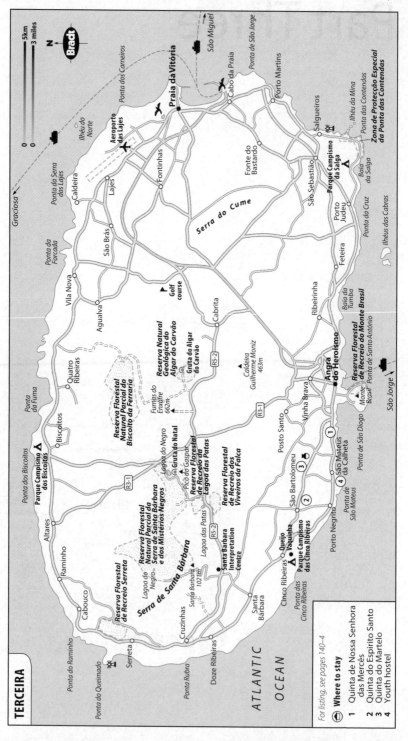

**TERCEIRA**

0 5km
0 3 miles

N

Bradt

*Graciosa*

*São Miguel*

*São Jorge*

**ATLANTIC OCEAN**

Ponta do Raminho
Ponta do Queimado
Serreta
Ponta Rubra
Ponta dos Biscoitos
Ponta da Fuma
Ponta da Forcada
Ponta da Serra das Lajes
Ponta dos Carneiros

Ilhéu do Norte

**Praia da Vitória**

**Aeroporto das Lajes**

Caldeira
Lajes
São Brás
Fontinhas
Ponta da Praia
Cabo da Praia
Ponta de São Jorge
Porto Martins

Vila Nova
Aguilva
Quatro Ribeiras
Biscoitos
**Parque Campismo dos Biscoitos**
Altares
Raminho
Cabouco

Ponta do Queimado
Cruzinhas
Doze Ribeiras
Santa Bárbara
Cinco Ribeiras
Ponta das Cinco Ribeiras
Ponta de São Mateus

*Reserva Florestal de Recreio Serreta*

*Reserva Florestal Natural Parcial da Serra de Santa Bárbara e dos Mistérios Negros*

Lagoa do Negro
Lagoa das Patas

Santa Bárbara ▲ 1021m

**Santa Bárbara Interpretation Centre**

Lagoa do Negro
Pico do Gaspar ▲
**Gruta do Natal**

*Reserva Florestal Natural Parcial do Biscoito da Ferraria*

Funhos do Enxadire 662m

*Reserva Florestal de Recreio da Lagoa das Patas*

*Reserva Florestal de Recreio dos Viveiros da Falca*

**Queijo Vaquinha**
**Parque Campismo das Cinco Ribeiras**

São Bartolomeu
Porto Negrito
**São Mateus da Calheta**

Posto Santo
Vinha Brava

**Angra do Heroísmo**
*Reserva Florestal de Recreio do Monte Brasil*
Monte Brasil
Ponta de Santo António

Ponta de São Diogo
Ponta de Santo Brasil

*São Jorge*

R3-1
R3-1
R5-2
R5-2

*Reserva Natural Geológica do Algar do Carvão*
**Gruta do Algar do Carvão**

Golf course ▲

Cabrita
Caldeira Guilherme Moniz 463m ▲

Serra do Cume

Fonte do Bastardo

São Sebastião
Salgueiros

Ilhéu da Mina
**Zona de Protecção Especial da Ponta das Contendas**

**Parque Campismo da Salga**
Baía do Salga

Porto Judeu
Feteira
Ribeirinha
Baía da Tumba

Ponta do Cruz
Ilhéus das Cabras

For listing, see pages 140–4

**Where to stay**

1. Quinta de Nossa Senhora das Mercês
2. Quinta do Espírito Santo
3. Quinta do Martelo
4. Youth hostel

136

# 5

# Terceira

Terceira is perhaps best known for two things: the international airport and American airbase at Lajes and the historic UNESCO World Heritage Site of Angra do Heroísmo. This is unfair because, like all the other islands, there is much else waiting to be discovered for those not in a hurry. As your plane comes in to land at the wide airport, you will be struck by the endless walled-off pastures that decorate the landscape as it gently rises towards the island's centre. Beyond, there are lovely villages, really wild country in the centre, volcanic caverns, vineyards, comfortable places to stay, some good restaurants to be sought out, an increasing number of land- and sea-based activities and even a golf course. It is an ideal island on which to hire a car and explore at your own speed: big enough to occupy you, but small enough to let you get to know it in just a few days.

It is easy to spend a whole day seeing the historic buildings of Angra do Heroísmo together with the fort and maybe take a walk around the whole of Monte Brasil. The drive along the beautiful west coast looking in at villages and charming museums is another joy and, if you choose to linger, a whole day can disappear in pleasant fashion. The island's rugged centre is a must, too; more or less in the middle of the island is the region known as Terra Brava, the Wild Land, and aptly named because of the bewilderingly broken country and, in places, dense vegetation. The island's highest point is Santa Bárbara (1,021m) in the west, and almost every day the summit is hidden in cloud. Its upper 300m is covered with typical scrub vegetation of juniper, erica, ling and bramble. On the northwest side of Santa Bárbara is the Serreta Forest, a mix of planted cryptomeria and eucalyptus and large patches of remnant native vegetation with endemic Azorean species. It is a good area for birds, as is the Lagoa Negra a little to the east. Praia da Vitória is another town to explore, smaller and very different, and if there is time, do seek out the view from the top of the Serra do Cume across the whole of the eastern part of the island. Between May and September some 220 Azorean bullfights will take place on the island, as well as bull-runnings in the streets, so there is a fair chance you will experience one or the other or both – remember, the bull is not killed or even wounded. It is the young men who run the risk of damage, but as the giant bull sculpture at the east of Angra evidences, Terceira has a very deep bull-related tradition to maintain. Generally known as the 'Purple Island', some other Azoreans prefer the slightly derogatory nickname 'Party Island'.

## BACKGROUND

**GEOLOGY** The oldest part of Terceira, composed of basalts from the last million years, is below sea level, plunging down more than 1,500m deep to the seabed; it comprises 90% of the island. The remaining tenth is much younger. Like São Miguel, Terceira is made from four volcanoes, the oldest being Cinco Picos which covers much of the southeast, a stratovolcano that was once a steep-sided cone made of layers of lava.

Its collapsed caldera is the largest in the Azores, about 7km across, and was formed some 300,000 years ago but it is now considerably eroded. The Serra do Cume in the northeast is the largest remnant, and the Serra da Ribeirinha is all that is left of the opposite rim, and between the two is the largest flat area in the whole of the Azores, disturbed only by five younger cinder cones in the crater bottom, the 'Cinco Picos'.

Behind Angra do Heroísmo is Guilherme Moniz volcano, another stratovolcano with a collapsed caldera. The crater's southern edge forms the Serra do Morião crescent which is still obvious and forms the hills seen looking north from Angra. In contrast, the north side of the crater has been completely destroyed by eruptions of the neighbouring Pico Alto volcano, whose lava flowed into the Guilherme Moniz crater, a rare occurrence of lava forming the floor of another volcano. The vertical cave called Algar do Carvão was formed around the same time, about 2,000 years ago. Pico Alto was also responsible for the grey, acidic rock and the more than 60 domes seen to its north behind Quatro Ribeiras and Lajes. Domes form when lava is very viscous and does not easily flow, and so accumulates in the vent.

Around 23,000 years ago, present-day Angra was covered by a Plinian eruption, a powerful explosion of gas, steam, ash and pumice followed by avalanches of hot gas, ash and rock debris. Associated with this were two later Surtseyan volcanoes, when seawater entered the vent to mix with the rising magma and the resulting steam caused the magma to shatter into fine fragments. These two formed Monte Brasil, creating the historically significant bay and associated anchorage and, just to the east, off the coast opposite Feteira village, the now much-eroded Ilhéus das Cabras.

In the west is the Santa Bárbara stratovolcano, about 12km in diameter at sea level, with a caldera that collapsed 25,000 years ago and collapsed further forming a smaller caldera inside some 18,000 years ago. This volcano's oldest eruptions suggest that there were many lava flows with cinder cones and spatter, cinder-sized lava fragments that are still molten when they hit the ground and therefore flatten, forming 'cowpats'; these can meld together and make steep-sided mounds, mostly less than 10m high. The latest eruptions over the last few thousand years on the flanks of Santa Bárbara are associated with trachyte flows, a pale greyish acidic rock whose molten viscosity can form rugged lava flows and domes, in this case more than 85 of the latter.

Between Santa Bárbara and Pico Alto activity along the Terceira Rift (page 5) created cinder cones and lava flows. Flows from Pico Gordo, located by the main road between Angra and Altares, reached the north coast to form the jagged black reefs of the Ponta dos Biscoitos and, now exploited, the Biscoitos vineyards. Along the same road, by the crossroad to Doze Ribeiras, the cone of Bagacina typifies the cinder cones, and between the two, near Lagoa do Negro, is a spatter cone.

In historical times, two eruptions occurred in 1761. The first created the Mistério Negro, near Pico do Gaspar, and the second, a few days later, a collection of cinder cones including Pico do Fogo, just to the east of Lagoa do Negro. The main Angra–Altares road runs conveniently between the two. In 1998, there was a submarine eruption 10km west of Terceira in a small area known as the 'Serreta High'. Surface signs were plumes of smoke coming from floating lava debris as it cooled. The basalt magma is rich in gases that are trapped inside, creating 'balloons' which float upwards towards the ocean's surface. As they rise the gases inside expand and cause the 'balloons' to explode. The debris floats on the surface for about 15 minutes and sinks when seawater enters as it cools. When great volumes of gas rise to the surface the sea becomes pale green, and it is very dangerous for boats, since they could easily sink. This surface evidence is not continuous, and its absence reflects quieter periods of submarine activity. The earliest eruptions detected were at 400m below sea level, and the magma has subsequently risen to 180m.

**HISTORY** Originally known as the Island of Jesus Christ, the island was later named Terceira or Third Island as it was the third island to be 'discovered'; it is also the third in size. The first settlers in about 1460 were led by a Fleming, Jácome de Bruges, with the first settlements around Porto Judeu and Praia da Vitória. Like the other islands, farming became of paramount importance with cereals and woad the prime crops. For centuries it was the most important island because of its sheltered harbour, protected by Monte Brasil. In 1534, Angra was the first settlement in all the Azores to be formally designated a town and in the same year Pope Paul III made it the seat of the bishopric. Terceira was a stronghold of resistance to the Spanish authorities when they annexed Portugal in 1580, holding out for the Portuguese claimant, Dom Antonio, who was being helped by the French. It was the last Portuguese territory to submit to Spanish rule, when the Spaniards defeated the French fleet at Terceira in 1582, overrunning the island the following year and inflicting a terrible retribution. As a consequence of the later 16th- and 17th-century Spanish exploitation of the New World, the island's harbour became even more important. Ships bringing back gold and silver at this time assembled off Terceira to form a convoy for escort to Cadiz, to reduce the danger of attack by pirates from the north African coast. Later in the 17th century, this practice ceased and the island's economy plummeted, followed by emigration to Brazil. After Portuguese liberation in 1640, the islands became a staging post for British trading ships, until the opening of the Suez Canal in 1863. Oranges also came to the rescue and their export led to renewed prosperity, but as in the other islands their demise led once more to further emigration.

Along with São Miguel, Terceira played an important role in the struggle of the Liberals and Absolutists; at one time Terceira was the only Liberal stronghold in all of Portugal. In 1829, the Absolutists attempted to land at what was then called Vila da Praia and their defeat by the locals was marked by the new name of Praia da Vitória. In 1832, it was from Terceira and São Miguel that the Liberal forces from the Azores left for northern Portugal in their fight against the Absolutists. In 1766, the government of the Azores had been unified and based in Angra, which remained the capital of the whole archipelago when the islands were divided into three districts. For a short time that year it was also the capital of Portugal when King Pedro IV was in residence – commemorated by the change of name to Angra do Heroísmo.

Lajes airport was constructed by the British RAF and local labour in 1943, for the Battle of the Atlantic and as a transit point for airborne troops flying to Europe, and today contributes, albeit with increasingly lesser importance, to NATO's strategic role. It has three runways, the largest 3,600m long, and is used by both civil and military aircraft.

On New Year's Day 1980, a severe earthquake inflicted substantial damage, affecting also Graciosa and São Jorge. Many of the important buildings in Angra do Heroísmo were badly damaged and have taken years to painstakingly restore. In 1983, Angra was declared a UNESCO Historic World Heritage Site.

## GETTING THERE AND AWAY

For travel to Terceira, see *Getting there and away*, pages 42–4, and *Getting around*, pages 48–9. Terceira's airport has a tourist information office (🕑 *09.00–21.00 daily*), plus half-a-dozen car-hire desks, ATMs and the ubiquitous free Wi-Fi. If you have time to kill, the souvenir shop often shows footage of the bull-runnings which take place at the island's major festivals. From Angra, a taxi will cost around €20, much less to Praia.

**Azores Airlines** [150 C2] Rua da Esperança 2, Angra; ☏ 295 212 016; ⊕ 09.00–18.00 Mon–Fri

**TAP Air Portugal** [150 C2] Rua da Sé 144, Angra; ☏ 295 206 460; ⊕ 09.00–17.00 Mon–Fri

# GETTING AROUND

If you are without a car, and especially if you are making a short visit, then Angra has the most accommodation and dining options and is probably the best place to base yourself. If you wish to be nearer the airport, then Praia da Vitória is the sensible alternative, with Angra then becoming a day trip by bus or taxi. Out of season, however, Praia is very quiet and Angra has more restaurant choices. There is a regular bus service on weekdays (first bus 06.15, then on the hour until 19.00) from the Praça Velha in Angra to Praia da Vitória, which takes less than an hour and is a pretty journey around the southeast corner of the island. The bus stops in Praia opposite the fire station; to reach the town centre, walk back in the direction from which the bus came and you soon come to a big junction; turn left and you are on the Rua de Jesus, whose undulating cobbles lead you to the main square. The return bus is from the same stop, leaving on the hour, between 06.00 and 19.00. Charles Darwin, when the *Beagle* put in at Angra for a brief visit on the journey home in September 1836, also made the excursion to Praia, but on horseback.

There are seven buses daily to and from Biscoitos leaving from in front of Angra's public garden; the route goes round the coast and takes 1½ hours. Note that, for all island buses, service is reduced on Saturdays and even more so on Sundays. The tourist office has the full timetable, though there is an English-language interactive screen on the Praça Velha in Angra, with timetables and fare information. Tickets are bought on the bus and are very reasonable (Angra–Praia is €2.43). To hire a taxi to ferry you around will cost about €18 per hour, but you might negotiate a better deal in low season. It is, however, an island more easily enjoyed if you have your own transport. From the airport down to Angra in your rental car will take you little more than 20 minutes on the smart dual carriageway. Taxis may be picked up at the places marked on the map of Angra [150 D2] or on the main square in Praia.

## ISLAND TOURS

**Comunicair** m 919 052 869; e info@comunicair. pt; www.comunicair.com. Excellent island tours, on bike or by jeep, plus walks, with a deep insight into the island's geology & botanical endemic species. With groups that never exceed 6 people, a worthwhile experience. Walks inc areas not covered by the official trails.

# TOURIST INFORMATION

Angra's office is at Rua Direita 74 (☏ *295 404 810;* ⊕ *09.00–18.00 Mon–Fri, 09.00–16.00 Sat*). Note there are also a number of private information kiosks around the island, earning their living from commissions on tour bookings. In Praia, one such kiosk operates from beside the marina (⊕ *winter 09.00–12.30 & 14.00–18.00 Mon–Fri, 09.00–13.00 Sat; summer 09.00–13.00 & 14.00–18.30 Mon–Sat*).

# WHERE TO STAY

June festival times and some of August can see prices rise on Terceira. The main hotels are in Angra, with a couple of good ones in Praia da Vitória, just five minutes' drive from the airport. The choice in Angra spans the range from the five-star overlooking the marina, through state-owned *pousada* housed in an old fort, to a city-centre hotel conveniently on the main square and a few smaller establishments in and around the centre. West of Angra town are a couple of resort hotels about 20 minutes' walk or five minutes' drive along a busy main road. Praia's options are modern, medium-sized hotels on the seafront.

As elsewhere in the Azores, **camping** is very cheap and you will pay very few euros to stay. For anyone planning to camp, a telephone call in advance is advisable. Some sites can get full at festival times.

## ANGRA DO HEROÍSMO AND AROUND

**Angra Marina Hotel** [150 D3] (130 rooms) Rua Pero Barcelos, Angra; 295 204 700; e angramarinahotel@gruposolpuro.com; www. angramarinahotel.com. The Azores' first ever 5-star hotel overlooks the marina; all rooms have a sea view & are large with satellite TV & free Wi-Fi. Indoor pool, full spa. Discos across the marina pump out noise till late on summer weekends, which can be intrusive. €€€€€€

**Angra Garden Hotel** [150 C2] (120 rooms) Praça Velha, Angra; 295 206 600; e geral@ angrahotel.com; www.angrahotel.com. On the main square, with restaurant, bar, lounge, health club, sauna, small indoor pool, gym, private parking. Free Wi-Fi & satellite TV. Perfectly sited for the exploration of Angra. Rooms to the rear are quiet, overlooking one of the best public gardens in the Azores. €€€€€

**Hotel Terceira Mar** [150 A2] (139 rooms) Portões de São Pedro, São Pedro; 295 402 280; e terceiramarhotel@bensaude.pt; www.bensaude. pt. West of town, 20mins' walk to the centre of Angra. Restaurant, bar, gymnasium, & splendid outdoor pool next to the sea, tennis courts, jacuzzi, Turkish bath, sauna, massage, hairdressers. Very comfortable. €€€€€

**Pousada de Angra** [150 D3] (28 rooms, 1 suite) Forte de São Sebastião, Angra; e reservas@pousadasaosebastiao@pousadas.pt; www.pousadas.pt. Formerly the Castelo de São Sebastião dating from 1555, it looks foreboding from the exterior but houses decent rooms, many with sea view. Seasonal outdoor pool, terrace restaurant. Satellite TV, free Wi-Fi. €€€€€

**Quinta de Nossa Senhora das Mercês** [map, page 136] (12 rooms, 1 suite, 1 s/c house) Caminho de Baixo, São Mateus da Calheta; 295 642 588; e geral@quintadasmerces.com; www. quintadasmerces.com. Between Angra & São Mateus, this farm goes back to the 16th century; the manor house & chapel are 17th century. Set

between sea & woodland it has spacious common rooms, b/fast & dining room, library, games room & an inner courtyard. Outdoor pool & tennis court, Turkish bath, jacuzzi, gymnasium & woodland walks. Also a s/c house with 2 bedrooms, kitchen & living room. Free Wi-Fi. Dinner available on request (24hrs' notice). B/fast inc. Stately manor house, a little quirky. €€€€€

**Hotel do Caracol** [150 A2] (100 rooms) Estrada Regional, Silveira; 295 402 601; e dap.reservas@hoteldocaracol.com; www. hoteldocaracol.com. About 30mins' walk from central Angra, with views across the bay to Monte Brasil, a resort hotel with restaurant & bars, leisure facilities inc spa, massage, therapy treatments, sauna, jacuzzi, gym, adults & children's outdoor pools, indoor heated pool. Free Wi-Fi. Sea bathing possible with access by ladder. €€€€

**Quinta do Martelo** [map, page 136] (10 rooms) Canada do Martelo, Cantinho, São Mateus da Calheta, just west of Angra; 295 642 842; e quintamartelo@mail.telepac.pt; www.acores. com/quintadomartelo. 'I don't want to be best, I want to be different,' says Gilberto, the owner. In this he succeeds. Once an orange farm, this *quinta* (estate) is set up as a series of workshops inc blacksmith/farrier, tinsmith, carpenter, & even a barber's shop – a private museum. Full of artefacts, Gilberto's 'project' is to give guests a feel for the atmosphere of an old rural house on Terceira, while providing comfortable s/c accommodation. Less traditional are the swimming pool, tennis court, gymnasium & sauna, but they do have traditional Azorean games. Luxury? No, but utterly different. Each room has a bathroom, there's AC/heating, TV & Wi-Fi. All are differently furnished. B/fast inc. Rates can inc car hire, specify when booking. €€€€

**Hotel Beira Mar** [150 C3] (23 rooms) Largo Miguel Corte Real, Angra; 295 215 188; e reservas@hotelbeiramar.com; www. hotelbeiramar.com. Good restaurant. A slightly old-fashioned feel to this waterfront hotel. Located by the marina, with a bit of noise in summer & at festival times. Pleasant, not luxury, but very central. Free Wi-Fi, satellite TV. €€€

🏠 **Quinta do Espirito Santo** [map, page 136] (4 rooms) Rua Dr Teotónio Machado Pires 36, west of Angra; ✆ 295 332 373; m 962 922 938; e geral@verdes-fragmentos.pt; www.quintadoespiritosanto.com. Just 15mins' drive from Angra, a welcoming, rustic *quinta* with charming host & hostess who are full of island information. Set in 3 acres, ecologically focused, with excellent b/fast featuring homemade products. €€€

🏠 **Casadangra** [150 C2] (3 rooms) Rua da Miragaia 9, Angra; ✆ 295 628 038; e casadangra@gmail.com; www.casadangra.wix.com/angra-bnb. Excellent renovated house, a peaceful place offering modern rooms with private bath, free Wi-Fi, communal kitchen with tea, coffee, etc, TV lounge area, roof terrace. Pleasant hostess, who has 3 friendly cats. A couple of mins' walk uphill from town. Sometimes a 2-night min stay in high season. Good value. €€

🏠 **Casas de Hospedes Isaias** [150 D3] (20 rooms, 10 apts, 1 house) Rua Ciprião de Figueiredo 35, Angra; m 914 397 676/914 246 206; e costaisaias@sapo.pt; www.cometoazores.com. Isaias is a real character, building a little empire with rooms & apts, the latter ultra-modern & suitable for up to 7 guests. Apts are s/c with washing machine, kitchen. Communal roof terrace with sea view, free Wi-Fi, TV. Off-season prices in particular make this a real bargain. Stand still for too long & Isaias will rent you a car, scooter or bicycle, too! Recommended for bargain-seekers. €

**Youth hostel**

🏠 **Pousada de Juventude de Angra do Heroísmo** [map, page 136] (70 beds) Negrito, São Mateus; ✆ 295 642 095; e terceira@pousadasjuvacores.com; www.pousadasjuvacores.com. Dorm beds, also has 1 s/c family room with bathroom, cable TV. About 7km west of Angra, on the seafront. Nearest restaurant is in São Mateus, 10mins'

walk. Swimming nearby, though some complain that it's a bit isolated. Budget option, rates inc b/fast. €

**PRAIA DA VITÓRIA**

🏠 **Hotel Apartamentos Praia Marina** [map, page 157] (31 apts) Av Beira Mar/Largo José S Ribeiro Santa Cruz; ✆ 295 540 055; e reservas@hotelpraiamarina.com; www.hotelpraiamarina.com. Overlooking the beach, very close to the town centre. Allergy-free rooms & apts with fully equipped kitchenettes. Some apts can sleep 4. B/fast inc. €€€€

🏠 **Hotel Atlantida Mar** [map, page 157] (28 rooms & apts) Boavista 11; ✆ 295 545 800; e reservas@atlantidamar.com; www.atlantidamarhotel.com. Only 5 years old, a very modern 4-star with view over the bay. High-quality fittings, outdoor pool (all year, but not heated), sauna, outdoor hot tub (all year), gym. Balconied rooms have AC/satellite TV & free Wi-Fi, good buffet b/fast inc. Also family suites/apts for 4 people. 15mins' walk from the town centre, 10mins from the beach. €€€€

🏠 **Hotel Varandas do Atlântico** [map, page 157] (30 spacious rooms) Rua da Alfândega; ✆ 295 540 050; e reservas.verandas@mail.telepac.pt; www.hotelvarandas.com. In front of the beach, 50m from the main square & the marina, 5mins' drive from the airport. Some rooms balconied, some with connecting rooms for children. AC, cable TV. €€€

**CAMPING**

🏕 **Parque Campismo da Salga** Caminho da Salga, near Porto Judeu; ✆ 295 905 451. Good facilities inc electricity. Sea swimming. Closed in winter. Popular, necessary to book in high summer. €

🏕 **Parque Campismo dos Biscoitos** Caminho de Santo Antonio, Biscoitos; m 963 501 574; ⊕ all year. Good site with amenities, close to natural swimming pool. €

🏕 **Parque de Campismo das Cinco Ribeiros** Canada do Porto, Cinco Ribeiras; m 964 758 051. All-year campsite on grass beneath tamarisk trees. Full amenities, inc laundry. €

✖ **WHERE TO EAT AND DRINK**

Angra in particular has some excellent restaurants in the centre, offering good traditional island fare or more inventive cuisine. *Alcatra* is a tasty, oven-cooked beef dish, done in red wine and a Terceira favourite. Like many other islands, there are excellent desserts and baked items guaranteed to worry your waistline. Some village restaurants are also mentioned under the car tours described later in this chapter.

In general, Praia's restaurants are in keeping with its resort image (or perhaps influenced by the nearby airbase), with burgers, pizzas and even a Mexican on the waterfront: a town crying out for a few more authentic options.

## ANGRA DO HEROÍSMO

**✗ Adega Lusitânia** [150 B2] Rua de São Pedro 63–65; ✆ 295 212 301; Mon–Sat ⊕ noon–15.00 & 19.00–22.00. Churning out traditional dishes for over 50 years, a family business always popular with locals. The soups are good, the *alcatra* (beef stew) sublime & if you have room for dessert, try *careta*, a gooey almond cake. Recommended. *€12*

**✗ Casa do Jardim** [150 D2] Inside the public garden; m 960 342 361; ⊕ Nov–Mar 10.00–17.30 Tue–Fri; Apr–Oct 11.00–19.00 Tue–Sat. An Azorean rarity: vegetarian! Serves up salads, light meals, lentil burgers, soups, etc, in a modern building perched above the beautiful gardens. No alcohol. *€8*

**✗ Pastelaria Pão Quente** [150 C2] Rua da Se 186; ⊕ 07.00–21.30. A good place for the budget-conscious to fill up, with *prato do dia* at €5. You serve yourself & your food gets weighed at the till, so take it easy! *€6*

**✗ Tasca das Tias** [150 C2] Rua de São João 117; ✆ 295 628 062; ⊕ noon–midnight daily. A newcomer in 2014, adding a bit of finesse to Angra's dining scene. Tuna is an excellent choice here & the side salads are a bit more inventive than the archipelago's norm. Soft music, stylish furnishings & some wonderful portrait photos on the wall. *€12*

**⌨ Made in Azores Café** [150 B2] Rua de São Pedro 12; ⊕ 07.00–20.00 Mon–Thu, 07.00–02.00 Fri & Sat. Daytimes, a pleasant café serving well-priced snacks & Azorean tapas, plus excellent coffee. Nearly everything ('except the whisky & beer') is indeed made in the archipelago. Good coffee, local products for sale, & on Fri, live music – starting around 22.00 – which could be anything from *bossa nova* to pop covers. *€8*

## PRAIA DA VITÓRIA

**✗ La Barca** [map, page 157] Av Marginal; ✆ 295 542 808; www.restaurante-labarca.com; ⊕ noon–15.00 & 17.00–23.00 Tue–Thu, noon–15.00 & 17.00–midnight Fri, noon–midnight Sat, noon–23.00 Sun. Just south of the Atlantida Mar hotel, a well-established pizza & pasta place, though daily specials are also offered.

Bright & light, with sea views, service is warm & welcoming. *€10*

**✗ Restaurante O Pescador** [map, page 157] Rua Constantino Jose Cardoso 1; ✆ 295 413 495. Reliable option, with 2 dining rooms serving traditional fish & meat dishes. If you can't decide from the menu which fish, they'll let you meet it before you eat it. *€13*

**✗ R3** [map, page 157] Boa Vista 40, opposite the Atlantida Mar; ✆ 295 513 879; ⊕ 10.00–16.30 & 18.00–22.00 Wed–Mon. An unusual name, in an unusual, space-age building, & for Terceira, an unusual restaurant. Actually, 3 restaurants: bistro, gourmet & salads. You'll pay a few euros more than elsewhere, but if you want to find some innovative culinary touches, start here. For example, octopus served with pear & bacon in a port wine reduction, or steaks with a choice of sauces. At lunchtimes, a selection of main-course salads. *€16*

## SÃO MATEUS

**✗ Beira Mar** Rua do Porto; ✆ 295 642 392; ⊕ noon–15.00 & 18.30–22.00 Tue–Sun. Take a turn-off the main coast road towards the São Mateus fishing port to find this gem. Often full of tourists, the sparklingly fresh fish is the reason; don't expect fancy sauces or sophisticated garnish. The fish is the claim to fame, landed in the harbour a few steps away & the cooking here is a reference point for the island. Meat dishes, too. Book in advance. *€12*

**✗ Quinta do Martelo** (page 141); ✆ 295 642 842; ⊕ noon–15.00 & 18.30–22.00 Thu–Tue. Good Azorean food in a typical farmhouse setting; reservations advisable. A bit pricey, but a splendid ambience, providing traditional & festive meals cooked on wood-burning stoves with home-baked bread. *€15*

## SERRETA

**✗ Ti Choa** Grota de Margarida 1; ✆ 295 906 673; ⊕ noon–14.30 & 19.00–21.30 Mon–Sat. On the west coast, look for a small sign on your left as you head north through Serreta. Serving a variety of island favourites, a traditional place with good cuisine & bread baked on the premises. Some rate it as the island's best, it won't disappoint. Occasional live music on Fri. Booking advisable. *€13*

## ALTARES

✕ **Restaurante Caneta** On the main road between Altares & Biscoitos, on the corner of the Canada José Romeira; ✆ 295 989 162; ⊕ noon–15.00 & 18.00–22.00 Tue–Sun. A smart restaurant with a well-deserved reputation, the speciality is the Aberdeen Angus beef. Fish also available. You pay a tiny bit more than elsewhere,

but it's worth the extra. The car park is down the side street. *€13*

## SÃO SEBASTIÃO

✕ **Os Moinhos** Rua Arrebalde, 9700-610 Vila de São Sebastião; ✆ 295 401 580; ⊕ 19.00–23.00 Wed–Mon. Restaurant with terrific ambience in a converted watermill. Charcoal-grilled meat & fish, an excellent *alcatra*, & top-quality desserts inc a chocolate mousse to travel for; finally an extensive wine list, with bottles from €9. In winter, wood-burning fires. Reservations recommended; it can be popular with tour groups. *€13*

# OTHER PRACTICALITIES

**Emergency** ✆ 112
**Police** [150 D2] Praça Dr Sousa Junior, Angra; ✆ 295 212 022
✚ **Hospital** [150 C1] Hospital de Santo Espirito, Canada do Breado, Angra; ✆ 295 403 200.

Large & modern, serves as a centre for other islands, too.
✉ **Post office** [150 C2] Rua Palacio, Angra; ⊕ 08.30–18.30 Mon–Fri

# WHAT TO SEE AND DO

## MUSEUMS
### Angra do Heroísmo
*Museu de Angra do Heroísmo* [150 D2] (*Ladeira de São Francisco;* ⊕ *09.30–17.00 Tue–Fri, 14.00–17.00 Sat & Sun; €2/1/free, adult/under 25s/under 14s; wheelchair accessible*) Housed in the old Convent of São Francisco, once the headquarters of the Franciscan Order of the Azores, the building itself is well worth the visit. Furniture and military exhibits, a room full of clocks, as well as an impressive collection of horse-drawn carriages and a useful bilingual chronology of the islands are included in the permanent displays and there are frequently changing exhibitions. The videos showing around the convent are currently only available in Portuguese, but English language information is available at reception (some at extra charge) and some wall panels are also in English.

*Os Montanheiros* [150 C3] (*Sociedade de Exploração Espeleológica, Rua da Rocha 6/8;* ✆ *295 212 992; www.montanheiros.com*) Currently closed for a refit, this geological museum includes topographical models of the islands, photographs and rock specimens. You can see similar exhibits if you visit the caves (page 156).

### Around the island
*Museu do Vinho dos Biscoitos* (*Biscoitos;* ⊕ *1 May–30 Sep 10.00–11.00 & 13.30–17.30; 1 Oct–30 Apr 13.30–16.00 Tue–Sun; closed 3rd week of Sep during the grape harvest; admission free, though a fee may soon be payable*) Good small private museum showing most interesting details of the Brum family business and wine production going back over 100 years. There are small demonstration vineyards, and other fruit orchards, plus a tasting and opportunity to buy.

**Quinta do Martelo** (*Centro Etnográfica e Gastronómico, Canada do Martelo, Cantinho, São Mateus;* \ *295 642 842;* e *quintamartelo@mail.telepac.pt; www. acores.com/quintadomartelo*) This is a private museum and restaurant just west of Angra with an excellent exposition of the traditional way of living. Open only to residents, and diners upon request. Telephone booking essential.

## GARDENS
## The Duque da Terceira Garden (⏲ *winter 08.00–17.30, increasing to midnight closing in high summer*) A charming historical urban space with some interesting plants, located in the centre of Angra (pages 65 and 151).

**BIRDS AND FLOWERS** A mix of bird hides and urban recreation is to be found near the town centre of Praia da Vitória. The coastline here was once the largest coastal wetland in the Azores, but when the town expanded most was destroyed. Now only a small area remains, the Ponds of Praia or Paúl Environmental Park, but they have recently been cleverly improved and are certainly effective as an urban landscape enhanced by habitats for waders, several species of waterbirds, herons, egrets and terns.

The best-known site among dedicated birders is a rather grotty disused quarry at **Cabo da Praia** that supplied the stone for the harbour at close-by Praia da Vitória in the 1980s. If you are visiting for the birds and not the scenery then it is regarded by many as the best place in Europe for spotting western Nearctic and Palearctic waders as well as ducks, egrets and seabirds; it is also an important breeding site of the Kentish plover. However, it is said that it is necessary to visit the quarry at the correct time since tidal times are important to your chances of success. The special thing about this quarry is that it was dug to a depth where the sea seeps through fissures in the rock and enters from underground. The twice-daily sluicing in rhythm with the tide has created a remarkable wetland habitat. Protected from the wind and excellent for waders, species usually seen only in Africa and North America seem to be able to find this quarry so if you visit two to five weeks either side of mid-September and go during the two- to three-hour period either side of low tide you could be rewarded with very interesting sightings. In 2016, notices at the site informed that it was being recovered as a wetland, with the promise of an interpretation centre. To find it, initially follow the signs for Porto Oceanico and park up at the oil tanks when the tarmac runs out. The quarry is 100m past the tanks.

To salve your aesthetic sense drop down to the Special Protected Area of **Ponta das Contendas** and the **Baía das Mós**, the southeast corner of Terceira. Originally there was a 500m-long peninsula created by lava flow and through erosion and chemical change it is now discontinuous, the furthest point being Ilhéu da Mina. Many species of both resident and migratory birds may be seen, but it is botanically uninspiring. Around the **Lagoa do Negro** (page 156), over 150 species (both resident and migratory) have been recorded and botanists will be pleased that this small lake and the surrounding **Mistérios Negros** provide them with rich pickings. West of centre, this remarkable volcanic area has formed a swamp and other special ecosystems rich in mosses and lichens; of special interest are the bog-lovers *Littorella uniflora* and *Isoetes azorica*. However, if birders continue on towards **Pico Alto**, 808m high with a collapsed caldera, woodcock and snipe might make a change from their usual observational menu.

**RECREATIONAL FOREST RESERVES** Monte Brasil, the volcanic peninsula overlooking Angra do Heroísmo (pages 152–3), and Serreta Forest (page 155) are the highlights.

## ACTIVITY TOURS

**Rope Adventures** Clube Naval, Av Beira Mar, Praia da Vitória; m 961 804 496; e ropeadventures@hotmail.com; www. ropeadventures.pt. A variety of activities, inc canyoning, coasteering, sea-kayaking & birdwatching.

## DIVING

✓ **Arraia Divers** m 914 241 939; e info@ arraiadivers.com; www.arraiadivers.com. Based inside the Hotel do Caracol, Angra da Heroísmo (page 141), a PADI 5-star development centre with shore & boat dives all year, subject to weather. Highlights might inc octopus, giant moray eels & eagle rays. Wreck-dives, courses, try-dives & dive packages all available. Open

Water courses from €380, single shore dive €60, equipment inc.
✓ **Octopus Diving Center** Clube Naval, Av Beira Mar, Praia da Vitória; m 965 431 985/912 513 906; e geral@octopusportugal.com; www. octopusportugal.com. PADI courses, shore & boat dives, snorkelling & boat trips. Near the marina in Praia.

## GOLF

✓ **Club de Golf da Ilha Terceira** Fajãs Agualva, Praia da Vitória; 295 902 444/299; e reservas@terceiragolf.com; www.terceiragolf. com; ⊕ Tue–Sun, email for tee-off times; green fees for non-members: 18 holes, inc club & trolley hire, €60. Large clubhouse with restaurant (⊕ Jun–Sep 08.00–19.00 Mon– Fri, 07.30–19.00 Sat, Sun & hols; Oct–May

08.00–17.00 Mon–Fri, 07.30–18.00 Sat, Sun & hols). Located just west of the Angra–Praia road. Small pro shop. Designed by Cameron & Powell & opened in 1954 at 350m above sea level, it is set in another beautiful Azorean landscape of tall trees, lakes, colourful azaleas & hydrangeas. With its wide fairways, reckoned to be the easiest of the 3 Azores courses. 18 holes,

### FESTIVALS ON TERCEIRA

The Holy Ghost Festival held on the eighth Sunday after Easter takes place not only in Praia da Vitória but also all over the island in villages wherever the crown of the Holy Ghost is held, either in church or in a private house. The Vine and Wine Festival in Biscoitos on the first weekend of September marks the grape harvest and also offers traditional foods. There are also many more, smaller celebrations held all over the island for saints' days and secular events. Praia da Vitória has a nine-day gastronomic festival over two weeks in early August.

**Carnaval** all over the island; can happen in Feb or Mar, but always 5 weeks before Easter
**10 Bodos** Praia; May. First event of the Holy Ghost Festival.
**Espírito Santo** different parts of the island; May to Sep
**Touradas á corda** throughout the island; May to end Oct. Endless bull-runnings & bullfights, plus wild revelry.
**São João** all over the island; 24 Jun
**Festa de Sanjoaninas** Angra; Jun. Includes many cultural activities & evening entertainments.
**Festas da Praia** Praia; end Jul/start Aug. Commemorates Praia's designation as a city; food fair with Spanish & Portuguese regions represented, bull-running, concerts & exhibitions. See www.festasdapraia.com.
**Festival Internaçional de Folclore dos Açores** Angra; Aug. Folklore festival with local & international performers, established for over 30 years. See www.cofit.org.
**Angrajazz** 1st or 2nd week in Oct. Jazz festival, with international acts. See www.angrajazz.com.

par 72. Handicap requirements: men 28, ladies 36, though production of handicap certificates not strictly enforced. There is also a driving range & golf lessons are available. Multi-day packages available. See also ad in 3rd colour section.

## SWIMMING   *Map, page 136.*

Around the coast there is a mix of semi-natural rock pools and artificial pools, many with toilets and changing rooms open in summer. The long sand beach at **Praia da Vitória** is popular, as is the smaller one on the other side of the marina. In **Angra** there is a small beach near the marina with facilities, a beach with a long history, for it was used for careening ships.

**Silveira** By the Hotel do Caracol at the western end of Angra, with a public bathing area in the deep inlet protected by Monte Brasil.

**Negrito** With harbour swimming facilities, changing rooms and a small café/bar.

**Ponta das Cinco Ribeiros** Harbour swimming, changing rooms and a small café/bar. Campsite nearby.

**Biscoitos** Natural rock pools amid interesting volcanic rock formations; changing facilities available.

**Baía das Quatro Ribeiras** Natural swimming pool, changing facilities and nearby campsite.

**Porto Martins** Near the harbour. A natural swimming pool, like a conventional pool but with a wave machine! There are changing rooms and a restaurant.

**Salgueiros** Sea swimming with changing facilities.

**Baía de Salga** Near Porto Judeu. Sea swimming with changing facilities. Campsite nearby.

**WALKING** There are now six official trails, with the Monte Brasil walk easily accessible for those staying in Angra, but without a car:

**Mistérios Negros** Difficult, 5km, 2½ hours. A circular walk from the Gruta do Natal cave, beside Lagoa do Negro (page 156). You will see plenty of native plants before you get to a difficult stretch over some 'recent' lava deposits.

**Baías da Agualva** Easy, 4km, 2 hours. With a bit of road walking at the end this can be a circular walk between Agualva and Quatro Ribeiras in the middle of the north coast, offering good birdwatching.

**Serreta–Lagoinha** Medium difficulty, 7km, 2½ hours. A circular walk including the lake of Lagoinha, and plenty of native flora. Care is needed at some steep places.

**Monte Brasil** Easy, 7.5km, 2½ hours. Beginning and ending at the Relvão park, by the Spanish fort.

**Relheiras de São Brás** Easy, 5km, 2 hours. A circular route from the picnic area in São Brás, near Lajes airport, revealing old oxcart tracks, evocative of earlier times.

**Rocha do Chambre** Medium difficulty, 9.3km, 2½ hours. A new, circular walk.

On Terceira, walkers should keep a wary eye open for bulls; these are not typical farm animals, but those raised for the Tourada à Corda. The **Mountaineering Society** offers a guided walk between March and October from 09.30 to around 17.00 on Sundays. Walks are announced a month in advance with details available from the Montanheiros website (*www.montanheiros.com*). There is no charge. You will need to be reasonably fit and with transport to get to the start of the walk. Comunicair (page 140) also offer guided walks, different from the official trails.

## TOURING THE ISLAND

The programmes suggested below take a total of three days, but can certainly be done in less time. Alternatively, you can easily select your own itinerary from the notes. Angra do Heroísmo is a must and will take you a morning. You could then spend the afternoon and early evening on Monte Brasil. Travelling slowly around the west coast to Biscoitos will never fail to delight, passing through small villages and past many houses, their whitewashed exteriors sparkling in the sun, even when the hills of the interior are covered with cloud. Including the museums and a reasonable lunch this will take an easy day. If the skies are clear or the clouds are not too low then a day could be spent exploring the wild hinterland, with many old volcanic cones and extensive areas of broken and tumbled land covered in grasses, mosses or tree heathers. This gives the opportunity to judge which day to do what, according to the weather. Since almost every visitor goes to Angra, the two car tours begin from the city.

**ANGRA DO HEROÍSMO** Given the setting and Renaissance urban planning, it is difficult not to slip back through time to the period when Angra was the centre of the Atlantic universe. Trading and treasure ships gathered and passed through here from both the East Indies and the New World, and the town grew ever more prosperous. It was central, too, to the Azores archipelago until usurped by Ponta Delgada. Ban the cars, change the shop windows, clamber into period costume, and all you need is a pirate ship to come sailing into the bay! Well, perhaps not quite, but it is fun to wander around at night when the streets are empty, and allow the imagination to fly.

The Duke of Cumberland's flotilla of English corsairs sank the Spanish galleon *Nuestra-Señora de Guia* off Terceira in 1589, an example of just one of almost 900 ships recorded lost from various causes in the Azores in the past 500 years. In the Bay of Angra alone there are some 80 shipwrecks, the deepest lying in 60m of water, the oldest from 1543. Angra provided the safest haven but, when storms blew in from the southeast, it became a dangerous dead end and disastrous for those ships too slow or unable to leave in time. It seems there are few doubloons to be found because any treasure was recovered soon after the shipwreck since such losses would severely impact upon the Portuguese and Spanish economies. These wrecks, however, represent the most marvellous sites of marine archaeology, time capsules because of the suddenness of their demise. There is also an 'anchor graveyard' near Angra, created by ships cutting their anchors in a hurry to avoid rough weather.

Although no-one wants to live in a theme park, what a stimulating centre Angra could become for the study and interpretation of a most exciting and vivid period of history. The exploration, exploitation and colonial expansion of new lands and the maritime consequences of politics and war on mainland Europe could become a major visitor site like the new one at Faial's Capelinhos.

**Angra city tour** (*This walk includes a bit of up & down & sections on the cobbled pavements. Suggested time: 1½hrs. At major sights, there are a number of new 'paddle-shaped' panels, giving additional information.*) During summer, several of the buildings are open to visitors and the tourist office has a helpful handout of which and when. They also have a leaflet with pictures, worth picking up before you start your tour. Begin at the centre of the city in the **Praça Velha** [150 D2], the most attractively paved square with a Renaissance influence. At the eastern end and built in the 19th century is the **town hall** [150 D2], which is open to visitors and has one of the largest and finest great halls in the whole of Portugal. Admire the tiled floors, chandeliers and the occasional art exhibition which takes place inside. Leave the square on its southern side by the Rua Direita and almost immediately on your right at numbers 113–119 is the balconied house (no sign) of the **Count of Vilaflor**, later Duke of Terceira, commander of the Liberal armies and leader of the Liberal army at the Battle of Praia in 1829. The visual unity of the long front elevation is satisfying. The house is no longer open to visitors. The Rua Direita is Angra's first main street and leads from the harbour directly to the main square and to the governor's house a little beyond.

At the lower end of the Rua Direita on the left is the dominating 18th-century **Misericórdia church** [150 D3] (*⊕ 09.00–noon & 13.00–17.00 Mon–Fri, 17.00–18.00 Sun (for Mass), closed Sat; donation of €1.50 expected, English-language information provided*). The first hospital in the Azores was built on this site in 1492, supported by the Brotherhood of the Holy Spirit; one of the founders was João Vaz Corte-Real, Governor of Angra, who is thought to have been the first to discover Newfoundland. The present building dates from the 18th century, built by an association of the earlier brotherhood and a charitable institution, the Misericórdia. It was badly damaged in the 1980 earthquake. Down in front of the church, towards the sea, is a stylish new fountain. Further round the harbour wall the small sandy beach was once the site of the shipyards that supported the early trading ships. The new yachting marina just to the east is seen by many as an ugly intrusion and violation of a historical patrimony, but brings activity to the waterfront, especially in summer.

Walk along the front, away from the marina and take one of the sets of modern steps beside the blue-and-white-painted building leading to the upper road. Walk a little bit further west and take the Rua Carreira dos Cavalos, the Way of the Horses, so named because a festival devoted to the horse was held here.

If you are interested in embroidery, before you turn right into this road, go along the Rua da Rocha and find a showroom called **Açorbordadas** (*⊕ 09.00–noon & 13.00–18.00 Mon–Fri, 09.00–noon Sat. May open weekend afternoons in high season*). All the product is made in houses across the island and finished here. After visiting, retrace your steps.

Halfway up Rua Carreira dos Cavalos on the left is the former **Episcopal Palace** [150 C3], now a government building with little remaining of the original dating from 1544. At the far end of the street on the right-hand corner is the **Bettencourt Palace** [150 C3]. Built at the turn of the 18th century, it has a fine portico above which is the Bettencourt family coat of arms. It is now a public library and open to visitors.

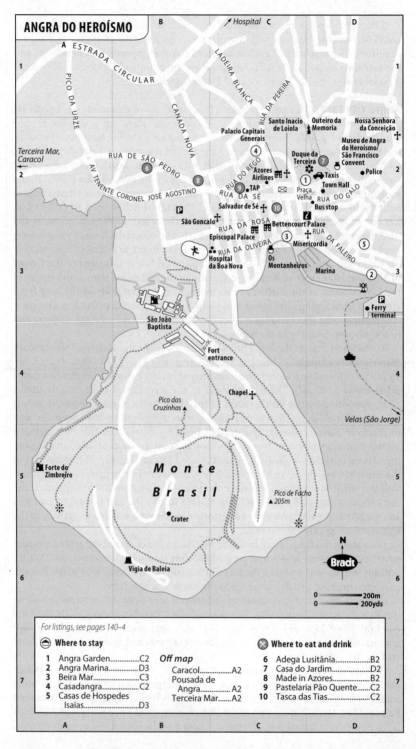

# ANGRA DO HERÓISMO

Hospital

A ESTRADA CIRCULAR

PICO DA URZE

CANADA NOVA

LADEIRA BLANCA

RUA DA PEREIRA

RUA DE SÃO PEDRO

*Terceira Mar,*
*Caracol*

AV TENENTE CORONEL JOSÉ AGOSTINO

Santo Inacio
de Loiola

Palacio Capitais
Generais

④

RUA DO REGO

Azores
Airlines

⑨ TAP

RUA DA SÉ

Salvador de Sé ✝

⑩

Outeiro da
Memoria

Nossa Senhora
da Conceição ✝

Museu de Angra
do Heroísmo/
São Francisco
Convent

Duque da
Terceira ⑦

① Taxis

Town Hall

Police

⑥

⑧

Praça
Velha

RUA DO GALO

Bus stop

ℹ

São Goncalo ✝

RUA DA ROSA

Episcopal Palace

RUA DA OLIVEIRA

Hospital
da Boa Nova

Bettencourt Palace

③ ✝

RUA

Misericordia

RUA DA FALEIRO

⑤

Os
Montanheiros

Marina

②

São João
Baptista

Fort
entrance

P Ferry
terminal

Chapel ✝

*Pico das*
*Cruzinhas* ▲

*Velas (São Jorge)*

Forte do
Zimbreiro

*M o n t e*

*B r a s i l*

*Pico de Facho*
▲205m

● Crater

☼

Vigia de Baleia

N

**Bradt**

0 ————— 200m
0 ————— 200yds

*For listings, see pages 140–4*

### 🛏 Where to stay

| | |
|---|---|
| 1 | Angra Garden...............C2 |
| 2 | Angra Marina...............D3 |
| 3 | Beira Mar...................C3 |
| 4 | Casadangra.................C2 |
| 5 | Casas de Hospedes |
| | Isaias...................D3 |

*Off map*

| | |
|---|---|
| Caracol...................A2 |
| Pousada de |
| Angra.................A2 |
| Terceira Mar.......A2 |

### ✖ Where to eat and drink

| | |
|---|---|
| 6 | Adega Lusitânia...............B2 |
| 7 | Casa do Jardim...............D2 |
| 8 | Made in Azores...............B2 |
| 9 | Pastelaria Pão Quente......C2 |
| 10 | Tasca das Tias.................C2 |

After the Bettencourt Palace go west along the Rua da Rosa and at the end on your right are the walls of the massive **Convent of São Gonçalo** [150 C2] (⏲ *09.00–noon & 14.00–16.30 Mon–Fri, 09.30–noon Sat*), founded in 1545 for the nuns of the Order of St Clare. It is Angra's oldest and the largest in the Azores. The small side door should be unlocked, and it is well worth entering. There are figured choir stalls, 18th-century Portuguese tiles, a 17th-century silver crucifix, paintings and an ornamental ceiling.

After visiting, turn left at the crossroads along the Rua da Boa Nova to quickly find the **Hospital da Boa Nova** [150 C3], a military hospital built by the Spanish for the soldiers stationed in the castle.

Now retrace your steps to the Bettencourt Palace. Across the road from its entrance is the rear of the cathedral church of Angra, **Santíssimo Salvador da Sé** [150 C2] (⏲ *10.00–17.30 Mon–Fri; €2*), founded in 1570. Of interest are the 16th-century painted panels, the Indo-Portuguese-style lectern made in the Azores of Brazilian jacaranda wood and whale ivory, and the altar's early 18th-century silver antependium made on Terceira. The church was finished in 1618 while Angra was under Spanish dominance, and its craftsmanship is influenced by Flemish, local and Spanish Baroque styles. There is also a museum of religious objects.

From the front of the cathedral, continue down the road in the direction of the Praça Velha, taking the first turning left into Rua do Palacio to find the splendid **Palácio dos Capitães Generais** [150 C2]. The original building was a Jesuit college, and the island's governor had it modified during the second half of the 18th century and made into a palace. Two kings have stayed here: King Pedro IV in 1832, and King Carlos I in 1901. The interior is richly decorated and furnished and is open to visitors (⏲ *10.00–13.00 & 14.00–17.30 Mon–Sat; guided tours available in English; €2*).

The entrance is on the Rua do Palacio and after visiting, proceed along the front on the Largo Prior do Prato, passing the church, the **Igreja Santo Inacio de Loiola** [150 C2] with beautiful wooden columns inside, to reach the entrance to a public garden, the **Duque da Terceira Gardens** [150 D2]. Initiated in 1862 as an experimental garden for agricultural development, it 20 years later also provided space for public use, which became a garden that was enlarged in 1888. This garden was developed by a Belgian, Francisco J D Gabriel, who began his early horticultural career in a Liège nursery before coming to the Azores aged 18 to work on São Miguel. He managed the garden for 15 years, until his death in 1897. A wonderful urban period garden of the late 19th century, it was noted in its heyday for its many exotic ornamental species. In February/March the magnolias are at their best and, of course, never get damaged by spring frosts. If you walk through the garden you can climb the steps that take you steeply up to **Outeiro da Memória** [150 D2], the Memorial Hill.

This was the site of the first fort built in the Azores around 1474; the obelisk was erected in 1846 in memory of King Pedro IV. The reward for making the climb is the fine view over Angra and across to Monte Brasil.

Go out of the garden and take the small road off on the right, the Rua do Pisão. Once there was a stream flowing in this area, and early in the town's development this was put into an open conduit and served for some 500 years the industries that sprang up alongside: watermills, tanneries and other enterprises. The narrow winding streets here are fun to explore and at the bottom you come to the **City Museum**, housed in the **Convent of São Francisco** [150 D2]; the entrance is off the Ladeiro de São Francisco, the road running up from the main square beside the public garden. The building alone is well worth seeing, and the museum offers permanent displays about the Azores and temporary exhibits. After, you can simply walk down the hill to the square where this walk began, or go up the hill, the Rua da Guarita, to see the impressive exterior of the 17th-century **Convent of Nossa Senhora da Conceição** [150 D2], built in the 16th century with 17th- and 18th-century alterations. According to the contemporary account by Edward Boid, when in 1832 King Pedro gathered his supporters in Angra prior to his invasion of Portugal, the monasteries were converted to military barracks but officers left the convents untouched: conventual infamy was shocking and the Conceição convent became the most fashionable resort of faithless husbands and amorous celibates, with the nuns in amorous communication through the grated windows and 'the grass was worn away under every window of this convent by the frequency of these communications'.

**MONTE BRASIL** During the Spanish occupation Sir Francis Drake unsuccessfully attacked Angra and eight years later, in 1597, the Earl of Essex with around 100 ships failed to seize a fleet of Spanish treasure galleons anchored in the bay. To defend the harbour against such attacks and at the same time secure control of Angra, King Filipe II constructed the Fort of São Filipe at the foot of Monte Brasil, later given its more familiar name of **São João Baptista** [150 B3]. The exterior wall is 4km long and some 400 artillery pieces defended it. Three other smaller forts along the coast, including that of São Sebastião, provided crossfire so completing the defence. Inside the fortress is the **Igreja de São João Baptista**, commemorating the restoration of Portuguese sovereignty in 1640 and the governor's palace.

If you are in a hurry, then drive or take a taxi up to **Pico das Cruzinhas** [150 B4] to enjoy the view of Angra. You can clearly see the old historical core; look for the last-century pyramid erected on the first fort to be built, then below the governor's palace, the Santissimo Salvador da Sé church, then down to the harbour at the bottom of the Rua Direita to the Misericórdia church. To the right on higher ground is the conspicuous Convent of São Francisco; to the left is the Convent of São Gonçalo, close to the large modern indoor sports complex. Note also the 17th-century Castelo de São Sebastião that once protected the eastern approaches, now a *pousada*. To the left, westwards, is an area known as Caminho de Baixo where the rich people of Angra once had their summer houses. Behind you on the grass mounds are British gun emplacements from World War II. The tall stone cross and the surrounding wall again incorporating the Cross is a typical monument that the Portuguese built wherever they landed and claimed new lands; this one was erected in 1946 commemorating the five centuries of settlement in the Azores.

Here you can spend a very enjoyable full day exploring this old volcanic hill on foot, walking easily from the centre of Angra, or from Pico das Cruzinhas. You can also incorporate a free guided visit of the Fort of São João Baptista, starting daily on the hour throughout the year. (In truth, there's not a lot to see inside, and your guide may be one of the soldiers, who may not speak a word of English. Still, he will take you round, duly unlocking the main entrance to the fort and letting you in to the church. Just ask the guard on duty, and if you're in a car, you can park inside beyond the barrier. The fort has been home to troops for over 500 years.)

Following the surfaced road, these are some of the walks you can do. The first signposted side road will take you to the little chapel of **St Antonio** [150 C4] at the end of the asphalt road. From here to the end of the unsurfaced track it takes about 45 minutes to walk there and back; you will have good views of Angra and views eastwards of the south coast. Alternatively, from near the chapel, you can take the signposted trail as described in the Tourism Authority's trails booklet.

Return to the main road and continue until you reach the rim of the caldera. The caldera itself is used by the military and you are not allowed to go down. Look for the signpost to the **Vigia da Baleia** [150 B6]; it takes about an hour to walk there and back. It is a good walk often in the shade of trees, and the reward is a commanding view seaward; if you have binoculars and the time, try your hand at whale watching. You can also walk in the other direction up to **Pico do Zimbreiro** [150 A5], Juniper Peak, on the west side of the caldera. The junipers have long gone, but endemic laurel and heather remain.

When you return to the main road continue round the caldera until you come to another large track on your right. There is a children's play area, picnic tables and a lavatory. From here it is another very pleasant walk up to **Pico do Facho** [150 C5], Signal Peak, the highest point of Monte Brasil at 205m. For four centuries it was a semaphore station; the lookout used large and small flags to signal the number of vessels approaching and from which direction.

## THE WEST-COAST TOUR: ANGRA DO HEROÍSMO TO BISCOITOS

**São Mateus**  Just two miles west of Angra is this pretty village and harbour, one of the most important fishing harbours in the Azores. Between 16.00 and 17.00 the boats land their catches to sell on the quayside. The colourful little vessels create a cheerful scene and there is a small fort overlooking the harbour. Take time, too, to explore the nearby backstreets. There are two good fish restaurants and also a boat shed, open daily, with a few of the whaleboats, some great old photos and usually with a few octogenarian ex-whalers hanging around; if you speak Portuguese, or can find an interpreter, they are willing to share some tales of derring-do. Nearby, their wives run a handicraft co-operative.

**Porto Negrito**  This is a small village with an old fort by the harbour, with swimming facilities and a small café/bar. An old small trying area has been preserved where in basalt are the fireplaces and pots for reducing the whale blubber. On the nearby headland is Terceira's youth hostel. As you continue, you should be able to see São Jorge on the horizon.

**Cinco Ribeiras**  Soon on the right-hand side of the main road you will reach the small ceramics studio of Aurelia Rocha, Azulart (*Estrada Dr Marcelino Moules 78;* m 967 529 099; ⊕ *10.30–18.00 Tue–Sun*). Her pots are all wheel-thrown and in stoneware are traditional Terceiran designs, and in earthenware traditional shapes and designs of the Azores. All are hand painted, and commissions are accepted. Reflecting the enterprise needed for life on an island in mid-Atlantic, she has built her own kilns. Ceramics in the early days on Terceira used clay imported from England, shipped over in the empty sailing boats coming for the orange crop, and clay is still imported from the continent as the island clay from Santa Maria does not take glazing and can be used only for *alcatra* pots and similar that do not need a glaze.

Further on, on the left, take the **Canada do Pilar**, a narrow road between houses going down to the coast, to reach the **Queijo Vaquinha** cheese factory (⊕ *08.00– 22.00 daily*), which makes the *vaquinha* cheese. You can sample and buy the three cheeses made and enjoy a coffee and a cake. *Queijo vaquinha* is the traditional cheese, made with salt only on the outside and sold in small blocks like butter. *O Ilha* cheese, the cheese of the island, has the salt incorporated into the milk, and the spicy *queijo vaquinha picante* has red peppers added. The dairy does not make any butter, so all the milk, not separates, goes into the cheese. Cheese was first made on Terceira in 1912, and *vaquinha* translates as 'small cow'.

At the end of the road you get to **Ponta das Cinco Ribeiras**, a harbour with swimming facilities, also the remains of a small fort that the sea has almost washed away. Close by is a camping site under trees with electricity and amenities.

Rather than return to the main road, you can continue parallel with the sea following always the asphalt road. It is a very pretty drive through a landscape of stone-walled fields and pastures, and eventually you will come to Pézinho da Senhora, a recently developed parking area with picnic tables and barbecue facilities, and an old-style oven for people to use who no longer have them in their modern houses. There is also a bullring, and the red-painted boards with white circles are the only means of defence from the bull! The arena is also used for music and folklore events.

From the picnic area take the road going inland and the left fork to quickly come to a little chapel with white tiles, with an adjacent large house on the Largo Nossa Senhora da Ajuda. There were no springs in this area, so water was at a premium. To the left of the large house is a small cistern; you will see steps going up to a small door. Look inside and you can see where a bucket can be lowered into the water, stored from rainfall falling onto the roof. The name Pézinho da Senhora comes from a rock in the river that has the imprint of a girl's foot; follow the steps down on the right of the chapel and you will see a small grotto, where the *senhora* is supposed to have appeared. The large house next to the church, originally a small priest's house but later enlarged, was for pilgrims to stay visiting these miraculous places, an equivalent to a *Romeiro* house on São Miguel.

Continue on the asphalt road to come into Santa Bárbara. If you missed all this, you can pick it up turning from the main road signposted to Largo Nossa Senhora da Ajuda, opposite the Mercado Bárbarense.

## Santa Bárbara
As you continue around the coast you come to the farming community of Santa Bárbara, with its white-painted houses so startlingly bright in the sunshine. The Spanish colonial influence in the architecture of the parish church suggests the 16th century. Inside there is a 17th-century organ from the Convent of Nossa Senhora da Conceição in Angra and the furniture in the vestry is made from jacaranda and other tropical hardwoods. You can find beautiful New-World woods used in often unexpected places, brought to the Azores as ballast. Near the church is a café and a 19th-century *império*.

## Doze Ribeiras
Some 200m before the church on the right-hand side of the road look out for the oldest house; there is no sign. In front of the stone building is a large tank for rainwater with a half-dome catchment roof; on the roof there is a washing tub and pots used for bread making. There is an oxcart, a windmill that would have ground *burra de milho* or donkey corn, used for feeding farm animals; note the sheets of zinc on the corn store to keep the rats away. In summer there are folk-dance performances. Nearly all the adjacent small houses were built with the help of the Portuguese military for the elderly unable to afford to rebuild after the disastrous earthquake in 1980. Houses are painted annually for the Holy Ghost or summer festivities.

## Serra de Santa Bárbara
Beyond Doze Ribeiras take the right-hand R5-2 turning inland, eastward, to the impressive volcanic area behind Santa Bárbara. On this trip, be sure to stop at the **Santa Barbara Interpretation Centre** (⌒ 295 403 800; ☉ 16 Sep–14 Jun 09.30–12.30 Tue–Sat; 15 Jun–15 Sep 10.00–18.00 daily), which is small, new and with excellent bilingual information on the geology of this

area, the most extensive natural park in the Azorean archipelago. If it's quiet, you may even get a free herbal infusion from the English-speaking staff. Look on the left-hand side of the road for a signpost to Serra de Santa Bárbara; take this side road (5km) to go to the top of the mountain where, if the weather is clear, you may see the most beautiful views of Terceira island. Note that beyond the radio masts, the caldera is a restricted area and only a few tour companies have permission to enter down into it. Stand at the top, admiring the views and the forest of juniper that lies before you. Return to the main road and turn right to rejoin the main road running along the coast.

**Serreta** This is a small village with its important Church of Our Mother of Miracles where promises are made by people from all over the island. Beyond the village you will come to a sign to a *farol* or lighthouse which makes a nice walk, or you can continue to Raminho and take the trail back to the lighthouse. It was off this stretch of coast that the undersea Serreta volcano was recently active, and the volcanic bombs could be seen coming to the surface. Roughly midway between Serreta and Rominha lies the much-visited Serreta Forest Recreational Reserve; of some 15ha, it provides numerous trails to picnic areas. The *Chafariz da Pomba* or Dove fountain is the focus for the feast of Nossa Senhora da Serreta from 13 to 18 September, peaking on *Serreta Monday* with afternoon bullfights. The village is home to a very good restaurant (pages 143–4).

**Raminho** The signposted Miradouro do Raminho is a substantial viewpoint looking along the coast and is a good place for seabirds, with toilets, parking and picnic tables beneath the trees. There is also a *vigia* (a simple lookout shelter) for spying whales. In the distance on a clear day you can see São Jorge and Graciosa.

**Altares** The local **ethnographic museum** (⊕ *14.00–17.00 Tue–Sun; admission free*) is right next to the blue-and-white church. This is a small village with a good restaurant, the Restaurante Caneta (page 144). You will see a hill on the coast called Pico de Altares (signposted Pico Matias Simão) with a monument at its summit. This was once a *vigia*. If you have time, climb to the top (153m) for the view along the coast.

**Biscoitos** This area was always intriguing because of its volcanic origins and black lava; *biscoito* means 'biscuit'. This came from the last eruption in 1761, when lava flowed down from the area around Pico do Gaspar. It was also known for its Verdelho wines, and is again becoming recognised in the Azores for its wine production and wine museum. Francisco Maria Brum (1860–1928) first began making wine over 100 years ago and was the first to graft grapes after the disastrous Phylloxera outbreak that decimated the vines. The years between 1910 and 1960 saw the maximum production. The family make white wines including a special small production of only 500 litres. However, by the time it is put into bottles only 400 litres are left, so it goes into half bottles to provide 800 for sale! The museum is signposted off the main coastal road in Biscoitos village.

From the west end of the village, you can follow signs for '*Zona Balnear/Porto da Pesca*' to reach the sea and find natural rock pools for swimming, with changing facilities, toilets and a small café. Turning east to continue parallel with the sea, you can then view the remains of defensive structures used in World War II, then the vineyards, tiny walled enclosures called *curraletas* where the vines grow horizontally. The houses here, built from black volcanic rock with white 'trim', are strangely attractive. This one-way road will bring you back on to the main coastal road again. If you take the inland road back to Angra, in July and August this road is made spectacular with all the flowering hydrangeas.

**THE WILD HINTERLAND TOUR, WITH PRAIA DA VITÓRIA** Setting out from Angra, take the R3-1 road heading across the interior of the island for Biscoitos. At the crossroads near Pico do Gaspar turn left to take the R5-2 leading to Doze Ribeiras; this road is called the Estrela dos Ribeiros. Continue until the road off to your left, signposted to São Bartolomeu; take this to reach a forestry park with picnic tables beside a lovely clear and sparkling stream beneath lofty cryptomeria trees. There is also a forest nursery here.

Returning to the Doze Ribeiras road, turn left and continue as before for a short distance to the turning off on your right to Lagoa do Negro; it goes across to the R3-1. This is a beautiful road, particularly in July and August when much of its length is lined with hydrangeas. First passing pastures, you soon enter wild country with native vegetation, especially the area called **Mistério Negro**, an extensive area of black cinders thrown out by the last major eruption on Terceira in 1761. The *mistérios* take their name from the locals being unable to understand why, on such a green island, vegetation refused to grow here; the answer lay in the acidity of the terrain. You will find the Lagoa do Negro on your right, and opposite is a stone house by the road. This is the entrance to the cave, the **Gruta do Natal** (⊕ *10 Oct–18 Mar 15.00–17.00 Mon, Wed, Fri; 19 Mar–31 May 15.00–17.00 Mon, Wed, Fri; Jun 14.30–17.45; Jul & Aug 14.00–18.00; Sep 14.30–17.45; 1–9 Oct 15.00–17.30; admission €6 adult, or €9 combined ticket with Algar do Carvão, see below; under 12s are free*), a 697m-long, branched horizontal lava tube with stalactite- and stalagmite-like structures. There is a small interpretation centre here, with volcanic materials and geological explanations, and information about the eruptions in 1761.

Continue on the same road until you come to a major junction. Turn right to go to Angra (left goes to Altares, opposite to Biscoitos). Just before you get to the crossroads you came to earlier, take a left turning to an area for car parking where there is a *tentadeiro*, an area where bulls are selected for the bullfight. On summer mornings you are likely to find plenty of activity here.

Now continue on the main road to the crossroads. At the crossroads, turn left towards Cabrito. If you would like a sharp reminder that you are on a volcanic island, then take the wide road you soon come to on your left signposted to **Furnas do Enxofre**; this road ends in a turning area/car park. The route can be slippery so take care. A small walkway takes you around this area, which has several small caves. Stay behind the wooden railings: the gases emitted are very dangerous. The ground around here is quite hot, and steam emissions have often turned the grass brown. The area is a geological protected zone. This was the first of the two excursions Charles Darwin made on Terceira when the *Beagle* put into Angra on their homeward voyage.

Return to the main road and continue, taking a turning on your left, signposted to **Algar do Carvão**. The **caves** (⊕ *as per Gruta do Natal, above; prices as per Gruta do Natal*) are a huge 'empty volcano'. As you descend the wet steps, above you is the mossy vegetation around the wide hole admitting daylight. The cavern is the remains of an eruption some 2,000 years ago; there are stalactites and stalagmites, formed by silica. The caves were opened to the public in 1968. Opposite is the Caldeira do Guilherme Moniz, a primary volcano with a crater perimeter of 15km that is among the largest in the archipelago.

As you return from the caves, look for the turning to Agualva, now off on your right. This is a really good drive passing a tumultuous volcanic landscape covered with native vegetation. Growing along the Ribeira Agualva are the most impressive tree ferns.

From Agualva, follow the main road along to Vila Nova and Lajes, and to Praia da Vitória.

**Praia da Vitória** In contrast with other towns in the archipelago, Praia always feels open and bright. It has an attractive main square and a long pedestrianised shopping street. In winter, it wears the clothes of an out-of-season resort, with slow business at the hotels and restaurants. In summer, its large, artificial beach and sheltered bay attract holidaymakers and the town kicks into life: the major festivals take it to a whole different level again. Seasonal ferries land visitors from other islands here and Praia is also home to the island's commercial port. The extensive lowlands of this eastern half of the island produced large quantities of wheat, and the wealth created is reflected in many fine houses in the town. At first called simply Praia, it gained town status in 1640. In 1581, after bombarding Angra, a Spanish fleet of ten ships was reconnoitring the Terceira coast and anchored in Salga Bay, in the southeastern corner. They were seen and the alarm given but by the time the Portuguese arrived 1,000 Castillians had landed and were already bent on destruction. After a morning's fierce but indecisive fighting an Augustinian friar had the idea to drive cattle at the enemy. Over 1,000 animals were stampeded at the Spaniards, who fell back in disarray and were either killed or drowned on the shore. Thus ended the Battle of Salga. Again battle came to Praia in 1829, when the town, supporting the Liberal cause, successfully resisted an attempted landing by an Absolutist fleet of 21 ships. In commemoration, the town was called Praia da Vitória in 1837. The nearby Lajes airport now covers much of what were the great wheatfields of earlier days.

In the main square, the **Praça Francisco Ornelas da Câmara**, is the Liberty Statue, erected on the first centenary of the 1829 battle won by the Liberals in homage to the heroes. Overlooking the square is the attractive town hall, and

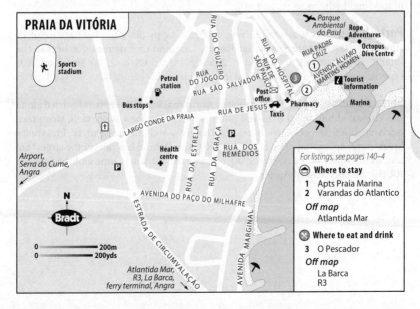

PRAIA DA VITÓRIA

Sports stadium

RUA DO CRUZEIRO

Parque Ambiental do Paul

Rope Adventures

RUA PADRE CRUZ

AVENIDA ÁLVARO MARTINS HOMEN

Octopus Dive Centre

Petrol station

RUA DO JOGO

RUA SÃO SALVADOR

RUA DO HOSPITAL

RUA DE SÃO PAULO

Post office

Tourist information

Bus stops

LARGO CONDE DA PRAIA

RUA DE JESUS

Pharmacy

Taxis

Marina

Health centre

RUA DA ESTRELA

RUA DA GRAÇA

RUA DOS REMÉDIOS

Airport, Serra do Cume, Angra

AVENIDA DO PAÇO DO MILHAFRE

ESTRADA DE CIRCUMVALAÇÃO

AVENIDA MARGINAL

N

Bradt

0 — 200m
0 — 200yds

Atlantida Mar, R3, La Barca, ferry terminal, Angra

For listings, see pages 140–4

**Where to stay**
1 Apts Praia Marina
2 Varandas do Atlantico

*Off map*
  Atlantida Mar

**Where to eat and drink**
3 O Pescador

*Off map*
  La Barca
  R3

further along on the Rua de São Paulo is the parish church, the **Santa Cruz church**. This was founded by one of the first settlers and has a 15th-century Gothic doorway and a 16th-century Manueline side doorway. Inside there are fine carvings, rich gilt ornamentation and various works of art. Further along on the same road on the left is the house where the writer **Vitorino Nemésio** (1901–78) was born. He held several senior academic posts in Lisbon and was a novelist, poet and scholar and also a popular television personality; his novel of 19th-century life on Faial and Pico, *Stormy Seas*, is in English translation.

In the opposite direction, towards the far end of the main pedestrianised Rua de Jesus, is the town market, built in the final quarter of the 19th century. Alternatively, in the opposite direction, take the Rua da Alfândega which leads down to the beach and along to the new marina.

The reduced strategic importance of Lajes airport has had an effect on the town, with the number of US personnel reduced from 2,500 to fewer than 200. For a small town like Praia, that is a significant dent to the economy. New direct flights from Boston and Madrid have helped to alleviate the damage, and the promise of budget flights from the Portuguese mainland will provide further stimulus.

**Porto Martins** The area was once covered in vineyards, of which there are still some small traces, but now there are many new houses, summer houses for people in Praia da Vitória. Near the harbour is a natural swimming pool and a restaurant.

**Salgueiros** Take the minor road to Ponta das Contendas, passing a field of *Strelitzia reginae*, the bird of paradise flower, grown for cut decoration. From the headland there are views of the three rocks, the Três Marias, which are a protected bird sanctuary.

**São Sebastião** The 15th-century parish church has interesting internal features including frescoes on the walls and unusual ceilings, and in the facing square is a monument to the Battle of Salga. Note also the nearby *império* with its depictions of food and hydrangeas (page 144).

**Porto Judeu** This is a small fishing village, a happy place to visit because of its simplicity. **Restaurante Snack-Bar Rocha**, Caminho da Esperança, is next to the infants' school on the main road (🖉 295 905 185; ⊕ 08.00–22.00 Thu–Tue). It is especially noted for octopus cooked in red wine (*polvo guisado*).

**Serra do Cume** If you have time, it is worth making the side trip to drive along this elongated hill top: the highest point is 545m. The view is of small, rich green fields enclosed by stone walls and hydrangeas, and the harbour of Praia with breakwaters appearing like a crab with two claws. Behind is a view of the largest flat area in the whole of the Azores, lying between the Serra do Cume and the Serra da Ribeirinha northeast of Angra.

# 6

# Graciosa

The general opinion is that Graciosa, meaning 'gracious', is the most relaxed of all the islands. Most certainly it would make for a great escape from the mainstream, a place to stay if ever strife and tribulation became too great to handle. Perhaps there has been little change, or at least slow change in the past few decades. A roughly oval-shaped island lying southeast/northwest and the least humid island of the archipelago, Graciosa's highest point is Pico Timão at only 398m. As a result, villages are distributed more or less equally across the countryside, and not located only around the coast – very different from some of its fellow islands. The pace is slow, men can still occasionally be seen travelling in pony traps or riding donkeys along the roads, there are at last some good restaurants, the walking is easy and everyone recognises the visitor second time round. The scenery is picturesque, an idyll of pastures and neatly walled enclosures, little clusters of whitewashed houses – with their peculiarly shaped chimneys – around village churches, occasional windmills with their distinctive red, onion-shaped domes (there were once 36) and all surrounded by a glittering blue sea. Like rare wine, it is an island to be enjoyed slowly. It is also, perhaps, a window into what the world could be like with fewer inhabitants.

Of greatest interest is the Furna do Enxofre, the cavern at the bottom of the caldera, first seriously explored in 1879 by Prince Albert of Monaco. The excellent, modern museum in Santa Cruz is worth your time. Otherwise, just relax and enjoy being on Graciosa, free from stress. The entire island is a UNESCO Biosphere Reserve.

## BACKGROUND

**GEOLOGY** Graciosa can be considered as having two main regions. The first is a mountainous zone comprising the Caldeira volcano, the Serra das Fontes and the Dormida and Branca *serras*. The second region, the northwest plateau, is generally flat and low; it is characterised by several cinder cones and associated lava flows now weathered enough for lava-walled vineyards, pastures and arable fields to thrive.

Starting from 1,500m below sea level, the oldest emerged rocks, at around 6,000 years old, are the stacks of horizontal flows forming the base of the Serra das Fontes. The Serra Dormida and Serra Branca date from around 350,000 and 270,000 years ago respectively. These uplands are steeply scarped, probably formed by faulting.

The Caldeira volcano started to build 50,000 years ago with violent eruptions caused by water mixing with magma and creating tuff deposits of ash and rock fragments, such as at Ponta da Restinga and Carapacho. During the course of several thousand years, many powerful explosions of gas, steam, ash and pumice took place, alternated with less explosive eruptions producing lava flows or highly dangerous avalanches of hot gas and rock fragments which together built the stratovolcano – a fairly steep-sided cone of layered lava fragments and flows and other emissions. On its flanks other eruptions formed the cinder cone Labeiro

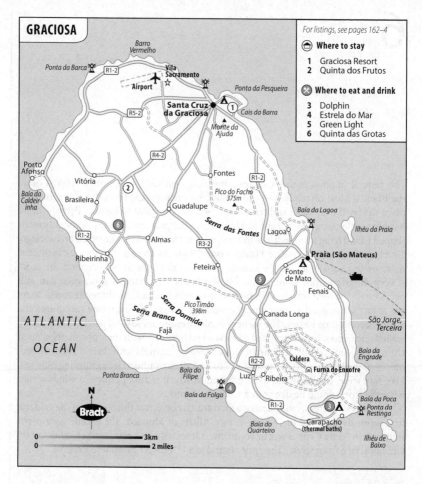

do Moro that dominates Praia and also, among others, what are now the eroded remnants of two offshore islets: the Ilhéu da Praia and Ilhéu de Baixo. The volcano's crater dates back 12,000 years and had a lava lake that might have overflowed from the shallow northwest flank and branched eastwards to the sea near Praia and west to Baía da Folga. The well-known Furna do Enxofre is a chimney or vertical vent left as the magma drained when still liquid. The associated cavern has two main fumaroles and an underground lake 22.5m deep below sea level.

The last eruption was 2,000 years ago, by Pico Timão at the end of the Serra Dormida. Its lava flow left a very rough broken surface known as *aa* lava (from the Hawaiian word), with a total length of 4km by 1km wide reaching the sea in the area of Arrochela, just north of Praia. In historical times an earthquake damaged Praia and Luz in 1730, and the Terceira earthquake of 1980 devastated Carapacho and Luz.

**HISTORY** There had always been a strong relationship between Graciosa and Terceira and so doubtless it was sailors from Terceira who first discovered the island and encroached upon it. The leading settler and man responsible for clearing tracts of vegetation was one Vasco Gil Sodré who came originally from Montemor-o-Velho in Portugal along with his family and household retinue and established himself at Carapacho. He was not, however, given the governorship; this went to Christopher Columbus's brother-in-law. It is thought many of the first settlers came from the Beiras and Minho regions of Portugal and from Flanders.

Graciosa soon proved very suitable for the cultivation of cereals and vines, and well within a century of first settlement was already exporting wheat, barley, wine and brandy. These exports were first shipped to Terceira, the economic and administrative centre that also hosted a harbour frequented by large ships. Needless to say the wealth this generated attracted pirates, and some 13 forts were built to protect the island and its women. Grain had to be stored in hidden underground chambers. The farming of crops remained dominant for very many years, but now, apart from grapes, like the rest of the islands, beef and dairy products are the main farming outputs. Fishing has become difficult in recent years because of the decline in fish stocks, though some of the islanders' catch is exported to Spain.

At one time the population numbered around 14,000 inhabitants, but emigration reduced this substantially and again there was a considerable exodus in the 1950s. At first only one member of a family was allowed to leave, but this was relaxed by 1959. Many ruined, abandoned properties can be seen in the island's interior. The population is now just under 4,400 and has stabilised somewhat, though as there is no tertiary education, some youngsters leave to study in Ponta Delgada or Lisbon and choose to stay there to seek job opportunities.

Graciosa proudly claims visits from three historical figures. Firstly Chateaubriand stopped over when fleeing to America from the French Revolution, afterwards to become known for his political writings as secretary to Cardinal Fesch and in 1822, ambassador to London. In 1814, the poet Almeida Garrett wrote some of his earliest poetry during his stay with an uncle on the island, and lastly the hydrographer Prince Albert of Monaco visited in 1879, and descended the Furna do Enxofre cave at the bottom of the caldera.

## GETTING THERE AND AWAY

For getting to Graciosa and away, see pages 42–4 and 48–9. Servicing a small population, Graciosa's airport dozes outside of flight arrival/departure times. The tourist information booth opens for both. An airport taxi is €5 to Santa Cruz, or €9 to Praia. Car hire can be obtained with **Medinha & Filhos** (*airport office, or Rua da Misericórdia 9, Santa Cruz;* m *919 289 538/969 996 644;* e *medinha_filhos@hotmail. com*). They also rent scooters, motor bikes (if you have the correct licence) and off-road bicycles.

**Azores Airlines** Santa Cruz; \ 295 730 160; ⏰ 09.00–12.30 & 13.30–17.30 Mon–Fri. On one corner of the Santa Cruz square.

**Airport information** \ 295 730 170. Worth trying outside of Azores Airlines office hours.

## GETTING AROUND

Having a car is the best option. Even though the island is small, the best restaurants are scattered and shops are few and far between. If you really don't want to drive, then bus, taxi or bicycle provide the other options. There are infrequent half-sized buses to every village with the service being geared towards locals. A printed timetable is available from the tourist information office, or the bus company in Rua Boa Vista, Santa Cruz (\ 295 732 363), and fares are nominal. Your hotel may also have details. You could make the outward journey by bus from Santa Cruz to your chosen destination, and return by taxi. Taxis are available in Santa Cruz, Luz, and Praia, and any bar will telephone for one, though there is no central number. The distances are not great and therefore taking a taxi is hardly expensive. Taking you to the caldera, waiting for you to visit the Furna do Enxofre and bringing you back will cost around €20 in a taxi from Santa Cruz, and hiring a taxi for 3–4 hours should set you back €60. Some accommodations have bikes for rent, otherwise you can get hybrid bikes from car-hire firm Medinha & Filhos (page 161). Expect to pay €9 per day for a bike, less for longer rentals or off-season. For location of towns, see map on page 160.

**ISLAND TOURS**  Any taxi will take you around the island, or to the start point of the walks. One English-speaking driver who offers island tours is **Marta Quadros** (m 967 677 445; e *martaquadros@yahoo.com*).

## TOURIST INFORMATION

There is an information kiosk tucked away with the car-hire companies inside the airport, which opens every day 30 minutes before flight arrivals. In Santa Cruz, the tourist office is close to the main square (*Rua Engenheiro Manuel Rodrigues de Miranda 11;* 295 730 240;  *09.00–12.30 & 13.30–17.00 Mon–Fri*), and in the square itself you will find a kiosk ( *09.00–noon & 13.30–17.30 Mon–Fri, 09.00–13.00 Sat*), though the staff there do not always speak English and the service is not as slick.

##  WHERE TO STAY

There is one large hotel, just out of Santa Cruz, plus a few other smaller options in town and elsewhere around the island. A movement to renovate and convert old family properties has seen the out-of-town options increase in recent years, and if you've ever wanted to stay in a windmill, then Graciosa can oblige. See map on page 160 for locations.

Apart from the Carapacho campsite, listed opposite, there are also other seasonal campsites at Praia (up the hill behind the town) and at Santa Cruz, on the coast road between the town and the Graciosa Resort Hotel.

### SANTA CRUZ

**Graciosa Resort Hotel**  (46 rooms, 6 villas with rooftop patios) Porta da Barra;  295 730 500; e info@graciosa.hotel.com; www.graciosahotel.com. Overlooking the pretty bay of Cais da Barra & surrounded by old vineyards, in part incorporated into the hotel grounds. Ask for a sea-view room. Restaurant, small gym, sauna, decent-sized pool (seasonal), free Wi-Fi, satellite TV & buffet b/fast. €€€

**Hotel Ilha Graciosa**  (15 rooms) Av Mouzinho de Albuquerque;  295 712 675/6; e gracitur@grwonline.com. Just 5mins' walk from town, a simple but well-restored manor house with lounge & bar with a lovely old basalt wine press. Wooden floors & shutters, this is not an option if you value modernity. A triumph of character over style, the pinnacle of quirk. Small garden courtyard. TV, free Wi-Fi. €€

**Hotel Santa Cruz**  (18 rooms) Largo Barão de Guadalupe;  295 712 345. The closest option to town, neat but old fashioned. Free Wi-Fi, all with private bath, some with AC/heating, b/fast inc. Also singles & triples. €€

### PRAIA

**Casa das Faias**  (6 rooms) Rua Infante D Henrique;  295 732 766; e casadasfaias@sapo.pt; www.gracipescas.com. In Praia, a highly rated place, 100m from the marina, 200m from the beach. Free Wi-Fi, TV, rooms in beautiful modern style. Roof conservatory, with views to the sea & Serra Branca. Pool table & table football to help pass the evenings. Convenient if you are arriving by boat. €€€

**Moinho de Pedra**  (4 apts) Rua Moinhos de Pedra 28;  295 712 501; e info@moinho-de-pedra.pt; www.moinho-de-pedra.pt. S/c, a typical island windmill, overlooking the sea in Praia, 200m from the beach. Can accommodate up to 4 people. €€

### ELSEWHERE AROUND THE ISLAND

🏠 **Quinta dos Frutos** (4 rooms) Rua Dr Manuel Correia Lobão, near the village of Vitória, 500m from Guadalupe; ☏ 295 712 557; www. casasacorianas.com/azores-es/casas/quinta-dos-frutos. Traditional basalt farm buildings set in a large orchard, charming owners, though little English spoken. Bicycle available. Sometimes 2-night min stay in high season. Free Wi-Fi, s/c & BBQ. Laundry service available. €€

### CAMPING

🏕 **Carapacho** ☏ 295 712 959; ⊕ Jun–Sep. In Carapacho, a lovely, basic small site on 3 levels with sea views & sheltered by trees, overlooking the Ilhéu de Baixo. Showers, toilets, electricity, stone BBQs. If unattended, you'll have to go to the post office building in Luz to make enquiries. Carapacho Spa is immediately adjacent, as is the sea swimming pool, but the nearest shop is in Luz. A pitch for a small tent is a paltry €3 per night! €

## ✖ WHERE TO EAT AND DRINK

The Graciosa Resort Hotel has a restaurant, but the Quinta das Grutas is probably the one place that adds some much-needed sophistication to the island's dining options. Although most of the accommodation is in Santa Cruz, almost all the better restaurants are out of town. However, a taxi to and from each is not expensive and takes only minutes. Fish is excellent but fresh, crisply cooked vegetables seem even more of a rarity on this island. Islanders living in Santa Cruz like to get out at weekends in summer, so the restaurants can be busy. Many of the places below are open early for café service; the times given are kitchen hours.

### SANTA CRUZ

✖ **Jal** Rua 25 da Abril 60; ☏ 295 712 344; ⊕ noon–15.00 & 19.00–22.00 daily. A basic place with old-fashioned dining room, bar & back room for playing pool. Food is average, prices reasonable. €10

✖ **Snack Bar Santa Cruz** Rua da Boa Vista; ⊕ noon–15.00 & 19.00–22.00 Mon–Sat. Specialities are *frango no churrasco* (a kind of barbecued chicken) & *alcatra peixe e carne* (a very slow-cooked stew). A tiny place, with a few tables & good prices. €10

☕ **Grafil** Largo Conde de Simas 4; ⊕ early till late daily. Opposite the line of taxis, just across from the *câmara* (town hall), in the main square, this virtually unsigned café is thoroughly modern & a good place for that unhealthy b/fast pastry & excellent coffee. No meal service. Free Wi-Fi.

### BAÍA DA FOLGA

✖ **Restaurante Estrela do Mar** Folga; ☏ 295 712 560; ⊕ noon–15.00 & 19.00–22.00 daily. Very simple small restaurant near the harbour. With a few outside tables, but you might prefer the interior on a windy day. Good fish selection, though you need to order in advance

for the fish stew. On summer weekends, booking advisable. A good place to watch the waves, & São Jorge & Faial are visible on clear days. €9

### FONTE DO MATO

✖ **Green Light** Canada dos Ramos, Fonte do Mato. To find Green Light, take the road from Praia towards Luz, then the right-hand fork when the road splits. It's then signposted after 100m. In a delightful rural setting, the chef barbecues up great fresh fish & generous meat. He owns 2 restaurants in Brazil but has recently returned to Graciosa & the food is excellent, though some locals doubt he'll be here long! English speaking. Good value. €10

### PRAIA

✖ **JJ's (Panificação Graciosense)** Rua Fontes Pereira de Melo 148; ☏ 295 732 855; ⊕ noon–14.30 & 19.00–22.30 daily. In the 1st street parallel to the beach, with tables outside. Behind the compact bar area is a large restaurant with a nice atmosphere. Menu with lots of fresh fish & seafood, good-value *prato do dia*. Not the highest sophistication level, but a good lunch option. In the front bar lurk some of the island's special pastries. €12

## CARAPACHO

**✕ Dolphin**  Just above the campsite;
☎295 712 014; ⊕ noon–15.00 & 18.00–22.00
daily. Modern, simple & good, both the
restaurant & an open terrace enjoy a great sea
view. Fish always very fresh, but plenty of steak &
other meat choices, inc hamburgers. Very
busy on summer weekends. Lunchtime specials
are excellent value here. Island wine is €2 per
litre! *€12*

## RIBEIRINHA

**✕ Quinta das Grotas**  Caminho das Grotas 28;
☎295 712 334; ⊕ 11.00–15.00 & 19.00–23.00
daily. Now well established, with the nicest
interior & probably the best choice on the island.
A delightfully rural situation in the island's west,
regional food with sophistication. Dishes served
on *telhas* (roof tiles!) can be recommended. Bread
freshly baked in traditional wood-fired oven. Can
get busy, booking advised. *€12*

## NIGHTLIFE

There is very little nightlife, and what there is is mainly found in Santa Cruz. On summer evenings many islanders gather in the spacious centre of town to stroll and talk until after midnight. There are several bars, some of which have small discos – identified by their music. Near the airport is a discotheque-pub, the **Vila Sacramento**, open in the evening on Saturdays. With the real action starting at midnight, it then stays open until 06.00. At the other end of the scale, a constant pleasure comes from just sitting on a wall above the harbour and listening to the sea, especially if there is moonlight.

## SHOPPING

A new initiative has introduced several kiosks into Santa Cruz's main square, selling Graciosa wines, lacework made by local women and other items. The best time to catch them open is on weekday mornings. The tourist office kiosk itself sells some good leaflets – on whaling, for example – plus other souvenirs of a tasteful nature. Graciosa cheese is another island speciality, quite strong for some tastes. *Queijadas da Graciosa*, small cakes, are delicious with an espresso coffee and are rather like a treacle tart mix in a crisp, thin pastry cup. With ingredients of flour, sugar, eggs, milk, butter and *canela e sal* (cinnamon and salt), they make a fantastic energy source when descending calderas. The little factory making them is in Praia and visitors are welcome, though there is no factory tour and you will stumble across their products in the island's cafés and shops.

## OTHER PRACTICALITIES

**Emergency** ☎112
**Police**  Santa Cruz; ☎295 730 200
**✚ Health Centre (Centro de Saúde)**  Rua Dr
Vasco Rodrigues; ☎295 730 070. With 24hr A&E,
though serious cases have to be helicoptered to
Terceira or São Miguel.
**✉ Post office**  Av Mouzinha Albuquerque, Santa
Cruz; Rua Rodrigues Sampaia, Praia

**INTERNET/WI-FI**  Free municipal Wi-Fi is available in Santa Cruz's main square and also in Praia. The Grafil café (page 163) also provides free Wi-Fi.

## WHAT TO SEE AND DO

**THE CALDERA AND FURNA DO ENXOFRE VISITOR CENTRE** (☎ *295 714 009;* ⊕ *16 Sep–30 Apr 14.00–17.30 Tue–Sat; 1 May–14 Jun 09.30–13.00 & 14.00–17.30 Tue–Fri, 14.00–17.30 Sat; 15 Jun–15 Sep 10.00–18.00 daily; €3.50/1.75/free adults/*

seniors & juniors/under 12s; guided tours available Oct–Apr 14.30 & 15.30; May–Sep 11.30, 15.00 & 16.30) The visitor centre provides information about the volcanology of Graciosa, especially the caldera and cavern, and generally about the Biosphere Reserve classification. The centre staff also survey the interior through CCTV cameras.

As you enter the caldera through the tunnel, built in 1953, a dramatic landscape confronts you. Small meadows are grazed by cows and all around cryptomeria forest climbs the steeply enclosing slopes towards the sky. The road soon forks, to the left down to a picnic site, to the right down to the visitor centre and entrance of the Furna do Enxofre. Please note the gas emissions are closely monitored and sometimes it may be too dangerous to visit; more likely in summer when the air may circulate less well. Unfortunately there is no way of knowing this until you get to the entrance.

In summer it is said by some that the best time to visit is between 11.00 and 14.00 when sunlight enters. Descend a concrete spiral staircase of 184 steps to the cave floor, stopping perhaps at one or two of the six 'windows' to admire the view. The staircase was officially opened on 30 July 1939, a great improvement over the rope ladder used on the first descent by Prince Albert of Monaco 60 years earlier. It seems that it was built to enable farmers to get water for their animals. The narrow opening allows a few ferns and mosses to grow. A little into the cave is a small gently bubbling mud pool, sounding rather sinister in the darkness. The ropes preventing further descent into the cavern result from the deaths of two visiting sailors some years ago who were overcome by an unexpected emission of sulphurous fumes deeper inside the cave. There is a lake, and at one time a rowing boat enabled further exploration when the lake was 130m across and 15m deep. In recent years the lake has gone down to a depth of 11m, though it varies with rainfall, and there is speculation there may be an underground connection with the thermal area of Carapacho. The floor of the lake is below sea level.

After leaving the cavern, a day can be spent very happily exploring and enjoying the peace of the caldera, or taking the walk described on pages 167–8.

## MUSEUMS
### Museu da Graciosa (*Largo Conde de Simas 17, Santa Cruz;* \ *295 712 429;* ⊕ *09.00–12.15 & 14.00–17.15 Mon–Fri; also Jun–Aug 14.00–17.00 Sat & Sun;* €1/0.50, adult/under 14s & over 65s) Established in 1983 and housed in a late 19th-century traditional building used for storing corn and making wine, the museum's frontage and modern extension were added in 2010. Here you will find furnished family rooms, various antiques and paintings, the tools of several important trades and all the gear to make wine in the old way, plus information on geology and agriculture. Information panels carry translations into English. Perhaps most impressive is the section devoted to carnivals, with bright costumes and some videos of the dancing that takes place during the island's big party. You can also see some examples of the island's renowned guitars, made by individuals and with distinctive heart-shaped holes in the body. In an annexe on the seafront signed *Barracão das canoas* there is a whaling boat and exhibits to do with whaling. It is often closed in winter months, due to the weather: ask at the main museum reception. Because this is so simply done and in a shed by the harbour you get the feeling that if a rocket were to be fired a crew would come rushing down to launch the boat. If you want to visit the restored windmill at Fontes, a short drive from Santa Cruz and standing resplendent in the landscape with its white base and bright-red cupola, access to this and the whaling-boat shed are by request at the main museum.

**Museu da Vida Rural da Ilha Graciosa** (*Caminho de Cima 97, Luz;* \ *295 732 787;* ⊕ *10.00–noon & 14.00–16.00 Mon–Fri; €1*) A restored house opened in May 2015, with original furniture left *in situ*, plus a separate building with old photos. In an outbuilding, there is an old oxcart. There is no English-language information, as yet.

**Atalho (Town water tank)** (*Rua da Boa Vista, Santa Cruz;* ⊕ *13.30–17.00 daily; admission free*) Full of water until around 20 years ago, this 1,800m² capacity water tank is now drained – and open to visitors! It is over 150 years old; with amazing acoustics, it is tempting the municipality to make it available as a venue for concerts. A guided tour is available, and is surprisingly interesting, given that you are standing in an empty tank. There is no archive material documenting the history of the tank, so the information for the guided tour has been constructed from word-of-mouth testimony passed down by locals.

**Loja Museu João Tomaz Bettencourt** (*Guadalupe;* ⊕ *08.00–noon & 13.00–16.00 Mon–Fri; admission free*) A small museum, recently opened, it is set out as the village shop, a few kilometres from Santa Cruz. Very genuine looking, it is tempting to want to buy one of the period hats or coats behind the counter. A sign claims there's a sale on – but the museum curator earnestly informs you that it ended in 1960.

**BIRDS AND FLOWERS** With little high ground and almost everywhere farmed, not many naturalists in the past have studied the island. The avian jewel in the crown here is the Monteiro's storm petrel (*Oceanodroma monteiroi*), which is endemic to Graciosa and of which there are only 200 specimens on Graciosa's two islets.

The basalt islet of **Ilhéu da Praia** is a Special Protected Area of 11ha and is said to have one of the richest and most diverse concentrations of seabirds in the Azores with many migratory species. It is a little more than 1km out from Praia. Breeding colonies have declined through human disturbance so while it is nice to know they are there, it is best they are left in peace. However, from the opposite shore or the harbour quay it is easy to observe the action with a good telescope. Another possibility, in the far southeast, is the Special Protected Area of the **Ilhéu de Baixo** and adjacent rocky shoreline.

Disappointed wildflower enthusiasts will just have to resort to applied botany – the grape vine and its products.

## ACTIVITIES

### ADVENTURE TRIPS
**Nautigraciosa** Porto Santo Cruz, Santa Cruz; m 966 060 969; e divingraciosa@gmail.com; www. divingraciosa.com; ⊕ May–Oct. Based in the Santa Cruz harbour but with a 2nd, bigger boat in Praia. Diving & diving with sharks. Also organises boat trips, kayak rental, big-game fishing & sea-based birdwatching trips. Some English spoken.

**BIKING** No-one as yet is doing guided bike excursions, but you can rent bikes from Medinha & Filhos (page 161) if you want to hire your own and devise your own circuit.

**BOAT TRIPS** Built in the early part of the last century, the *Estefânia Gorreia* played an important part in Graciosa's economy during the whaling period when it went out supporting the small boats, towing the whales back to shore. The last whales were caught in 1974. At Cais da Barra, by the Clube Naval, you can usually see the boat on the slipway in winter, and next to it the trying area. The large buildings nearby are all to do with whaling. The boat also played an important role in emergencies, taking people to the hospital in Terceira before the time of the air services. Beautifully restored, it nowadays takes the island's rowing team to other islands to compete, towing the team's vessel behind. Very occasionally, it makes trips round the island; check at Clube Naval or the tourist office for further details. More promising opportunities for boat trips, kayaking, dolphin watching, fishing and diving are provided by the companies listed below.

## FISHING

**Calypso** Rua Rodrigues Sampaio 10, Praia; 295 098 389; m 917 566 500; e info@ calypsoazores.com; www.calypsoazores.com; ⏲ winter 09.00–12.30 & 13.30–17.00 Mon–Fri, 09.00–noon & 13.00–17.00 Sat; summer 08.00–12.30 & 13.30–18.00 Mon–Fri, 09.00–noon & 13.00–17.00 Sat. Based in Praia, organises sport fishing, dolphin watching, snorkelling & boat trips, inc inter-island cruises. English spoken.

**Gracipescas** Rua Serpa Pinto 11, Santa Cruz; m 912 154 370; e turismo@gracipescas.com; www. gracipescas.com. With 2 boats, prices depend on the season & number of passengers. Also available for non-fishing boat trips. English spoken.

**SWIMMING** Santa Cruz has a tiny pool in front of the harbour, plus a seasonal saltwater pool beside the Rua Corpo Santo on the way to the airport.

There is a natural, partially enclosed rock pool at **Barro Vermelho**, with showers and changing facilities, as well as picnic tables and barbecues, less than 2km north of Santa Cruz, and the area is backed with tamarisk trees which makes it more attractive. **Praia** has Graciosa's only beach – small, and almost white sand – and this is very popular, although the sand can sometimes disappear after a winter storm. There are changing rooms and showers, and a counter selling ice creams, etc; across the road are a couple of café/bar/restaurants. Carapacho has good access to protected sea swimming, in a walled-off pool.

**Carapacho Spa** ⏲ noon–18.00 Tue–Fri, 10.00– 17.00 Sat & Sun, all year; €1. Located in Carapacho, in the island's southeast, unfortunately the spa's 16 individual immersion rooms & a medical consulting are closed, with no immediate prospect of reopening. At time of writing, this has left only a modestly sized indoor hot swimming pool. The spa dates back to 1750. Despite its currently limited facilities, there is also the natural rock pool nearby, & it is altogether a very popular place in summer.

**WALKING** There are three official trails, summarised below, with a promise of a couple of new ones being developed. The trail guides for the routes below are handed out, free of charge, at the tourist offices and also at some of the hotels. Route maps may also be printed off from the trails section of the Visit Azores website (*www.visitazores.com*).

### Around the caldera and Furna do Enxofre Easy, 9km, 3 hours. See map, page 170. A torch is recommended. Take a picnic and you can happily spend most of the day exploring this route. If you have no car, a taxi from Santa Cruz into the caldera and down to the entrance to the cavern is the easiest way to start this walk. From the visitor centre (pages 164–5), walk back up the road and through the tunnel, and down the road to take the first turning off on the left (with red and yellow waymarking). This gives access to the intermittently tarmac-surfaced road that runs round the outside of the caldera. After a few hundred metres, take a very sharp left-turn to follow the route in a clockwise direction. After 100m, take a diversion up some rough steps to your right, signposted Furna Maria Encantada; this is a lavatube some 60m long and was probably formed when the

lava lake that was inside the caldera reached its highest point. After visiting it, descend the steps and continue clockwise as before.

If you are feeling lazy, you can simply drive the route round the exterior of the caldera. Whether walking or driving, be sure to stop to enjoy the views over the coast and later on, over to São Jorge and Terceira.

**Serra Branca–Praia** Easy, 7km, 2½ hours. Crosses the island from west to east, with good views across the island.

**Baía da Folga** Easy, 2km, 1 hour. Quite fun to do after a good meal at the little restaurant in Folga (page 163).

## TOURING THE ISLAND

**FULL-DAY DRIVING TOUR** Whether driving or being taken by taxi, a day tour should take in the caldera and Furna do Enxofre, the view of Santa Cruz from **Monte da Ajuda**, Praia with its windmills and beach, the lighthouse at **Ponta da Restinga**, Carapacho and the Serra Branca. In the northwest, you can then also take a short side trip down to Porta Afonso (the track is often too rutted for cars and you may have to walk). Here the sea churns and boils, and an offshore wind skims the tops of the waves in spectacular fashion, making for some great video footage. The lighthouse at Farol da Ponta da Barça, with its whale-like rock formation, might be your final stop before returning to Santa Cruz. As an alternative, and if you like to swim, you could undertake an itinerary which includes a longer stop at Carapacho, swimming or – if the building works are ever completed – a dip in the hot baths. As soon as you arrive there, book your lunch at the Dolphin Restaurant (page 164), then have a swim and a shower before lunch. After dining, continue the tour clockwise around the island, visiting the places listed above, before returning to Santa Cruz in the early evening. If you don't want to swim, then take your midday break at Folga and enjoy exploring the tiny harbour and its surrounds and isolation, maybe incorporating the official trail, before returning back to base.

If you are on the island for a few days, you might want to visit the Furna do Enxofre (pages 164–5) itself as a separate trip, perhaps combining it with a walk (pages 167–8), rather than trying to cram it into a day tour. After all, there is no rush on Graciosa.

**SANTA CRUZ DA GRACIOSA** The town focuses on the spacious main square of cobbles laid beneath large metrosideros trees, elms and araucarias, and two large water reservoirs, originally used for watering cattle accessed by a sloping cobbled road. There are several understated small bars and cafés nearby, and some shops. The shops are rather scattered and are not always obvious, which is inconvenient if you need something in a hurry, but a most charming and welcome contrast to the ubiquitous commercial units emblazoned with neon. The taxi rank is in the square, with telephones each housed in a little model windmill. Roads leading off are often lined with grand town houses and domestic buildings with interesting wrought-iron balconies and other architectural detail.

The tiny harbour with its simple quay and a semi-natural swimming pool has some charm; above is a narrow cobbled street and pairs of seats in the wall. It is on a small and intimate scale. Further round is a modern quay, built in the 1960s. In winter, the harbour will be devoid of boats: it doesn't take much of a swell for the water to spill over the quay, so caution is advised. On the hill above, the **Monte da Ajuda**, are three chapels: São João, São Salvador and Nossa Senhora da Ajuda, all

In August, the weekends start early and finish late, with an extended party to celebrate each of the saints' days which come thick and fast. In particular, the **Festival of Santo Cristo** is celebrated with boat races, *touradas* (bullfights) and cultural and musical happenings. Santa Cruz really decorates itself for the celebration, and becomes uncharacteristically busy (by its own standards) with visitors from the other islands as well as returning North American emigrants. One feature of the more raucous events is that various associations – musical, sporting or other – dance until they drop, then take photos of their 'survivors', namely the members who last the pace. The one with the most 'survivors' in their photo is the unofficial winner, and owner of the bragging rights!

When the **Espírito Santo** or **Holy Ghost** celebration takes place seven weeks after Easter, one can enjoy participating in the island's hospitality, taking the special bread and local wine. This occurs widely over the island, but especially in Santa Cruz, Luz, Guadalupe and Praia (São Mateus). **Carnaval** starts to build as early as January, reaching a crescendo, a riot of colour and costumes, in February or early March. On 24 May, there is a **procession** from Guadalupe to Monte da Ajuda and back, to pray for the prevention of future earthquakes.

floodlit at night. The last can be likened to a castle; it is 16th century and has 18th-century *azulejos*. All three are usually closed, but sometimes, if anyone is around to ask, a key may be found. (The priest lives to the right of the town's main church, and is the best bet.) There is a surfaced road to the top where a splendid view can be had of the whole town. A little below the chapels is a small bullring, used during festivities in August; a stepped path leads down and continues on into town.

From the town square, if you take the coastal road leading to Praia, Rua Infante D Henrique, and walk for about ten minutes, you will pass the island's dairy co-operative and a power station. On the same road is the **Associacão de Artesãos da Ilha Graciosa** (Artisans' Association of Graciosa Island); you will see a silver nameplate on the building, though they now have a sales kiosk in the town square. The entrance is towards the end of the side passage. Here you will find the women working, and a display of their completed work and items for sale. It is open weekdays during normal business hours.

Take the turning to the left down to the old harbour, the **Cais da Barra**, just near the hotel. It is a pretty bay with several small boats moored during the summer. Here you will find the Clube Naval building and maybe refreshments. You will soon realise this is on the site of an old fort, **Forte de Santa Catarina**, which dates from the period before 1800, and there are old rusty cannons still threatening the ghosts of long-dead pirates. Peer over the wall and in the black lava you will discern an old ramp where the whales were once hauled ashore. On the headland beyond (reached by the farm track along the coast) are the remains of a large building and defensive walls, which the sea is slowly undermining. This was once a Jewish settlement, the **Forte Deis Judeus**, and there is a tiny cemetery in black basalt engraved 'Cemiterio Judaico' nearby. This coastal stroll makes for a good after-dinner perambulation for those staying at the Graciosa Resort Hotel. For those who are not, the stroll back along the asphalt road following the coast is a pleasant return walk into town.

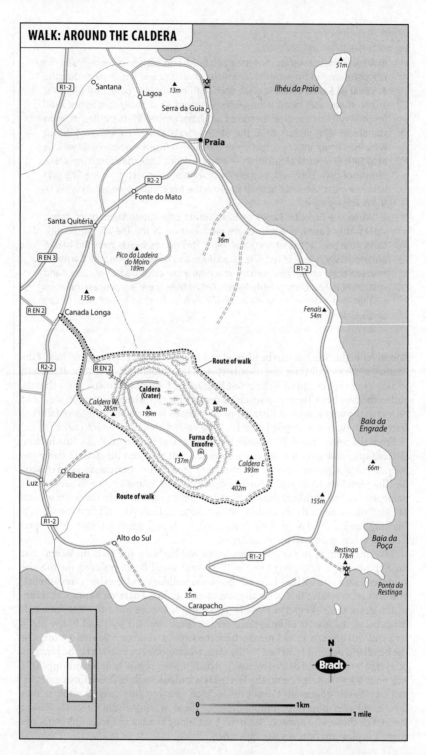

# WALK: AROUND THE CALDERA

R1-2

Santana

Lagoa

Serra da Guia

13m

51m

*Ilhéu da Praia*

**Praia**

R2-2

Fonte do Mato

Santa Quitéria

R EN 3

*Pico da Ladeira do Moiro*
189m

36m

135m

R EN 2

Canada Longa

*Fenais* 54m

R1-2

**Route of walk**

R2-2

R EN 2

**Caldera (Crater)**

*Caldera W* 285m

199m

382m

**Furna do Enxofre**

137m

*Caldera E* 393m

402m

*Baía da Engrade*

66m

Ribeira

Luz

155m

**Route of walk**

R1-2

Alto do Sul

R1-2

*Restinga* 178m

*Baía da Poça*

35m

Carapacho

*Ponta da Restinga*

N

Bradt

0 — 1km
0 — 1 mile

**PRAIA** Also known as São Mateus, Praia is a fishing and ferry port with a high sea wall (necessary in the wilds of winter), and an arched gateway leading from the beach through the wall into a long, arcing street. The houses are small and pretty, some a bit weather-beaten. The usual cobbled square is in the road behind, before the **Church of São Mateus**, rebuilt in the 19th century; inside there are Flemish images of St Matthew and St Peter and a *pietà*, all 16th century. The beach itself is almost white sand and very popular, with a café and other amenities. In the near distance is the modern **Negra Quay**, the island's main port and where the inter-island ferry comes in during the summer. A little further on and there is a collection of picturesque windmills, of which a couple are now converted into accommodation options.

**ILHEU DA BALEIA** If you walk out of Santa Cruz along the north coast you first pass what was once the main vine-growing area and a stretch of coastline that is a popular bathing area among the rocks near the few houses of **Barro Vermelho**. Beyond this you come to **Ponta da Barca**, with its lighthouse, about 5km from town. Close to the shore is a rocky islet that looks, without much imagination, like a whale; there may be some seabirds as well. Unless you have a car, you have to walk along the road to get there, but there is little traffic; in summer the best time to do this is in the cool of the evening.

**VIEW OF THE OTHER ISLANDS** The best and most readily accessible view is from the main road as it skirts the Serra Branca following the southwest coast between Luz and Ribeirinha. Pico, São Jorge, Faial and Terceira can all be seen on a clear day. Other great views can be had from the walk around the exterior of the caldera.

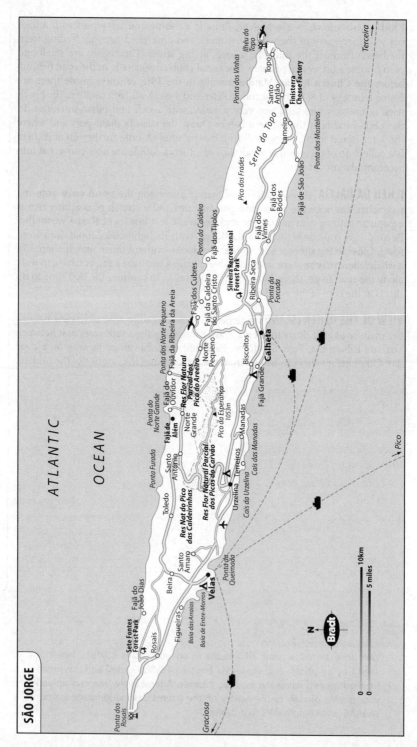

SÃO JORGE

ATLANTIC

OCEAN

Ponta dos Rosais

Ponta da Queimada

Graciosa

Pico

Terceira

# 7

# São Jorge

Town of Velas so beautiful
Leaning on the sea side
More beautiful I have yet to see
Not kissed by the moonlight

Oh, island of infinite grace
Far away from you, thinking with
    obsessive thoughts
My longing has no end

In my beating heart
The days: eternity
In the heart separation …
being more 'cold' in the friendship,

is more 'warm' the absence to be
    alone …
when the sweetest is the missing
the heart is more crucified.

Anselmo da Silveira, Angra, November 1949.
On an *azulejo* in the town garden, Velas.

An islander used to greet visitors with 'Welcome to São Jorge, my island with 10,000 people and over 20,000 cattle'. Known widely beyond its shores for its delicious, strong, Cheddar-like cheese, the other attributes of this long, cigar-shaped island are far less recognised. To some, São Jorge is an island of mystery, sometimes disappearing into cloud or mist. Arriving at the Velas quay, the imposing sea gateway and walls dating from the time of pirates promise quiet pleasure. Velas town itself features narrow streets, small shops, an impressive church, some manor houses, a little square or two, the sound of voices coming from tiny bars.

Elsewhere, there is an intense pleasure to be derived from walking along little-used farm roads in utter silence with stone walls, hedgerows, cows and occasional trees giving depth to the stage. In sunshine and with a deep-blue sea beyond, the cliff paths are magnificent for scenery, combining landscape grandeur and intimate vignettes together with unexpected human interest, while steep descents to isolated *fajãs* on tiny tracks give a tender appreciation of the hardships of the islanders.

Although it is an island with good walks, graded unsurfaced roads have in recent years ramified throughout the island and in reasonable weather allow the motorist to explore many of the previously hidden beauties of the island. Many very happy days can be had exploring the island back roads as well as the little-trafficked main roads from which side roads lead into small, often charming villages.

On a full moon the island comes into its own; the channel across to Pico island reflects and shimmers, while the great black unequal-sided triangle of Pico mountain massively provides the theatre setting. In Velas, drop down to the harbour, and on the tiny terrace, if you are lucky, thrill to the haunting mew of Cory's shearwaters as they fly just above your head in the dark.

By car, São Jorge is an island on which to spend slow days relaxing, stopping to explore the accessible little settlements along the coast – or walking to the more isolated ones – and pausing to enjoy the scenery. On the southern coast, it can be difficult to tear your eyes away from the imposing pinnacle Pico. The *fajãs*, while not unique to São Jorge, are a very special feature of this island. Now classified as a UNESCO Biosphere Reserve, their microclimates and settlements are most rewarding to explore – some are only accessible on foot. There are numerous viewpoints, the two ports of Velas and Calheta, lovely sites for picnics, and opportunities to make easy short walks – there are plenty to take you to lovely places. One can also take the ferry and visit Pico and Faial islands, the other two islands that make up the so-called *triangulo*; see page 49 for details.

## BACKGROUND

**GEOLOGY** The **cigar-shaped** São Jorge is 56km long but only 8km at its widest. A long ridge running its length characterises the island, arising abruptly from the sea and ascending to Pico da Esperança (1,053m) at about the centre. The average height of this central ridge is 700m. The coasts are very steep, in places over 400m and almost vertical, particularly on the north side. Much of the land surface is above 300m and villages are at much higher altitudes than anywhere else in the Azores.

Different from all the other Azores islands, São Jorge originated from fissures, cracks or faults so deep in the Earth's crust that magma rises to the surface. From these, lava usually erupts with little or no gaseous explosions and so mostly produces lava flows; however, they can also erupt explosively, forming cinder cones. There are no stratovolcanoes like on Pico or on Faial, nor are there any big calderas or craters. Initially, though, these fissural eruptions, some 1,000m down on the sea floor, would have been very explosive as the hot magma met the seawater, but as the island built up above the sea, the thermal shocks ceased.

The island has a northwest–southeast orientation which reflects the regional plate tectonics and fault lines. Two areas make up the island, separated by a fault line cutting obliquely across the middle, which is now covered with recent volcanic emissions. Wearing deeply into this fracture is the Ribeira Seca creek, just east of Calheta.

The Topo complex is the island's oldest, up to 600,000 years old, but the relief of this eastern side is more difficult to interpret and it is harder to identify the volcanic features and lava flows because it is so eroded. The younger areas to the west of the Ribeira Seca fault mirror the same eruption style of Topo; lava flows and explosive eruptions, leaving cinder cones. The wide spine of the central and western region comprises the Manadas complex and the Rosais complex, at around 24,000 and 30,000 years old respectively. From fissures lava welled out and piled up to thicknesses of over 500m, burying older cinder cones under newer flows. The glorious walk or drive along the island's spine passes the cones of the youngest eruptions from just a few thousand years ago.

The sheer cliffs of the coast are probably due to faulting. The island's *fajãs* are caused in two ways: detritus *fajãs* are gravity deposits produced by landslides caused by erosion of the base of the cliff such as Fajã dos Cubres, while lava *fajãs* are created by lava flowing over the cliffs into the sea making a platform, as with Fajã do Ouvidor. São Jorge has over 70 in total, the majority on the north coast, but many were abandoned following the 1980 earthquake and now only the larger and safer ones are inhabited. They are much valued for their microclimate and the cultivation of vegetables and fruit.

During historical times there have been several volcanic eruptions, the first in 1580, east of Velas, whose lava flows formed the Ponta da Queimada. It also emitted hot gas and ash that spread quickly close to the ground, burning those unfortunate enough to be caught, and killing many cattle. In 1808 came the infamous eruptions at Urzelina that continued for six weeks, with 13 large cinder cones exploding over several days together with lava flows. This was followed by avalanches of hot gas and stones that extended over Urzelina as a dense black cloud. Terrified villagers cowering in the church were protected, but endured the sound of falling debris on the roof. Not long after came a lava flow half-burying the church, whose tower can still be seen in the village today. The survivors said they had seen a vision of hell.

**HISTORY** Topo, at the island's far eastern extremity, was settled by a Flemish nobleman, Van der Hagen, who had first been made Captain of Flores, but this was so remote no-one wanted to settle there and he asked the king if instead he could have São Jorge. Velas was founded around the middle of the 15th century and within 50 years developed sufficiently to be given its town charter, with an economy based on exporting wool and archil, a lichen used for dyeing, and growing wheat and grapes. Three centuries later, oranges became an important export crop, with schooners coming to Urzelina from England to load the boxes of fruit. As with some of the other islands, the lack of a good harbour meant isolation until the airport was built. The principal products are now cattle and, most importantly, three large co-operatives and one private factory now make cheese for which São Jorge is renowned. Like all the other islands, São Jorge suffered from the predations of pirates; its history has also been ravaged both by earthquakes and the two major volcanic eruptions of 1580 and 1808.

## GETTING THERE AND AWAY

For travel to São Jorge, see pages 42–4 and 48–9. Ferries arrive and depart in Velas throughout the year from nearby Pico and Faial, and in summer from other islands. The sleepy island airport lies a few kilometres to the east of Velas and is equipped with café, car-rental companies (page 176), free Wi-Fi but no ATM. Taxis to Velas cost €8.

**Azores Airlines**  [Map, page 184] Rua Maestro Francisco Lacerda 40, Velas; ☎295 430 350; ⊕ 09.00–noon & 13.00–17.30 Mon–Fri

**Airport information (Azores Airlines airport office)** ☎295 430 360

## GETTING AROUND

**BY BUS**  There is a limited, mainly weekday bus service which brings passengers into Velas from all the significant villages in the morning, returning in the evening. One morning service from Velas runs to Calheta, returning in the afternoon. It is designed to take workers to the tuna factory, and they take priority over mere tourists! The other morning service from Velas runs to Rosais in the west. You can get all the way to Topo in the far east, by taking an afternoon bus: this takes well over two hours and the return is early the following morning. The Velas tourist office has the full timetable. Buses leave from opposite the Velas Auditorium, on the waterfront.

**BY TAXI**  If you want to make a tour of the island by taxi, or use taxis to access the walks, then taxi rates start at around €17 per hour, but drivers should be able to show you a set price list for island tours as well as specific destinations. One English-speaking taxi driver is **Carlos Brasil** (m 914 209 612; e carlosbrasil@outlook.pt). For a guided island tour by vehicle, try **Discover Experience** (page 180; prices from €185 for four people, other prices on request).

For the location of Velas listings see map, page 184, and for the location of other towns see map, page 172.

In Velas, taxis can be found behind the main church, or you could call m 910 539 621 or 966 780 383. A full list of taxi-drivers is displayed in the airport. Bars and restaurants in other villages will also summon a cab, if you need one.

**BY CAR** Rental cars should be pre-booked, as the companies' desks will sometimes only be staffed to receive pre-booked customers. In high season, cars get booked very quickly. São Jorge has half-a-dozen car-hire companies, including:

**Autoturistica Sao Jorge (Rent-a-Car Velas)** Based both at the airport & opposite the Hotel São Jorge Garden in Velas; ☎ 295 430 159/129

**Ilha Verde Rent-a-Car** Largo João Pereira 21, Velas, & at the airport; ☎ 295 432 141; e rentivsaojorge@ilhaverde.com, www.ilhaverde.com

## TOURIST INFORMATION

The office [Map, page 184] (*Rua Conselheiro Dr José Pereira 3, Velas;* ☎ *295 412 440;* ⊕ *09.00–17.00 Mon–Fri; summer hours may be longer*) is efficient and well organised. At the airport, there is a minuscule kiosk (⊕ *10.00–noon Mon, Wed, Fri; 08.00–10.00 & 15.00–17.00 Tue, Thu*). There is also a kiosk in Calheta (⊕ *09.00–noon & 13.30–17.30 Mon–Fri, 09.00–13.00 Sat*).

## WHERE TO STAY

There's a good variety of accommodation options on São Jorge. In addition to the hotels and hostels below there are a number of camping options. Out of season, it's essential to ring ahead, as the sites may be unmanned. In each case, pitching a tent will cost no more than a few euros per person. Hot showers available at all three listed sites. See map, page 184, for Velas listings, and map, page 172, for other locations.

### VELAS AND AROUND

 **Quinta das Figueiras** (3 apts) Figueiras; ☎ 295 438 121; e quinta.das.figueiras@gmail.com; www.quintadasfigueiras.com. S/c apts sleeping 2–8 people, a few km west of Velas on the road to Rosais. Seasonal pool, free Wi-Fi. B/fast provisions inc in rate. Could use a lick of paint, but off-season prices are good value. €€€€

**Cantinho das Buganvilias Resort** (19 apts) Rua Padre Augusto Teixeira, Queimada; ☎ 295 432 271; e cantinhodasbuganvilias@gmail. com; www.cantinhodasbuganvilias.com. Beautiful coastal location 5km from Velas & 1.5km west of the airport. Spacious modern s/c apts with lots of light, but the positions of some & large windows may compromise privacy. Indoor & outdoor pools, fitness centre, bar & seasonal restaurant. Free Wi-Fi. No b/fast inc. €€€

**Casa do António** (8 rooms) Rua Infante D Henrique, Velas; ☎ 295 432 006; e antonio@ viagensaquarius.com; www.viagensaquarius. com. This is a wonderfully eccentric & personal well-designed, well-built new extension to an old building so there are quirky stairs & corners & the whole thing comes together in a mock Art-Deco style. A really fun place & right by the harbour with, in summer, Cory's shearwaters whipping by overhead to their nesting sites in the nearby cliff face. The owner/designer has put considerable thought into making guests comfortable, & the rooms are all en suite. There is a b/fast room (with excellent varied b/fast), & a small elevated garden. AC, free Wi-Fi – a good choice. €€€

**Hotel São Jorge Garden** (58 rooms) Av dos Baleeiros, Velas; ☎ 295 430 100; e info@hotelsaojorge.pt; www.hotelsaojorge.pt. In a good situation overlooking the sea & across the channel to Pico, just a few mins' walk from the centre of town. Rooms have balconies & AC, cable TV. Swimming pool (seasonal), bar, b/fast room, but no restaurant. Wi-Fi is available in public areas. €€€

**Quinta do Canavial** (4 rooms in main house, 20 rooms in annexe) Lugar do Canavial, Velas; ☎ 295 412 981; e quintacanavial@hotmail.com;

www.quintadocanavial.com. High up above the football ground, overlooking the bay of Entre-Moros on the very western edge of Velas, this is an old manor house in a garden setting, with most rooms in an annexe. Pool, restaurant serving evening meals on request, courtesy transport – will pick up from port or airport. Free Wi-Fi. Rooms are full of characterful antiques. B/fast inc. €€

🏠 **Residencial Neto** (23 rooms) Rua Cons Dr José Pereira, Velas; ☎ 295 412 338. In the very centre of town, close to the harbour. Simple rooms, few frills, though with TV, free Wi-Fi, bar & small seawater swimming pool (seasonal). B/fast inc. €

## CALHETA

🏠 **Pousada de Juventude (Youth hostel)** (6 dorms, 9 rooms, 9 family rooms) Canada da Vinha Nova, Fajã Grande; ☎ 295 460 000; e saojorge@pousadasjuvacores.com; www.pousadasjuvacores.com. Communal TV, bar & free Wi-Fi. €

## FAJÃ DA CALDEIRA DO SANTO CRISTO

🏠 **Casa Tio João** (5 rooms) m 969 153 722; e casa.do.tio.joao@outlook.pt. A true wilderness experience; you need to walk here or get a quad-bike (see box, page 186, owners can arrange, extra cost). Double rooms & triples, fully s/c but you need to bring your own food (cooking oil, salt, etc, provided). The setting is unique, a peaceful place for those genuinely seeking a retreat. Power is by generator, part-time; rooms are simple, no Wi-Fi, no TV, shared bathroom. Communal wood-burning stove, garden. Open year-round, subject to weather. €€

## TOPO

🏠 **Casa do Topo** (1 s/c cottage) Rua da Ponta; e casadotopo@gmail.com. In the far east of the island, a delightful little house which sleeps up to 5, at a low price. Heated, with TV, kitchenette, terrace & patio, overlooking the Topo islet & close to natural swimming pools. €

## CAMPING

⛺ **Fajã Grande** Calheta; ☎ 295 417 366; m 963 797 170; e camping.cht.siz.2014@gmail.com; ⊕ May–Sep. Just west of Calheta close to the sea, there is a good natural rock pool with European Blue Flag status. The campsite has a children's playpark, & tents can be hired. There are also bungalows for 4 people. It is very attractive with a pergola & belvedere, a great place to sit & watch the sunset. To find the campsite take a steep cement road down to the sea. Free Wi-Fi available. Shops are very limited; there is no bakery, but there is a kiosk & a snack bar (⊕ 09.00–23.00). €

⛺ **Urzelina camping ground** ☎ 295 414 401. All amenities & resident warden. Swimming pool & natural rock pools. Clothes washing facilities. Close by are restaurants, grocery, bakery & coffee shop. €

⛺ **Velas** ☎ 295 412 721. Located next to the football ground in the Baía de Entre os Morros about 15mins' walk west of town & providing free transport to & from the harbour. It has a freshwater swimming pool & tents, with sleeping bags for hire. Clothes washing facilities. €

# ✗ WHERE TO EAT AND DRINK

It's probably fair to say that the island has no stand-out restaurants. Velas (map, page 184) has enough places to eat around the centre, though with little variety and a standard that rarely exceeds average.

If you want to eat outside Velas, then some better options are listed below. For the location of towns see map, page 172.

## VELAS

✗ **Cervecaria São Jorge** Rua Francisco Lacerda 31; ☎ 295 412 861; ⊕ 08.00–17.00 Mon–Fri, 08.00–15.00 Sat. A daytime option with friendly staff serving up soups, snacks & burgers, plus more traditional fare. Bargain lunches served noon–14.30. Free Wi-Fi. €9

✗ **Clube Naval** Rua Conselheiro Dr José Pereira 9; ☎ 295 098 091; ⊕ 08.00–22.00 Mon–Fri, 09.00–22.30 Sat, 17.00–22.30 Sun. Serves meat & fish dishes, plus sandwiches & snacks while the locals watch football on the TV. Dish of the day is a cheap option at weekday lunchtimes. €10

## SANTO AMARO

✗ **Fornos de Lava** Travessa de S Tiago, Santo Amaro, not far from Velas; ☎ 295 432 415 ⊕ noon–15.00 & 18.00–23.00 daily.

A delightfully rural place, with luxuriant views over pastures; the owners are really trying hard &, a true novelty for the Azores, they grow their own vegetables & herbs for the restaurant. €13

## QUEIMADA

✖ **A Quinta da Akafona** 100m west of the airport, on the main road; ✆ 295 432 590; ⏰ 10.00–22.00 daily. In a characterful, stone building, definitely one of the island's better options. Menu is fairly standard, but off-season it can draw a midweek crowd when other places are empty. €12

## FAJÃ DO OUVIDOR

✖ **Café O Amilcar** Close to the harbour; ✆ 295 417 448; ⏰ (meal service) noon–15.00 & 19.00–22.00 Wed–Mon. This simple café offers good fish – the owner is also a fisherman – plus standard meat dishes. €12

## RIBEIRA SECA

✖ **Café/Restaurante Ponto de Encontro** ✆ 295 416 240; ⏰ 07.30–midnight Wed–Mon. Located at Canada dos Vales, on the main road just before Ribeira Seca, this place does a buffet meal at lunch, à la carte for dinner. An inviting restaurant with views across to Pico & a good place to try the island's famous clams – cheaper here than elsewhere. €10

## NIGHTLIFE

The plush **auditorium** in Velas sometimes has events such as *fado* – ask at the tourist office for information of upcoming shows.

## OTHER PRACTICALITIES

**Emergency** ✆ 112
**Police** Velas; ✆ 295 412 339

**Health centre** Velas; ✆ 295 430 220. Open 24hrs for emergencies.

**WI-FI** Free access is available in the Jardim da Republica in Velas, at the Velas marina, in Calheta and at the airport.

**PARKING** Free of charge and away from high season, generally available in the centre of Velas. There is a large, free car park behind the courthouse.

## WHAT TO SEE AND DO

### MUSEUMS

**Museu de Arte Sacra (Sacred Art Museum)** (⏰ *10.00–noon & 14.00–18.00 Mon–Thu, 10.00–noon & 14.00–17.00 Fri, 10.00–noon Sat; €1*) Housed in a musty annexe of the Matriz de São Jorge church, Velas. The opening hours do rather depend on whether one of the volunteers is working in the museum at the time. Exhibits include sacred images, silver, censers and monstrances.

**Museu da São Jorge/Francisco Lacerda Museu** (*Rua Jose Azevedo da Cunha, Calheta;* ⏰ *09.00–18.00 daily; €1/free adult/under 12s*) On the main road down to the harbour, occupying a house built in 1811, there is a permanent exhibition about the history and ethnography of the island and a supporting library, as well as details about this Azorean composer (1869–1934) who worked and studied in Lisbon and Paris. Plans are afoot to move the museum to the former tuna factory down in the harbour, but whether it will happen during the lifetime of this edition is debatable. English-language information is available. What is currently lacking is a musical backdrop, playing some of Lacerda's compositions during your visit.

**Eco-Museu da Ilha da São Jorge** (Santo Antonio Eco-Museum) (*Santo Antonio; on the left, just after taking the Fajã da Ouvidor turn-off from the northern coast road;* ⊕ *16 Sep–14 Jun 14.00–17.30 Tue–Sat; 15 Jun–15 Sep 10.00–13.00 & 14.00–18.00 daily; free*) With English-language information on plant life and wildlife plus a short video with subtitles.

**FINISTERRA (CHEESE CO-OPERATIVE)** (☏ *295 415 216;* ⊕ *09.00–noon & 13.30–16.00 Mon–Sat; €1.50 inc tour & tasting*). You can look round this cheese factory, located on the main road, just west of Santo Antão There are three dairy co-ops on the island, but this is the only one making both the famous São Jorge cheese *and* the Topo cheese, the latter being softer and smoother. The tour is in English, modest, and the cost is merely to cover the hygiene-related clothing you have to wear. Tour guide Mary-Lou is very entertaining, and the cheese is tasty and authentic. Around 50% of the product is exported, much to the USA.

**BIRDS AND FLOWERS** The most interesting areas are undoubtedly the *fajãs*. Best known is **Fajã dos Cubres** on the north coast east of Norte Pequeno, formed largely by the 1757 earthquake and subsequent erosion and with a biologically rich, very indented lagoon. Groundwater enters the lagoon but causeways built across it have created two habitats, essentially marine to the west and fresh water in the east. It is among the most important wetland habitats in the Azores. Growing among the pain-inflicting sharp rush, *Juncus acutus*, is goldenrod, *Solidago sempervirens*, or cubres after which the *fajã* is named. Wild celery, wild carrot, orache and the submerged herb beaked tasselweed are among the varied plants. Eurasian coot and greenshank, snipe, terns and a long list of rarities can make this a rewarding site for birds, especially coming as it does at the end of a beautiful cliff walk (page 181).

A little further eastwards along the coast is the **Fajã da Caldeira do Santo Cristo**. Its lagoon is well known for being the only place in the Azores where clams are found. Although remote, it is also one of the best places for surfing in the islands. This nature reserve has one of the largest populations of endemic scabious, *Scabiosa nitens*.

**Ilhéu do Topo** off the far eastern end of São Jorge is a Special Protected Area because of its birdlife. The islet has in excess of 2,000 Cory's shearwaters among its many breeding seabirds.

At the other island extremity, the high coastal cliffs at **Ponta dos Rosais** support an interesting vegetation that can only without difficulty and danger be glimpsed from a distance. It is an important site for migratory birds and is a passage point for whales, dolphin and turtles.

## RECREATIONAL FOREST RESERVES
**Sete Fontes Forest Park** Signposted from the Velas to Rosais road. Here, at the Seven Fountains, the forestry department has laid out an attractive 12ha park with ornamental planting sheltered and shaded by trees. There are picnic tables, a barbecue area, and some animals. The surrounding countryside is a mixture of meadows and forestry. Many of the roads are unsurfaced, and a relaxing day can be spent exploring the area on foot (see also page 183).

**Silveira** Off the EN–2 main road, from Velas 5km beyond Calheta. This 10ha forest between 300m and 375m altitude on a steep south-facing hill is picturesquely crossed by several streams, once used to power watermills. There are numerous paths and shady walks, picnic areas, a deer enclosure, and some amusing exercise equipment. It is quite charming (page 188).

## ACTIVITIES

### CANYONING
**Discover Experience** Fajã dos Vimes; m 967 552 354/968 481 448; e geral@discoverxperience.com; www.discoverxperience.com. A young company with a range of activities, inc canyoning (from €55 pp) & coasteering (from €65 pp) – prices depend on group size. All activities inc insurance; min age limit may apply.

### DIVING
**Urzelinatur Dive Centre** Rua do Porto, Casteletes, Urzelina; 295 414 287; e victor_ soares@sapo.pt; www.urzelinatur.com; ⊕ 09.00–17.30 Mon–Sat

## FISHING

🐟 **Velas Fishing Tur** 📱 919 821 513;
✉ jaimefbpereira@hotmail.com. Big-game fishing

or bottom-fishing. Groups from 2 to 6 people, durations from 2 to 8 hrs, €40 pp.

## KAYAKING

🛶 **Discover Experience** (page 180) Sea kayaking from €50 pp, price depends on group size.

## SWIMMING  See map on page 172 for locations.

**Velas** Natural pools at Poça dos Frades, just west of the auditorium, and at Preguiça, just west of the Hotel São Jorge Garden.

**Urzelina** Natural pools and harbour swimming with changing facilities. About 100m further on at **Portinhos** is another access to the sea with facilities and a grassy relaxation area.

**Fajã Grande** Natural rock pool with all facilities.

**Fajã do Ouvidor** The Simão Dias natural swimming pool is in a dramatic setting near the harbour, with restaurant nearby (don't confuse it with the rather dirty pool further down).

## WALKING  São Jorge has some memorable walks; several are long established and so fairly clear to follow. There are seven official trails, summaries of which are given below. Although all routes are downloadable from www.visitazores.com, you should always check at the tourist office to ensure that your chosen route is open and safe before setting off. At the time of writing, a long-distance trail that will cross the entire island from Topo to Rosais was under construction.

### Serra do Topo, Fajã da Caldeira do Santo Cristo, Cristo–Fajã dos Cubres
(Map, page 182) Medium difficulty, 10km, 2½ hours. Down to and along the north coast, starting at the wind farm. Steep downhill sections will not suit the weak-kneed. A car park has been built at the start of the walk; there are restaurants at both Fajã da Caldeira do Santo Cristo and Fajã dos Cubres.

### Serra do Topo–Fajã dos Vimes  (Map, page 182) Hard (recently upgraded from medium difficulty), 5km, 2½ hours. Mostly downhill, on the south coast. Use the car park detailed above, a few hundred metres east of the trailhead.

### Fajã de São João–Lourais–Fajã dos Vimes  Hard (recently upgraded from medium difficulty), 10km, 3½ hours. Along the south-coast cliffs.

### Pico do Pedro, Pico da Esperança–Fajã do Ouvidor  Medium difficulty, 16.8km, 4 hours. Along the spine of the island.

### Fajã de Além  Medium difficulty, 6km, 3 hours. A shortish, circular walk down to the *fajã* from near the Santo António chapel, west of Norte Grande.

### Trilho do Norte Pequeno  Medium difficulty, 11km, 3 hours. A circular walk from Norte Pequeno descending the cliff face to the *fajã* settlements.

7

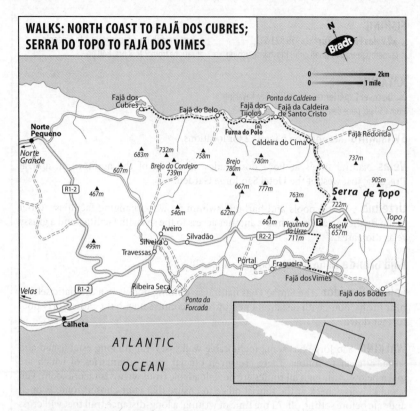

## Fajã dos Vimes–Fragueira–Portal
Medium difficulty, 3km, 1½ hours. Short linear walk on the south coast.

## Guided walks
**Discover Experience** (page 180) Offers guided walks between 4km & 18km, off the beaten track, giving insights into island history, geology & culture. Prices (from €40 pp) depend on group size, though they will go with a 'group' of only 1. Overnight expeditions also possible.

## TOURING THE ISLAND

São Jorge is skinny and elongated so, unlike in many of the islands, to travel places seems to take a disproportionate amount of time. Many visitors are based in Velas and content themselves with seeing Rosais in the far west, and then undertake a central circuit taking in both north and south coasts but not going further east than Calheta. There is a considerable amount of 'up and down' and roads are narrow and twisting; beware of injudiciously parked tractors and pick-up trucks.

**VELAS** [Map, page 184] Velas, the main town of São Jorge, remains very small, and the old part around the pretty harbour has been generally well cared for and retains its charm. The narrow backstreets, some fine houses with their wrought-iron balconies, the little shops, and the inviting, intriguing and imposing 18th-century gateway, or **Portão do Mar** [Map, page 184], all go to make a pleasing whole. You will even find a boat or two parked on the road along with the cars. Some of the little streets have been very prettily pedestrianised, and paved in the traditional manner of small black setts with designs in white depicting activities of the island. One street, Rua Maestro Francisco Lacerda, is now an attractive shopping area, replete with banks and souvenir shops, hanging baskets filled with flowers, a good cake shop at one end and the attractive town square at the other, where a fine replica now replaces the time-battered classic old bandstand. At a little distance the unmistakable and very modern community building declares Velas is really part of the 21st century; inside is the public library, meeting rooms and a splendid 220-seat theatre. There is an imposing parish church, the **Church of São Jorge** no less, which has been built and modified from the 17th century and of particular note is the carved wooden retable. The 17th-century **Church of Nossa Senhora da Conceição** was a former Franciscan monastery and is now cared for by nuns and well worth seeing. Tucked away inside the parish church is a tiny museum of sacred art, showing Indo-Portuguese items and silver altar vessels. Built upon a *fajã*, the harbour and old town is beautifully set against surrounding high cliffs, and the new marina complements it. Ferries from other islands arrive here throughout the year.

**ROSAIS** Rosais itself is a very linear village running along the road, but this is also the name given to the whole of the end of the island west of Velas. After you pass through the village you will come to the signposted Miradouro Pica da Velho, and at 493m this gives a commanding view over this part of the island. The viewpoint is generously planted with camellias, hydrangeas, azaleas and agapanthus so it is also very pretty when they flower; it is part of the Sete Fontes Recreational Reserve.

**FAROL DOS ROSAIS** This lighthouse is at the far western end of the island, and is also the end of the road. It is now abandoned, after the earthquake of 1980 made the cliffs unstable. Be very careful if you walk near the lighthouse as there are deep holes in the ground.

**THE CENTRAL PART OF THE ISLAND BETWEEN VELAS AND CALHETA** Leaving Velas, take the road to the north coast signposted to Norte Grande, and go first through **Beira**; continuing on the north road you pass through **Toledo**, now just a tiny village, which was probably first settled by Spanish immigrants soon after King Philip of Spain invaded Portugal. Next along the road is the settlement of **Santo António,** destroyed in the earthquake of 1980, and rebuilt.

**Norte Grande–Velas** Norte Grande is the largest village in the north. Do visit the church, Nossa Senhora das Neves, Our Lady of the Snows, dated 1762; it has a quiet and beautiful interior with splendid *azulejos* and modern stained-glass windows. Note the weathervane in the shape of a fish; this is peculiar to São Jorge and is the symbol adopted by early Christians. Fifty metres past the church, take a left where signposted to **Fajã do Ouvidor**. Stop in at the eco-museum (page 179), then continue down to the *miradouro* for a fine view of the village below: you will appreciate how inaccessible these *fajã* settlements are. (On a clear day you can see Graciosa and to your right, further along the coast, Fajã da Ribeira da Areia.) Now continue down to the *fajã* where there is a small harbour, a natural swimming pool and a restaurant (page 178). Even on a fairly calm day, the swell creates quite a spectacle as it crashes into a circle of rocks with rock-arches, a sort of semi-submarine Stonehenge. You can't help but wonder at the shelf life of the houses built precariously close to the edge. From the harbour, yams were once exported to Graciosa in exchange for clay roof tiles. There are waterfalls along the coast; if

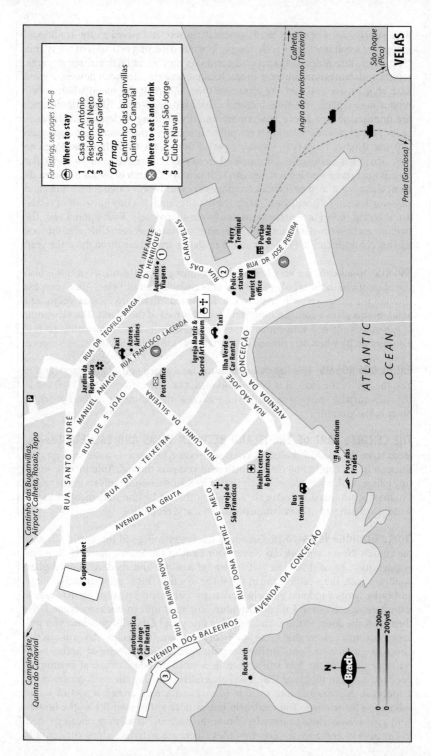

VELAS

Calheta,
São Roque (Pico)
Angra do Heroísmo (Terceira)
Praia (Graciosa)

ATLANTIC
OCEAN

For listings, see pages 176–8

**Where to stay**
1 Casa do António
2 Residencial Neto
3 São Jorge Garden

Off map
Cantinho das Buganvillas
Quinta do Canavial

**Where to eat and drink**
4 Cervecaria São Jorge
5 Clube Naval

Ferry
Terminal

Portão
do Mar

Police
station

RUA DAS CARAVELAS

RUA DR JOSÉ PEREIRA

Tourist
office

Aquárius
Viagens

RUA INFANTE
D HENRIQUE

RUA DR TEOFILO BRAGA

Taxi

Azores
Airlines

Jardim da
Republica

RUA FRANCISCO LACERDA

Taxi

Igreja Matriz &
Sacred Art Museum

RUA MANUEL ANIAGA

RUA DE S JOÃO

Post office

RUA CUNHA DA SILVEIRA

RUA DR J TEIXEIRA

RUA SANTO ANDRÉ

Cantinho das Buganvillas,
Airport, Calheta, Rosais, Topo

Ilha Verde
Car Rental

RUA SÃO JOSÉ

AVENIDA DA CONCEIÇÃO

Auditorium

Poça das
Frades

AVENIDA DA GRUTA

RUA DONA BEATRIZ DE MELO

Igreja de
São Francisco

Health centre
& pharmacy

Bus
terminal

Camping site,
Quinta do Canavial

Supermarket

Autoturistica
São Jorge
Car Rental

RUA DO BAIRRO NOVO

AVENIDA DOS BALEEIROS

Rock arch

AVENIDA DA CONCEIÇÃO

N

Bradt

0        200m
0        200yds

you are enjoying a gloriously sunny day and a period without rain, you will not see much evidence of them, however. The lava here came from what is now called Pico da Esperança (1,053m), which you can see high above you, but the details of the eruption are lost in pre-history. There are two short walks you can do here over the lava, taking the path next to the house with the new conspicuous stone driveway.

Having returned to the main road, in the middle of the next village, **Ribeira da Areia**, there is a stone sign pointing the way down to Fajã da Ribeira da Areia – another dead end, twisting and turning its way down to the ocean. By the waterside is a community of tiny houses, inhabited by hardy islanders. It makes you appreciate just how isolated some of these communities were and still are. A memorial on the rocks pays homage to a villager who disappeared in the ocean.

Move on to the large village of **Norte Pequeno** where the road turns south to Calheta. Look out for the asphalt road signposted down to Fajã dos Cubres; from the top there is probably one of the finest views of the coast. The *fajã* beyond dos Cubres is Fajã da Caldeira de Santo Cristo (page 186), another isolated settlement with its nearest road nearly an hour's walk from the road ending below you.

Cross the island to Calheta, but before you get there take the main road left signposted to Topo and then go down to **Ribeira Seca**. On the skyline above you will see five wind turbines generating 15% of the island's energy requirement. The road is very pretty, lined with flowering azaleas, hydrangeas, escallonia and tibouchina shrubs. Near the church is a large private house covered with painted tiles, and a 17m-tall chimney inspired by the Royal Palace at Sintra. It was built in 1905, in French colonial style, by Gaspar de Silva, a Hawaiian emigrant who returned very wealthy – the current epidemic of pretentious new building would seem to be nothing new! Another house belonging to him with the same kind of exterior tiles may be seen in the centre of Velas. Francesco Lacerdo, the Azores' greatest composer and friend of Claude Debussy, was born here in 1869 and later lived in Urzelina.

Go along the lower road into **Calheta**, in size second only to Velas. Calheta developed as a town, but Velas has the better harbour and so became the principal town, later reinforced by the construction of its nearby airport. There remains a healthy rivalry. Calheta is on Fajã Grande, one of the flat coastal plains around the island. There is a recently extended busy harbour, with its small fishing fleet, near which may be seen an old tuna factory. There are public toilets, a post office and a café/bar serving light meals. There is also the museum (page 178), a tourist information office (page 176), and you can even visit the Santa Catarina tuna

## DECORATIVE PAVING

Decorative paving has long been a feature of Moorish Spain and Portugal, although today it is the latter where it is most popular. It first appeared in the Azores in 1825, when the governor had it laid in front of his residence in Horta. The idea soon spread but most of the present paving dates from the 1940s. The black stones are, of course, basalt from abundant local sources but the white are limestone and have to be imported. On mainland Portugal the situation is reversed, and white dominates. A knapping hammer is used to shape the individual stones which are then laid on a thick layer of sand and dry cement, with the gaps filled with dry sand. It is always fascinating to watch the paviors at work as they apply their considerable skill in a seemingly most nonchalant manner to give great charm to the archipelago's streets.

Seven people reside permanently in Santo Cristo, safely out of reach of the road network. Having been destroyed by earthquake and abandoned, it was then resettled, but following a further quake, social housing was built for the villagers on the south side of the island and many never returned.

Until now, perhaps. You have three options to get to the village, two of which involve walking and the other clinging on to the back of a quad bike as it negotiates the bumpy 4km along the side of the ocean, a couple of hundred metres below. Best not to look down.

No new-built properties are currently allowed in the village, but many of the abandoned houses are now being renovated, all the building materials being brought on the snarling quads. A second restaurant is underway, and there are a couple of surf-houses and a guesthouse. Part-time power is by generator, meals taken by candlelight. With no shops, you need to bring your own provisions with you.

In the mixed salt/freshwater lagoon in front of the houses, a diver looks for the famous clams which adorn the menus across the island.

It's a beautiful place, free of vehicles, free of Wi-Fi and without television. Electricity is on its way, however, though surely not a road. In summer, the snap and snarl of those quads disturbs the peace; in winter, those seven hardy residents are joined by few outsiders, making it the ultimate retreat.

Will it change? Undoubtedly, but the locals currently call the shots, determined to keep it as something special. An otherworldly place, a unique atmosphere. Just don't forget the tea bags: there are no shops, and it's a long way back.

factory, the island's biggest private employer at the west end of town ( 295 416 220; e geral@atumsantacatarina.com; ⊕ visits at 10.00 & 14.00 Mon–Fri, advance notice required; €1.50), though you'll need to be comfortable with a very strong fishy smell. The factory is on the lower road from Calheta, and you pass through **Fajã Grande** itself. Santa Catarina is held to be among the best brands and the product is exported to Europe, the USA and now China.

Following the main road back to Velas, you will come to **Manadas** (meaning 'a group of cows'), where you must stop to see the **18th-century parish church** dedicated to Santa Bárbara, assuming that the extensive renovation works have been completed (⊕ Sun only for mass, but call m 911 110 060 & Senhora Gina will open up). It is very small and in a most beautiful setting by the sea adjacent to the ruined remains of a fort that once defended the little harbour. This gem of Azorean Baroque is the finest in the archipelago, and the interior has remained almost unchanged for many generations. There are splendid tiles telling the story of Santa Bárbara, a rich gilt carved altar and a cedarwood ceiling. Legend has it that in 1485, a sailor, Joaquim António da Silveira, found an image of Santa Bárbara in a wooden box off the coast of São Jorge and thought a church in her honour should be built. Work started in 1510, but it was later enlarged to its present form in about 1770, and of the original there remains a window and a font.

At **Terreiros** there is a small harbour with picnic tables and two restaurants. **Urzelina** suffered tremendously in the eruption of 1808 when the lava flowed down and buried everything except the church tower and this remains today as a monument to the buried village. Many of the villagers sheltered inside the church and were either buried or suffocated. It is on the right, close to the main road, surrounded by a pretty little garden. Overlooking the small harbour is a seating area with two commemorative stones. The first concerns a former harbour master. A British schooner, the *Tamar Queen*, anchored offshore and was boarded by the harbour master Amaro Soares but bad weather quickly blew up and the ship set sail for England. Sadly, Senhor Soares was murdered, and the crew later punished. The second gives the names of early settlers. Immediately above the harbour are the remains of an old Portuguese fort, now a summer café/bar. On the harbour's other side is a house with a large tile picture on its wall; this was once a temporary store for oranges before they were exported to England. There are some manor houses in the village that reflected the wealth of the orange farmers. Urzelina gets its name from the lichen that was such an important export in the early days after settlement. A small ethnographic museum by the harbour was severely damaged by waves in 2016, but may reopen.

**Ribeira do Nabo** is a small village beyond Urzelina where the **Cooperativa Artesanato Sra da Encarnação** (*signposted off the main road, then located beside the church;* ⊕ *09.00–18.00 Mon–Fri; at weekends, call* ◣ *295 414 296 or* m *962 296 734 & someone will open up*). It offers a good range of nicely handmade goods including knitted pullovers, appliqué, macramé, ceramics, items in wood, jams and many other things. Only three local women still operate the weaving looms here, making a total of five in the whole island. In a few years, their skills may be lost forever. After you reach the airport at Queimada there is a road going down to the sea and a very primitive landing place called **Porto da Queimada**. In summer there used to be a boat that ferried between here and Velas, long before construction of the new marina. The blackened stone tower that looks as if it might once have been a windmill is in fact an old lime kiln. The best thing though is the sea-level view of Velas, worth seeing if you travel by air and do not come or go by the ferry.

**THE EASTERN PART OF THE ISLAND** To reach **Fajã dos Vimes**, going down from the main road to Topo, is a most beautiful drive through luxuriant forests of largely acacia, the high humidity offering shelter for ferns and mosses. Stop at the Miradouro dos Vimes; 300m below is Fajã Fragueira and in the distance your immediate destination of Fajã dos Vimes. As you further descend note two old watermills and the overhead wires still used today for transporting forage and fuelwood to the houses way below. In the village, find the **Café Nunes**; here they make arabica coffee from beans grown in the village. The beans are picked between May and September. Above the café, there is a small weaving centre where Senhora Nunes and her sister make the famous woven woollen bedspreads. Made with natural colours and traditional designs and looms, and wool imported from Santa Maria and mainland Portugal, they are not only collectors' items, but also a great pleasure to use. Sadly, there are now only two people weaving here and it takes a week and a half to make a double bedspread. These cost around €550. Other people also make them at the co-operative in Ribeira do Nabo (see above), and they can be found in the shops in Velas. Towards the cliff you will see growing many pollarded willows that are used for basket making; *vimes* means 'withy' or 'osier'. From the eastern end of the village there is an obvious footpath eastwards to make the short walk to **Fajã dos Bodes** and its waterfall and mill.

Return to the main road and continue eastwards; if you have time, drop down to **Fajã de São João** with its mixed orchards enjoying the microclimate, the watermills and dragon trees. Back on the main road, you will reach the **Finisterra cheese factory** (page 179), then pass extensive areas of pasture to come to **Santo Antão** and finally **Topo** with its lighthouse. Take the road to the right of the lighthouse to find a viewpoint over the **Ilhéu do Topo**, a strictly protected sanctuary for birds which they share with some hardy sheep. The very first settlement on São Jorge was at Topo, but the Serra do Topo so separated the people from the rest of the island that it was easier to go by boat to Terceira for their supplies rather than travel by land.

On the way back to Velas, above Fajã dos Vimes, you will see a surfaced road going off on your right by the side of the turbine parks. This ranks highly among the many beautiful roads of the Azores, as it winds along through a gentle landscape of small pastures surrounded by hedges, especially lovely in July and August when the hydrangeas are flowering. It is not a long drive, so do stop along the way and enjoy late-afternoon shadows and the tranquillity. You will come to a junction. Turn left to Silveira; if you turned right you would go to Norte Pequeno. Soon you will see signs marking the way to the **Silveira Recreational Forest Park**, a beautifully green semi-gardened area to stroll around. Should you arrive earlier in the day, then it is a cool place to enjoy a picnic (page 180).

# 8

## Faial

Known as the Blue Island because of its many hydrangeas, Faial is quite spectacular when they are blooming from mid-July through August. One taxi driver said he had calculated there are 56km of hydrangea hedges. Some years ago a letter appeared in *The Times* London newspaper bemoaning the abundant hydrangeas in the Azores and appealing for something else to be planted!

Much of the landscape is pasture, although there is now some forest; at one time the tree cover was so depleted that wood for fuel was imported from Pico. At the time of settlement the island was luxuriously forested, including an abundance of what the Portuguese called *faya*, and so named the island Fayal. The plant was later collected by Kew's first paid plant hunter Robert Masson in 1777, who introduced it to the gardens where it was scientifically named *Myrica faya*.

Although the island is dominated by its central caldera and nearby highest point of 1,031m, the visitor is not really aware of this, travelling around the island past its pretty villages, lush pastures and vigorous hedgerows.

If you arrive from a tour of the smaller islands, approaching Horta from the airport can fool you into thinking you are at the entrance to a city: a smattering of industry and a spate of large villas line the way into town. Once in town, this impression soon disappears in the face of simple, elegant Portuguese architecture and cobbled streets and pavements. Picturesque Horta has long been a major port of the Azores and the town has dominated the island; today its marina is a major tourist attraction and the harbour has the largest maritime painting collection in the world. Around 1,100 yachts put in each year for supplies and repairs as they make the Atlantic crossing and this influx of around 5,500 mostly young crew members certainly enlivens the evenings, especially between May and August.

History is everywhere among the streets and old buildings, and always across the channel is the great cone of Pico. Sometimes it is totally clear, seeming arrogantly to challenge the elements to renew their erosive attacks. More often, it is adorned with a fast-changing wardrobe of clouds, engulfing its summit, encircling its midriff, or clothing it from apex to base, and obscuring it from our sight but not our consciousness; you never tire of glancing across the channel. In winter with its uppermost quarter dusted with snow and fronted with a travel-brochure blue sea, the mountain is breathtakingly beautiful.

Horta, the only town, will take at least a half day to explore, easily a full day with the museums. Seeing the highlights of the rest of the island can be done by taxi or hire car and could occupy a day. There are now a few more official walks too, to stretch the legs. The view into the caldera, green and a nature reserve, and the reverse view down to Horta, across the channel to Pico island and up to its volcano summit with São Jorge beyond, make it well worth a drive up. Then there is Capelinhos, the site of the major 1957 eruption which added another 2km² to Faial; the devastated lighthouse and half-buried village houses, slowly becoming exposed once more

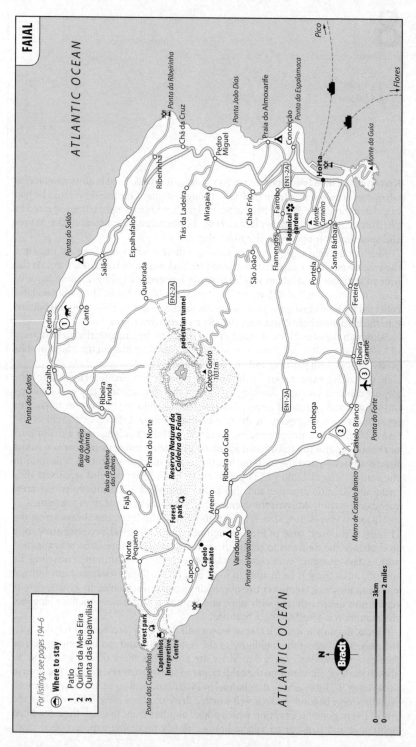

FAIAL

ATLANTIC OCEAN

ATLANTIC OCEAN

For listings, see pages 194–6

**Where to stay**
1 Patio
2 Quinta da Meia Eira
3 Quinta das Buganvílias

Ponta dos Cedros

Ponta do Salão

Ponta da Ribeirinha

Ponta João Dias

Ponta do Almoxarife

Ponta da Espalamaca

Ponta dos Capelinhos

Baía da Areia da Quinta

Baía da Ribeira das Cabras

Ponta do Varadouro

Morro de Castelo Branco

Ponta do Forte

Monte da Guia

Pico

Flores

Cedros
Canto
Cascalho
Ribeira Funda
Praia do Norte
Fajã
Norte Pequeno
Capelo
Capelinhos
Interpretive Centre
Forest park
Varadouro
Areeiro
Ribeira do Cabo
Forest park
Reserva Natural da Caldeira do Faial
Cabeço Gordo 1031m
pedestrian tunnel
Salão
Espalhafalos
Quebrada
Trás da Ladeira
Ribeirinha
Chã da Cruz
Pedro Miguel
Miragaia
Chão Frio
São João
Flamengos
Farrobo
Botanical garden
Monte Carneiro
Conceição
Praia do Almoxarife
Horta
Santa Bárbara
Portela
Feteira
Ribeira Grande
Lombega
Castelo Branco
Capelo
Artesanato

EN2-2A
EN1-2A
EN1-2A

N
Bradt

0       3km
0       2 miles

by wind erosion from their smothering of ash, bear witness to the human drama. All of this is now enhanced by the high-tech interpretative centre spectacularly built below ground in the fallout from the eruption, for which you should allow 1½ to two hours. Recently there have been many new developments and Faial now offers a good range of interests and maritime and land-based activities. There's a new museum and a small aquarium situated at Porto Pim.

## BACKGROUND

**GEOLOGY** Faial is the nearest island to the Mid-Atlantic Ridge, some 100km to the west, and grew up on its flanks from a depth of 1,500m from the same northwest–southeast-aligned fissures that gave rise to Pico. It was formed by four volcanic complexes. First, the Ribeirinha complex in the northeast of the island, part of a shield volcano (one that is gently sloping, built of very fluid basaltic lava from many closely spaced vents) and forming the oldest rocks of Faial at around 700,000 years ago. Associated are two major fault lines or scarps, to the north and to the south of Pedro Miguel village. Second, the Cedros complex in the north and linked to the development of the central Caldeira volcano; Horta Formation, the third stage of Faial's construction, began around 11,000 years ago, with what at first were Surtseyan eruptions when seawater could enter the vent, mix with the rising magma, and create steam causing the magma to shatter into fine fragments. Once the vents were above water, eruptions changed to more moderate types. Monte Queimado and Monte da Guia, which protect what is now Horta harbour, date from this period. Monte da Guia, consisting of thin layers of yellowish ash, often compacted or welded into tuff, erupted in shallow water whereas the burnt cinders of adjacent Monte Queimado burst on to dry land. Finally, there is the Capelo Formation, the most recent complex. The Capelo Peninsula grew westwards from a series of eruptions on land, remaining evidence being the alignment of domes starting from near the Caldeira volcano that are a continuum of the Pedro Miguel Fault. Only two eruptions at the very end of the peninsula occurred underwater: these were Costa da Nua and the latest, Capelinhos. The Ilhéus dos Capelinhos were evidence of an earlier eruption, but they were destroyed by the Capelinhos eruption. In historical times, the Cabeço do Fogo (*cabeço* meaning 'head') and Picarito erupted in 1672; they caused seven months of intermittent earthquakes spreading ash over the island and lava flows which buried houses and farmland in and around Praia do Norte and formed the present Zona do Mistério. It is assumed some of the four systems may have been active simultaneously.

The Caldeira volcano that today dominates the island began as a stratovolcano, a steep-sided cone with a medium or low basaltic explosive activity forming bedded layers of lava fragments and flows. Some 16,000 years ago, this eruptive pattern changed to a mainly explosive acidic form, producing a pale viscous acidic rock which often formed rugged lava flows and domes. During this later period the Caldeira volcano erupted at least 14 times, one of them coinciding with the opening of the caldera 1,000 years ago. This was a Plinian eruption, a highly dramatic and powerful explosion of gas, steam, ash and pumice rising kilometres into the air, together with pyroclastic flows – avalanches of hot gas, ash and rock debris. The caldera is now 400m deep and 1,450m in diameter with almost vertical walls. The highest point of the island is Cabeço Gordo at 1,031m, a basaltic cinder cone on the side of the Caldeira volcano.

Future events will most likely occur in connection with the Capelo Formation and the Caldeira volcano. At a second level, the Horta platform or the faults of Pedro Miguel might offer excitement.

**HISTORY** Early maps present the island as *Insule de Ventura*, and the Portuguese discovered it in the first half of the 15th century and began settlement. Led by Josse Van Huerter, a few Flemish settlers came to Faial in 1468, and just 20 years later their number had grown to 1,500. Establishing themselves first at Praia do Almoxarife, they soon moved inland to the Vale dos Flamengos ('Valley of the Flemish'), not far from Horta, and the parish now called Flamengos evidences this early settlement. The first two areas developed were at either end of what is now the main port and marina of Horta. The Azores have always played an important role in the history of the Atlantic. Laden Portuguese ships returning from the West Indies would seek protection from the many pirates awaiting them off the African coast. As both the new English settlements in North America and the West Indies and the Portuguese Empire grew, Horta became a busy sea port, then the only really safe anchorage in the Azores. Horta was not only trading but also victualling, supplying good fresh water and vegetables, repairing ships and providing crews for East Indiamen, West Indiamen, codfishers, slavers, ships carrying wine, or sugar, or salt, or miscellaneous cargoes, and men-of-war. In addition, there has always been a great deal of inter-island trading, as well as between the islands and mainland Portugal.

Of course, it was not always peaceful; in 1583, the Spanish attacked and fought a battle for the Santa Cruz fortress. This still overlooks the harbour, but is now a *pousada* (state-owned hotel). During Spanish rule English privateers attacked several times; Sir Walter Raleigh razed Horta by fire, carried off the governor and either captured or destroyed all of a Spanish fleet home-bound from Mexico. A far more peaceful English visitor was Captain James Cook who, in 1775, merely checked his navigational instruments onshore before sailing off to explore the South Seas.

Early whaling fleets came to Horta for supplies, anchoring in Porto Pim to rest, to offload whale oil and recruit crews. Later, entrepreneurs developed warehouses and other facilities to further attract ships to Horta. Among these was American John Dabney who arrived at the beginning of the 1800s, and whose family influenced commerce for 100 years. The family house, lookout, wine cellar and whaleboat house are all preserved today. Oranges and Pico wine were two important exports they handled, as well as whale products, whale fishing, ships' chandlery, and much else. Extremely successful, they lived life on a lavish scale, building several large houses, entertaining and exchanging latest news with ships' officers, and being generous benefactors to the islanders. The number of whalers increased, especially from New Bedford, which is now twinned with Horta. Work began in 1876 on the docks and sea wall to better protect the port so that steam ships could also call as well as sailing ships, and so bunkering services were added with much of the coal shipped out from Liverpool, England.

The world's first reliable transatlantic telegraph cable connection was laid in 1866, and more quickly followed during the next 50 years linking many regions of the world. In 1893, the first cable was laid linking Horta with Ponta Delgada and on to Carcavelos on the Arrabida coast south of Lisbon. This was operated by an English company, the Europe and Azores Telegraph Co, which eventually became, in 1934, part of Cable & Wireless.

These early telegraph cables had a relatively short operational range, and Horta's mid-Atlantic position was ideal for a relay station for transatlantic cables. It was also a good interchange location, and Deutsch-Atlantische Telegraphengesellschaft, founded in 1900, laid its first cable to link the USA and Germany via the Azores. Further cables followed, between Horta and Waterville in Ireland, Horta and

Porthcurno in Cornwall and on to Mindelo in the Cape Verde Islands to connect with other cables to Africa and South America.

In the early 1900s, there were some 300 employees – British, Germans, Americans and Portuguese. The last cable connecting Horta was laid in 1928, the latest technology allowing simultaneous transmission of five messages in each direction, a total of 500 words per minute. Now Horta was one of the most important cable centres in the world. It was in 1969 that the last cable company left, superseded by new technology. The 1893 cable linking the Azores with mainland Europe also meant the meteorological observations made in the Azores, so far out in the Atlantic, could be transmitted rapidly; this had a tremendous influence on the development of weather forecasting. In 1901, construction of the Prince Albert of Monaco Observatory began on the summit of Cabeço das Moças, above what is now the Faial Resort Hotel, and it is still in use today. Colloquially, *moça* means 'mistress', and the hill was thus named because it was where visiting sailors courted the town's young women.

The first transatlantic crossing by seaplane was made in 1919 by the American Albert C Read, who landed off Horta *en route*, to be followed by many others. In 1933, Charles Lindbergh flew to Horta seeking an acceptable year-round route for Pan-Am's seaplanes from America to Europe. Soon after Horta became the regular stopover for the Pan-Am clipper flights, to be followed by Lufthansa, Air France and Imperial Airways, now British Airways. However, there were disadvantages: the harbour was not large enough for landings and take-offs and the big flying boats had to use the open ocean, taxiing in and out of the harbour. Ocean swells could delay flights and in December 1939, four clippers were stranded for three weeks. This romantic era of travel ended with improved land-based aircraft and a runway constructed on Santa Maria.

Now the summer maritime traffic crossing the Atlantic enhances the cosmopolitan life of Horta, the giant cruise ships berthed on one side of the harbour facing off with the sleek yachts on the other. Tourism generally is the new growth industry. Meanwhile, cattle and fishing continue in the background.

## GETTING THERE AND AWAY

For travel to Faial, see pages 42–4 and 48–9. Compared with some of the smaller islands, Faial's airport is a step up, receiving as it does international flights from Lisbon. It can offer an ATM, gift shop, cafeteria, a couple of car-hire firms, **Ilha Verde** (✆ *292 943 945; www.ilhaverde.com*) and **Autoturistica Faialense** (✆ *292 292 308; www.autoturisticafaialense.com*), a tourist office and free Wi-Fi. With luggage, a taxi to Horta will cost around €12.50. (Airport buses are infrequent.)

**Azores Airlines** [204 C3] Largo do Infante, Horta;
✆ 292 202 290; ⏰ 09.00–18.00. Also at the airport
✆ 292 202 310

## GETTING AROUND

Within Horta itself, there are four bus lines tootling around, on weekdays only. For most visitors, these will be unnecessary, given the modest dimensions of the town, but all of them go to (or very near to) the ferry terminal, so could be useful if you have luggage. There are infrequent public buses around the island, but you will need to obtain the current timetable with the tourist office, or search online (*www.farias.pt*). They are inexpensive, but not of great help to the visitor. Most frustratingly, the new interpretative centre at Capelinhos is not well served; currently you can either get out there by or leave at around 12.30. If you get stuck, you will find local drivers amenable to hitchhikers.

The best way to see the island is to hire a car for a day or two, or to take a taxi tour. Taxis cost around €17 per hour.

If you are pushed for time and literally just want to *see* the island, without stopping, you can take the 11.45 bus which goes westwards from the stop close to the tourist information office. This will take you round the coast to Ribeira Funda, from where it continues clockwise in line with the coast back to Horta. The whole circuit takes two hours, costing €5.95. When you board the bus, ask for a ticket to go right round the island. First following the coast and a sparkling blue sea you get to Capelinhos, and a good view of the 1958 eruption site and the half-buried lighthouse. Twenty years ago the area was pretty well deserted, with damaged or destroyed houses lying abandoned or buried in ash. Now people are returning, and either restoring the old houses or building new ones and it is becoming very attractive. On to Praia do Norte and to Cedros, passing through some well-forested areas, it is then down to Ribeirinha before climbing up to Espalamaca, looking down to Praia do Almoxarife on your left, to Pico, and opposite, the splendid view of Horta.

**EXCURSIONS TO OTHER ISLANDS** To travel to Pico by ferry, there are regular 30-minute sailings from Horta to Madalena throughout the year. In winter, Atlântico Line (*www.atlanticoline.pt*) runs ferries four-times daily (*07.30, 10.45, 13.15 and 17.15*), with two more crossings added in summer (*09.00 & 20.15*). Returning ferries from Madalena depart at 08.15, 11.30, 14.00 and 18.00 in winter and additionally at 09.45 and 21.00 in summer. A single fare costs €3.60. Less frequently, there is also a service to São Roque, on Pico's northern coast (*1hr 10mins*). In summer, ferries also leave Horta daily or twice daily for Velas on São Jorge (*2hrs 20mins*), with a few boats also calling at Calheta. Similarly, there is a summer service thrice weekly leaving Horta for Angra do Heroísmo on Terceira, a 7-hour journey. Again, check the website for the latest information. For location of listings see map, pages 190 and 203.

## TOURIST INFORMATION

The main tourist information office is opposite the Pousada de Santa Cruz on the Rua Vasco da Gama in central Horta [203 C3] (✆ 292 292 237; e pt.fai@azores.gov.pt; ⊕ 09.00–12.30 & 14.00–17.30 Mon–Fri). An additional office serves the cruise-ship hordes and ferry passengers in the Maritime Terminal and an airport office opens to meet incoming flights.

 ## WHERE TO STAY

Horta has several large hotels, plus a few smaller, characterful options, plush apartments and budget choices. Out of town, you'll find some tasteful, relaxed places, together with *casas* which can be rented by the week. All prices can rocket during Sea Week, in early August.

The Tourism Association (*www.casasacorianas.com*) lists many inviting rural tourism establishments around the island, offering from two to ten rooms. Some of these may be bookable only by the week. However, there are three pleasant places which can be booked by the night.

# HORTA

**🏠 Faial Resort Hotel** [203 C4] (143 rooms) Rua Consul Dabney; 📞292 207 400; e centraldereservas@investacor.com.com; www. investacor.com. Bar, snack bar, lounge, shop, games room, spa, conference rooms, indoor pool & outdoor pools, fitness room. Going since 1973, with part occupying buildings once belonging to one of the cable companies, plus addition of new wings. Copious buffet b/fast. €€€€€€

**🏠 Apartamentos Kósmos** [203 C2] (12 apts) Av 25 de Abril; 📱 927 517 518/962 374 761; e kosmosreservas@sapo.pt. Spacious, modern, fully equipped s/c apts in an unnumbered blue building on the waterfront. Free Wi-Fi & cable TV. Rooms are land or sea view. €€€€€

**🏠 Estrela do Atlantico** [203 B1] (5 rooms) Calçada de Santo Antonio; 📞292 943 003; e info@edatlantico.com; www.edatlantico.com. Individualistic, stylish rooms in a large manor house, set in rich gardens & less than 10mins' walk from town. Soft colours & tasteful furnishings enhance the relaxed ambience. Large living room with myriad books & an honesty bar. Duplex rooms can accommodate families. Free Wi-Fi, excellent, inventive b/fast inc. Recommended. €€€€€

**🏠 Hotel do Canal** [203 C4] (103 rooms) Largo Dr Manuel de Arriaga; 📞292 202 120; e reservas@ bensaude.pt; www.bensaude.pt. Friendly staff, in a large, international-class hotel. Located by the busy harbour. Large rooms enjoy AC, cable TV & free Wi-Fi. Reasonable restaurant, bars, winter garden, games room, fitness centre, sauna, jacuzzi, Turkish bath, hairdresser, conference room, garage. Excellent buffet b/fast inc. €€€€€

**🏠 Pousada Forte Horta** (formerly Pousada de Santa Cruz) [203 C3] (28 rooms) Rua Vasco da Gama; 📞210 407 670; e recepcao.stacruz@pestana.com; www.pousadas.pt. A 16th-century fort declared a national monument in 1947. Renovated to the high standards of Pousadas de Portugal, only the balconied superior rooms have a sea view; the restaurant offers regional dishes at prices a little more than elsewhere, & there's also a bar with terrace & pool overlooking the harbour, with views across to Pico. €€€€€

**🏠 Vila Bélgica** [203 A1] (3 rooms) Caminho Velho da Caldeira 13; 📞292 392 614; e villabelgica@sapo.pt; www.azoresvilabelgica. com. On the outskirts of Horta, a charming B&B with views across to Pico. €€€

**🏠 A Casa do Lado** [203 C1] (14 rooms) Rua D Pedro 23; 📞292 700 351; 📱 961 964 414; e geral@acasadolado.com; www.acasadolado. com. Decent budget option; go for a standard room but specify a balcony. Cable TV, free Wi-Fi, private bath. B/fast inc in mid & high season. Low-season rates are excellent. €€

**🏠 Faial Marina Apartments** [203 C3] (6 apts) Rua Conselheiro Medeiros 8; 📞292 391 313; e torrinhasazuis@gmail.com. Spacious modern apts, some of which can accommodate up to 10 people. Fully s/c, with AC, free Wi-Fi, cable TV & private parking. Very central & good value. €€

# ELSEWHERE ON FAIAL

**🏠 Patio** [map, page 190] (8 rooms & apts) Quinta do Moinho, Rua da Igreja, Cedros; 📱 917 428 111; e bookin@patio.pt; www.patio.pt. Linked to the horseriding centre on the north coast (page 200), you can stay here in these brand-new (2016) rooms & apts, without jumping on a gee-gee. Pleasant outdoor space, free Wi-Fi & a relaxed ambience. €€€

**🏠 Quinta da Meia Eira** [map, page 190] (13 rooms) Rua dos Inocentes, Castelo Branco; 📱 965 435 925; e info@meiaeira.com; www.meiaeira.com. Set well off the main road, west of Horta, with views down to the sea. A pleasant rural retreat with lovely rooms. Half-covered, year-round swimming pool, spacious gardens. Free Wi-Fi, cable TV, AC. B/fast inc. Excellent reputation, good value. €€€

**🏠 Quinta das Buganvílias** [map, page 190] (8 double rooms) Castelo Branco, by a bus stop on the EN1–1A, above the airport & 6 miles from Horta; 📞292 943 255; e qta-buganvilias@hotmail.com; www.quintadasbuganvilias.com. An old family property, with the *quinta* converted into what is now a long-established guesthouse with a lounge & bar – which doubles up as a museum – all in a pleasant garden & orchard setting of 5 acres. Free Wi-Fi. €€€

# CAMPING

**⛺ Praia do Almoxarife** 📞292 949 855; www. urbhorta.pt; ⏱ Jun–Sep. Near the small beach, with a lovely view across to Pico. A 15min taxi drive from Horta, or reachable by local bus. Tents can be hired. €

**⛺ Salão** 📞292 946 042; ⏱ Jun–Sep. Near Salão, on the north coast. €

**⛺ Varadouro** 📞292 945 339; e campismo. hortaludus@mail.telepac.pt; ⏱ Jun–Sep. Close to the tidal swimming pools. €

In Horta, there are plenty of so-called snack bars and still not enough good restaurants. Some recommended places are listed below.

## HORTA

**✗ A Arvore** [203 C1] Rua da Conceiçao 23; ☏ 292 392 500; ⏰ noon–15.00 & 18.30–22.00 Tue–Sun. At the town's northern end, open buffet served at lunch & dinner, fill up as often as you like for €7. Desserts & drinks extra, but still a real bargain & a good choice for the hungry. Established for 23 years. *€7*

**✗ Atletico Restaurante** [203 B4] Rua Luis Camões, Loco 8a; ☏ 292 292 492; ⏰ noon–15.00 & 19.00–23.00 daily. First, finding it: don't confuse it with the previous location (the sign's still up!), nor the Atletico Bar. Keep heading away from the sea & it's a few hundred metres further, on your left. Fish & meat is all cooked over a wood fire. A simple place, but reliable. *€10*

**✗ Canto da Doca** [203 C4] Rua Nova; ☏ 292 292 444; ⏰ noon–14.30 & 19.30–23.00 daily. Located in the corner of the harbour, this offers a very different meal where you cook your own dinner of seafood or meat on a very hot lump of basalt. It is great fun, albeit noisy & rather expensive for the experience, but at least there are no complaints about the chef! *€15*

**✗ Clipper Restaurant (Hotel do Canal)** (See page 195) ⏰ 12.30–15.00 & 19.00–22.00 daily. In a swish, modern setting, good fresh fish & other dishes at prices a bit above the norm. A set dinner is also on offer, changing daily. *€15*

**✗ Genuino's** [203 C5] Areinha Velha 9; ☏ 292 701 542; www.genuino.pt; ⏰ noon–15.00 & 19.00–23.00 daily. Overlooking Porto Pim & the beach, a place top-rated for its fish, & while you pay a bit more, you can contemplate the achievements of Portugal's only solo round-the-world sailor. Even better, talk to him – this fine gentleman will greet you at the door. Serves everything from fish stew to lobster – you could spend a lot of money in here, but you don't have to. Save some appetite for dessert, as the *perdiçao do Genuino* (chocolate cake with passion-fruit ice cream) is a must. *€16*

**✗ Taberna de Pim** [203 C5] Rua Nova 3, by Porto Pim; ☏ 292 700 905; ⏰ 11.00–01.00 daily. Small, nice atmosphere, food cooked to order. *€12*

**⌨ Café Porto Pim** [203 C5] Rua Areinha Velha 5; ☏ 292 292 979; ⏰ 07.00–21.00 daily. Overlooking the sea in Porto Pim, great for its location, outdoor tables & proximity to the beach. Excellent for a snack lunch offering good soup & a welcome range of sandwiches. *€9*

**⌨ Casa Tea House** [203 C2] Rua São João, 2 streets above the main post office; ☏ 292 700 053; ⏰ noon–22.00 Mon, Tue, Thu, noon–02.00 Fri, 16.00–02.00 Sat, 16.00–22.00 Sun Refreshingly different, young owner Eugene creates a super ambience. With a delightful garden & roof terrace with town views, the perfect place for a pot of tea; take your choice from Asia, Africa, South America, plus herbal, flower & fruit infusions. Eugene bakes up cakes as wicked as his sense of humour. Soup, snacks & sandwiches, inc smoked salmon & goat's cheese & other offerings. Daring to be different, also offers cocktails, coffee, wines & beers. *€4*

## PORTO DO VARADOURO

**✗ Vista da Baía** On the way to Capelo; ☏ 292 946 155; ⏰ noon–15.00 & 18.00–21.00 (until 16.00 Sun) Thu–Tue. Serves the best barbecued chicken on the island at a very reasonable price, with great sunsets thrown in. *€12*

## CEDROS

**✗ Aldina** Estrada Regional 54; ☏ 292 946 155; ⏰ 07.30–22.30. Sharing its premises with a supermarket, located on the main road, a bright & modern dining room with daily dishes at decent prices. *€10*

## NORTE PEQUENO

**⌨ Fim do Mundo** On the main road. The 'End of the World' is how this bar's name translates. Surely one of the world's smallest, it is run by English-speaking Domingos, a returned emigrant from the US. Located on the main road, it's 'drinks only' & the opening hours are strictly to suit himself. Good entertainment value, if you're passing by. Try some island liquors. No coffee: 'You can make it at home!' says Domingos.

**AUTATLANTIS**
*Rent a Car*

# EASY TO RENT
## DRIVE TO EXPLORE

## BOOK HERE

TEL. (+351) 296 205 340    FAX. (+351) 296 287 146

info@autatlantis.com    www.autatlantis.com

### AVAILABLE IN

TERCEIRA   SÃO MIGUEL   SANTA MARIA   FAIAL   PICO   GRACIOSA   FLORES   SÃO JORGE

Quality Service
**Best Price Guaranteed**

In sailing season, there's always lively chatter amongst the crews taking downtime in **Peter's Café Sport** [203 C4] and weekends can feature live music there, too. The **Casa Tea House** (page 196) is a mellow place to unwind with friends, with its backdrop of world music. Horta's renovated **cinema** [203 C1], near the main square, has a bar and with its ornate music-hall-style rows of boxes and Art-Deco ceiling, offers a mix of Hollywood and art cinema, together with occasional orchestral and jazz music.

## SHOPPING

**CAPELO ARTESANATO (CRAFTS SCHOOL – ESCOLA DE ARTESANATO DO CAPELO)** (*Alto dos Cavacaos, Capelo;* ℡ *292 945 027;* ⊕ *Jul & Aug 09.00–19.00 Mon–Fri, 14.00–17.00 Sat & Sun; Jun & Sep 10.00–18.00 Mon–Fri, 14.00–18.00 Sat & Sun; Jan–May, Oct–Dec 10.00–17.00 Mon–Fri, 14.00–17.00 Sat & Sun*) Near Capelo, on the way to Capelinhos, you'll find this centre, promoting local artisans' products, traditional to the island: incredibly intricate fig pith and fish scale sculpture, lace, embroidery, corn dollies, basketry and much else. There is also a fascinating book of black-and-white photos of the various stages of the Capelinhos eruption: the photos are for sale, but you can browse for free.

## OTHER PRACTICALITIES

**Emergency** ℡ 112
**Police** [203 B5] Largo Duque d'Avila e Bolama, Horta; ℡ 292 208 510
**Hospital** [203 A4] Estrada Princípe Alberto do Mónaco, Horta; ℡ 292 201 000

**Post office** [203 C2] Largo Duque d'Avila e Bolama, Horta; ⊕ 08.30–18.30 Mon–Fri

## WHAT TO SEE AND DO

Wandering through the streets of Horta, enjoying the present and past harbours, and making a tour to see the caldera and the scene of the last eruption is what most visitors do. One thing you should not miss is the Capelinhos Interpretative Centre, an outstanding design concept packed with information about volcanoes. If you have a car, then there are little villages to explore, tempting places to stop from which to make your own short walks, and whale watching from the clifftops.

For pleasure-boat and fun fishing trips, see *Activities* on page 200 for some ideas. The tourist office carries a full list of the many operators.

### MUSEUMS
**Horta** If you are in the mood for museums while in Horta, the ones below are listed in an east-to-west order, starting with the Museu da Horta in the town centre. The last three are clustered together on the shore of the Monte da Guia.

***Museu da Horta*** [203 C2] (*Largo Duque d'Avila e Bolama;* ⊕ *winter 09.30–17.00 Tue–Sun; summer 10.00–17.30 Tue–Sun; €2/1/Free adult/under 25/under 15s & seniors*) Housed in a former Jesuit college, it is noted for its collection of incredibly detailed fig-wood sculptures, one of the island's traditional handicrafts, but now has excellent new rooms dedicated to the transatlantic seaplane crossings and the submarine cables that once made Faial so important in intercontinental communications. Other

By far the busiest celebration is Sea Week at the beginning of August. Primarily a yachting regatta with whaling-boat, kayak and even jet-ski races, the channel between Faial and Pico is a mass of fluttering sails and buzzing craft. Different musical groups perform each evening, including bands from mainland Europe, local bands and folklore groups; everything from brass bands to reggae. There are exhibitions too, and the road along the seafront is closed, allowing thousands of people to promenade. On the first Sunday at the beginning of Sea Week the Festival of Nossa Senhor da Guia, Protector of the Fishermen, takes place with a procession from Porto Pim. The dates of many festivals vary each year, so please check with the tourist information office, or www.marinasazores.com for the Sea Week.

**Sports and Cultural week** Horta; end of Apr
**Festa de N Sra Angústias** Horta; 6th Sun after Easter
**Festa de São João da Caldeira** Horta; 24 Jun
**Sea Week** Horta; the week between the 1st & 2nd Sun in Aug. *Horta's big party*.
**Festa de N Sra Lurdes** Feteira; last week in Aug
**Festas do Espírito Santo** From May until Sep, intermittently
**Festa de N Sra Saúde** Varadouro; 1st week Sep
**December festival** Horta; exact date varies

rooms focus on paper cut art, religious art, while the main corridor exhibits antique furniture and paintings. Most of the information panels are bilingual.

*Casa Manuel de Arriaga* [203 B3] (*Rua Jose de Freitas Fortuna;* \ *292 202 576;* e *museu.hort.info@azores.gov.pt;* ⊕ *09.00–12.30 & 14.00–17.30 Tue–Fri; €2/1/free adult/under 25 & senior/under 15*) Opened in 2011, this well-laid-out museum is in the home of the Faial-born first President of the Republic of Portugal, elected in 1911. A humanist and political intellectual, the museum celebrates his life, private ideals and Republican values. There are permanent and temporary exhibitions, library and other resources, but most of the information is only in Portuguese, save for a couple of videos.

*Museu Scrimshaw Café Sport* [203 C4] (*Rua Tenente Valadim 9;* ⊕ *09.00–noon & 14.00–16.00 Mon–Sat; €2.50*) A private collection of over 300 scrimshaw items, upstairs in the famous Peter Café Sport. It is illegal to use bone from dead whales to make scrimshaw, so the artists who still produce these pieces use material from days gone by; an ever-decreasing stock, of course, so prices stay high.

*Fabrica da Baleia (Whale factory)/Centro do Mar* [203 C6] (*Monte da Guia;* \ *292 292 140;* e *geral@oma.pt; www.oma.pt;* ⊕ *1 Nov–15 Apr 09.30–17.30 Mon–Fri; 16 Apr–14 Jun & 16 Sep–31 Oct 09.30–17.30 Mon–Fri, 14.00–17.30 Sat & Sun; 15 Jun–15 Sep 10.00–18.00 daily; €3/2/free adults/juniors & seniors/under 13s; family tickets available; the museum may be closing for up to 9 months, from Jun 2016*) This new museum focuses on the story of whaling in the Azores. In addition to all the machinery *in situ*, there are videos (some in English) to watch, self-guided tours and an enthusiastic staff. Begun in 1943 with Norwegian-made equipment, the former whaling station processed sperm whale oil, bonemeal, and meatmeal for cattle feed and functioned for 30 years. Around the same time factories were also established in Capelas on São Miguel and Santa Cruz on Flores. In addition to the museum, in a different space, concerts, theatre, art exhibitions, conferences and ecology/marine workshops are held, plus a children's programme on environmental subjects. There is also a shop and bar. To get there either follow the road to Monte da Guia at the southern end of the harbour, or simply walk across the beach from Porto Pim.

**Antiga Adega/Antiga Casa Veraneio/Antiga Casa das Botes das Dabney** [203 C6] (*Monte da Guia;* ⊕ *16 Sep–14 Jun 09.30–13.00 & 14.00–17.30 Mon–Fri, 14.00–17.30 Sat; 15 Jun–15 Sep 10.00–13.00 & 14.00–18.00 daily; €3.50/1.75/free adults/juniors & seniors/under 12s*) Ticket includes aquarium visit. The former wine cellar, summer house and boathouse of the Dabneys contain bilingual information about this family whose influence was important in the island's history.

**Aquario da Porta Pim** [203 B6] (*Monte da Guia;* ☏ *292 207 381;* ⊕ *as Antiga Adega, above*) Ticket is combined with the visit to the Dabney properties, prices as above. A small collection of sea creatures, which varies as the commercial company running the operation buys and sells with other aquaria worldwide. You might see barracuda, dusky grouper or sea turtles brought in for recuperation after injury.

## Around the island
**Centro de Interpretacão do Vulcão dos Capelhinos (Capelinhos Interpretative Centre)** (*www.vulcaodoscapelinhos.org;* ⊕ *15 Jun–15 Sep 09.30– 18.00 daily; 16 Sep–14 Jun 09.30–16.30 Tue–Fri, 14.00–17.30 Sat & Sun; €10/5/free adult/juniors & seniors/under 12s; visits are by self-guided, or guided tours (summer: 11.00, 13.00, 15.00 & 16.30 daily; winter: 11.00 & 15.00 Tue–Fri, 14.30 & 16.00 Sat & Sun); you can buy a combined ticket for €15, which gives admission also to the Dabney house (see above) & the Faial Botanical Garden (pages 206–7)*) Your visit begins with a 15-minute, 3D film in English. The 13-month story of the destructive 1957/58 Capelhinos eruption is then explained using an 8-minute holographic projection dramatically showing the stages of eruption. A series of galleries follow, illustrating the Azores microplate and how the islands began to form, highlighting some of the key elements of volcanology on each island, explaining the different sorts of eruption, and covering some of the most active volcanoes around the world as well as the volcanic peculiarities of each Azorean island. The centre is built underground, in the ash and debris that buried the nearby villages and half the nearby Capelinhos lighthouse; all that appears in the bare landscape is a very low raised circle that allows natural light to the main chamber below. The internal design creates a great feeling of space and swirling lines and is aesthetically both stimulating and pleasing. The final section is the lighthouse itself, and one can climb the 140 steps to the upper balcony for the view. The spiral ascent is steep and narrow, so be warned. The building was opened in 2008 to coincide with the 50th anniversary of the eruption, and one should allow two hours to do justice to the presentation. There is a shop and a café. Since it opened it has deservedly gained many national and international awards for its design and content.

**BIRDS AND FLOWERS** The **Caldeira do Faial Nature Reserve** is good for the smaller endemic or rarer plants and in the grassland by the footpaths and around the viewing area inside the tunnel *Lactuca watsoniana, Daboecia azorica, Thymus caespititius, Centaurium scilloides, Hypericum foliosum*, yellow pimpernel and more can be found. The two most common birds are chaffinch and blackcap. The new volcano at **Capelinhos** regularly has nesting common terns and the roseate tern has also been recorded. Waders and ducks put into the beach at **Porto Pim**, and at the back of the beach grow sea daffodils. The protected area of **Monte da Guia** supports several native plant species.

## RECREATIONAL FOREST RESERVES

**Capelo** An 80ha area of woodland with numerous trails, including much of the walking trail from Capelo to Capelinhos Interpretative Centre. In the early days after settlement, woad was cultivated here, but the good land was lost when the 1672 eruption of Pico do Fogo covered all with lava and it became another area of Mistério. It is now a protected area, and in the woodlands on higher ground Azores endemics can be found. Picnic tables, etc, make this a very popular place on summer weekends.

# ACTIVITIES

## DIVING

**Norberto Diving** 292 293 851; m 962 824 028; e norbertodiver@mail.telepac.pt. With dives from €45 & with a 'menu' of over 20 dive spots around the islands, plus longer trips to the offshore Princess Alice sea bank.

## FISHING

**Brasilia Fishing Charters** m 966 783 101; e les@fishpics.info; www.azores-fishing.com. Tuna fishing from May to Jun & blue marlin from Jul to Sep. Coastal fishing Apr–Oct. Reserve well in advance essential – even though they have 5 boats, these get fully booked in season.

## HORSERIDING

**Patio** See *Where to stay*, page 195; m 917 428 111; e anja@patio.pt. With 15 horses, organises day rides & riding holidays which could inc a week-long circuit of the island. Good, solid reputation, well-looked-after horses. Accommodation on site, for those who want it. English, French & German spoken.

## SWIMMING

**Varadouro** On the southwest coast, on the way to Capelinhos. Natural rock pools, changing facilities and occasional lifeguard. There was also a thermal bath here, but the spring stopped flowing after the 1988 earthquake; the hunt is now on to find where it is presently coming out.

**Porto Pim** The relatively long sandy beach in the bay with almost sand-coloured sand, was once the original harbour. Shallow water, often calm, for some way out, so the water is warmer. Very popular, and on the edge of Horta town; there are facilities at the far end of the beach, towards the Centro do Mar, and cafés nearby.

**Praia do Almoxarife** Very small sandy beach, near the camping site. Some 15 minutes by taxi from Horta, with facilities and a restaurant nearby.

**WALKING** There are now eight official walks, of which two are long, linear hikes (full details of all walks are on the 'Trails' section of www.visitazores.com). The others are summarised below:

**Caldeira** Easy, 7km, 2½ hours. A circuit of the crater starting at the caldera viewpoint. Only to be attempted in settled weather with good visibility. Note that the caldera itself is a nature reserve and descent is not permitted, unless you are with a specially licensed guide.

**Caminhos Velhas** Hard, 15.5km, 5 hours. Starts in Ribeirinha, in the eastern side of the island.

**Levada** Easy, 8km, 2½ hours. A new, linear walk starting in Capelo.

**Rocha da Fajã** Easy, 5km, 2 hours. A circular walk out of Praia do Norte, reaching the coast before returning.

**Capelo–Capelinhos** Medium difficulty, 5km, 1½ hours. Beginning from the forest park at Capelo and taking in two optional ascents of volcanic cones.

**Rumo ao Morro de Castelo Branco** Easy, 4km, 1½ hours. A circular walk from Lombega village, in the island's southwest, to Morro de Castelo Branco, a headland noted for its birds and flora. Be aware that ascent of the headland itself is dangerous, and should not be attempted.

**WHALE WATCHING** Quayside cabins in front of the Peter Café Sport in Horta are home to operators of all sea-based activities, including those listed below. Around the island, locations of old *vigias* (whale lookouts) are signposted – look out for them, especially near Cedros. This is a splendid initiative, for they are the perfect places for a picnic and binoculars; it is amazing how many waves turn into dolphins by the end of a bottle of wine.

🐋 **Hortacetáceos** m 962 432 694/965 351 422; e info@hortacetaceos.com; www. hortacetaceos.com. With 1 boat, a small but reputable whale- & dolphin-watching operation run by enthusiastic owners. Also do trips that combine sea & land-based activities, such as jeep tours.
🐋 **OceanEye** m 966 140 608; e info@oceaneye. pt; www.oceaneye.pt; €32/22 adult/under 12. The *Ana G* is a special James Bond-style modern version of the glass-bottomed boat & allows easy underwater observation around the islands of Faial

& Pico. Expect to see in their natural habitat fish & other marine creatures, as well as geological features. The trips last 1½–1¾hrs & have both a recreational & an educational role, highlighting the conservation & biodiversity of this marine environment.
🐋 **Whalewatch Azores** ✆ 292 293 891; e info@whalewatchazores.com; www. whalewatchazores.com. For the serious or avid whale watcher, week-long holidays between May & Oct, focusing on whale & dolphin observation. Will take day trippers, if they have space.

## TOURING THE ISLAND

**CAR TOUR** Faial is small, and this itinerary provides a fascinating half-day tour. If you can, take a picnic to enjoy in the forest park at Capelinhos. See map on page 190 for locations.

### Horta–Espalamaca–Ribeira Funda–Praia do Norte–Capelinhos–Castelo Branco–Horta
Leave **Horta** and begin by driving up to the ridge that overlooks the town from the north and stop at the belvedere at **Espalamaca**. Here you have a fine view over Horta, the harbour, and of fields nudging their way up to the houses, so quickly does town end and countryside begin. Along the ridge of Espalamaca are several windmills and, neatly nestling in its valley, **Flamengos** village. Turn around and look down upon a pretty valley and Praia do Almoxarife.

Take the EN1–2a on your way to the caldera, and the little **Chapel of São João** is your next stop, after a cool drive beneath cryptomeria trees. São João is at the junction, where you have a view down over meadows to Horta and across the channel to Pico. In early summer the hedgerows here are bedecked with tiny double red roses, coinciding with the Festa do São João in June (page 198).

Turn right in front of the chapel (EN2–2a), and follow signs up to the **caldera** along a narrowing road lined with tall hydrangeas. You will pass a road off to your right leading to Quebrada and Ribeira Funda on the north coast. There are wonderful views across to Pico and São Jorge.

The road ends by a **tunnel**, at an altitude of 900m. The tunnel is very short, and sometimes windy and cold. Walk through and view the caldera which is now a nature reserve, with access restricted to properly licensed guides and their small groups. The large crater is 400m deep and 1,450m in diameter. Common native shrubs here include juniper and erica. Above the tunnel on the caldera's rim is the Oratory of São João. On a clear day Pico, São Jorge and Graciosa can be seen; almost due west from the summit is a line of cinder cones marking the fracture along which eruptions have occurred in recent geological time. To the east you can make out the impressive Pedro Miguel Graben, where the earth's crust has been displaced downwards between faults on either side of it. From the German *graben*, meaning 'trench', and orientated west northwest–east southeast, it is a major volcanic feature of the island.

Drive back down to the turn-off previously mentioned, now on your left, leading to **Ribeira Funda**. For flowers, this is one of the prettiest roads, and during July and August the hydrangeas are at their best. There are good views from two viewpoints along this road, and between trees and hydrangeas there are glimpses of villages and the sea beyond. Stop and enjoy, too, the glorious view over the Ribeira das Cabras and note the extensive lava beds before coming to **Praia do Norte**.

Praia do Norte is a good place to stop for coffee before going to **Capelinhos**, held to be one of the most interesting volcanic sites in Europe and well captured in its state-of-the-art museum.

Continue more or less parallel with the coast on the EN1–1a to **Castelo Branco** where there is a fine view of the coastline before proceeding to **Feteira**. You will often see this place mentioned in brochures. Lying between the airport and Horta, it is a length of coast with contorted lava rocks and rock arches of some curiosity.

**HORTA** The island's only town is made up from two adjacent bays: one small and rounded, Baía do Porto Pim; the other larger and more open. The remains of a volcano crater, known as Monte da Guia, divide them, and splendid views can be had from the top. The smaller bay is intimate, seemingly almost separate from the town, and was an American whaling centre from the end of the 18th century and during the 19th century. As many as 400 ships have been recorded in the harbour. Even by the beginning of the last century, two-thirds of all sperm whales harpooned were caught off the Azores. The old whale factory and the slipway where whales were landed and hauled up for processing after being caught by the Azorean open boats is now an excellent museum. In the town itself there are some fine buildings, and there is a walk northwards along the esplanade out to a little park. Work is now finished on the new €35 million quay to complement the existing one dating from 1876 on the south side of the bay; it now takes medium-sized cruise ships, and, as in Ponta Delgada, cruise passengers are able to walk from their ship straight into town.

**Town trail** This conveniently divides into two walks, and we begin with the central and northern parts of town. Do keep an eye on the information panels on the town's

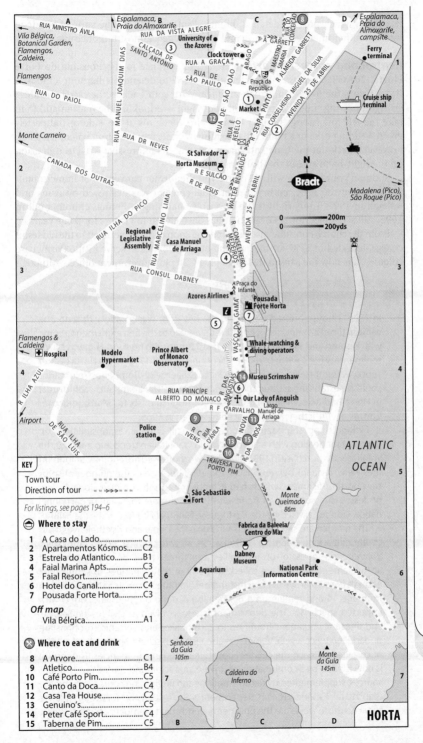

**KEY**

Town tour     ·········
Direction of tour     ·⇒⇒⇒⇒·

*For listings, see pages 194–6*

🛏 **Where to stay**

| | | |
|---|---|---|
| 1 | A Casa do Lado | C1 |
| 2 | Apartamentos Kósmos | C2 |
| 3 | Estrela do Atlantico | B1 |
| 4 | Faial Marina Apts | C3 |
| 5 | Faial Resort | C4 |
| 6 | Hotel do Canal | C4 |
| 7 | Pousada Forte Horta | C3 |

*Off map*
Vila Bélgica ................................ A1

🍴 **Where to eat and drink**

| | | |
|---|---|---|
| 8 | A Arvore | C1 |
| 9 | Atletico | B4 |
| 10 | Café Porto Pim | C5 |
| 11 | Canto da Doca | C4 |
| 12 | Casa Tea House | C2 |
| 13 | Genuino's | C5 |
| 14 | Peter Café Sport | C4 |
| 15 | Taberna de Pim | C5 |

Faial TOURING THE ISLAND

8

**HORTA**

bus stops, which provide detailed, bilingual information on the various points of interest: rather unexpected, useful and unfortunately almost unnoticeable!

**Central and northern Horta** Start at the entrance to the **Pousada de Forte Horta** [204 C3], the *castelo* (castle) built in 1567 to defend the harbour. Opposite the *castelo* is the tourist information office. With your back to the castle entrance, go right, passing the little garden on your right overlooking the marina and then take the left fork along the Rua Conselheiro Medeiros at the side of the pastel-green wedding cake of a building, charming with its wrought-iron balconies. First, however, check out the **Café Internacional**, with its impressive Art-Deco interior, on the right-hand side of this building.

Soon on your left you will see above you the former convent of St Francis, built at the end of the 17th century; the original convent was destroyed by Essex and Raleigh in 1597. To its right is the towering, charming St Francis church, built in 1696; still scheduled for restoration, it has been closed to visitors for some years.

From the church continue eastward and you soon come on your left to the old Jesuit college, founded in 1719 for the training of missionaries to serve in the Portuguese colonies. It is now the **Museu de Horta** [204 C2], plus government offices. Although

## HORTA'S VOLUNTARY FIRE SERVICE

In 1875, a house burned down and the governor was so angry that no-one came in time to extinguish it he offered a reward to the first eight men to come with a pump and a lesser sum to the first 12 men with buckets. This was how a rudimentary fire service began, and continued until 1912, when Horta's water supply was improved and the Associaçao Faialense de Bombeiros Voluntarios could be established. Church bells would sound the alarm and each district in Horta had its own signal; four bells for Angusuas, six for Matriz, eight for Conceição, until they were replaced by a siren in 1966.

Extinguishing shipboard fires was and still is their responsibility. Their payment for dealing with a fire on a World War I Italian troopship enabled the volunteers to purchase in 1930 their first two motorised fire engines. Shipboard fires were frequent between 1958 and 1968 because of the number of ships transporting fishmeal, which had a tendency to self-combust. Today's very professional association of *bombeiros* is one of more than 450 departments nationwide supervised by the Portuguese National Fire Authority, the SNB.

The firemen are still volunteers who give their time and risk their lives, thus continuing a long tradition. Horta has 54, all with understanding employers. Volunteering tends to run in families, sometimes three generations serving at the same time. They are called by the siren that continues to sound until enough firemen arrive to crew the engines. Volunteers can join the association from age 14 and remain until 60. Training is done on the island, often with imported specialists. The department is also involved in civil rescue service, and disaster simulations from fires to earthquakes and volcanic eruptions are undertaken twice a year. Volunteers also visit each school on the island at least once a year to teach the children how to respond in emergencies. The service is now funded by a combination of private, municipal and central government sources, supplemented by demonstrations and firefighting courses around the island to raise money. The fire department is also responsible for the ambulance service, whose crews are the only permanently paid members of staff.

a small museum, it is well worth visiting. Among its exhibits is statuary of several centuries, some originating from Flanders but many carved from cedarwood in the Azores. The Friends of Heart School in Angra made figures which were taken to the other islands and the figures come not only from churches and chapels no longer extant, but also private homes. Next door is the **Church of São Salvador** [204 C2], the principal or Mother (*Matriz*) Church of Horta, begun in 1680 and completed in 1760.

Leaving the Horta Museum turn left and take the road along the right side of the post office, the Rua Serpa Pinto, to come to the marketplace on your left. Next to this is a little garden square, the **Praça da República** [204 C1]; on the diagonally opposite corner is another wedding cake of a building, this time pink, with splendid white balustrades. In earlier times houses painted pink were owned only by the aristocracy. Almost equally smart is the fire and ambulance station to its right. Take the narrow road that leads uphill next to the pink building, then take the first right, and you will see a clock tower at the top. This is the **Torre do Relógio** [204 C1] (clock tower), built in the early 18th century; it is a symbol of Azorean perseverance in the face of seismic forces which destroyed the 16th-century Mother Church. The adjacent public garden dating from 1857, the **Jardim de Florêncio Terra**, has a fine dragon tree, while the massive building behind is the former **Hospital da Misericórdia**, now usefully housing the oceanography and fisheries faculty of the **University of the Azores**. Leave this area by the road below the clock, taking you steeply down towards cobbles. At the bottom go left, passing the A Arvore restaurant (page 196) and at the end crossing a small stream, the Ribeira da Conceição, near which Faial's first settlement was begun in the 15th century. You will see the small, pretty white church, the **Igreja de Nossa Senhora da Conceição**, inscribed with the dates 1527, 1597, 1749, 1926 and 1933. This church has suffered a traumatic history. Originally built by the early settlers, it was destroyed during the first sacking of the town in 1597. A church built much later was destroyed in 1926. Its replacement was built in the Art-Deco style of the time and this in turn was damaged in 1941 by an explosion in a nearby army barracks. Following a major restoration, it is now pristine and most elegant. From here, either return along the roads through the town, or go south to the sea and return along the esplanade.

**Southern Horta** To explore the second, southern sector, again leave from the **Pousada de Forte Horta** [204 C3]. This time turn left and walk down the road to pass the Peter Café Sport. Many years ago this was a small bar known to all sailors who called in at Horta, and a visitors' book was maintained which had many amusing entries. Now there is a shop and other enterprises including a museum of scrimshaw, whale-watching tours and restaurant, and the guest book with all its early entries is posted on the internet; with good self-publicity the café is now known to a much wider circle around the world – almost a global brand!

Proceed on and keep to the higher road and you will soon come on your left to the **Igreja de Nossa Senhora das Angústias** [204 C4], the Church of Our Lady of Anguish, just recently restored. Continue straight and you will soon reach **Porto Pim**, the original harbour of Horta. Note the defensive walls and the remains of the **Fort of São Sebastião** [204 B5], constructed during the 17th century as protection against pirates and other attackers. You should try to visit at night when the gateway is floodlit and very pretty. Construction of the new harbour began in 1876.

Take the road running behind the sea wall left of the gateway to access the beach. You will see the small houses of one of the oldest remaining parts of Horta, all nestling at the foot of **Monte Queimado** [204 C5]; *queimado* means 'burned', referring to the cinders. Walk along the beach to the far end to visit the old whale factory. This was built only about 50 years ago and there is an earlier factory dating from 1836 built originally for drying cod. It is now a whaling museum with machinery intact and cultural centre (page 198), with occasional events and exhibits to do with the sea. This small area is full of history, for you can find near the museum the point where the submarine cables came out to connect to relay stations. This area is indelibly linked to the influential Dabney family. A new museum devoted to the family and their role in the development of the island is now open (page 199), and a bit further along is a new aquarium.

From the whale factory, take the road that climbs to the summit of **Monte da Guia** [204 D7]. On the way you will pass a little chapel, dedicated to Senhora da Guia, also once used as a lookout for whales. The actual summit of Monte da Guia is 145m but it is closed to visitors. To return, follow the road all the way down and as you descend enjoy the splendid views of Porto Pim and Horta. Look also across Porto Pim Bay and to the hill behind, **Monte das Moças**, where you will see an observatory. The building dates from around 1901, and has been in use as a meteorological observatory since 1915. It was named **Prince Albert of Monaco Observatory** [204 B4] in 1923, a year after the prince's death. Just below this are the buildings and tennis courts of what is now the Faial Resort Hotel; previously these buildings were the residential compound belonging to the American Western Union Telegraph Co, built in the 1920s with reinforced concrete to withstand earth tremors. Hotel Faial opened in 1973, and has had new buildings added in recent years.

As you return to town and pass the harbour, pause to view the drawings and cartoons on the walls left by visiting yacht crews. This free outdoor art gallery exists because it is said to be bad luck to sail away without leaving your mark. Sadly, however, one or two have become memorials. Considerable care and time have clearly been taken by some artists, others are rushed scrawls, but all show a record of the many crews that have put in at Horta on their travels across the oceans.

**PRAIA DO ALMOXARIFE**  Just the other side of the ridge immediately to the north of Horta is one of the prettiest valleys on the island. Long settled, the large houses have charming gardens and there are a few restaurants, mainly open in summer. There is a small sandy beach with changing facilities, and the camping site is nearby. It is a relaxing place from which to enjoy a fine view of Pico. A bus runs to Praia do Almoxarife from the stop at the northern end of the Horta marina.

## FLAMENGOS
**Jardim Botânico de Faial** (✆ 292 307 282; ☉ 15 Jun–15 Sep 10.00–18.00 daily; 16 Sep–14 Jun 09.30–13.00 & 14.00–17.30 Tue–Fri, 14.00–17.30 Sat; €3.50/1.75/ free adult/juniors & seniors/under 12s; family tickets available) Based in Flamengos, this is in the grounds of the Quinta de São Lourenço, with an extensive area of old gardens sheltered by magnificent hedges to protect them from the salt-laden winds. Established in 1986, the small botanic garden, the Jardim Botânico do Faial, is devoted to the endemic and indigenous plants of the archipelago, and is most attractively designed with gentle hills and a ravine filled with ferns. Because of its location the garden is able to grow species that are found at both sea level and at various altitudes in the mountains, and four altitudinal zones are represented. Here some of the more showy species such as *Thymus caespititius*, the native thyme, *Azorina vidalii*, the native campanula, dramatic *Euphorbia stygiana* and the most desirable shrub of all, the endemic bilberry *Vaccinium cylindraceum*, can be enjoyed in season. In addition, if you (understandably) have been struggling to identify all the different evergreen shrubs native to the islands, here is an excellent opportunity to study them close at hand and compare them: they have labels. A new extension

Earthquakes started on 16 September 1957 and on 27 September, the sea began to boil near the Capelinhos rocks. On 29 September, explosions began and cinders were thrown into the air. By 1 October, cinders were being projected some 600m high, the eruption cloud rose to 6,000m and an islet began to form round the crater. Six days later, there was a cone-shaped island 60m high and 640m across, but already the sea was starting to destroy it. Two days more and it was 100m tall and over 700m across in the shape of a horseshoe, opening to the south. The sea entered this break so that the vent of the volcano was underwater, causing very violent explosions and fragmenting the new lava into ash and cinders. By 30 October, the sea had washed away the entire island.

In early November, eruptions began again and by the middle of the month a new island was linked to Faial by a narrow bar of black ash. Eruptions continued through the winter and by March 1958, more than $2km^2$ of land had been added. During the following months lava flowed into the ocean, and, with the vent protected from the sea, incandescent lava was thrown up most spectacularly more than 500m, continuing intermittently until 24 October. In one period of 36 hours over 300 earth tremors were registered, shaking the whole island. In total some 300 houses were destroyed and almost every house on the west side of Faial was damaged; 2,000 people were rehoused. Crops were destroyed and a 5m layer of ash and rocks buried houses and many of the fields around the villages of Capelo and Norte Pequeno. Wind erosion is now slowly exposing these once more. The eruption changed the lives of many islanders, with hundreds emigrating to the US and Canada. Now, some have returned and houses have been renovated for holiday letting.

was underway in mid 2016, to provide more display space for the collection of orchids. A short film in English is shown, and there is a small gift shop and café.

**CAPELINHOS** This is the site of the 1957 eruption and it is fascinating to see how it is, years later, with a few hardy pioneering plants trying to establish themselves, and the effects of wind erosion. Come here on a blustery day and you see the fine particles blowing on the wind and indeed feel them stinging your face. The stunning new visitor centre explains it all (page 199). It is worth walking or driving down to see the small fishing harbour below Capelinhos. Also near the village is the forest park which is a pleasant place to walk.

Faial  TOURING THE ISLAND

8

You can post your comments and recommendations, and read the latest feedback and updates from other readers online at www.bradtupdates. com/azores.

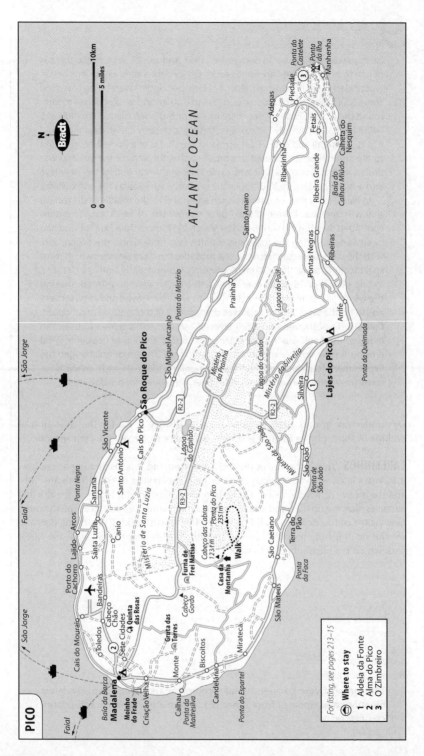

PICO

ATLANTIC OCEAN

São Jorge

Faial

For listing, see pages 213–15

Where to stay
1  Aldeia da Fonte
2  Alma do Pico
3  O Zimbreiro

# 9

## Pico

Pico is to most visitors Pico mountain itself, a remarkable, steep-sided, dormant volcanic cone rising to 2,351m, and Portugal's highest mountain. Certainly this peak and the numerous black lava flows in different parts of the island make Pico the most distinctive of all in the archipelago. The finest views are to be had looking across the channel head-on from Faial, or the long side view from São Jorge; on the island itself, there's also a superb view of the summit to be had from Lajes. In the western end of the island you are always aware of Pico's overshadowing presence, whether dense clouds hang just above Madalena's rooftops obscuring everything above 40m, or the sky is at its bluest and all is revealed. As late as April, it can wear a snowy covering. The mountain always looks over your shoulder.

Of all the islands this is the most obviously volcanic, especially around Madalena and along the coast by the airport where the black stones have been gathered and made into tiny walled enclosures, square ones for vines, round ones for figs. Long ago, red and pink scrambling roses, the dark purple-blue trumpet flowers of the climbing ipomoea, and carpets of nasturtium escaped from cultivation, and now add wild colour for many weeks if not months of the year. Houses are of black stone, dressed around the windows, whitewash on the walls. Pico, with nearby Faial, was the centre for land-based open-boat whale hunting; some seven years after the last whale was killed, boats again went to sea looking for whales, only this time just to watch, and Pico has become one of the main centres.

The southern slopes of the island are more sheltered and less windy and so protective enclosures go high above the coastal villages. In contrast, the northern slopes are far more forested. Pittosporum and native myrica have invaded the lower slopes where there were once extensive vineyards among the stones, adding further large areas of tree cover. On the uplands most of the native vegetation has been cleared for cattle pasture, helped by subsidies from a then embryonic European Community – a dubious investment, since the resultant grass is very poor. However, there are pockets of native and endemic plants and hopefully current measures will be sufficient to save them; 1,500ha above the 1,200m contour are a designated protected zone. These remnants provide Pico with the most easily accessible areas of indigenous vegetation where you can begin to imagine just how the islands might have appeared to the very first settlers.

To explore the island's uplands by car, to find the lakes and other beautiful areas, just to stop and enjoy the grand scenery and the ever-changing cloud patterns around the mountain, is reason enough to come to Pico. But added to this are the cultural and historical interests and, for the experienced walker, the extraordinary experience of being on the summit of Pico where on a clear day the stupendous views embrace the sister islands of Faial, São Jorge, Graciosa and Terceira. Much closer, below, daughter cones and craters pockmark the plateau giving a tiny hint of what an extraordinary scene this must have been when it was most active. The mountain is only dormant; at the very summit on Piquinho, also called Pico Pequeno, the little peak that is a small cone in the summit crater, there are fumaroles, rocks are very warm to the touch and there is a smell of sulphur. Escaping gases and flowing hot magma when the surface lava was cooling have created caves and tube-like tunnels; several are known and named, but others are buried beneath vegetation or a thin tumble of rocks so great care is needed and it is essential not to wander from paths. The second-largest island in the Azores surely has something for everyone.

An island tour by car or taxi is a must, driving as high as the road reaches on Pico mountain and down to sheltered areas by the sea, enjoying impressive landscapes and exploring villages and country life, while the coast has numerous headlands, some of which provide spectacular *miradouros*. The central mountain road running the length of the island offers endless interest, with side excursions off to small lakes and viewpoints. The museum in Lajes tells the fascinating story of whaling in the Azores, as does that in São Roque. The more adventurous can go whale watching or attempt the ascent of Pico. The island was once famous for its fortified Verdelho wine and, in the last several years, new methods of cultivation and production are once again making saleable table wine. Originally the vines were grown in very small stone-wall enclosures to protect the plants from salt winds and to gain extra heat, and they are an extraordinary memorial to the tenacity and hard work of the earlier settlers. Extensive areas stretching along the western coast from just outside Madalena are so impressive that in 2002, UNESCO designated them a World Heritage Site. A visit to the winery followed by a tasting completes the picture.

## BACKGROUND

**GEOLOGY** Given that the channel between Pico and Faial is only 100m deep it is quite likely the two islands could be part of the same volcanic complex. Pico mountain is 2,351m above sea level and rises 3,500m above the surrounding ocean floor.

The island of Pico can be viewed as three sections: the stratovolcano of Pico mountain that dominates the western part of the island; Topo volcano, a shield-like structure located on the southern part of the island above the town of Lajes do Pico; and the 29km-long westnorthwest–eastsoutheast-orientated plateau, the Planalto da Achada, located between the central part of the island and its eastern end and characterised by scoria and spatter cones and associated lava flows.

**Pico mountain** began as a shield volcano, a broad and gently sloping volcano formed by repeated eruptions from a cluster of vents at different time intervals creating a large plinth some 16km wide at sea level and about 1,100m altitude. Extensive lava flows have completely covered the base of the volcano, thought to be around 240,000 years old. Most of the conspicuous cinder cones of the lower slopes originate on this shield, and are relatively recent.

The magnificent summit cone was created by eruptions from vents clustered closely together, forming a stratovolcano, a steeply sided cone of lava fragments and flows. Its development can be divided into three phases. The first was terminated by the formation of the older summit collapsed crater at 2,050m, presently 550m across and 25m deep. The second phase was the creation of Piquinho, the small lava cone 125m high in the larger crater, some 17,000 years ago. This, too, has a very small collapsed crater, which gives off occasional fumes from between warm rocks. The third phase included eruptions from the nested lava cone (Piquinho) 1,300 years ago, and from an eruptive fissure on the top of the stratovolcano. The larger crater was once much deeper, but has filled with *pahoehoe* lava discharged from Piquinho, a smooth lava usually formed from basalts emitted in a hot fluid state. Wherever plants have so far failed to gain a foothold on the steep slopes, basaltic cinders, ash, small stones and scree dominate the landscape.

**Topo volcano** rises 1,022m above sea level and 2,500m above the ocean bottom, and its oldest formation not under the sea has been dated at 250,000 years old. Topo is a basaltic shield volcano and has two subsidiary structures: Terra Chãs and Santa Bárbara, which some authors have interpreted as volcanic calderas. While the Santa Bárbara area does correspond to the remains of an old collapsed crater, or caldera, it has been suggested the Terra Chãs depression could be due to lateral movement of the flank driven by gravity and tectonic instability.

The **Planalto da Achada** is an elongated plateau occupying the central part of the island from Pico mountain in the west to its eastern termination; as one very apt description has it, stretching out eastwards like a comet's tail. Numerous volcanic cones lie along the axis of the plateau with a general westnorthwest–eastsoutheast orientation. These are mostly made of cinders, with a wide range of size and shape. The largest cone has a diameter of 900m at its base and a height of 190m, while the smallest represent fissure eruptions building small spatter ramparts, ie: lava fragments spewed upwards as a fountain that are still molten when they hit the ground and thus form 'cowpats' which often weld together building ramparts or cones. Lavas issuing from sources along the plateau are mostly *aa* flows, lavas with a very rough broken surface, and have cascaded down the steep slopes of the plateau either towards the north or south coast and then spread, sometimes into the sea such as to form the Ponta dos Biscoitos near Santa Bárbara, between Lajes and Ribeiras.

The plateau's oldest above-sea-level formation is 230,000 years old, which means the oldest sections of Pico island are the Topo volcano, followed by Pico mountain.

Data shows 14 eruptions have occurred on Pico island in the last 1,000 years and more than 35 in the last 2,000 years, with longer quiet periods on the Planalto da Achada than on Pico mountain. Historic volcanism and carbon dating of lavas suggest that eruptions are not evenly distributed through time, but that events are separated by alternating short and long periods, and that peace reigns on average for 130 years. Since settlement, eruptions occurred in 1562, 1718 and 1720.

Visitors arriving on Pico soon hear about the **Mistérios**, extensive areas of sharp, broken and often forbidding black lava. These puzzled the first settlers arriving from 1466, who had yet to witness an eruption and experienced almost 100 years of volcanic tranquillity before they saw their first eruption in 1562. This eruption created the Cabeços do Mistério cinder cones and sent a basaltic lava flow into the sea to form the Ponta do Mistério, east of São Roque on the north coast. It must have been terrifying as the surrounding forests caught fire and sometimes as many as 40 glowing hot streams of lava illuminated the night, all over a period of two years. The 1718 eruption left an inheritance of several cinder cones and a lava flow that created Cachorro, near the present airport, a dramatic formation as though inspired by a punk hairstyle. At the same time, on the opposite south coast a lava flow destroyed the then village of São João and formed the headland of Ponta de São João. The 1720 eruption occurred just northeast of São João and created the Mistério da Silveira.

**HISTORY** The first houses are thought to have been built in Ribeiras, but real settlement began in the area of what is today Lajes, in about 1460, and this for many years was the principal port and town. Later it was to develop as the centre of the whaling industry in the Azores. São Roque dates back to 1542 and is thought to have been first populated by people from Graciosa. Later, it too was a whaling base with a large processing factory.

Until the latter half of the 19th century, wine production was a very important economic activity and the island's Pico Madeira wine was exported in substantial volume, to England, the US, and famously Russia. The vineyards, especially those along the west coast south from Madalena, were owned by some half-dozen families from Horta who came over for the summer to oversee the grape and wine production. Their large summer houses may still be seen today. Ever-increasing use of the important harbour on the adjacent island of Faial brought greater prosperity to that island and allowed the development of Horta, which in turn influenced the development of Madalena. Horta was the export centre for Pico's wine. Facing each other across the channel, the two towns have always been closely linked. In 1852, disease (*Oidium tuckeri*, a mildew) nearly destroyed the vines and 20 years later when the aphid insect Phylloxera struck the remaining vines were destroyed. This was the final blow to a very valuable export, for already the market had been declining. In the US the fashion for fortified wine was losing out to American-made whiskey, and the belief that wine was good for one's health was under question, along with increasing movements for total abstinence. Sadly, with the loss of the vines, exactly what was the Pico wine so extolled by the tsars is now a mystery. The Madeiran wine trade did, however, slowly recover, although minus the American market. This collapse of the wine trade brought terrific hardship to the islanders, causing a mass emigration of many of Pico's then population of 32,000 to Brazil and California. Those who could afford to paid their way onto passing ships, while the less fortunate embarked illegally on whaling ships serving a minimum contracted term of two years. With the vines gone, the families sold their large land holdings and so people were able to acquire small plots of their own. Later, returning islanders brought with them the American Isabela grape, which thrived, and so the smallholdings began producing low-alcohol, partly fermented wine for local consumption, known as Vinho de Cheiro. Around this time, with skills gained from working on the American whalers, land-based whale hunting began from Pico, using small open boats. This soon spread to other islands, and whaling made a substantial contribution to the economy until world demand fell for the oil for lamps and machinery when cheaper synthetics became available. Many factories closed, while hunting continued on an ever-decreasing scale until the final whale was killed in 1984.

Today, like all the other islands, cattle and dairy produce drive the economy, despite the relatively poor quality of the land. In Madalena there is a tuna-fishing fleet, and tourism is increasing.

## GETTING THERE AND AWAY

For travel to and from Pico, see pages 42–4 and 48–9. Pico's sleepy, modern airport, 7.5km east of Madalena, is only occasionally disturbed by a flight arrival, rarely in low season. There are a few car-rental companies, including **Autatlantis** (*www.autatlantis.com*) and **Ilha Verde** (*www.ilhaverde.com*) and a tourist office, all open only to meet incoming flights. A cafeteria, free Wi-Fi and an ATM are also available, as is that rare species, free airport parking. A taxi will take you to Madalena for around €12, or to either Lajes or Piedade for €30.

**Azores Airlines** Rua D Maria da Glória Duarte, Madalena; ☎ 292 628 391; ⏱ 09.00–18.00

There is a bus service which follows two routes: the north-coast Madalena–São Roque–Piedade, and the south-coast Madalena–Lajes–Ribeirinha, but they run only twice daily in each direction and only once on Sunday. Nevertheless, they do allow budget travellers to make an island circuit. Take the south-coast bus going to Ribeirinha at 10.00, arriving at 11.45, and after a quick lunch, return via the north-coast route to Madalena, leaving Ribeirinha at 13.40. From Lajes to Madalena the respective times are 06.45 arriving 08.00, and 14.05 arriving 15.15, and return from Madalena to Lajes 10.00, arriving 11.00, or 17.45, arriving 18.55. The tourist office will provide an up-to-date timetable.

The island divides quite easily into a half-day car tour – Madalena–Santa Luzia–São Roque–Lagoa do Ciado–Lajes/Madalena or variations – and a full-day tour taking in most of the above plus going down to the little-visited far eastern end of the island. The price for a taxi is around €110 for a day, €70 for a half-day tour (up to four passengers), and the tourist office has a full list of taxi drivers and their linguistic abilities. One English-speaking driver whose vehicle can carry up to eight passengers is Carlos Costa (m *962 525 517*). Car hire is available from the airport or the ferry terminal and you could explore the whole island very comfortably in three days.

**EXCURSIONS TO OTHER ISLANDS** To travel to Horta on Faial by ferry, there are regular sailings from Madalena throughout the year, a 30-minute journey, operated by Atlântico Line (*www.atlanticoline.pt*). In winter they run ferries four-times daily: 08.15, 11.30, 14.00 and 18.00, with two more crossings added in summer (09.45 and 21.00). Returning ferries from Horta depart at 07.30, 10.45, 13.15 and 17.15 in winter, and additionally at 09.00 and 20.15 in summer. A single fare costs €3.60. You can also visit Velas on São Jorge, with a boat or two departing Madalena each day (*1hr 20mins*). Less frequently (mainly at weekends), there is also a service to Horta from São Roque, on Pico's northern coast (*1hr 10mins*), and weekend boats between São Roque and Velas on São Jorge, a 40-minute journey. Careful study of the Atlântico Line website is advisable, as there are certain exceptions to the schedules.

In Madalena (✎ *292 623 524*; ⊕ *09.00–17.00 Mon–Fri*), this is based inside the ferry terminal. In Lajes, the office was, at the time of writing, being relocated to the harbour, and due to reopen in late 2016.

 # WHERE TO STAY

There is one hotel in Madalena, two in Lajes, and one in nearby Silveira. New guesthouses are springing up, especially in and around Madalena. Piedade has one excellent accommodation option. Many of the private homes offering lodging will pick up guests from the ferry. Check with the tourist office for details of all rural tourism accommodation and guesthouses. For locations, see maps pages 208 and 218.

## MADALENA AND AROUND

⌂ **Hotel Caravelas** (137 rooms) Rua Conselheiro Terra Pinheiro, Madalena; ✎ 292 622 500; e geral@hotelcaravelas.net; www. hotelcaravelas.com.pt. The island's only truly large hotel sits right opposite the harbour. Ask for one of the newer (slightly larger) rooms & a balcony. AC, free Wi-Fi, cable TV. B/fast inc. €€€€€

⌂ **Jeiroes do Mar** (10 apts) Rua Alexandre Herculano, Madalena; ✎ 292 638 310;

e info@jeiroesapartamentos.com; www.
jeiroesapartamentos.com. On the southern side of
the harbour, spacious & fully equipped apts, each
named after a grape varietal, close to the ocean &
the public sea swimming pool. Cable TVs in lounge
& bedroom, free Wi-Fi, 1 apt suitable for those with
limited mobility. No b/fast. Can sleep up to 4 per
apt. Restaurant across the road. €€€€€

⌂ **Alma do Pico** (13 apts) Rua dos Biscoitos
34, Madalena; m 914 231 436; e info@
almadopico.com; www.almadopico.com. Set in a
delightful wooded surrounding, with great views
to Faial. Fully s/c apts. Outdoor pool, yoga classes.
Each apt is set well apart from the others. Run by
an enthusiastic Italian couple. €€€

⌂ **Calma do Mar** (5 rooms) Av Padre Nunes
da Rosa, Madalena; m 910 952 409/914 443 408;
e info@calmadomar.com, www.calmadomar.
com. Set in a quiet location, a few mins' walk from
central Madalena. Spacious rooms with tiled floors,
free Wi-Fi, communal kitchen & TV lounge with
wood-burning stove. Guests can use the garden,
with BBQ, or hire bikes (extra cost) & use the trails
provided by the young owners, who also have
strong connections to activity companies & can
further advise on suitable walks from the doorstep.
Buffet b/fast inc. €€€

⌂ **Villa Madalena** (11 rooms) Rua Cecilia do
Amaral 15, Madalena; ☎292 628 030; e info@
villamadalena.com; www.villamadalena.com.
Very smart doubles, family rooms & triples in a
new, villa-style building just south of Madalena
centre. Plenty of space & light, some rooms have
balconies, all with TV (international channels),
free Wi-Fi. Buffet b/fast inc. Plans are underway to
build apts next door, due for opening 2017. €€€

## LAJES AND AROUND

⌂ **Hotel Apartamentos Aldeia da Fonte**
(16 rooms, 8 suites, 16 studios) Silveira; ☎292
679 500; e info@aldeiadafonte.com; www.
aldeiadafonte.com. A series of basalt-built
s/c cottages & bedrooms 5mins by car west of
Lajes, with a central restaurant & lounge bar in
a charming garden/woodland setting on cliffs
a few metres above the sea. A great effort has
been made to integrate the buildings with the
landscape. Offers a very wide range of leisure
activities, inc whale watching & climbing Pico, & a
series of self-guided walks from the hotel. Fitness,
sauna, seasonal outdoor pool. Free Wi-Fi, cable TV

& b/fast inc. The suites are s/c. Excellent restaurant
(see opposite). €€€

⌂ **Hotel/Alojamento Bela Vista** (16 rooms
& apts) Rua do Saco, Lajes do Pico; ☎292 672 000.
A hotel nestled in the town centre, with apts close
to the sea near the whalers' museum, & remodelled
in 2007, providing rooms or s/c apts. TV with
international channels, free Wi-Fi. Some rooms have
balconies with sunloungers. Apts have washing
machine, cooker, fridge, microwave. B/fast inc for
both hotel & apts. €€–€€€

⌂ **Residencial Whale'come ao Pico** (12
rooms) Rua dos Baleeiros, Lajes do Pico; ☎292 672
010; m 917 405 630; e viallelle@espacotalassa.
com; www.espacotalassa.com. Situated next to &
run by the Espaco Talassa whale-watching base,
right on the harbourfront. With TV, free Wi-Fi,
buffet b/fast inc. Ideal base for whale-watching
enthusiasts. Great off-season rates. €€

## PIEDADE

⌂ **O Zimbreiro** (5 rooms) Caminho do Cruzeiro,
Ponta da Ilha; ☎292 666 709; e lebonj@zimbreiro.
com; www.zimbreiro.com. Almost at the extreme
eastern tip of the island, a Belgian/French run
guesthouse in a lush rural paradise, overlooking the
channel between Pico & São Jorge. Rooms, which
can be made to accommodate families on request,
are spacious & stylish. B/fast is different every day,
with produce from the garden. Evening meals on
request, verging on the gourmet. Swimming pool.
Delightful owners can advise on nearby walks, or
you can simply enjoy the active birdlife or try to spot
a passing whale. Recommended. €€€

## CAMPING

⋏ **Lajes** ☎292 679 700; www.cm-lajesdopico.
pt. At the far end of town within easy walking
distance of all amenities. €

⋏ **Madalena** ☎292 628 700; e claudiabrasil84@
hotmail.com. 200m beyond the medical centre;
showers & lavatories, though a bit exposed to all &
sundry. €

⋏ **Santo António** São Roque; ☎292 642 884;
e furna@outlook.pt. Excellent 24hr supervised
sheltered site amid pine trees with all amenities,
BBQ, tennis court, children's playpark, deer
enclosure. Within 200m are restaurants, a disco &
the sea. Close by are the Furnas pools. €

Pico now has more than 30 restaurants, over half in Madalena. Many serve up buffet-style feasts, good value but of variable quality. Listed below are a few which offer something a bit different and of a better standard, though not always Azorean. The further east you go, the fewer options there are. For location of listings see maps, pages 208 and 218.

## MADALENA AND AROUND

Most of the larger restaurants offer a self-service buffet at lunchtimes with a set price of around €9–10.

**✗ A Tasca O Petisca** Av Padre Nunes da Rosa, Madalena; ☎ 292 622 357; ☉ 07.00–02.00 daily. Full meals noon–15.00 & 19.00–22.30. Styled as a 'tidbit house', very popular with locals, serving snacks & tapas, plus grilled fish, meat & lobster. Daily specials work out slightly cheaper. *€12*

**✗ Atmosfera** ☉ 19.30–22.30 Wed–Mon. 10mins' drive from town, with just 18 seats, so book early if you want some Italian/international dishes in a rural setting. *€15*

**✗ Cella Bar** Just north of Madalena, signposted off the coast road; ☎ 292 623 654; ☉ noon–midnight Wed, Thu & Sun; noon–02.00 Fri & Sat. A short selection of tapas-style dishes, plus favourites such as oven-cooked octopus, steaks with a choice of sauces, BBQ ribs & other dishes. Occasional live music. Good for a drink & snack, mixed reviews on the meals. *€15*

**✗ Restaurante Marisqueira Ancoradouro** Rua João de Lima Whitton, Areia Larga, Madalena, 400m beyond the wine co-operative, heading out of town; ☎ 292 623 490; ☉ noon–15.00 & 19.00–22.00 Tue–Sun. Most rate it as the island's best. Seafood & traditional dishes such as black pudding with pineapple, along with a view of the lights of Horta across the channel. *€13*

**▢ Caffe 5** Rua Carlos Dabney 5; ☎ 292 623 970; ☉ 08.00–midnight Mon–Fri, noon–midnight Sat. A popular little central café, with freshly squeezed orange juice, pastries & light meals. Even kebabs can be found here! Free Wi-Fi, a pleasant place to browse the web, or people watch from the few outdoor tables. *€10*

## LAJES AND SURROUNDING AREA

**✗ Restaurante Aldeia da Fonte** (page 214); ☎ 292 679 504; ☉ May–Sep noon–15.00 & 19.00–22.00; Oct–Apr noon–15.00

& 18.30–21.30. Belongs to the Aldeia da Fonte Hotel & offers a traditional menu, & also international specialities. Nice ambience, good surroundings; definitely trying to do things differently & deserving of its good reputation *€16*

**✗ Restaurante Lagoa** Largo São Pedro, Lajes; ☎ 292 672 272; ☉ noon–15.00 & 19.00–22.00 daily. Focusing largely on buffet meals, you can go for 'all-you-can-eat' or something more modest with soup & a simple *prato do dia*. Fresh fish also available. *€11*

**✗ Whale'come ao Pico** (page 214); ☉ restaurant noon–16.00 & 18.30–22.00, bar 08.00–midnight, Apr–Oct. Everything from soup to fish, with baguettes, pasta & snacks in between. If you've been craving a decent, main-course salad since you left home, you'll find it here. Subscribes to the 'slow food' movement. Great variety, decent prices. *€12*

## PRAINHA

**✗ Canto do Paço** Rua do Ramal 4; ☎ 292 655 020; www.cantodopaco.com; ☉ noon–15.00 & 19.00–22.00 Wed–Mon. Well rated for its traditional cuisine. *€12*

## SÃO ROQUE

**✗ Clube Naval** On the harbour, by the museum; ☉ noon–15.00 & 19.00–22.00 daily, but snacks always available. Cheap eats, predominantly a male clientele at lunchtime. No great finesse. *€10*

## PIEDADE

**✗ Ponta da Ilha** Caminho de Baixo, Manhenha; ☎ 292 666 708; ☉ noon–15.00 & 19.00–22.00 Tue–Sun. A fish restaurant at the extreme east of Pico, with a good reputation for grilled fish, squid & shrimp. *€12*

9

⚏ **Artesanato Picoartes** Estrada Regional, São Mateus. On the main Madalena/Lajes road in São Mateus; ☏ 292 699 276; www.picoartes.com. 3 industrious family members produce genuine Pico handicrafts, inc embroidery, woodwork, artwork from fishscales, cowbone & whalebone.

⚏ **O Oleiro** Ponta da Ilha, Piedade; ☏ 292 666 020. Although from Belgium, this potter takes his inspiration from Pico & its surrounding waters, having resided here for 18 years.

## OTHER PRACTICALITIES

**Emergency** ☏ 112
**Police** Estrada Regional, Lajes; ☏ 292 672 410; Rua Secretário Teles Bettencourt, Madalena; ☏ 292 622 860; São Roque; ☏ 292 642 115
✚ **Health centres** Largo Vigário Gonçalo G Lemos, Lajes; ☏ 292 679 400; P Á Dr Caetano Mendonça, Madalena; ☏ 292 628 800; Rua do Cais, São Roque; ☏ 292 648 070

✉ **Post office** Rua Gen Lacerda Machado, Lajes; Rua Visconde Leite Perry, Madalena [Map, page 218]; Rua do Cais, São Roque

## WHAT TO SEE AND DO

Essential to Pico's past, and very much to the present because of the tourism that is keeping the island's history in the forefront of consciousness, are wine and whales. Their history and significance are presented through the extensive vineyards around the coast near Madalena, the wine museum and three very different whale museums. Then there is the landscape itself, and of course all the little villages that can be visited on a car tour (pages 223–7).

## MUSEUMS
### Madalena
***Museu do Vinho (Wine Museum)*** (*Rua do Carmo, Madalena;* ☏ *292 672 276;* ⊕ *10.00–17.30 Tue–Sun & hols; €2/1/free adult/senior & under 21s/ under 14s*) Take the coastal road north past the smart sports stadium, then turn right (signposted 'Museu') and find this museum beneath some tall araucaria and metrosideros trees at the next junction. It's part-housed in an old Carmelite convent enclosed by a high stone wall. There are fascinating old photographs and early equipment, a game to let you test your 'nose', and English-language information on laminated sheets and some translated wall panels. You can also purchase Pico wines, though tastings are sadly no longer offered. A real bonus in the garden is a small grove of dragon trees and their seedlings, totalling around 70 stems. The largest individual tree is over 850 years old and has a canopy spread of about 16m and a stem diameter of 1m. Pico's wine co-operative (see below) has over 230 active member-producers, growing around 500 tonnes of grapes annually.

***Cooperativa Vitivinícola (winery/co-operative)*** (*Av Padre Nunes da Rosa, a short walk past the Madalena municipal swimming pool;* ☏ *292 622 262; www. picowines.net;* ⊕ *09.00–17.00 (last visit 16.30) Mon–Fri; €2*) Here you can see the production and bottling plants, with tastings of five of their products included: two aperitifs, two whites and a brandy. Guided tours should be available without advance booking. English is spoken.

***Moinho do Frade (windmill)*** *(⊕ Jun–Sep 09.00–17.00 Tue–Sun; Apr, May, Oct 16.00–17.00 Sat, 09.00–10.30 Sun; Nov–Mar 09.00–10.00 & 14.00–15.00 Sun; when not open, you can still climb the steps to get a good view & take a photo)* The historically important UNESCO World Heritage wine-growing area just south of Madalena starting at Criação Velha captures an important economic and social period of the Azores. This recently restored windmill provides a splendid elevated view over an extraordinary landscape. It is claimed elsewhere that if all the stone walls of Pico island were joined end-to-end, they would go twice around the globe. Hard to prove, but the effort that must have gone in to clearing the ground and creating the walls is quite astounding.

## Lajes
***Museu dos Baleeiros (Whalers' Museum)*** *(Rua dos Baleeiros, Lajes; ☏ 292 672 276; ⊕ 10.00–17.30 Tue–Sun & hols; €2/1/free adult/under 25s & seniors/under 15s; optional audio-guide is €2 extra)* In front of Lajes harbour, this is a fascinating exhibition about whaling as it was in the Azores until 1985. The exhibits are appropriately displayed in three original 19th-century boathouses plus ancillary areas. They include full-size boats, tools and other artefacts, photographs, many good examples of scrimshaw, a blacksmith's workshop and much else. Displays are constantly being improved. An essential experience for any visitor wishing to understand the role of whaling in the social and economic history of the islands. There is English-language information on laminates and some wall panels, and temporary exhibitions from time to time.

***Centre for the Arts and Marine Sciences*** *(Rua do Castelo on the outskirts of Lajes, coming from Madalena – beside the tall chimney; ☏ 292 679 330; e cacm-sibil@ sapo.pt; ⊕ winter 09.00–18.00 Mon–Fri; Jun–Sep daily; €2.50/1.25/free adult/senior & under 18/under 12)* A former whale-processing factory, in this large restored building can be seen some of the original processing machinery, video and multi-media presentations about cetaceans (some in English), plus a good book- and gift shop, and a small snack bar. It also has facilities for exhibitions, research and teaching, and holds evening events.

## São Roque
***Museu da Indústria Baleeira*** *(Rua do Poço, São Roque; ☏ 292 622 147; ⊕ 10.00–17.30 Tue–Sun & hols, times may be 30mins earlier in winter; €2/1/free adult/under 25s & seniors/under 15s; free to all on Sun)* Housed in the old whale factory that was built in 1946 and closed in 1984 to become a museum ten years later. The original US-manufactured machinery is well oiled as though it had only just finished working. You can begin to see what it must have been like when a huge sperm whale was brought in for processing; definitely missing is the smell, not even a lingering whiff, which would really have brought it to life. Of all the many Azorean whaling museums, it probably wins the prize for having the most gruesome photos of whale dismemberment on display – and set in such an elegant building, too, down in the harbour by Clube Naval. Ask at reception about the small scrimshaw museum (Casa das Sofias) nearby.

## GARDENS
**Quinta das Rosas** *(East of Madalena; ⊕ Jun–Aug 08.00–20.00 Mon–Fri, 10.00–20.00 Sat, Sun & hols; Oct–Apr 08.00–16.00 Mon–Fri only; May & Sep 08.00–19.00 Mon–Fri, 10.00–19.00 Sat, Sun & hols; free)* This was a private garden and once quite beautiful and filled with plants, especially roses (hence the name). It was bequeathed

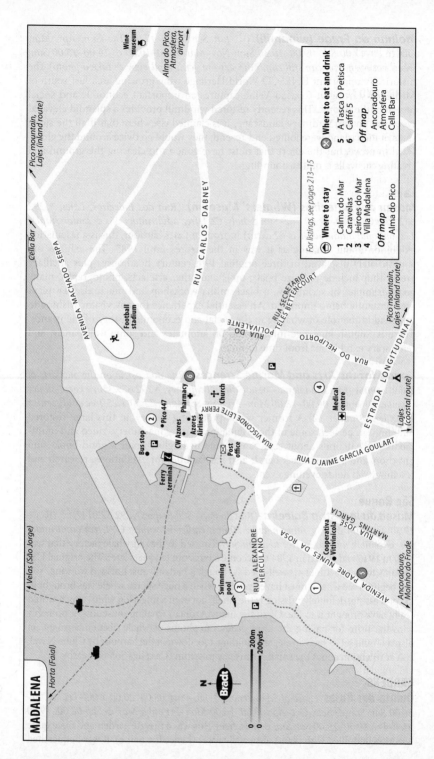

MADALENA

Wine museum

Alma do Pico, Atmosfera, airport

Pico mountain, Lajes (inland route)

Celia Bar

RUA CARLOS DABNEY

AVENIDA MACHADO SERPA

Football stadium

RUA SECRETARIO TELES BETTENCOURT

RUA DO POLIVALENTE

Pico mountain, Lajes (inland route)

RUA DO HELIPORTO

ESTRADA LONGITUDINAL

Lajes (coastal route)

Medical centre

Church

Pharmacy

CW Azores

Azores Airlines

Pico 447

Bus stop

Ferry terminal

Post office

RUA VISCONDE LEITE PERRY

RUA D JAIME GARCIA GOULART

RUA ALEXANDRE HERCULANO

Swimming pool

Velas (São Jorge)

Horta (Faial)

RUA NUNES DA ROSA

RUA JOSÉ MARTINS GARCIA

Cooperativa Vitivinícola

AVENIDA PADRE NUNES DA ROSA

Ancoradouro, Moinho do Frade

N

Bradt

0       200m
0       200yds

For listings, see pages 213–15

Where to stay
1 Calma do Mar
2 Caravelas
3 Jeiroes do Mar
4 Villa Madalena

Off map
Alma do Pico

Where to eat and drink
5 A Tasca O Petisca
6 Caffé 5

Off map
Ancoradouro
Atmosfera
Cella Bar

218

by its owner to the government and some interesting exotic plants remain, while efforts have been made to restore it. A visit will pass an hour or so if you have time to fill; it is about ten minutes by taxi from Madalena. Children's play area.

**BIRDS AND FLOWERS** Pico offers the easiest access to remnant laurisilva forest and provided there is no thick fog, the road passing **Lagoa do Capitão** will reveal a good number of the typical Azorean species including superb specimens of the handsome *Euphorbia stygiana*. The various lakes in this highland area can attract ducks and waders. The harbours offer good opportunities for birding, especially Madalena; the recommended place is **Ponta do Arieiro**, just to the south, which also gives sight of two small islands. **Lajes** has a number of habitats beyond the harbour thanks to a large eroded lava flow that offers intertidal pools and marshland. Vitally, it helps protects the town from winter storms, but has suffered badly in recent years. It is rated one of Pico's best sites for shorebirds, herons, terns and rarities.

## RECREATIONAL FOREST RESERVES
**Mistérios de São João** Along the south-coast EN–1 between São Caetano and São João, this small area is a narrow lava flow stretching down almost to the sea. Originally mainly heather, it was planted in the 1960s with various conifers and now dominated by the Mediterranean maritime pine, *Pinus pinaster*. Now adapted for leisure use, with trails, barbecues and picnic tables, exercise facilities, an observation tower for birdwatching and an interpretation centre for volcanism.

**Prainha** Along the northern EN–1 from São Roque to Piedade, Prainha offers extensive recreation facilities beneath the pines including children's play area, a multi-sports facility with showers, deer enclosure, footpaths and some restored typical rural buildings.

## CAVES
**Gruta das Torres** (m *924 403 921;* ⊕ *1 Jan–14 Jun & 16 Sep–31 Dec 14.00–17.30 Tue–Sat, guided tours (compulsory) 14.30 & 16.00; 15 Jun–15 Sep 10.00–18.00 daily, guided tours 10.30, noon, 13.30, 15.00, 16.30; €7/5.60/free adult/student & senior/ under 14; family ticket €13)* A 10-minute drive south from Madalena, the cave is signposted near Criação Velha. This lava cave is a fascinating volcanic phenomenon arising from lava flowing from the eruptions of Cabeço Brava and appears as a tunnel running through and emerging from an old lava flow. The principal tunnel is 4,480m long and mostly around 15m high. There are much smaller lateral secondary tunnels that show greater geological diversity. There is good public access and explanation and the entrance has been built of basalt rocks cleverly designed to blend into the landscape. The maximum tour group size is 12; an initial briefing is given, followed by a 450m walk, which all takes about an hour. Hard hats and lamps are provided, and you will need strong shoes.

The surfaces of lava flows often develop into two types which have been given the Hawaiian names of *aa* and *pahoehoe*. The *aa* is formed from the more viscous lava which soon congeals and does not travel far and the surface is a jumbled mass of angular and rugged rocks. A *pahoehoe* surface is formed from more fluid lava and frequently resemble huge coils of rope; as the lava cools it often produces a skin-like surface beneath which the lava is still liquid and as this continues to flow the smooth skin gets wrinkled and ropey. The image comes to mind of a dollop of hot jam on a plate to test the setting point from the wrinkles when pushed by the cook's finger. Occasionally this skin-like solidified crust gets attached to the sides of the channel and

On 22 July and around, Madalena celebrates its patron saint, Santa Maria Madalena, with several days of cultural and musical events. Coinciding with the Festival of Our Lady of Lourdes is the week-long Semana dos Baleeiros or Week of the Whalers. This is celebrated every August in Lajes by a whaling boat regatta and with *fado* and other traditional music as well as modern concerts, an arts and crafts fair and other cultural events. São Roque celebrates Cais de Agosto at the end of July with music and guest bands, guided excursions on Pico mountain, other guided walks, and exhibitions. Especially popular are the boat trips in restored whaleboats belonging to the São Roque Yacht Club.

**Espírito Santo**  Lajes; 7 weeks after Easter
**Domingo do Espírito Santo**  São Mateus, Candelária & other villages; 7 weeks after Easter Sun
**Terça-Feira do Espírito Santo**  Madalena; Tue following the 7th Sun after Easter
**Festa de Santa Maria Madalena**  Madalena; towards the end of Jul (inc 22 Jul)
**Cais de Agosto**  São Roque do Pico; last week of Jul/start of Aug
**Festa do Sr Bom Jesus Milagroso**  São Mateus; 1st week of Aug, with 6th being the highpoint
**Festa de São João Pequenino**  São João; middle of Aug
**Semana dos Baleeiros**  Lajes; 4th week of Aug

when the molten lava beneath drains away the crust is left suspended, thus forming an empty tunnel. Liquid lava dripping from the roof congeals into stalactites and other curious shapes and the tunnel may present numerous different manifestations of the lava flow. With time they can also develop secondary features such as stalagmites and stalactites of limonite, an iron mineral, or silica. This tunnel shows good examples of both lava types and is rich in geological forms. The temperature inside the tunnel is a constant 15°C throughout the year, and a high humidity is maintained by water filtering through the roof.

## ACTIVITIES

**CLIMBING PICO MOUNTAIN**  Ascending Pico mountain is a serious business and the first thing to do is to decide whether to 'go solo' or book an authorised guide through one of the outdoor activity companies (page 221). The registration process thereafter is handled at the **Casa da Montanha** (m *967 303 519*; ⊕ *16 Oct–30 Apr 08.00–18.00 daily; 1 Jun–30 Sep 08.00–20.00 Mon–Fri; May & 1–15 Oct 24hrs daily; €10 'park entrance fee' to climb, plus €2 extra to climb the 'little Pico', the final 100m rock scramble to the summit*). You will also be issued with a compulsory GPS, at no extra charge, but which you can optionally insure against loss for €25 (a replacement will otherwise cost you €275!).

The ascent and descent of Pico mountain, a round trip of about 9km, can take between six and seven hours, depending upon how fit you are and the weather conditions, with the descent usually taking more time than the ascent. You can go on your own, without a guide, but it is strongly recommended to go with one of the official guides, who from May 2016 can be contracted only through the outdoor activity companies licensed by the government. If choosing the latter option, expect to pay around €55 per person, which should include transport to and from the Casa da Montanha, park entrance fee and insurance. Guides are trained in mountain rescue and first aid. Taking a guide means you are their responsibility; without a guide you are responsible for yourself and if you get into trouble and need rescuing there is a very substantial fee to pay (around €1,500 to get you off the mountain; with a proper guide, such an eventuality should be covered by their insurance, but do ask).

Beginning at Cabeço das Cabras at 1,231m it is an ascent of over 1,100m, in part over loose stones and scoriae. There are marker posts at approximately 100m intervals but in poor weather they could be difficult to see. It is not a technically difficult climb but you need to be a strong walker and capable of coping with fast-changing weather conditions. You will need boots or substantial shoes with a good gripping sole and layers of clothing including a windproof jacket and waterproofs. At the Casa da Montanha, there is a briefing room with two videos, one on safety and another more general one. There are also photographs with explanations about Pico and its ecology, also a small bar with coffee and emergency-type snacks, and lavatories. The GPS, which you will be loaned, gives a signal every ten minutes or so which is traced on a computer monitored by the rescue service. The above precautions are imposed because climbing Pico has become very popular and walkers do get into trouble. Increasingly popular, over 10,400 people climbed the mountain in 2015 and some people have been killed as the ground can be dangerous off the small footpath and the weather changes very quickly. Incautious visitors have had to be rescued by the Civil Protection Service and a cavalier attitude to the mountain is irresponsible. The best time is in June, July and August; later it can get very cold, with snow on the summit as late as April.

To watch the sunrise from the summit, start out at 02.00, or to see both sunset *and* sunrise, go up the evening before, between 17.00 and 19.00, and bivouac (a maximum of one night on the mountain is permissible). Note that outside the Casa da Montanha office hours, you will have to perform the registration procedure with the fire station in Madalena, situated on the Estrada Regional to São Roque, about 20 minutes' walk from Madalena harbour.

However many mountains you might have climbed, to be on the top of Pico is to be 2,351m high in mid-Atlantic, and that is an experience to stay with you for life. To the south is Antarctica, 9,000 miles away and with nothing in between. In other directions and given luck with the clouds you should be able to see Faial, São Jorge, Graciosa and Terceira. In June and July the two native species of thyme and heath, *Thymus caespititius* and *Daboecia azorica*, are in full flower and the higher slopes are a spectacular pink and wine, a veritable rock garden of massed colour.

Before setting off it is wise to see what the day's weather is likely to be, for to make the ascent without the views would be terribly disappointing. Therefore make your decision by 08.00. Alternatively be bold and arrange to be taken up to the start of the climb by 02.00 so you can be high on the mountain, if not at the summit, for sunrise. The early morning light has a special quality and as the sun catches the lower daughter volcanic cones and slowly spreads up the mountainside to strike you, banishing the cold of dawn, it vindicates the decision to make the effort. The ultimate, of course, is to watch the sunset, then bivouac and wait for the sunrise. As with all mountains, it is a mixture of luck and timing as to what rewards you reap.

## Pico climbing companies
A full list of licensed companies is available from the tourist office. The two companies below come recommended:

**Caminhando** m 962 408 417; e caminhandoazores@gmail.com. A well-known company run by João Xavier, an English-speaking guide who is often recommended by locals & visitors.

**CW Azores** (page 223) Well-established company which can offer guides.

## CYCLING

**&#9895; Autatlantis** Rua Carlos Dabney 57, Madalena, or inside the ferry terminal; m 926 210 120/967 681 470; www.autatlantis.com. Hybrid bikes available to hire from around €13 per day, discounts if you hire a car from them & prices decrease for longer rentals.

**&#9895; Pico 447** Rua da Gare Maratima, Unit 1 (opposite the ferry terminal), Madalena; m 961 101 404; e info@pico447.pt. Hybrids & road bikes, €17/20 per day respectively, helmet inc. Can provide a variety of suggested trails/routes.

## DIVING

**&#10003; CW Azores** (page 223). PADI centre based on the harbourfront in Madalena, with everything from beginners' dives up to Divemaster courses.

Trips to Princess Alice Seamount available, to see mobula rays. Dives from €45, snorkelling from €40.

## SWIMMING

**Madalena** Right in town, by the harbour, there is a swimming pool with sea views and Faial across the channel. There is also a good natural rock pool, where even with a swell the surface is stable. There are changing facilities, showers, etc, and all for no charge, and there are bars and restaurants nearby. Further south, by the Jeirões apartments, there is a manmade pool, only operational in summer. There are numerous sea bathing areas around the island.

**WALKING** Pico so far has 14 official trails, all detailed on the Azores Tourist Board website (*www.visitazores.com*), but the daddy of them all is of course the ascent of Pico mountain (for further details, see pages 220–1). There is some glorious countryside with a lot of hidden history and of course landscapes unique to Pico, especially among the forested land, vineyards and on higher ground. You do have to be on guard for quickly descending cloud and mist, not forgetting there are 81 known cavities in the lava and many holes well concealed beneath the moss, ferns and other vegetation, so keep to obvious paths. As of 2016, all the official trails were well waymarked, but a quick check with the tourist office is always advisable. The three walks summarised below are all circular.

**Ladeira dos Moinhos** Easy, 3.4km, 1¼ hours. A circular walk beginning and ending in São Roque, passing on the way six watermills, some rebuilt, some in ruins, and an old threshing floor.

**Prainha do Norte** Easy, 8km, 2½ hours. A short circular route beginning and ending in the public garden of the village of Prainha (also known as Prainha do Norte). It passes old houses and beautiful stone bridges and down to Pico's only sandy beach and the Caso do Fio, a building used for the early transatlantic communications cable. Then following the coastline, reach a natural swimming pool in the rocks, and so back into the village.

**Calheta do Nesquim** Medium difficulty, 12km, 4 hours. A circular walk from the church in Calheta do Nesquim, a village with a long history of whaling. The route goes along the coast, climbs up through pastures and woodland to high points giving good views, and past a whale lookout.

**WHALE WATCHING** Both at the harbour of Madalena and at Lajes, many companies vie for your business with offers of trips to observe cetaceans. Pico is a major whale-watching centre; Lajes is where it all began. Approved boat operators are listed on noticeboards by the quay. The boats are generally smaller here than some across the channel in Horta.

## Madalena

🦭 **CW Azores** Cais da Madalena; 📞 292 622 622; 📱 911 133 658; ✉ info@cwazores.com; www.cwazores.com. Well established with 2 RIBs, theoretically open all year, but with Mar–Oct being the main season. Swimming with sharks also offered, plus land-based trips. Whale-watching trip from €65.

## Lajes

🦭 **Espaco Talassa** 📞 292 672 010; ✉ espacotalassa@espacotalassa.com; www. espacotalassa.com. Over 25 years ago, Frenchman Serge was a pioneer in Azorean whale watching. His enthusiasm undimmed, his business has also grown, but the personal touch remains. Evening talks on subjects such as island geology, sea turtles & whales (of course) are executed professionally. Recommended. Whale-watching trips are €64/49 high/low season.

## TOURING THE ISLAND

**MADALENA–SÃO ROQUE–LAJES–MADALENA** Madalena years ago was a little sleepy sort of place and because it had not been touched for ages had a pleasing air. With the new harbour, large hotel, increase in activity companies and the opening of a couple of stylish restaurants, it has stirred from its slumber and can be a hive of high-season activity. Viewed from the sea at a distance, with mighty Pico mountain in the background, it still looks very picturesque.

Depart from **Madalena** and first take the main road to the airport at Bandeiras and from near the airport follow the road signs to **Porto do Cachorro** on the northern coast. The tiny harbour, no more than just a slipway, is set among a tumble of black lava – a rather unique landscape, even by Azorean standards. An explanatory signboard maps out the points of interest, helping you to find the *rolas pipas*, the ramps made in the lava for rolling wine barrels to the sea. Lava here is contorted into many weird shapes (look for the dog's head!) and rock arches where the ocean rushes in; in fact the sea has obviously at one time rushed in rather too effectively: notice how the original cement pathway that once led the visitor safely through has been destroyed, precariously resting on a crumbling natural stone arch and with its days surely numbered. Thankfully, a new path has been constructed, letting you get close to the foaming ocean below. A distinctive whooshing noise emanates from seawater being sucked in and spat out by the flat concrete building at the edge of the sea, used for experiments in harnessing wave power for generation of electricity. The black lava buildings are mostly *adegas*, places where village wine, the *vinho de cheiro*, is made and stored and in September it can be very jolly here. One of them is now a small museum and shop, another was under development in 2016 to be reopened as a new distillery. You will also find a sunken, grassy area and a larger stone house with a well in front that at one time served the nearby communities of both Santa Luzia and Bandeiras. Such wells, known as tide wells, were dug near the sea so that seawater entering it would be filtered and at least made brackish for general use and, in times of severe drought, drinking. Note also the typical stone and cement cisterns with their roofs sloping down to the centre to catch and store rainwater. Near the museum is the church, dated 1460.

Continue parallel with the coast, coming first to **Lajido** where there is another communal well, this time in the middle of the road. An old distillery, *adega* and manor house have been restored. You have been passing through an area of *mistério*, a tumble of lava from the 1718 eruption emanating some 900m up the side of Pico. The

9

lava took two years to cool and prevented travel between São Roque and Madalena so that people were obliged to go by sea. Right by the roadside just before you get to **Arcos** you should be able to make out the wheel tracks of oxcarts in the lava flow. You will come to **Santa Luzia**, a traditional wine-producing area, and then **Santana**. Some of the large, pretentious, and totally out-of-scale new houses intruding upon the landscape are summer holiday homes, some of their owners still working in North America. Beyond **São Vicente** but before Santo António, look out on your right for *Adega 'A Buraca'*, a restored wine cellar, which offers tastings and the chance to see around a small, family-run, wine-orientated museum. For groups of four or more, they will cook meals of a traditional nature, given notice (◖ *292 642 119; www. adegaaburaca.com;* ⊕ *winter 09.30–17.30 Mon–Thu; summer 09.30–20.00 Mon–Fri*).

Just past **Santo António** you come to an area called **Furnas**. Here the lava solidified as it flowed down and met the sea, and the smooth swirls of rock resemble congealed chocolate sauce. Continue to **São Roque** where there is a café in the centre of the village. If you want to visit the impressive whale factory, turn left down to the sea just before the centre of São Roque to reach the harbour where you will find the museum and the Clube Naval. The club is popular with locals for its low-cost daily buffet.

From **São Roque** take the R2–2 signposted to Lajes and head for the mountains. There are glorious views behind you back to the coast as you climb. When the road stops climbing at around 700m the landscape is of rounded hills, pastures and remnants of the original forest that once covered much of the island. You will come to a junction with the EN–3 (also called the R3–2 on some maps) heading back to Madalena. Turn right, taking the EN–3 for about 2.5km to come to a small road off at 90° on your right leading to **Lagoa do Capitão**. This is just a small lake with a few isolated endemic junipers still withstanding the winds; walk anticlockwise round and follow the path leading off right uphill. Go behind the hill to be rewarded with a magnificent view of the whole length of São Jorge and, below, the coast of Pico around São Roque, something most visitors miss.

Retrace the way you came to rejoin the previous road (EN–3), back to its junction with the R2–2, and turn right in the direction of Lajes. Soon you come to a narrow side road off to your left, signposted to **Lagoa do Caiado**. Drive down this road for a few hundred metres and here you will see some of the important native plant species, many of which are endemic, found only in the Azores. While botanically fascinating, do be very careful if you wander from the road because there are many deep hollows between the rocks under the covering of mosses for the unwary to fall into and possibly disappear!

Return (again) to the main R2–2 road and descend to **Lajes**. It is a pretty drive; do allow time to take it slowly. Images that come to mind are of tall, stately cryptomeria trees, green meadows, hills, rounded hills, conical hills and glimpses through trees of hills going on higher up. Sunshine and shadow on the road; shining bright leaves; leaves of large-leaved gingers give a subtropical effect; and occasional camellia trees 5m tall are in full red bloom in January. Just before you get to Lajes on your right is the SIBIL former whale-processing factory, now the Centre for the Arts and Marine Sciences (page 217).

Lajes was the first settlement on the island and is well worth an hour's exploration. The 17th- and 18th-century houses offer interesting architectural details and the little chapel of São Pedro at the far end is a delight inside, built around 1460 by the first settlers. Regrettably it has been rendered with cement so that it could easily be mistaken for somebody's outbuilding; for centuries it had a thatched roof. Next to the Church of Our Lady of the Conception is the town hall, formerly a Franciscan convent. From the harbour there are fine views of Pico mountain; the whalers' museum is also just by the harbour (page 217).

As you drive back to Madalena following the coast, you will see in the woodlands around **Mistério de São João** inviting picnic areas built by the forest services. Then, before you reach Madalena, turn off the main road towards the coast to the village of **Criação Velha**. (If you have time, turn off before this and explore some of the coast and its settlements.) Criação Velha begins the wine-producing area along to the small port of **Areia Larga**, formerly used whenever bad weather closed nearby Madalena. This UNESCO-recognised heritage area captures something of former times when Pico wine was in full production and would have been swarming with hundreds of workers. You will see clearly above all the stone walls the **Moinho do Frade**, a restored mill which provided an elevated view over the vineyards (page 217). Continue round the coast, coming to the wine co-operative on the outskirts of Madalena near the municipal swimming pool.

**AROUND THE COAST OF THE EASTERN PART** With a whole day stretching ahead of you, a tour of the eastern sector is really a journey of gentle exploration following the main road that encircles the island and dropping down to explore little places on the coast that appeal as and when you get to them. Coming from Lajes along the southern coast, drop down from the main road to Calheta de Nesquim following the steep winding road and stop at the Church of São Sebastião. This is a typical Roman Catholic village church immediately overlooking the harbour, dated 1856. In front, note the statue to the man who led the first whale hunt on Pico. There is also a whaleboat house nearby, with six refurbished whaleboats. Return to the main road by the road you came down and when you come to conspicuous blue tourist signs take the first right to **Ponta da Ilha** and the immaculately kept lighthouse at the eastern tip of Pico. From here there is a fine view of the eastern sector of São Jorge and in the distance Terceira looking almost circular with a central plateau. Return to the main road and immediately take the tourist sign to **Parque Matos Souto** and the **Desenvolvimento Agrario**. Awaiting you at the end of the winding road is a delightful garden with shade trees and ornamental flowers, lily pond and picnic tables maintained by the forestry service. Even if you are not ready for your picnic, it is charming to visit.

Once more return to the main road and shortly you will come to **Piedade** where there is a bank and some shops. Along the very straight stretch of road following look out for a small viewing point of **Terra Alta**, a narrow concrete belvedere 330m atop the steep sea cliff; it provides a fine view across the channel of São Jorge while directly below you is a forest of pittosporum and a few native laurels trying to compete with the invader.

Take the turning down to **Santo Amaro** and stop in the square by the Church of Nossa Senhora do Carmo. About 100m along the road following the sea wall is the **Escola Regional de Artesanato** (⊕ *09.00–17.00 daily; donation expected*), a most charming crafts museum and school, set in a traditional house and dedicated to keeping traditional crafts alive. Very original corn dollies, straw hats, embroidery, fish-scale flower pictures, weaving and other crafts are displayed, together with three rooms furnished in traditional manner. Another house is a craft workshop while a third is a small shop selling many crafts plus angelica liqueur and delicious fig jam. Near the slipway is the boatbuilding yard, the main centre for the whole of the Azores. Access to the sea at this point is very gentle, something so rare in the islands that this may be the reason boatbuilding began here. You can usually see someone building or repairing wooden craft. In the Rua António Maria Teixeira

Not surprisingly, the extraordinary appearance of this tree has ensured it a place in parks and large gardens wherever there is a suitable Mediterranean climate. However, in its native state it is classified as endangered. The tree is endemic to the Canary and Cape Verde islands, where already it is extinct on some individual islands, and there are just two surviving wild trees on Madeira, where it was once widespread in the arid lowland areas, especially on adjacent Porto Santo where it is incorporated into the town's coat of arms. So abundant was it on Porto Santo it seems that when the first settlers arrived they felled trees in large numbers without learning how to propagate them, and flooded the market with resin until the price dropped so low they ceased harvesting, thus inadvertently saving whatever trees remained. The fruits became famous for fattening pigs, but here, too, the tree is now extinct.

Bound to mythology, it would seem Hercules might have been the first plant hunter associated with it. His 11th and last Labour was to seek and bring back three golden apples from the Garden of the Hespérides, and after searching all the known world he is thought to have located the garden on an island beyond the Atlas Mountains. The garden was guarded by Landon, the hundred-headed dragon, and when Landon was killed his blood flowed out across the land and from it trees sprung up which we now know as dragon trees.

With the scientific name of *Dracaena draco*, this very slow-growing umbrella-shaped tree grows to a height of 15m or more, develops a hugely wide crown, and produces numerous branched inflorescences of small greenish-white sweetly scented flowers followed by 1cm-wide fleshy orange fruits. After each flowering, the tree then branches. Their trunks do not have annual rings like most other trees so to determine their age one has to know roughly how often they flower, once every ten to 15 years (maybe more frequently in the Azores), and count the number of branches. Once thought to live for very many hundreds of years, this has been revised downwards to 600 or so. It would be fun to determine the oldest specimen in the Azores, since they have been cultivated here for at least 500 years, and used as nail varnish as well as medicinally.

From the dragon tree comes dragon's blood, the sap of the tree that upon drying becomes a reddish resin, and in the Canary Islands this was used by the aboriginal Guanche to embalm their dead. Dragon's blood was widely known in ancient times, used as a dye and medicine, but this probably came from *Dracaena cinnabarini* on the island of Socotra, and from Somalia. Other plants produce resins also known as dragon's blood and *Daemonorops*, a palm, from Sumatra, is the main source of the dragon's blood varnish for violins.

That *Dracaena draco* is now an endangered species is probably due to habitat loss and other human influences, but before the Spanish invaded and colonised the Canary Islands, we are told a flightless bird related to the pigeon and about the size of a turkey used to feed upon the fruits of the dragon tree. It soon became extinct, and one theory is that the dragon trees there declined because the seeds had to pass through the bird's digestive system before they would germinate. If this is true, it would be interesting to know if anything eats the seeds in the Azores, because they certainly seem to germinate well in the garden of Pico's wine museum!

there was a **private museum** explaining the art of wooden boatbuilding and aspects of Azorean maritime history, but it seems that the owner has emigrated to the US and locals doubt whether he will return.

Stay on the lower road and continue to **Prainha** and the square and its cafés at the side of the church, with its little garden. From the main door of the church is a good view of São Jorge. Take the road that continues on behind the church which quickly turns steeply uphill to rejoin the main road and continue to São Roque. You will pass by the **Prainha Forest Park**, a splendidly manicured and laid-out picnic and recreation area beneath the trees.

# Part Four

## WESTERN GROUP

Corvo ✈
Vila do Corvo

Santa Cruz das Flores
Lajes
*Flores*

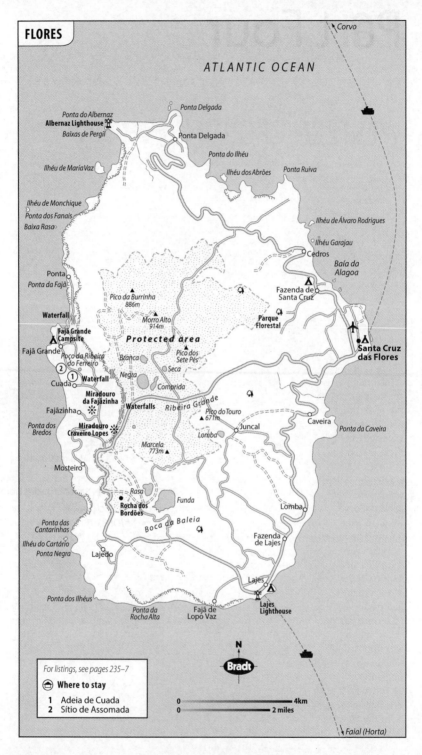

# FLORES

ATLANTIC OCEAN

Corvo

Ponta do Albernaz
**Albernaz Lighthouse**
Baixas de Pergil

Ponta Delgada
Ponta Delgada

Ponta do Ilhéu

Ilhéu de Maria Vaz

Ilhéu dos Abrões
Ponta Ruiva

Ilhéu de Monchique
Ponta dos Fanais
Baixa Rasa

Ilhéu de Álvaro Rodrigues
Ilhéu Garajau
Cedros

Baía da
Alagoa

Ponta
Ponta da Fajã

Fazenda de
Santa Cruz

Pico da Burrinha
886m

Morro Alto
914m

*Protected area*

**Parque
Florestal**

**Waterfall**

**Fajã Grande
Campsite**
Fajã Grande
Poço da Ribeira
do Ferreiro
② ①  **Waterfall**
Cuada
Branca
Negra
Seca
Pico dos
Sete Pés

Comprida

Santa Cruz
das Flores

**Miradouro
da Fajãzinha**
Fajãzinha
**Waterfalls**
Ribeira Grande
Pico do Touro
671m

Ponta dos
Bredos
**Miradouro
Craveiro Lopes**
Lomba
Juncal

Caveira
Ponta da Caveira

Marcela
773m

Mosteiro

Rasa
**Rocha dos
Bordões**
Funda

Lomba

Ponta das
Cantarinhas
Ilhéu do Cartário
Ponta Negra
Lajedo
Boca da Baleia

Fazenda
de Lajes

Lajes

Ponta dos Ilhéus
Ponta da
Rocha Alta
Fajã de
Lopo Vaz
**Lajes
Lighthouse**

N

**Bradt**

For listings, see pages 235–7

⊖ **Where to stay**

1 Adeia de Cuada
2 Sítio de Assomada

0 ——————— 4km
0 ——————— 2 miles

Faial (Horta)

# 10

# Flores

For many visitors, certainly for those seeking nature and tranquillity, Flores will be your favourite island. Not only have you now reached the westernmost island of the archipelago, you are also at the western extremity of Europe. Europe ends at Flores, the Isle of Flowers, on longitude 31° 15' W, and 1,380 miles from Lisbon. Given the island's small area, only 17km long and 12.5km wide, it is probably the most intensively rugged of the archipelago, with peaks, valleys, crater lakes, waterfalls and precipitous cliffs. Small pastures and arable fields all surrounded with hydrangea hedges or lichen-encrusted stone walls tie these together. Like Graciosa and Corvo, Flores is now a UNESCO Biosphere Reserve.

Although it is a long way from almost anywhere, Flores is an island of quite spectacular natural beauty and well worth the effort to reach. July and August are the peak times, June and September are busy, then tourism fades away. Come in winter, see no other tourists, enjoy sharp lighting, cloud effects, rainbows, storms, waterfalls, brilliant sunshine, wonderful conditions for photography – for in winter there is tremendous clarity – and simply escape from the madding crowds. Today, however, all too often the tourist is in a hurry to see everything and move on. Having invested travel time and fares to reach Flores, do stay at least three nights, even if you are not a walker; if you are, then think of five nights. If you want to visit nearby Corvo, you should allow an extra day. Ideally, you would spend a whole week. In winter, be tempted to rent an old restored comfortable cottage with wood-burning stove, bring books and CDs, and retreat for a month or three.

Whatever you do, make sure you have spare days in your itinerary to allow for cancelled flights due to bad weather. It is bad luck when this occurs, but it can happen at any time of the year, especially in winter when Flores bears the brunt of the Atlantic winter gales. There is a lovely story about a consul in Flores who had never left the island and, in the mid 1800s, boarded a ship that had called to take on fresh provisions. The weather became too rough for the ship to remain at the anchorage and stood out to sea for safety; the wind became stronger and it was impossible for a small boat to go ashore. Being short of provisions, the ship sailed away with the consul to its intended destination, arriving a few days later in England!

The main highlights are the landscape and geological features: the peaks of Sete Pés, Burrinha, Marcela and Flores's highest point at 914m, Morro Alto, all best seen from the viewpoint overlooking the Fazenda da Santa Cruz Valley; the Rocha dos Bordões basalt pipes; the seven different lakes in the centre of the island; several waterfalls, spectacular after rain; sea cliffs 600m high; and, for navigators, the islet of Monchique used as one of the main reference points to check navigational aids when sailors relied upon astronomy. Everywhere the countryside is beautiful, and there is constant temptation to stop the car and quietly take in the atmosphere. For walkers, there is the ultimate in conversation stoppers: walking almost the entire length of Europe's westernmost coastline (unless you count Greenland). In the calmer weather of summer, one of the finest ways to appreciate the island is to take a boat trip around the coast, part of which you will see anyway if you go to Corvo by sea.

This rugged island defiantly stands proud of the ocean, with many lengths of precipitous cliff challenging the sea to do its worst. In a few places the land descends less abruptly to meet the ocean, resulting in ravines and narrow river mouths, and just occasionally the descent could almost be described as sharply gradual, for example in the northeast and the odd point of flat land in the east, providing just enough space for the airport and main town of Santa Cruz. All the villages lie around the island's circumference, either close by the sea or perched upon the clifftops. Flores is unique among the Azores for being without a large caldera or dominated by long fissures. The chance of history made Flores the frontier post of Europe rather than of the US. Less than 3,800 people live here and Flores draws about the same number of visitors each year. It deserves more, though savvy locals are fearful of their beautiful mid-Atlantic nugget being tarnished by a sudden rush of uncontrolled mass tourism.

## BACKGROUND

**GEOLOGY** Flores is the westernmost island of the Azores and with Corvo rests upon the North American Plate. Both islands are on a nine- to ten-million-year-old oceanic crust. Flores's volcanic build-up occurred in two phases: first a complex that formed the embryonic island mostly below sea level with the oldest rocks around 2.5 million years old and the youngest some 650,000 years old, which were partly emergent and influenced by sea-level changes. The second complex, all above sea level, was active between 670,000 and 3,000 years ago, and created a diverse geological landscape. It consisted of thick, sometimes very thick lava flows which alternated with lesser pyroclastic (rock and ash) deposits, with a final eruptive stage of considerable lava flows from two or three volcanic centres.

One of the special features of Flores is the 'Lake District', consisting of Lagoas Lomba, Funda, Rasa, Negra, Comprida, Seca and Branca. These are *maars*, shallow, flat-floored craters caused by multiple explosive steam eruptions when rising magma comes into contact and interacts with groundwater or surface-derived water below the original ground surface. No cone is formed, and ejected material can form a low rim around the crater and the resulting depression often fills with rainwater. In all the tourist brochures are photographs of the Rocha dos Bordões, a fine example of columnar jointing located near the road between Mosteiro and Lajedo. These arise in the inner part of very thick lava flows when the hardening process proceeds relatively slowly to the flow's outer surface and sets up tensional stresses during contraction. Hardening along numerous parallel axes, usually perpendicular to the flow's surface, breaks the lava down into pentagonal or hexagonal prisms. Later weathering exposes them as 'basaltic organs', 'elephant roadways', and other suggestive forms. More familiar examples are Scotland's Fingal's Cave and Ireland's Giant's Causeway.

There have been no eruptions during historic times and geological evidence suggests the island's volcanoes are now extinct.

**HISTORY** The name Flores, meaning 'flowers', is thought to derive from the many yellow flowers of *Cubres* that adorned the sea cliffs at the time of Portuguese discovery. This is the local name for *Solidago sempervirens*, a North American species that might have been introduced, but has certainly been in the Azores for a very long time.

Diogo de Teive and his son João discovered the island around 1452, much later than the other two island groups. The first settlement was attempted by a Flemish nobleman Willem Van der Hagen at the bottom of the Ribeira da Cruz, a deep and dramatic valley with a small rocky beach giving access from the sea. The settlers tried to grow woad for export but because of the island's isolation and lack of a good natural harbour this failed after a few years, and Van der Hagen retired to Topo on São Jorge. **Permanent settlement** began only in around 1504 with people mainly from Portugal, Terceira and Madeira together with slaves from Cape Verde, and supplemented by Spanish, German, English, Jewish and Moorish families. Possibly by 1515, Lajes was already a small town, and 30 years later so was Santa Cruz, and by the end of that century the parish of Ponta Delgada on the north coast was also well established. Many places in Flores owe their names to settlers from towns in other Azorean islands. Contemporary accounts tell us the population of Flores was around 1,300, and conditions primitive. The houses were straw-thatched huts, the paths were muddy and so bad they could not be used by wheeled carts. Seldom did they get a boat visit from Terceira, and then only between March and September because of the winds.

However, the Azores were good hunting grounds for **pirates and corsairs** and in June 1587, five English vessels destroyed Lajes. Each year the Spanish organised two major convoys called the *Flota* and the *Galeones* to protect ships bringing back bullion from South America. In 1591, a British squadron waited to intercept the *Flota* on its way back from Mexico. The British crews had suffered greatly from illness and were largely ashore when a Spanish fleet sent to the Azores to meet and protect the *Flota* hove into sight. The British rapidly embarked but one ship, the *Revenge*, was slow to escape and was cut off. Single-handed the ship, under the command of Sir Richard Grenville, a wealthy landowner and cousin of Sir Walter Raleigh, fought the entire Spanish fleet for 15 hours, sinking two enemy ships before surrendering; an action immortalised by Tennyson's poem, *The Revenge*, beginning 'At Flores in the Azores Sir Richard Grenville lay …'. Sir Richard was mortally wounded and buried ashore but, being Protestant, not in consecrated ground. About the end of World War II, a storm exposed near the shore the buried remains of a man much taller than the islanders, together with a big sword. Could this have been the long-lost grave of Sir Richard? If it was, the remains are again lost.

By 1770, the island was no more peaceful, for in that year two American privateers badly bombarded Lajes, but were eventually fought off with a cannon firing broken crockery, bottles and stones and finally a cannonball. However, by the end of the century the relationship changed, and the islanders ended by trading with the pirates to mutual advantage.

The early economic activity was survival; yams were the mainstay, plus potatoes and other vegetables together with fish and bread, with the export of woad and minor products such as archil (lichen) and dragon's blood, while sheep produced wool. There was also casual trade and repairs with those ships that by losing their longitude came to Flores by chance. By the middle of the 18th century, supplying whalers and other shipping provided an income to the island, which peaked around the middle of the 19th century with meat, fruit and vegetables being exchanged or sold for export to the other islands, Madeira and beyond. Reflecting the economy, the population also peaked at this time, and since then over the last 150 years has gradually declined, largely through emigration, from over 10,000 to the present total of around 3,800. Open-boat land-based **whaling** began in 1860 and reached its peak in the late 1930s; there followed construction early in the next decade of the whale factory in Santa Cruz and a second one in Lajes, but these were always handicapped by the lack of a good harbour. Whales killed by Corvo men were towed to Flores for processing, and the last whale killed in the Western Group was off Corvo in 1981.

Roads within the island were bad or non-existent for a very long time, and only in the 1950s did this begin to change. What really ended the isolation of the island was the building of an airport, port improvements and the opening of a French **meteorological observatory** and satellite-tracking station in the 1960s. The French have gone, made redundant through new technology, and the economy depends upon meat and tourism. Fishing is small and enough for the island; tourism is very slow in winter but in the peak of summer the infrastructure struggles to meet demand.

## GETTING THERE AND AWAY

For getting to Flores, see pages 42–3. Certainly one of the smaller airports in the Azores, here you'll find a couple of car-hire companies, **Autatlantis** (✆ 292 542 278; m 961 393 996) and **Isla Verde** (✆ 292 542 372), a tourist office which will open to meet all incoming flights (except at weekends during November to March), a cafeteria, free Wi-Fi, a gift shop and not too much else. There's a solitary urinal in the gents' toilet.

To get to town, or any of Santa Cruz's accommodations, it's less than a ten-minute walk, or two minutes in a taxi.

**RIAC (Ferry ticket office)** ◷ 09.00–noon & 13.30–17.30 Mon–Fri. Sells tickets for the public ferry only.

**Azores Airlines** Rua Senador André Freitas 5, Santa Cruz das Flores; ✆ 292 590 340/341; ◷ 09.00–18.00 Mon–Fri.

## GETTING AROUND

**BY CAR** A rental car (see above) lets you stop for photo-shoots whenever you want, and gives maximum flexibility. Flores is not overblessed with petrol stations, and while you'll have to work hard to use a full tank in a week's visit, don't get caught out. Santa Cruz has two petrol stations, one on each of the roads that run parallel with the airport runway.

**BY BUS** There are public buses connecting most of the towns for a few euros, but they are infrequent and do not always operate every weekday, and certainly not at weekends. A published timetable is available from the tourist office. If you're a walker, the most useful buses are likely to be the Santa Cruz to Fajã Grande (Line 5) bus which departs at 08.35, arriving at 09.20, thus allowing you to do Stage 2 of the west-coast walk (page 243–7). An evening bus (Line 1) from Ponta Delgada (departs 17.45,

> ### FLORES'S TROUBLED AUTOMOTIVE HISTORY
>
> It can hardly be an 'urban' myth, as there's nothing urban about the island, but a story is told by locals about the first vehicles on Flores. In 1939, the first car arrived. In 1947 came the second one … and in that year, the first head-on collision was recorded.

arrives 18.38) at the end of the walk would then return you to Santa Cruz, but note that these convenient times are in June, July and August only. If you're staying in Fajã Grande, an 08.00 (winter 07.45) departure on Line 3 will drop you 20 minutes later at Lajedo, from where you can complete Stage 1 of the west-coast walk, arriving back on foot in Fajã Grande at the stage end. The logistics are mind-blowing: if you're not on a tight budget, a taxi to any trailhead is around €25 to/from most places.

**BY TAXI** Taxi hire for a day's sightseeing tour costs around €18 per hour from Santa Cruz. Most likely your driver will follow the route (Car Tour 1) described on pages 250–4, which takes about four hours. The tour to Ponta Delgada on the north coast (Car Tour 2, page 254) takes around two hours.

## ISLAND TOURS

**WestCanyon Turismo Aventura** m 968 266 206; e info@westcanyon.pt; www.westcanyon.pt. Local company offering jeep tours, guided walks & trips to nearby Corvo. Great enthusiasm for the island & its natural delights. Also bike rental & canyoning (page 240). Jeep tour €65/50 full/half day pp, guided hiking from €40 pp (based on group of 4). Prices for Corvo trips, inc trip up to its caldera, depend on numbers.

**Passeios Turisticos Ilhas das Flores** m 918 804 210/926 532 014; e toursofflores@gmail.com; www.toursofflores.com. English-speaking tour company who will drop-off/pick up at trailheads, & also do tours of the island in car or minibus, depending on group size. €120/80 half-/full-day tours for up to 4 passengers. Will also do shorter, customised tours on request.

## TOURIST INFORMATION

**Z Tourist office** Rua Dr Armas da Silveira, Santa Cruz; ☎ 292 592 639; ⊕ Oct–Mar 09.00–17.00 Mon–Fri; Apr–Sep daily; may occasionally be closed for an hour at lunchtime. English spoken,

up-to-date, helpful & informative staff. In Lajes, the tourist *quiosque* only opens for cruise ship arrivals, which are rare.

## WHERE TO STAY

In Santa Cruz das Flores there are three conventional hotels, but few other options. There is good-quality rural accommodation in Fajã Grande, and choices are on the increase here in what is the island's tourism hotspot. In the peak summer months, especially July and August, demand is such that you will have to book well in advance. The Santa Cruz tourist office carries a full list.

There are now four sites set aside for camping and theoretically they are open all year. As with everything, your ability to camp is subject to weather and in winter you might wake to find that your tent has taken off in the direction of Lisbon. **Fajã Grande**, **Santa Cruz**, **Lajes** and **Lagoa** are the locations and they are all basic with public showers and toilets. It is advisable to contact the tourist office in Santa Cruz to get further details. At most, there will be a nominal charge, but often they are free.

### SANTA CRUZ DAS FLORES

🏠 **Hotel das Flores** [map, page 251] (26 rooms) Zona do Boqueirão; ☎ 292 590 420; e inatel.flores@inatel.pt; www.inatel.pt; ⊕ Apr–Sep only. Offers gymnasium, games room, outdoor pool & restaurant. On a headland with views of Corvo island. The closest you'll get to a medium-sized luxury hotel on Flores, rooms are smart &

spacious. Free Wi-Fi. 15mins' walk into town. B/fast inc. €€€
🏠 **Hotel Ocidental** [map, page 251] (36 rooms) Av dos Baleeiros; ☎ 292 592 552; e hotelocidental@hotmail.com; www. hotelocidental.com. Good location, next to the sea. Many rooms have balconies & a splendid sea view. TV, free Wi-Fi in public areas only. The hotel is tiled

throughout & although spotlessly clean, it looks cheerless & b/fast is uninspiring. Has a restaurant (page 237) & boat tours. €€€

🏠 **Hotel Servi-Flor** [map, page 251] (34 rooms) Bairro dos Franceses; 📞 292 592 453; e hotelservi-flor@mail.telepac.pt; www.servi-flor. com. Converted from the old accommodation & restaurant building that once belonged to the French-operated communications relay station, & known as the 'French Hotel'. Rooms have AC, TV with international channels, free Wi-Fi & fridge. Rather dark & gloomy, but well heated in winter. Bar, outdoor pool (seasonal), children's play area & minigolf. B/fast inc. €€€

🏠 **Casa de Hespedes Malheiros** [map, page 251] (5 rooms) Rua do Hospital 8; 📞 292 592 201; m 963 165 190; e malheirosserpa@hotmail.com; www.malheiros.net. In the centre of town, 4 rooms with private bath, 1 without. Kitchen available to guests. Free Wi-Fi & TV in rooms. Gets cheaper for longer stays. €

## FAJÃ GRANDE AND AROUND

🏠 **Adeia da Cuada** [map, page 230] (18 cottages) Cuada, Fajã Grande; 📞 292 590 040; e aldeiacuada@mail.telepac.pt; www. aldeiadacuada.com. On the west coast, 2km from Fajã Grande. Through emigration, Cuada village became deserted. Now, 18 of the abandoned houses have been tastefully refurbished to a high standard, with free Wi-Fi, TV, kitchen (cooker, fridge, microwave) & heated by wood-burning stoves, offering 1-, 2- & 6-bedroomed accommodation. No b/fast inc though can be supplied (extra cost). Each cottage has a small simple garden, BBQ, & access is by narrow paths between walls. It is charming, in a delightful pastoral setting near the sea. €€€

🏠 **Residência Argonauta** [map, page 251] (5 rooms) Rua Senador André de Freitas Fajã Grande; 📞 292 552 219; e info@argonauta-flores. com; www.argonauta-flores.com. This charmingly refurbished traditional & characterful house, over 300 years old, has retained many early features, while providing a high standard. A new owner in 2016 has not diminished its charm. There are 5 en-suite rooms in the main house with b/fast room & bar. 1 unit is s/c. Free Wi-Fi, TV lounge & a great selection of books to browse. If the budget stretches to it, the top-floor suites are recommended. The owner is an interesting & hospitable Italian photographer & photography courses are available, too. Airport pickups & transfer service to trailheads can be organised. B/fast inc. €€€–€€€€

🏠 **Sítio da Assumada** [map, page 230] (5 chalets) Estrada Regional da Fajã Grande; m 924 195 407; e sitiodaassumada@hotmail.com; www. sitiodaassumada.com. Just outside Fäja Grande, ultra-modern chalets, an ecotourism award winner. The site is solar powered, the garden plants all endemic. AC, kitchen (fridge, cooker, microwave), free Wi-Fi, TV with international channels. Chalets are either 2 or 3 person, extra bed may be possible. No b/fast available. €€€

🏠 **Palheiro da Assomada & O Palheiro** (1 cottage, 1 studio) Fajã Grande; m 964 257 731; e neilking84@hotmail.com; www.fajagrande.com. Both beautifully renovated, a compact studio & a larger cottage on the peaceful west coast, with full s/c facilities inc oven, plus outdoor space to enjoy the sun. Free Wi-Fi. English-speaking owners. To rent by the night, week, or any period in between. Attractive off-season rates. Closed Dec & Jan. €€

## ✖ WHERE TO EAT AND DRINK

The options for dining out are fairly limited, more so in winter when some close due to lack of business. Most offer the basic Azorean fare without much variation in presentation. There are many 'snack bars' and insufficient restaurants. For ocean views in Santa Cruz, the **Buena Vista** (⊕ *11.00–21.30 Mon–Fri, until midnight Sat, until 18.00 Sun & in winter*) near Santa Cruz's natural pools offers coffee/salads/snacks, with outdoor tables and a glass pod for the (many) windy days. While Santa Cruz has the biggest choice, the best options are in Fajã Grande and elsewhere.

### SANTA CRUZ DAS FLORES
At lunchtime, poking around the streets behind the church will reveal a clutch of canteen-style

places full of locals. They offer cut-price plates of unexceptional food, filling for those on a budget. Otherwise, try the following:

**Hotel Café Restaurant** [map, page 251] Av dos Baleeiros, next to the Hotel Ocidental (page 235); 292 542 083; m 915 939 302; (restaurant) noon–15.00 & 19.00–23.00 Mon–Sat. The food is better than the deeply unimaginative name, but no better than average. A modern dining room, limited starters & a few fish & meat main courses. *€12*

**Lucino's Bar** [map, page 251] Praça 25 de Abril; 292 592 633; 07.00–22.00. Usually has the most buzz of anywhere in town, serves good coffee & you can also pick up a bowl of the soup of the day for next to nothing. Cheap eats. *€6*

**Pastelaria Snack Bar Amanhecer** [map, page 251] Rua Dr Armas da Silveira 21; 292 542 111; 08.30–21.00 Tue–Sat, 10.00–21.00 Sun. A few Azorean standards are enhanced by an Indian twist or two from the Mozambican owner. Grilled fresh fish, some vegetarian choices, too. *€9*

**Restaurante Sereia** [map, page 251] Rua Dr Armas da Silveira 30; 292 592 220; noon–15.00 & 18.00–21.30 Mon–Sat. At lunchtimes, select a decent *prato do dia* from a choice of 4 at a bargain price: €6 will buy you a main course & a drink. *€6*

**Servi-Flor Restaurant** (page 236); 292 592 454; noon–14.00 & 19.00–21.00 daily. A limited but daily changing menu in the Hotel Servi-Flor. *€13*

### LAJES

**Casa do Rei** Rua Pixote Pimentel 33 (on the road towards Fāja Grande); 292 593 262; m 922 259 289; www.casadorei.com; 18.00–21.30 Wed–Mon. 'House of the King' is how the name translates & this German-run establishment probably wears the crown as the island's best. A Teutonic touch can be detected in the cuisine, but the food is nearly all sourced on the island, some from their organic farm. English spoken. Fish, meat & vegetarian options, too. A good evening choice. *€13*

### FAJĀZINHA

**Pôr do Sol** [map, page 242] Rua dos Rolos; 292 552 075; 9 May–Sep noon–14.00 & 19.00–21.00 Tue–Sun; Oct–8 May noon–14.00 & 19.00–21.00 Sat & Sun only. Generally accepted as being the best traditional restaurant on the island & with friendly service, too. *€12*

### FAJĀ GRANDE

**Jonah's Snack Bar** (formerly Costa Ocidental & signed as such) Rua Senador André de Freitas 20; 292 552 043; 07.30–23.00 daily. Halfway up the main cobbled street, the popular hangout for locals lingering over a coffee. Inside is a nicely renovated dining room, with fish & meat choices – more options in summer. Outdoor tables too. *€13*

**Restaurante Casa da Vigia** On the main street, just north of where the cobbles run out; 292 552 217; may close in winter. A small restaurant with lots of atmosphere & some Italian dishes, dine indoors or in the enclosed garden; inc homemade pasta & vegetarian options; more expensive but very enjoyable. *€14*

**Restaurante Maresia** Rua do Porto (by the bathing area); m 965 665 649; (restaurant) Apr–Oct 13.00–16.00 & 19.00–22.00, (bar) noon–02.00 daily. With a great location down by the sea, a limited but quality menu is served in an alternative atmosphere. Expect some world music & relaxed service. Steaks are good here. Tables out front catch the best views of the mesmerising waves. Free Wi-Fi. *€15*

**Restaurante Papadiamandis** Rua do Porto (by the bathing area); m 917 947 118; noon–15.00 & 19.00–22.00 daily. A good place to watch the waves. Casual bar area & smarter dining room, serving everything from pizza & hamburger to fish & meat mains. *€13*

### PONTA DELGADA

**O Pescador** 292 592 692; noon–22.00 daily. A small restaurant owned by a fisherman, serving well-priced though mainly unexceptional food in a basic dining room. Limpets, beef & goat all feature on the menu, but the lamb is the dish to choose here. House wine is a bit rough: trade up to the inexpensive bottled stuff. *€9*

## NIGHTLIFE

The **Hotel Café Restaurant** (also known as the Toste), behind the Hotel Ocidental, is a popular 'pub' which often puts on live music at weekends, drawing in artists from other islands. It opens late (sometimes till 06.00) and has seating outside where people can dance until dawn in summer. The **Buena Vista Café**, above the swimming pool, occasionally has live music in summer. If that's not enough, then the disco **Epyka** struts its stuff at weekends. You'll find it signposted off the Santa Cruz to Ponta Delgada road, in Fazenda: it doesn't get going until midnight.

## OTHER PRACTICALITIES

**Emergency** ☎112
**Police** Santa Cruz das Flores; ☎ 292 592 115; Lajes; ☎ 292 553 186
**✚ Health Centre** Someone is always in attendance at the health centre in Santa Cruz; ☎ 292 590 270

(24hrs). There is no hospital on Flores & emergency cases are flown to Terceira.
✉ **Post office** Rua Senador André Freitas 13A, Santa Cruz das Flores; ⊕ 09.00–12.30 & 14.00–17.30 Mon–Fri

**BANKS/ATMS** Stock up with cash in Santa Cruz, as there are no facilities elsewhere on the island!

**WI-FI** You'll find open-access Wi-Fi in the centre of Santa Cruz [map, page 251], in the airport, the port at Lajes & even along the cobbled main street of sleepy Fajã Grande.

## WHAT TO SEE AND DO

Santa Cruz das Flores (page 250) is the principal town, though Fajã Grande is the biggest draw for visitors, being a useful base for walking, with better-quality accommodation and restaurants.

**MUSEUMS** As well as the flagship whaling museum in Santa Cruz, there are also tiny museums in Lomba, Lajes and Fajã Grande, but the opening hours are sporadic and the exhibits of fairly limited interest. The whaling museum is a must, a testament to what can be achieved with a will and some funds. Unless it's raining and you've run out of things to do, don't waste time on the **Museu e Auditório Municipal** (*Av Principe de Monaco, Santa Cruz;* ⊕ *10.00–noon & 14.00–16.30 Mon–Fri*). It does occasionally have temporary exhibitions, or show films in its auditorium, otherwise the exhibits amount to four old printing machines. The locals tell you that the 'museum' tag was simply added to obtain EU funding.

### Fábrica da Baleia do Boqueirão (Whaling Museum) (*Rua do Boqueirão 2, Santa Cruz;* ☎ *292 542 932;* ⊕ *Jun–Sep 09.00–17.00 Mon–Fri, 14.00–17.30 Sat & Sun; Oct–May 09.00–12.30 & 14.00–17.30 Mon–Fri, 14.00–17.30 Sun; guided tours (in English) available at 10.00, 11.30, 14.30 & 16.00; no guided tours on Sun in winter; €2.50/1.50/free adult/adolescent/under 12s; family tickets available*) Even without the guided tour, a truly excellent new museum, with a chronology of whaling, superb French-made videos (with English subtitles) showing an actual whale hunt, a full-sized whaleboat, 'talking heads' of old whalers spinning their tales and bilingual informative wall panels outlining the relationship between American whalers and their recruitment of Azorean crew. It's all housed in the town's former whale-processing factory, with the original but renovated Babcock and Wilcox machinery eerily left *in situ*, accompanied by an explanation of the gruesome process. Possibly the best whaling museum in the archipelago. Recommended.

**BIRDS AND FLOWERS** There are three protected zones: the extensive central area of lakes; the south coast from Lajes and along the west coast up as far as near Mosteiro; the northeast coast from Santa Cruz to the Albernaz lighthouse and down to include the Ilhéu de Maria Vaz. These include the islets where the largest European colonies of roseate tern nest. It is thought that with their potential for Nearctic land birds and storm-tossed American vagrants, the westernmost islands offer the greatest birding excitement. A noted area for the land birds, with its small fields and woodlands, is around **Fajã Grande**. The central area has considerable and complicated geological interest while its humid Atlantic climate of fogs, strong winds and high rainfall has created boggy habitats dominated by juniper and sphagnum moss and other parts good for laurisilva species. Resident birds include canary, goldcrest, chaffinch, blackcap and grey wagtail and the whole wetland complex is regarded as an important area for regular migratory birds and also for the common tern.

## RECREATIONAL FOREST RESERVES
**Parque Florestal da Fazenda de Santa Cruz** (*Signposted off the main Santa Cruz to Ponta Delgada road, in Fazenda, 10mins' drive from Santa Cruz;* ⊕ *May, Sep & Oct 10.00–18.00; Jun–Aug 10.00–20.00; admission free*) This is a charming park set in a valley surrounded by evergreen forest, dating from the time when the then extensive common lands were cleared and converted to more productive pastures and timber in the early 1960s. In addition to a small formal garden with azaleas, there are picnic tables, a barbecue area, children's play area and toilets. There are also strutting, barking peacocks, some handsome chickens, caged birds and a deer enclosure. There is a building with an exhibition about the birds, but no café or shop. A short walk leads up to a viewpoint overlooking a small dam. You could also go slightly further on and ask to be put down at the dam. This is a peaceful spot with picturesque views, good for a picnic, and you can easily walk back to the park. If you cross the dam you will see a cobbled path leading steeply uphill beneath the trees. Should you follow this it goes between stone walls and hydrangeas and comes out after about 30 minutes into pastures where you get a fine view of the Ribeira da Badanela. Return the way you came. A longer linear walk from the park, returning to Santa Cruz, is detailed on pages 247–9.

## ACTIVITIES

**BOAT TRIPS** On a small and remote island what is available is inevitably going to vary each year, but trips in summer around the Flores coastline make a fascinating excursion to see the rock formations and seabirds; you can also see islets and various caves, including the intriguing Gruta dos Incharéus below Caveira, 50m long and 25m wide. In winter, when the public ferry schedule is limited, two of the operators below are worth contacting. If they have enough people interested, they will run a boat over to Corvo, and you can hop on board for a €25 adventure. All boats leave from Santa Cruz.

**Elisario Serpa** m 964 220 645; viagemailhadocorvo.blogspot.com. Worth contacting as an alternative to the public ferry.

**Hotel Ocidental** ℡ 292 590 100; e hotelocidental@hotmail.com. Worth contacting as an alternative to the public ferry.

**Jeroninvest** ℡ 292 552 009; e rui@ azoresferias.com; www.azoresferias.com. Also does diving trips.

**Zagaiaflores** ℡ 292 592 521; e zagaiaflores@gmail.com; www.zagaiaflores.pt. Can arrange fishing expeditions.

**Trips to Corvo** In summer there is a public ferry service on Tuesday, Thursday and Saturday, and in winter on Tuesday and Saturday. The single/round trip costs €10/20 and one way takes 40 minutes to cover the 13-mile journey.

## FESTIVALS ON FLORES

In July, the Festa do Emigrante (Emigrant's Festival) is Flores's biggest celebration, with music and folklore groups coming from other islands as well as Flores; there are exhibitions and various cultural events and a Carnival Ball. Other lesser festivals occur, mainly in late summer.

**Festa de N Sra Lourdes**  Santa Cruz; 2nd week of Feb
**Festa do Espírito Santo**  throughout the island; end of May
**Festa de São Pedro**  Santa Cruz; end of Jun
**Festas do Emigrante**  Lajes; middle/late Jul
**Cais das Poças**  Santa Cruz; 1st week of Aug, now the 2nd most important after the Emigrante festival
**Festa de Santo Cristo dos Milagres**  Fazenda dos Lajes; 1st/2nd week of Aug
**Festa de N Sra dos Remédios**  Fajãzinha; 3rd week of Aug
**Festa de N Sra Saúde**  Fajã Grande; 1st or 2nd week of Sep
**Festa do Bom Jesus**  Caveira (Santa Cruz); 3rd week of Sep
**Festa de N Sra Rosário**  Lajes; 4th week of Sep/1st week of Oct
**Festa de N Sra Conceição**  Santa Cruz; 1st/2nd week of Dec

See www.atlanticoline.pt for the latest information and times as there may well be more sailings. All crossings are subject to weather conditions on the day. Tickets should be bought in advance from the RIAC office (page 234). Note that the ferry terminal is the Porto das Poças, a simple quay at the end of Rua Dr Armas da Silva; don't wait at any of the other, former quays – the ferry will not arrive!

### CANYONING
**WestCanyon Turismo Aventura**  m 968 266 206; e info@westcanyon.pt; www.westcanyon. pt. Focusing on canyoning, also with a few bikes for rental. Most activities go with a min 2 people. Canyoning (half day) from €55 pp.

### DIVING
**Flores Dive Center**  292 552 009; m 964 794 943; e miguel@floresdivecenter.com; www. floresdivecenter.com. A summer-only activity, based out of Fajã Grande. Boat & shore dives, min 2 people required. Dives from €35.

### SWIMMING
**Santa Cruz das Flores**  There is a great natural rock pool halfway between the Ocidental and Servi-Flor hotels with showers and toilets. The Buena Vista Café is up above.

**Fajã Grande**  Black-pebble beach and a quay for access, with facilities and restaurants open, mainly in summer. You can also take a dip in the freshwater Poço do Bacalhau, north of town.

**WALKING**  There are four official waymarked trails, though plans are afoot to expand these. Three of these are described in full later in this chapter, as is an 'unofficial walk' from the Parque Florestal back to Santa Cruz (pages 247–9). The fourth of the official walks is graded medium/hard and spans the 7km between Miradouro das Lagoas and Poço do Bacalhau. Clear weather is needed for this three-hour walk, as low cloud could make way finding difficult. Details are on the www.visitazores.com website.

An extension is planned to the west-coast walk, so that it loops around from Ponta Delagada and ends up in Santa Cruz; eventually, there may be a circular walk around the entire island. As it is, any stroll into the countryside within sight of the sea carries the added frisson of excitement on account of the distance from anywhere else (Corvo excepted) – half the Atlantic before major landfall. Always check beforehand with the local tourist office if the trails are open and safe, as landslides can make them impassable.

**Waymarked trails** For the west-coast walk below, starting at Ponta Delgada in the north would mean descending to Fajã Grande, but many prefer the other direction, ascending from Fajã Grande since the path can be wet and slippery, thus difficult on the downslope. To cover the entire west coast, you could start from Lajedo and end in Ponta Delgada as described below; this can be done either as a tough single hike, or over two days, overnighting in Fajã Grande.

*Flores west-coast walk* (*Time (both stages together): about 7½hrs; total distance: about 24km*) By far the grandest walk to undertake. The walking is not too strenuous, but there are steep ascents and, more importantly, steep descents which can be slippery in wet conditions or when smooth cobbles are hidden by soft juicy foliage. There is also some boulder-hopping to do and a few streams to cross. After rain it will be muddy in places, and sometimes the path may be running with water. You should avoid this walk on very windy days, especially in winter. Otherwise it is straightforward and you will be rewarded by wonderful ever-changing views of coast and countryside, and experience walking a route that has been in use for 500 years. Should your schedule only allow time to do one of the stages detailed below, then the second one is definitely the more beautiful, though slightly harder. For walkers who are scared of heights, the first stage is the one to choose.

**Stage 1: Lajedo–Mosteiro–Fajãzinha–Fajã Grande** (*Time: about 3½hrs; distance: 12km. For a shorter walk, simply arrange to meet a taxi in either of the villages en route. This first stage crosses a series of hills & river valleys & passes within sight of the Rocha dos Bordões, the famous basalt rock formation, as well as giving some excellent coastal views. It includes a long & steep descent into Fajãzinha.*) To start, take a taxi to the church in the centre of Lajedo, or park your car at the village post office near the church. If you're staying in Fajã Grande, a third option is to take the early-morning school bus and get dropped off in Lajedo. Opposite the church is an *império* with brown-painted doors. Follow the road that rises steeply to the right of this building, and then go left. The road levels off and you continue to where it ends. Continue straight on and you are on the footpath. There is a signboard marking the official start of the walk.

Follow the cobbled trail keeping left at the junction you come to in a couple of minutes. From here, clear red and yellow waymarking makes route finding straightforward, always on a trail that varies from cobbles to grass. A couple of streams, usually easily negotiable, have to be crossed. Gurgling water later announces another stream, which is partially hidden by dense vegetation. You cross it on an old stone bridge said to have been built by the Castillians some 500 years ago. Once across, look back to see the narrow arch through which the water rushes.

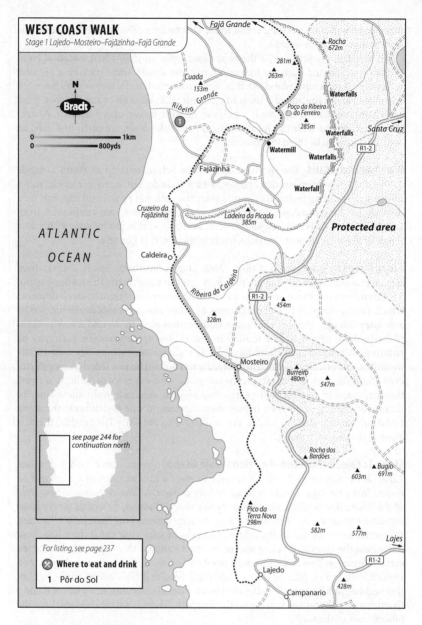

see page 244 for continuation north

For listing, see page 237

❌ **Where to eat and drink**

1    Pôr do Sol

**WEST COAST WALK**

*Stage 1 Lajedo–Mosteiro–Fajãzinha–Fajã Grande*

The route changes at times from being narrow and grassy, at times entering wooded areas, to wide cobbled track which can be slippy, but the path is always obvious. The Rocha dos Bordões formation becomes visible high up to your right (you'll get a better view later on) before you cross another stream and proceed downwards. After a cobbled section, you reach a wider stream which needs careful crossing on a series of boulders. Your path now climbs sharply up to the left, taking you up and out of the valley. Soon you get that promised closer view of the Bordões basalt rock, before continuing onward to Mosteiro. On reaching the asphalt road, turn left and walk downhill, soon reaching the church and a tiny square with seats, a good spot for a break after 1½ hours.

Continue on downhill on the asphalt road; when it bends right you go straight ahead on a wide paved path which then quickly bends right and crosses a river bridge. Continue on the grassy path which soon climbs uphill and joins the asphalt road. Turn left and continue along this quiet coast road. Follow this road but look out for the waymarking for the path which takes you downhill through vegetation and then turns right into the abandoned hamlet of Caldeira, before climbing again towards another hilltop, rejoining the asphalt road. Approximately three-quarters of the way uphill watch carefully for the grassy path off to the left, just before a left-hand bend in the road. It is signed to Fajãzinha. Follow this path all the way. You will get spectacular views ahead of the next deep valley, the Ribeira Grande and some impressive waterfalls. The path down is mostly in trees and vegetation; it is steep but not difficult, though not to be rushed as the rounded cobbles demand respect. Once in Fajãzinha you will soon reach a tiny square with a tree, and in summer a table and chairs. There is a shop/café, but it seems to have a fairly random schedule and should not be relied on – consider it as a bonus if it's open! A short diversion to the Pôr do Sol restaurant (signposted) is an option, though this is no longer directly on the route; for opening hours, see page 237. You are now about 2½ hours into the walk.

Previously, the route now proceeded downwards towards the sea, past the Pôr do Sol, but the weather destroyed the bridge and the new route turns you inland. From the square, pass the shop/café on its right-hand side, follow the road down for 50m and turn sharp right towards the distant waterfalls to pick up the waymarking. At the junction where the Queijaria Tradicional (cheese factory, page 253) is signed left, you turn right uphill then take an immediate left on to the Rua do Espinhaço. Where the tarmac runs out, you turn right on to a cobbled path. Ignore paths to left and right, heading roughly towards those cliffs and waterfalls. The path eventually joins the main road, opposite the small watermill, and you turn left. Follow the road across the two bridges, then take a sharp right uphill (waymarked) on to another road. (If you are fed up of hills by this point, an alternative finish to the walk is to simply continue along the main road all the way down to Fajã Grande.) Continue upwards for around 1km to the end of this dead-end road, then take the waymarked grassy path to the right, by the side of a stone wall. The walk is now around 40 minutes to Fajã Grande, mainly downhill and flanked by stone walls. At times it takes you very close to the foot of the cliff face, allowing you to fully appreciate the density of the vegetation. After a few minutes, be sure to keep right at a Y-junction. After less than 15 minutes from leaving the dead-end road, the path reaches another road, but instead of joining it, look out for the waymarking which ushers you down to the right again, between two more stone walls. Soon, the first buildings of Fajã Grande village will become visible to your left. Again, the path reaches a tarmac road: this time, you simply cross over it and continue again between yet two more stone walls. Keep a lookout for a sharp turn to your left (waymarked) and take it to proceed on a narrow path between two more stone walls. Away to your right, you can now see the distant church of Ponta da Fajã village, which you will visit on Stage 2 of the walk, if you choose to do it. The grass path soon brings you out next to a large modern house. Fifty metres beyond it, you turn left on to a tarmac road which after 400m deposits you on to the cobbles of Fajã Grande's main street. Turn right to find a café, shop or to continue onto Stage 2 of the walk.

## Stage 2: Fajã Grande–Ponta da Fajã–Ponta Delgada (*Time: about 4hrs; distance: 12km. There are ways of shortening the distance, which can make sense as the middle*

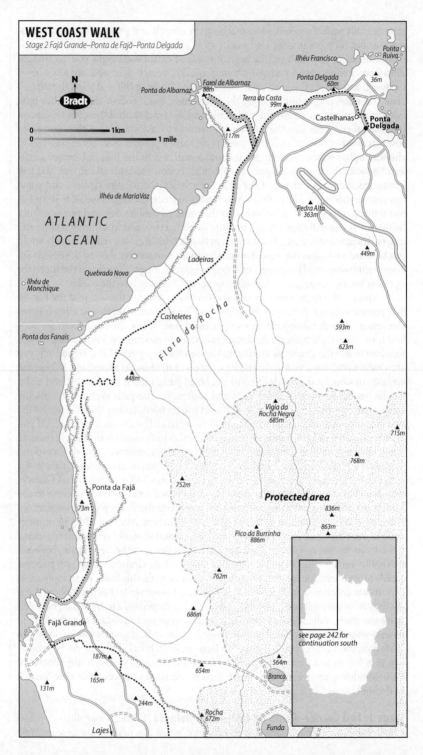

# WEST COAST WALK
*Stage 2 Fajã Grande–Ponta de Fajã–Ponta Delgada*

**Bradt**

N

0 ——————— 1km
0 ——————— 1 mile

ATLANTIC
OCEAN

Ilhéu de Monchique

Ilhéu de Maria Vaz

Quebrada Nova

Ponta dos Fanais

Ladeiras

Casteletes

*Flora da Rocha*

Ponta do Albarnaz

Farol de Albarnaz
88m

117m

Ponta Delgada
60m

Ilhéu Francisco

Ponta Ruiva

36m

Terra da Costa
99m

Castelhanas

**Ponta Delgada**

Pedra Alta
363m

449m

593m

623m

448m

Vigia da
Rocha Negra
685m

715m

768m

Ponta da Fajã

73m

752m

**Protected area**

836m

863m

Pico da Burrinha
886m

762m

686m

Fajã Grande

187m

165m

131m

244m

654m

564m

Branca

Rocha
672m

Lajes

Funda

*see page 242 for
continuation south*

244

*section is the most interesting. To do so, either take a cab to Ponta da Fajã (or park your car behind its church), or else phone a taxi when you reach the concrete road 3km from the end of the walk, rather than walking into Ponta Delgada – or do both! The description below is for the full walk from Fajã Grande to Ponta Delgada centre.)* From the north end of Fajã Grande, simply follow the tarmac road to Ponta da Fajã, with its church always visible in the distance. You soon pass the turn-off for Poço de Bacalhau (Codfish Pool), but it's maybe too early for a swim. On reaching the church at Ponta da Fajã, take the path to its left and pick up the waymarking. You set off down a wide grass and dirt track, cross a stream bed and continue across grass. After going through a gap in the stone wall, the path turns slightly right up towards the cliffs. Be sure to look back for the first of many excellent views of Fajã Grande. Ahead and offshore is the lonely pinnacle of Baixa Rasa, stranded mid ocean.

After a gradual climb of a few hundred metres, the waymarking takes you sharp right on a couple of stone steps, then left on a grassy track and zig-zags up towards a small waterfall (except in really dry times). Go left along a grassy ridge, still climbing. The path climbs more steeply as you enter the first of a series of low forests. You exit this on rough stone steps. You enter another wooded area, zig-zagging upwards. Watch carefully for the waymarking as it steers you off to the left. You enter a narrow grassy track lined with trees. Reach some rough wooden steps with a handrail, with cliffs towering above. The path levels out briefly, skirting along the front of the rockface, before turning inland and climbing on rough stone steps in another wooded area. On exiting the trees, turn round again for more stunning coastal views. Up to your right, you will soon see a handrail and some stone steps leading to a wooden stairway. This leads you to a small grassy plateau, an ideal resting place after your climb. You now head across the grassy clearing, but halfway head left through bushes. Continue to climb on rough steps. This section can be muddy in places. Reach a stream and a gate (fallen down at time of writing), cross another stream bed and go through another gate. The path now levels across moorland and soon you will catch your first sight of Corvo (assuming the weather is being friendly).

Waymarking takes you sharply left towards the sea, then right again to continue your descent through bushland. Follow the waymarking through this moorland, peppered with bushes. Soon the whole of Corvo island should be visible. Briefly you head back towards the sea, then right again opposite the rocky islet of Baixa Rasa. Descend to a stream, usually easily passable, then climb up again alongside a stone wall. Go through a gate and up through more bushland. A further muddy section comes next; continue in the same direction between two stone walls. Reach a grassy clearing, from which on a clear day you will have a truly breathtaking view of the Ilhéu de Maria Vaz, the various other islets, the Atlantic waves, the Albernaz lighthouse and with Corvo as a backdrop.

Continue through more bushland. You now cross moorland, crossing the occasional stream – in spring, these streams play host to some vociferous frogs! With the giant heather, this could be Scotland on steroids. The path now descends over rough stones – very slippy when wet – and the gap between the two stone walls becomes wider, levelling then descending to a narrower, stony path. Down to your left, you will see ahead the concrete road which you will eventually join. When the path emerges on to this road, you will have about 4km to (mainly) descend to the end of the walk. (If you have had enough, taxi drivers know this spot and will pick you up: a return from here to Fajã Grande will cost around €35.) Turn left on to the concrete and follow this cement road. Continue straight on and soon the cement road reaches a T-junction. (If you divert left here, it is a 0.5km walk to the Albernaz

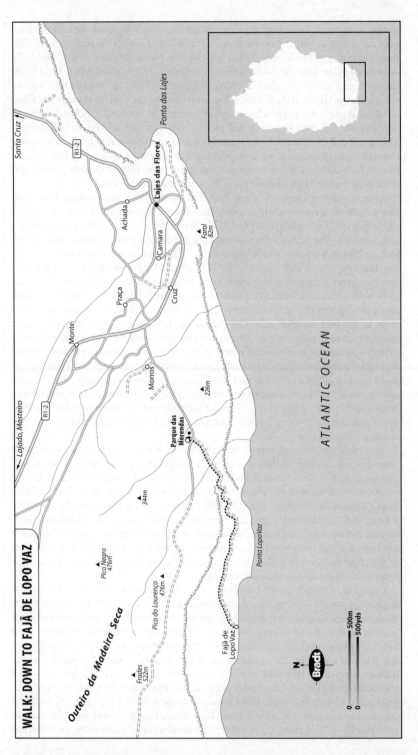

# WALK: DOWN TO FAJÃ DE LOPO VAZ

Santa Cruz

R1-2

Lajado, Mosteiro

R1-2

Monte

Praça

Achada

Câmara

Cruz

Morros

Lajes das Flores

Ponta das Lajes

Farol 82m

226m

Parque das Merendas

344m

Pico Negro 476m

Pico do Lourenço 476m

Frades 522m

Outeiro da Madeira Seca

Fajã de Lopo Vaz

Ponta Lopo Vaz

ATLANTIC OCEAN

Bradt

N

500m

500yds

0

0

lighthouse, where you get a good close view of the large Ilhéu de Maria Vaz just offshore, and, beyond, Ilhéu de Monchique. If you take the diversion, you will have to return to the junction.)

Turn right and simply follow the asphalt road, contouring past pastures and hedgerows with Corvo getting ever closer, and keep descending gently to the road end, ignoring any tracks coming in from the right. Reach a T-junction. If you turn left here, in 100m you have a view of the tiny harbour below you and the village to your right. Return to the junction and continue straight uphill. Continue up until you come to the *império* building on your right and the O Pescador Restaurant on your left. You can ring for a taxi from here, or from the blue-and-white café, Café do Sr José Adao, a few hundred metres further on, down to your left.

**Down to Fajã de Lopo Vaz** (*Time: 45mins each way from the clifftop, total 4km; 1½hrs each way from Lajes, 8km*) This waymarked walk descends from a small attractive picnic park to the largest beach on Flores (pebbles and sand) some 300m below. It claims to be the hottest area with a 'microclimate tropical' and bananas are grown.

You can take a taxi or drive the short distance from Lajes up to the picnic site above the *fajã*, the Parque das Merendas. This is a pleasing spot, with lovely views over the countryside and out to sea, with picnic tables, barbecue and toilets beneath myricaria trees. Stand in front of the stone cross and look down to get a preview of your walk.

The walk down the cliff to the beach takes approximately 45 minutes each way as the descent needs care. The path down has more than 300 uneven stone steps; there are also well-formed sections of path on grass or earth. At times the drop off to the left is sheer but it is mostly well protected by vegetation, though not recommended after rain. There is no onward path from the beach, no road access and no facilities, so bring your own water. There is an occasional house and parts of the beach may be suitable for swimming when very calm – there is a strong undertow. It was one of the sites adopted by the early settlers, and gives a good feel of how hard life must have been in such an isolated place. The path is one of the oldest manmade constructions on Flores; some 500 years old.

If you started in Lajes, simply follow the road back up to the main road and descend back into town.

**Parque Florestal da Fazenda to Santa Cruz das Flores walk** (*Time: about 2½hrs; distance: about 7km*) This is a glorious, easy, rural walk through magnificent pastoral country surrounded by high valley sides and largely sheltered from wind. Magnificent on a sunny day if you want to be idle and take a long time over an easy walk, splendid on a windy or cloudy day, and absolutely perfect in winter. Although much is on the road, you are unlikely to meet a vehicle until the end. Although the distance can be covered in a couple of hours, try to allow longer because it is so tranquil. You could extend the walk by combining it first by visiting the Parque Florestal (page 239) and then walking back to the road fork to the start of the walk.

At the Parque Florestal, where the carved wooden signpost points down to the park, instead of descending continue to walk up the road to the next Y-junction where you choose the left fork, which is a cinder road, going uphill between trees. You slowly climb up the valley of the Ribeira da Fazenda. This road is used by dairy farmers, but not by many others. Look back from time to time and you will glimpse the ocean and Fazenda church. Towards the head of the valley the road turns briefly to tarmac, and you have glorious pastoral views all around you,

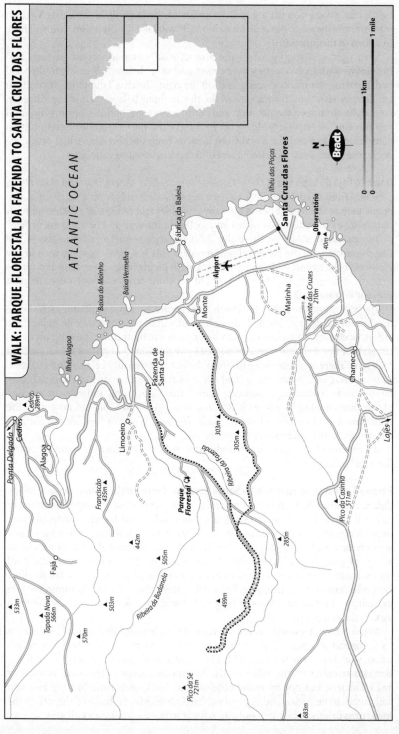

# WALK: PARQUE FLORESTAL DA FAZENDA TO SANTA CRUZ DAS FLORES

ATLANTIC OCEAN

Ponta Delgada
Cedros
Cedros 289m
Alagoa
Ilhéu Alagoa

Fajã
Tapada Nova 566m
533m
570m
503m

Francisção 435m
442m
505m

Ribeira da Badanela

Pico da Sé 721m

499m

Parque Florestal

Limoeiro

Fazenda de Santa Cruz

683m

285m

Pico da Casinha 511m

Ribeira do Fazenda

303m
305m

Baixa do Moinho
Baixa Vermelha

Fábrica da Baleia

Monte

Airport

Matinha

Monte das Cruzes 210m

Santa Cruz das Flores

Ilhéu das Poças

Observatório
40m

Charmeca

Lajes

N

Bradt

0        1km
0        1 mile

Each of these can be incorporated into a day's car tour, as they are very short.

**SHORT WALK 1: ALAGOA** (*Time: about 20mins*) From Santa Cruz take the road to the north towards Ponta Delgada and at Alagoa, before you reach Cedros, leave your car by the main road where you see a large rock-crushing depot, and walk down the unsurfaced road starting by the notice declaring the area has special protection for wild birds. This leads you between the scattered houses and down to the beach. There are five islets in the bay and for centuries this was the island's only accessible natural harbour when a strong southwest wind was blowing.

**SHORT WALK 2: POÇO DE BACALHAU (THE CODFISH POOL)** (*Time: about 10mins*) After you turn right to take the cul-de-sac to the village of Ponta da Fajã (page 253), you immediately come to a small bridge over the pretty little Ribeira das Casas and its gurgling stream. There is a signposted footpath nearby; simply follow the stream past two old watermills. Finally you have to scramble over a stone wall to reach the pool and its waterfall.

**SHORT WALK 3: POÇO DA RIBEIRA DO FERREIRO** (*Time: about 20mins*) Signposted off the main road (page 252), a short walk on a red-and-yellow waymarked stone track through forest takes you to a stunning vista, especially after rain. A whole series of waterfalls, perhaps up to 70m plummet down the rock face. A small lake completes this essential photo opportunity. There is usually some water, though in dry periods it may be a trickle.

except eastwards where lies the sea. At a double green gate on your left you see a *levada*, or water conduit, contouring off up a small side valley. Look up and slightly to your right and you will see the Pico da Sé, the highest point. You soon reach the highest point of the road, the tarmac runs out again and you descend for a short distance on a rough, grassy track to where it finally ends by some trees. By now, you'll have heard the gurgling of the stream, so follow the tiny path down and you reach the waters. There is a pool deep enough for a refreshing splash (if you're brave enough) and to leave a bottle of wine to cool in time for your picnic. Endemic plant species you can find around here include juniperus, rhamnus, faya, tree heath, vaccinium and viburnum.

To return to Santa Cruz should take you no more than 1½ hours. When you are ready to continue, walk back down the road for just over 1km. After the tarmac finishes and you rejoin the rough track, in 500m take the wide cinder road which descends, first weaving right, left, then right again until it reaches a concrete bridge crossing a stream. Climb steeply on what becomes a tarmac road and then dirt again and wends its way along the valley side. Santa Cruz will eventually become visible down to your right after a couple of kilometres. The road descends seawards to the village of Monte and reaching a T-junction you turn right, then left soon after. After 100m, at a square stone tower with a noticeboard, take a right turn to descend steeply to another T-junction where you turn right down another steep road which you follow to join the main road. Cross this carefully to immediately find a path to the left of a house. This very soon becomes stone steps which you take to be returned to Santa Cruz at the end of the airport runway.

Flores  ACTIVITIES

10

**SANTA CRUZ DAS FLORES** This is the island's principal town and includes the airport, whose landing strip runs the town's entire length. It's an enjoyable enough place to potter for an hour or two. The most striking building is certainly the 19th-century **Nossa Senhora da Conceição church**, of substantial, solid architecture made more imposing by two towers framing the front elevation. Equally substantial is the charming Baroque **Convento de São Boaventura**, now the **Flores Museum** which has been shut for four years, undertaking painstaking renovation. It is due for a reopening in early 2017, with much of the ethnographic collection shunted off into storage and new multi-media exhibits installed in their place. Begun in 1642 for the Franciscan Order, in 1734 it became a hospital and then later a school. Set around an internal cloister, prior to closure the rooms formerly displayed items to do with whaling, including scrimshaw, old hand tools of various trades, linen and wool production and weaving, agricultural implements, and other ethnographic items. They had too, a collection of religious statues plus jewellery and other objects concerned with the cult of the Holy Spirit. See also the **Church of São Boaventura** which is integral to the convent, once it reopens. Look for the Hispanic-Mexican influence in the chancel, the plant motifs and allegorical figures painted on the magnificent, cedarwood ceiling, and a 16th-century Portuguese School *Annunciation*. Two British visitors, Joseph and Henry Bullar, described Santa Cruz in 1839: 'The streets are long and narrow, and fields intervene between the houses. There are no large private dwellings, the great majority being cottages of the poor. Above them all rises the church, which is one of the largest in the Azores …'.

⸳ Traditionally, visiting strangers were accommodated in the convents in rooms set aside for guests. Nearby is Pimental Mesquita's house, built in the 17th century for the then governor of Flores and Corvo, and now a public library. This is thought to be the oldest home on Flores and the first to have a tiled roof and glazed windows.

**CAR TOURS** One suggestion is to do the lakes area in the high country and the south and west coast in one day; in fact this is about a four-hour tour. On another day, drive up to the northeast corner, to Ponta Delgada, about a two-hour tour. If you have enough days on Flores, then time your journey to the lakes and high country when there is no fog. If the day is not clear but very windy this could be a good time, for often low clouds will be travelling quickly and you will get windows of clarity, often in spectacular light. The beautiful new tarmac from near Lagoa Comprida which connects to the east coast between Cedros and Ponta Delgada in the far north, has cut journey times considerably. You should also include one of the shorter walks on your touring schedule (page 249).

## Car Tour 1: Touring the high country together with the south and west

Leave Santa Cruz by the Lajes road and take the first major turning off to your right, signposted to **Fajãzinha** and **Fajã Grande**. You will soon get marvellous views on your left of the Ribeira da Cruz as you ascend, followed by a view to your right of Fazenda Valley. Look out for the Miradouro Pico da Casinha; here you might notice steep grassy slopes with narrow terraces running along the contours; these were made by hand 50 or more years ago to make the pasture accessible for cows. The landscape soon becomes open wet grassland and trees and you pass through an area called Castanheiro. Continue, and after passing a pretty little chapel (Our Lady of Flores) on your right, turn left at the intersection on to a roughish road

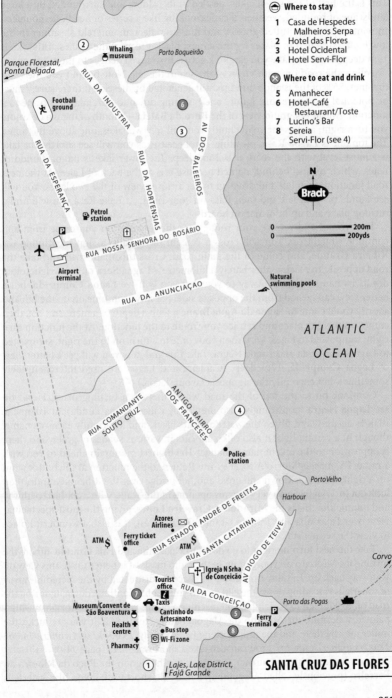

For listings, see pages 235–7

⊖ **Where to stay**
1  Casa de Hespedes
   Malheiros Serpa
2  Hotel das Flores
3  Hotel Ocidental
4  Hotel Servi-Flor

⊗ **Where to eat and drink**
5  Amanhecer
6  Hotel-Café
   Restaurant/Toste
7  Lucino's Bar
8  Sereia
   Servi-Flor (see 4)

Parque Florestal,
Ponta Delgada

Whaling museum

Porto Boqueirão

Football ground

RUA DA INDUSTRIA

RUA DA ESPERANÇA

RUA DA HORTENSIAS

AV DOS BALEEIROS

Petrol station

RUA NOSSA SENHORA DO ROSÁRIO

Airport terminal

RUA DA ANUNCIAÇAO

Natural swimming pools

ATLANTIC OCEAN

N
Bradt

0                    200m
0                    200yds

RUA COMANDANTE SOUTO CRUZ

ANTIGO BAIRRO DOS FRANCESES

Police station

Porto Velho

Harbour

Azores Airlines

RUA SENADOR ANDRÉ DE FREITAS

ATM $

Ferry ticket office

ATM $

RUA SANTA CATARINA

AV DIOGO DE TEIVE

Corvo

Igreja N Srha de Conçeição

Tourist office

Taxis

RUA DA CONCEIÇAO

Museum/Convent de São Boaventura

Cantinho do Artesanato

Health centre

Bus stop

Wi-Fi zone

Pharmacy

Porto das Pogas

Ferry terminal

Lajes, Lake District,
Fajã Grande

**SANTA CRUZ DAS FLORES**

(signposted for Lagoa da Lomba). At the next junction turn right on to smooth tarmac, following the sign to Lagoa da Lomba which you soon reach on your right. This is the first of the seven lakes, nestled in its caldera and surrounded by a large landscape of rounded, weathered cones looking like a series of headless shoulders. In winter the boggy tufted grasses and mosses reflect an emerald shimmer in the low light, darkened in places by the almost black-green of the rushes. This lake is 15m deep. From the lake you can look across hydrangea hedges to the south coast.

Follow the road on, with views of the sea to the left. Note behind you the wind turbines; 85% of the island's power is still generated by diesel, but there surely must be potential to change this. Ignore a left turning down to Fazenda, and come to a junction. Ahead is a grand view of the **Boca da Baleia** – 'mouth of the whale'. Soon, you turn right, and as the road climbs you will see two lakes, one above the other. The top one is **Lagoa Rasa**, meaning 'flat', because, as you will see shortly, the lake is almost level with the road; it is 16m deep. The lower lake is **Lagoa Funda** of Lajes, which means 'behind', named because it is at the back of Lajes. At the next road junction, turn left and drive up to get a closer view of the two lakes. You will see Funda on your left and then Rasa on your right. At Lake Rasa you will find a turning place and an information board.

Turn round and retrace your route; pass the intersection you came from and continue straight on. You will cross a cement bridge and a sign identifying the **Ribeira Grande**, and come to the main road. Cross this main road and take the road opposite to reach – after barely a kilometre – **Lagoa Seca** on your right, often dry as its name suggests. Away to your left you will see **Lagoa Comprida**, but a better view can be had from the opposite side. For now, continue on up the hill and shortly you'll come to **Lagoa da Água Branca**, with a depth of a mere 2m. You then come to a turning place and retrace your route to the junction. At the junction turn right, signposted to Lajes. Very soon you come to a turn-off to the right, signposted to Lagoa Comprida and Lagoa Negra. Take this and now you will get a better view of **Lagoa Comprida**, 17m deep. (Caldeira and Lagoa are used interchangeably sometimes, but currently the signposts favour 'lagoa'.)

Continue on to the top of the road where there is a turning place. Here you see **Lagoa Negra** (confusingly, also previously called Lagoa Funda), at 108m the island's deepest lake. Often the water appears black, and it certainly earns its name, though in a certain light it also often appears in various shades of green and there is opposition to the recent name change! The highest mountain ahead of you with a radio/TV mast is Morro Alto, at 914m. Return to the junction at the bottom and turn right. Continue down and cross another bridge over the Ribeira Grande, then look out for a layby and a very narrow opening in the 'walls' with a cobbled pathway and *miradouro*; this is the **Miradouro Craveiro Lopes**, giving the most spectacular view over Fajãzinha and Ribeira Grande. Facing west, it is also a wonderful place to view the setting sun.

Take the next turning right to go down to **Fajãzinha** and **Fajã Grande**. Ignore the turning for Mosteiro on your left up to the radio masts; it is better to see this view on your way back up. In rainy times, you will become distracted by the incredible array of waterfalls cascading down the cliff face to your right. Continue down, ignoring the road off to your left to Fajãzinha, and reaching a bridge you see on your right a white-painted watermill, the **Moinho da Alagoa**, dating from 1862. If you are lucky, the miller may be there and the mill working (⊕ *generally, 13.00–17.00 (winter), 14.00– 18.00 (summer), Sun–Fri*). You can also take a short walk here (page 249).

A few hundred metres further, watch out for the sign to the **Poço da Ribeira do Ferreiro** (previously called Alagoinha), a must-do short walk if you like waterfalls (page 249). The road then descends. Now look out for a road off to your right, signposted Moinho da Cascata/Casas da Cascata. Take this; it is an upper road around Fajã Grande. You will pass a rock-crushing enclosure on your left and the road descends through dense pittosporum and acacia trees, and then past many whiteish stone walls enclosing small fields. These have now gone to pasture, but presumably in earlier times they grew vegetables and other crops. Continue down until you find a road going off to the right. Take this turning and at the bottom reach a junction where you will find a small bridge. (Starting at the bridge, you can also make a short walk to the so-called **Codfish Pool** – see page 249. It is also near the start of the second stage of the west-coast walk to Ponta Delgada.) Turn right to go to the village of **Ponta da Fajã**, but it is a cul-de-sac so you will have to return the same way when the road runs out beyond the church. Returning to the bridge, this time keep straight on to reach the natural pools of **Fajã Grande** and then the main cobbled street which courses up through the village itself. There are restaurants both by the pools and in the village.

Looking north along the coast there is a good view back to Ponta da Fajã with its high cliff backdrop and to more incredible waterfalls and, out to sea, the **Ilhéu de Monchique**.

Retrace your route and if you have time, divert and go down to **Fajãzinha**, a very charming village where time seems to have stood still. Signposted by the village shop is the road to the **Queijaria Tradicional** (*signposted;* ⊕ *14.00–17.00 Tue–Sat*), the tiny village cheese factory. You will find it at the end of a very narrow road, passing many small houses and their productive gardens. Cheese is made here all year round: a soft cheese every day and a dry cheese when there is sufficient milk. Both are delicious. You can buy, but there are no free tastings, and no English is spoken by Ilda Henriques, the cheesemaker. In the village, down towards the sea you will also find the traditional restaurant, Pôr do Sol.

To leave, head back up towards the main road you came by and climb the hill, this time taking the turn-off to the right, and stop at the viewpoint **Miradouro da Fajãzinha** beneath the radio/TV mast to enjoy the superb aerial view of Fajãzinha and Fajã Grande. Continue on this road, descending parallel with the coast, and you will soon see the deserted village of **Caldeira**. Shortly afterwards you come to the village of **Mosteiro**, the white-painted houses and church running down the side of a ridge with its background of 'organ pipes', the Rocha dos Bordões. It is a charming scene, with the village surrounded by small fields enclosed by stone walls. The population numbers about 70.

Once you have passed through the village you come to a T-junction where you turn right on to the main Lajes road. Soon you get a good close view of the **Rocha dos Bordões**, and you can stop the car to better study the formation. The road continues on, curving round beneath the rocks and soon the hillside above the tarmac is covered in dense vegetation. There were once fields and pastures, all hedged with hydrangeas and you can still make out these boundary hedges in amongst all the aggressive invading growth of pittosporum, tree heather and myrica. The next village to come into view on your right is **Lajedo**; the road then curves away and you follow a straight stretch into **Lajes**.

Lajes has no real focus but you will see the church on your right surrounded by a cluster of buildings, so turn into the village and park near the church. From the front of the church is a good view down to the harbour, where wooden boats are still built. There are also public toilets. To explore the harbour either walk down, or drive back to the main road and turn left soon to find a road off left signposted to the port. Park on the spare ground opposite the Beira Mar Café, and take the narrow road in front of the café. In a minute or two you will be at the beach, where there are picnic tables. There are a few seasonal snack bars. Tackling the last, short sector of this island tour, note as the road climbs beneath dense evergreen trees on the road between Fazenda and Lomba two privately owned watermills by the side of the road. The first on the right is the **Moinho do Rei** and the second, on the left in a bend, **Moinho do Brisita**. Then you pass the village of **Lomba**. Just after that is the small village of **Caveira** and you come into the **Ribeira das Cruz** and get a view to Santa Cruz. This *ribeira* you are crossing is dramatic with its broken topography and dense evergreen vegetation. Look down to the coast and see the small and sheltered **Fajã do Conde**, the site of the very first settlement on Flores and a fertile place where oranges and strawberries are grown. Minutes later you pass the first houses of **Santa Cruz**.

## Car Tour 2: Touring Ponta Delgada and the northeast
Leave Santa Cruz from the northwest corner of the airstrip and quickly climb, getting views of the rugged coastline. Soon you are crossing ravines filled with evergreen pittosporum and myrica trees, and all is cool and humid. The pretty little village of **Fazenda de Santa Cruz** is unmistakable thanks to its conspicuously sited church. On the clifftop high above you will see the rooftops of Cedros village. Below, in the bay, are many rocks including the largest, Ilhéu Alagoa. Drive round the **Ribeira do Cascalho** passing the tiny settlement of **Alagoa** and ascend to **Cedros**; just before the top of the climb there is a viewpoint marked by a low stone wall giving a fine view to Alagoa and Santa Cruz. As you continue you will get constant views of Corvo to your right – on clear days, anyway. Leaving Cedros the road travels inland, but gives you a fine view of Ponta Ruiva way below on its exposed *fajã*. After about 8km you will see **Ponta Delgada** village below you; this is the largest village on Flores. From above, the land looks flat but this is deceptive for when you descend to explore the village you will find there are plenty of steep hills. The road forks towards the bottom of the descent and by following the left fork you will get a good view of the tiny harbour.

Head back on the same road: turn right (it is signposted), to go to the **Farol do Albernaz**. This is a narrow asphalt track going to the lighthouse which was built in 1911 and is the most westerly navigational aid in Europe. There is a good view of the precipitous coast, and the large rock just off the boulder-strewn beach is the **Ilhéu de Maria Vaz**, while out to sea is the **Ilhéu de Monchique**, which can also be seen from Fajã Grande. Come back on the same road and this time continue going on straight into Ponta Delgada village until you reach the municipal building marked **Casa do Povo on your right.** You can park here, since the streets below are very narrow, and exploration is better on foot. Don't forget the fisherman's restaurant O Pescador (page 237). Return to Santa Cruz by the same main road, or, if you have plenty of time and light, you could take the road off on your right just over midway between Ponta Delgada and Cedros and go south through the centre of the island via the 'Lake District'.

# 11

## Corvo

Corvo is by far the remotest island of the archipelago and must surely rate as one of the most isolated places in all Europe. This ancient volcanic remnant is surrounded by an often cruel and savage ocean, and remained inaccessible for months at a time, even from its nearest island neighbour, until the advent of the aeroplane. It is the tiny elusive gem at the apex of the Azores crown. Day visitors from Flores making the boat crossing in settled summer weather account for most of the visitors, but for the true traveller intent upon getting a feel for this island (and for ardent birders who arrive in October looking for American 'vagrants'), there are a slowly increasing number of accommodation options giving opportunities for longer stays.

Whether you arrive by plane or boat, you land in the island's only settlement, Vila do Corvo. It is the only suitable place to host a town, a lava delta where the last eruption occurred. Little has changed in the eastern segment of the town, the narrow cobbled streets between dark basalt walls of the houses all huddle tightly together in mutual protection against winter storms and to save valuable arable land much as they have always done. The only road snakes steeply up the hill to the cow pastures, and continues ever upwards to the caldera, a distance of some 6km.

On a day visit there should be time enough to walk to the road's end to enjoy the view down into the crater which, at 300m deep and 2km across, is among the largest in the Azores. However, be warned: it is often shrouded in cloud. For those with more time, there are two official walks to do, and it is an Azorean highpoint for autumn birdwatching. But the greatest delight must surely come from simply being on Corvo and freeing your senses to absorb its atmosphere of truly splendid isolation.

As well as being the remotest island in the Azores, Corvo is also by far the smallest, at just 17.13km². It is also the smallest parish in Portugal: 430 people, 1,200 cows, and if you stayed for a week then you'd probably meet them all. The island consists of a volcano summit in the northern half with a caldera, in the bottom of which are small lakes. Given its size and isolation it is perhaps just as well that today there is no noticeable seismic activity and it is considered to be inactive. Since the western islands are the first obstacle that the Atlantic Ocean meets for over 1,000 miles, Corvo has been substantially eroded, so that the island now confronts the ocean with precipitous cliffs 700m tall, especially in the north and northwest. These are the highest in the Azores.

In 2009, UNESCO declared the island a Biosphere Reserve, encompassing all the land area above sea level and a surrounding marine zone totalling 25,853ha. The landscapes and biological value are considered to be of regional, national and international importance, and take in the previously protected sites.

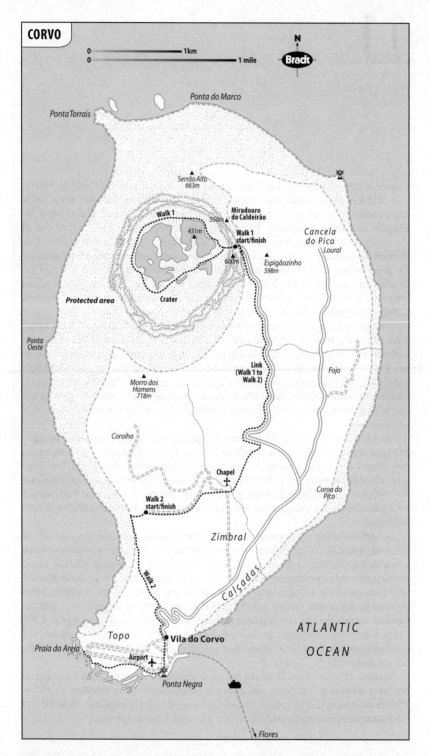

CORVO

0 ————— 1km
0 ————— 1 mile

N
Bradt

Ponta do Marco

Ponta Torrais

Serrão Alto
663m

Walk 1

Miradouro
do Caldeirão
550m

431m

Walk 1
start/finish

600m

Espigãozinho
598m

Cancela
do Pico

Loural

Protected area

Crater

Ponta
Oeste

Morro dos
Homens
718m

Link
(Walk 1 to
Walk 2)

Fojo

Coroiha

Chapel

Coroa do
Pico

Walk 2
start/finish

Zimbral

Walk 2

Calçadas

Topo

Praia da Areia

Vila do Corvo

ATLANTIC

OCEAN

Airport

Ponta Negra

Flores

**GEOLOGY** Like Flores, Corvo can be divided into two complexes, the older comprising submarine eruptions one to 1.5 million years old, and a superior complex of above-sea-level volcanism dating from around 700,000 years ago. The island appears to have a much simpler structure than Flores, and is the emerged summit of a basaltic stratovolcano (one that is a steeply sided cone of alternate layers of lava and other basaltic fragments). It would have been about 1,000m high before the caldera collapsed, and the highest point is now 718m.

The caldera's smooth and gently sloping sides suggest it could be one of the oldest in the Azores. The cinder cones within it, some up to 30m tall, are the result of later eruptions.

The last eruption occurred 100,000 years ago in the area of Pão de Açúcar ('Sugar Loaf') and its lava flows created the lava delta where Vila do Corvo and the airstrip are now located.

**HISTORY** Corvo means 'crow' or 'raven', but the name probably derives from a pre-Portuguese designation of Corvimarini or similar. Along with Flores it was the last of the islands to be discovered by the navigators, sometime around 1450. Initial attempts at colonisation failed and it was not until 1548, when its donatory, Captain Gonçalo de Sousa, imported slaves, probably from Cape Verde, that permanent settlement was achieved. Because of its size, isolation and lack of safe harbour, it has remained an agricultural-based society, and today livestock farming and fisheries, both subsidised, together with subsistence agriculture, are the mainstays.

## THE TRIALS OF ARRIVAL AND DEPARTURE ON CORVO

*David Sayers*

To make my first visit I had to charter a boat, and I gave a lift to an emigrant who had returned from California to Flores for the first time in 26 years. He was desperate to get to Corvo to see his 84-year-old aunt. Arriving at the little jetty, a small drama ensued with much embracing and tears between him and about a dozen islanders, and it was equally emotional when we departed four hours later. The boat's captain was given bunches of onions, and as we drew away from the harbour we were all sadly watching the tiny town grow smaller and smaller and the mists come down ever lower.

On one December trip to the Azores, I had ten days of magnificent weather, changeable and exhilarating. Exactly according to schedule SATA Air Açores – as it was then called – flew me from Ponta Delgada via Terceira to Flores and a week later from Flores to Corvo. This time it was just me and a policeman as passengers. An hour later a storm blew in, and the next day I watched fascinated as 12m waves crashed over the end of the runway and I began to see myself on Corvo for Christmas. Just 24 hours later and so typical of the Azores, the wind dropped long enough for the plane to land, fly to Flores and back, and take me to Faial exactly as printed in the timetable and displayed on the airline's website. At the same time high seas had prevented the usual supply-ship crossing from Flores for over three weeks, and the island was very short of fresh fruit and vegetables, though I was assured there was still three months' supply of beer in stock. It was a fun experience, but a visit in summer should be easier!

11

Early communication with Flores was by lighting fires, the number lit being code for a doctor, priest or other urgent need. Money entering the island's economy had to come from outside and in the time of the pirates and corsairs it seems an unofficial relationship was established with them to everyone's mutual advantage. In exchange for water, food supplies and ship repairs, the islanders gained protection and luxury items.

The advent of the American whalers in the 18th and 19th centuries attracted able men to help crew the ships, and later land-based open-boat whaling generated some cash income. In 1830, there were some 3,000 sheep grazing the island. The first boys' school opened in 1845, followed by one for girls in 1874, thanks to a bylaw passed in Lisbon. Around the turn of the century imports included sugar, flour, coffee, wine, vinegar, *aguardente*, port wine, cheese from São Jorge, figs, candles, soap and leather. Important exports were cows and hides, but it was also a time of yet more emigration, to Brazil, the other islands, but mostly to North America. In 1864, the population was 1,095; now it is a little over 400 and occupies just one page in the Azores telephone directory. Beef cattle are winched from the quay into a boat during the summer months for transfer to Flores, where a larger ship takes them onwards to Lisbon. With an excellent new school, easily identified by its windows and doors most attractively framed in traditional blue and yellow, the new generation maintains contact with the outside world via the very latest technology, and has far better internet access than is available in parts of rural England. Inhabitants of other islands comment on how the Corvo islanders are adept and adroit at getting their share of government spending. Until recently, children at 14 had to go to Terceira or São Miguel to complete their schooling, but can now complete it on their home island thanks to new facilities. Cast an eye across the townscape of white houses and your gaze may be halted by a dark, square building. This is Corvo's multi-purpose community hall; even bigger is a beautiful new sports centre.

## GETTING THERE AND AWAY

This is not always a straightforward process, whether you plan to arrive by plane or boat. Weather conditions are all-important, crosswinds and waves being the enemies, and the visitor should always allow for delays when planning a holiday itinerary. However, just because it is too windy for a plane to fly or the sea is too rough for a ship to come into port does not imply bad conditions on land.

Azores Airlines flies up to three-times weekly in winter, daily in summer, connecting Corvo with Flores, São Miguel, Faial and Terceira. General information on inter-island travel is given on pages 42–4 and 48–9. Apart from the public ferry operator, whose tickets can be bought at the RIAC office in Flores (page 234) or in Corvo (*opposite the post office*; ⊕ *09.00–17.00 Mon–Fri*), other private boat companies are based on neighbouring Flores. See pages 239–40 for information.

## GETTING AROUND

There is no car hire, so … walk! If this really does not appeal, you will find someone who is willing to take you to the start of one of the two walks, or simply to peer down into the caldera. After that … well, where else would you go on tiny Corvo?

**Carlos Reis** m 964 577 765. Limited English, but will transfer you up to the caldera for €5.

**João Mendonça** m 969 568 941/917 763 029. Provides a similar service.

## TOURIST INFORMATION

The tourist information office (**Casa do Bote**) (*Rua Jogo Bola;* ☏ *292 590 200; www.cm-corvo.pt, in Portuguese only;* ⊕ *09.30–17.00 Tue–Fri, 14.00–17.00 Sat & Sun;*) is located in the rather strangely shaped 'boathouse' building on the sea-side of the airport terminal building. It contains an old whaling boat.

##  WHERE TO STAY

Accommodation is very limited, but there is a good reason for that: there are few visitors even in high season. Nevertheless, advance booking is advisable: the arrival of one moderately sized group of birdwatchers could take up the island's capacity and leave nothing left for others! Addresses are superfluous for the listings below, as they will all pick up from port or airport; alternatively, in a place this size, everyone knows everyone and everything. If you want to camp on Corvo, look out for the signpost 'Parque de Campismo' near the airport. Here you'll find a good, flat, grass field at the end of the airstrip, by Corvo's tiny boulder-and-sand beach. There are simple facilities including a barbecue, all free of charge.

⌂ **Guesthouse Comodoro** (13 rooms) ☏ 292 596 128; e corvoazores@yahoo. com. Everyone can tell you the way, but the guesthouse offers a free transfer for pre-booked guests from either airport or ferry, each 5mins' walk away. Rooms come with private bathroom, free Wi-Fi & cable TV in a communal lounge area, with myriad books on the island & welcome coffee- & tea-making facilities. Quiet, well established: Manuel – a former town mayor – is a delightful host. B/fast inc. €€

⌂ **Joe and Vera's Place** (2 rooms) m 914 112 097; e vera.camara@sapo.pt; www. joeveraplace.pt. In a brand-new yellow house just beyond the Comodoro, 2 twin-bedded rooms with private bath, free Wi-Fi, cable TV & b/fast inc. €€

⌂ **Paula's Place** (3 rooms) m 917 763 012; e paula_cvu@hotmail.com. Painted pink & next to the Commodoro, 2 twin rooms with shared bath. Free Wi-Fi, TV. B/fast inc. €€

⌂ **Pirates' Nest** (3 rooms) m 963 731 953; e info@thepiratesnest.com; www.thepiratesnest. com. At the top of town, pass the post office heading uphill & look to your right for the welcoming skull- &- crossbones flag. TV & free Wi-Fi, shared bathrooms. No b/fast, but communal kitchen with hob lets you self-cater. Washing machine, too. €€

## ✕ WHERE TO EAT AND DRINK

✕ **Restaurante A Traineira** Rua da Matriz, by the harbour; ☏ 292 596 207; ⊕ 08.00–21.00 Mon–Sat. With fish soup a speciality & always offering fresh grilled fish. €12

✕ **Restaurante O Caldeirão** Caminho dos Moinhos; ⊕ restaurant: noon–14.00 & 19.00–21.00; bar: 07.30–21.00 Wed–Mon. On the sea-side of the airstrip, serving up fairly standard meat dishes, plus slightly more expensive fish. The owner is an ex-fire-eater. €12

## OTHER PRACTICALITIES

Everything is within spitting distance of each other and a map is unnecessary to find the **Health Centre** (Centre de Saúde), **post office** and the two banks with **ATMs**, all central. Free municipal **Wi-Fi** can be had at the airport or in the central area around the post office. ·

Corvo is so small and with so few people that celebrations here seem like a big house party. The most important festival is that of Our Lady of Miracles in August. The dates of festivals may vary each year, so please check with the tourist information office.

**Festa de Santo Antão** last weekend of May
**Festa de São Pedro** last weekend of Jun
**Festa do Dovino Espírito Santo** 2nd weekend of Jul
**Festa da Sagrada Família** last weekend of Jul
**Festival dos Moinhos and Festa de Nossa Senhora dos Milagres** 13–15 Aug

## WHAT TO SEE AND DO

**ENVIRONMENTAL INTERPRETATION CENTRE** (*Canada da Graciosa;* \ *292 596 051;* e *parque.natural.corvo@azores.gov.pt; parquesnaturais.azores.gov.pt/corvo;* ⊕ *09.00– 12.30 & 14.00–17.30 Mon–Sat; admission free*) The exhibits and custodians provide the visitor with an understanding of life on the island, an experience that will enhance any visit. The recently restored old building shows the traditional architecture, and is appropriately located in the town's compact historic core. The exhibition area contains a relief model of the island, letting you understand at a glance why there's only level space for the one town! It also features bilingual wall posters with information on the bird and marine life. An adjacent building houses a treadmill, with explanatory information. Guided tours are offered free, so take advantage.

**VILA DO CORVO** There is only one town, **Vila do Corvo**, and no villages or other settlements. If you have come just for the day, as do most visitors, then Vila do Corvo certainly justifies an hour or two. Wander around the old part of town enjoying the details: from the harbour, the narrow streets called *canadas*, the play of sun and shadow on the cobbles, and the Church of Nossa Senhora dos Milagres – Our Lady of Miracles – with origins dating back to the 16th century. The present church was built between 1789 and 1795, and paid for by the Corvo population together with remittances from emigrants; in 1796 the first priest was appointed, arriving from Urzelina on São Jorge. Corvo was the first island to publish and have approved in 1984 a strategic development plan and all the old part of Vila do Corvo is a conservation area. The new half is not without interest, and reflects the enterprise of the islanders. If you explore the south coast below the airport you will notice the old slipway by the windmills; this was where whales were brought up before the factory was built on Flores, and the blubber was reduced on the shore in the open. If the clouds are high, then the main attraction is to visit and preferably to walk around the caldera, the crater with its lake and small islands. See *Walk 1*, pages 261–2, for details.

**BIRDS** In October every year, a faithful band of British birders arrive in Corvo, on the hunt for vagrant birds blown on to the island on their way from the US to Africa. For some, it seems, the Atlantic storms can indeed be good news, while for the birds themselves, the lakes in the caldera provide a welcome place for ducks and waders to recuperate after the Atlantic squalls have blown them off course. British birder Peter Alfrey has written detailed descriptions of his visits to the island, highlighting Azorean birdwatching on Corvo (page 282). In 2005 alone, some 16 species of mostly Nearctic passerines new for Macaronesia were recorded, and more have followed since.

## ACTIVITIES

**WALKING** The best way to explore the island is to walk. The two official walks, both very easy and very satisfying, are well waymarked (as of 2016) and are described in this section.

Most visitors will want to go to the highest accessible point and see the caldera. A taxi to the caldera edge then a circular walk around the inside is the best recommendation. The summit is frequently in clouds, but do not be put off as these often clear for short moments, enough to give you a window to see down into the caldera. The second walk is also easy, and is both picturesque with all the pastures and at the same time dramatic because of the rugged coastline and views down over town and airport. You can marvel at being in such a glorious place and yet in the middle of the Atlantic Ocean.

### Walk 1: Around the inside of the caldera *(Time: 2hrs; distance: 4.7km. Easy/ medium, with descent at the beginning, ascent at the end. This walk assumes you get a taxi to the crater & that you get picked up again. However, you could choose to walk back down to town on the tarmac, which will add an extra 1½hrs to the time. Winds around the crater can be bitter, so a windproof jacket is usually a good idea.)* Corvo attracts so few visitors that you may have the caldera entirely to yourself, apart from numerous cows, blackbirds and the occasional seabird. From the official start of the walk at the crater edge, simply descend down a well-marked path following the red-and-yellow waymarking, usually visible on short wooden posts at intervals of 50–100m. You'll notice that the crater is valuable grazing land for cattle, some of which stay here even in winter. Many of them spend the winter in the numerous stone buildings you will have passed while being driven up from town. The road itself was completed in 1995, replacing a previous dirt track. On reaching the foot of the crater, these instructions now take you clockwise, though counterclockwise is equally possible. Follow the waymarked posts towards a large grassy mound. The undulations in the caldera floor quickly make you realise that it is not as flat as it seemed from the top! From the top of a mound, you descend to a rough stone bridge next to a small pond. Continue straight ahead towards the caldera wall. The path veers round to the right, taking you to the western end of the lake, boggy at times, then close enough to the lake shore to hear the croaking of frogs in spring. You cross the end of a wide peninsula, and pick up the waymarking on a large, isolated boulder, before continuing down and resuming close to the lake's edge. You will have noted how few trees grow inside the crater, though there is a rich variety of moss and grass for the cows. Keep to the lake shore, the path leading you round the right-hand side of a rocky hill. By now you can see the lowest point of the eastern caldera rim, where you started your walk. Follow the waymarking, being sure to find the designated solid path that leads upwards; trekking uphill on spongy moss will tire your legs considerably!

*If you fancy a much longer walk, you can link up walks 1 & 2 by following these instructions, taking you to the trailhead of walk 2:*

From the start/finish of walk 1, simply walk down the tarmac for around 25/30 minutes until you reach (on your left) a white building with a cattle grid just beyond. At the end of the building, and without crossing the cattle grid, turn right down a grassy slope in the direction of a rough road which you can see before you. At the foot of the grassy path, reach a concrete road and turn right. Proceed between two stone walls, and after ten minutes you reach a junction with a shrine on your right. At this point, turn right uphill on a wide dirt road. Continue up this road then take the first road off to your left and follow this until you see the signboard on your left, marking the start of walk 2.

## Walk 2: Caro de Indiano ('the Indian's face') to Vila do Corvo (*Time: 2½hrs; distance: 4km to Vila do Corvo, 4½km to the west end of the runway. You could alternatively do this as an 'out-&-back' walk, but it is better to take a taxi to the start & walk downhill, thus avoiding a long initial uphill trudge & seeing the same scenery twice: the instructions below assume that you start at the top. Starting from the top also ensures you see the spectacular views of the west coast, the town, & across to Flores.*) From the signboard, go through a wooden gate and down a narrow grassy/cobbled path between stone walls. After 200m, the waymarking takes you sharp left down a narrow path beside a barbed-wire fence. After a further few hundred metres, you go sharp right, the path narrowing even further between stone walls. A bit of wall climbing may be required, as farmers sometimes block gaps with string, wire or even stones to prevent cattle from wandering. Again, the path takes you sharply right, along a wall and hedge. Go through a gap in a wall, proceeding upwards with a wall on your right, waymarked in places.

Soon you will see the sea far below, and you follow the waymarking to the left towards the distant end of the runway. Caution: keep well clear of the edge at this point, especially in high winds!

Head for a wooden gate, through which you now pass. Cross grassland, again away from the cliff edge, before heading slightly inland to pick up the waymarking on a series of rocks which occupy the grassy pasture. Soon, the markings take you again inland, before you head briefly right to reach the end of a wall and barbed-wire fence. Hop over the wall, to find the waymarking. At a second wall, by two new wooden posts, cross it and continue in the same direction, with the town of Vila do Corvo now spread out before you.

You now cross a wooden bridge, perhaps having to step over some more string or wire, before continuing in the same direction, following the waymarked wooden posts. You now descend, fairly steeply and often between stone walls. The narrow downhill path eventually joins the main road, where you turn briefly right, before very quickly leaving it again to your left to descend on a wide grassy path with the tiny harbour ahead of you. You also get excellent views of the town's cramped old quarter. This path takes you on to tarmac again, before veering left again (waymarked) on to another descending grass track.

Soon, this turns to concrete and you begin to pass the first buildings of the town. Reaching cobbles, you turn right and descend into town. You can stop here, or continue to follow the waymarking which will take you past the eastern end of the runway, then along the airport road before turning left a few hundred metres after the windmills to take you down to the sea, along the shore and eventually to the runway's western end and the town's two black-sand beaches, where the walk officially ends.

# Appendix 1

## LANGUAGE

Portuguese is notoriously difficult to pronounce, takes much practice, and ought to be mastered before trying to use any vocabulary. Fortunately, you will meet plenty of friendly Azoreans happy to coach you to say a phrase to the point where they can recognise it!

Many words can be guessed from English or Spanish and some Spanish speakers get along quite well with a mixture of *português* and *espanhol*. Examples include many words ending with -ion or -on in English and Spanish respectively which are similar in Portuguese but end in -ão (plural usually -ões) – *televisão*, *associação*.

Take care, though, for some similar Spanish and Portuguese words have completely different meanings: *niño* (Spanish = child) versus *ninho* (Portuguese = nest); and it is best not to describe an ordinary man as *ordinário* as this implies he is common or vulgar.

### PRONUNCIATION

| | |
|---|---|
| ã + a followed by m | nasal (similar to 'ang'). |
| c | ss before i or e; k elsewhere |
| ç | ss |
| cc | ks |
| ch | sh |
| g | soft j before i or e; hard g elsewhere |
| j | soft j (as in French) |
| lh | ly (as in Spanish ll) |
| nh | ny (as Spanish ñ) |
| o or ô | oo when unstressed |
| o or ó | o when stressed (as in hot) |
| ou | o sound (as in both or window) |
| õ + o followed by m | nasal (similar to 'ong'). |
| qu | k before i or e; kw elsewhere |
| s | z or sh (at end of word) |
| x | sh or s |
| z | soft j |

### ESSENTIALS

| | | | |
|---|---|---|---|
| Hello | *Olá* | Yes | *Sim* |
| Good morning | *Bom dia* | Yes please | *Sim, por favor* |
| Good afternoon | *Boa tarde* | No | *Não* |
| Good evening | *Boa tarde* | No thank you | *Não obrigado* |
| Goodnight | *Boa noite* | (masculine) | |
| Goodbye | *Adeus* | I am sorry | *Desculpe* |

| | | | |
|---|---|---|---|
| That is all right | *Está bem* | excellent | *óptimo* |
| good | *bom* | | |
| Excuse me (to pass someone) | | *Com licença* | |
| What is your name? | | *Como se chama?* | |
| My name is … | | *Chamo-me* | |
| You're welcome | | *De nada* | |
| | | (ie: 'it's nothing' – reply to thank you) | |
| Please | | *Por favor* | |
| Thank you (masculine) | | *Obrigado* | |
| Thank you (feminine) | | *Obrigada* | |
| Thank you very much (masculine) | | *Muito obrigado* | |
| Thank you very much (feminine) | | *Muito obrigada* | |
| It is very kind of you | | *É muito amável* | |

## QUESTIONS

| | | | |
|---|---|---|---|
| How? | *Como?* | How much (cost)? | *Quanto custa/é isso?* |
| How much? | *Quanto?* | What? | *O quê?* |

## NUMBERS

| | | | |
|---|---|---|---|
| 0 | *zero* | 16 | *dezasseis* |
| 1 | *um* | 17 | *dezassete* |
| 2 | *dois* | 18 | *dezoito* |
| 3 | *três* | 19 | *dezanove* |
| 4 | *quatro* | 20 | *vinte* |
| 5 | *cinco* | 21 | *vinte e um* |
| 6 | *seis* | 30 | *trinta* |
| 7 | *sete* | 40 | *quarenta* |
| 8 | *oito* | 50 | *cinquenta* |
| 9 | *nove* | 60 | *sessenta* |
| 10 | *dez* | 70 | *setenta* |
| 11 | *onze* | 80 | *oitenta* |
| 12 | *doze* | 90 | *noventa* |
| 13 | *treze* | 100 | *cem* |
| 14 | *quatorze* | 1,000 | *mil* |
| 15 | *quinze* | | |

## DAYS, MONTHS AND TIME

| | | | |
|---|---|---|---|
| Sunday | *Domingo* | Thursday | *Quinta-feira* |
| Monday | *Segunda-feira* | Friday | *Sexta-feira* |
| Tuesday | *Terça-feira* | Saturday | *Sábado* |
| Wednesday | *Quarta-feira* | | |

| | | | |
|---|---|---|---|
| January | *Janeiro* | July | *Julho* |
| February | *Fevereiro* | August | *Agosto* |
| March | *Março* | September | *Setembro* |
| April | *Abril* | October | *Outubro* |
| May | *Maio* | November | *Novembro* |
| June | *Junho* | December | *Dezembro* |

| | | | |
|---|---|---|---|
| after | *depois (de)* | now | *agora* |
| before | *antes (de)* | today | *hoje* |

| day | *dia* | tomorrow | *amanhã* |
| never | *nunca* | yesterday | *ontem* |

## GETTING AROUND

| aeroplane | *avião* | right | *à direita* |
| bus | *autocarro* | road | *estrada* |
| car | *carro* | Stop here, please | *Pare aqui, por favor* |
| closed | *fechado* | straight on | *em frente* |
| here | *aqui* | street, road, highway | *rua* |
| left | *à esquerda* | there | *ali* |
| lorry, truck | *camião* | Where is it please? | *Onde é que é, por favor?* |
| open | *aberto* | Which way? | *Para onde?* |

## ACCOMMODATION

| bathroom, toilet | *casa de banho* | cold/hot water | *água fria/quente* |
| bed | *cama* | hotel | *hotel* |
| guesthouse | *residencial* | toilet paper | *papel higiénico* |

**EATING AND DRINKING** This includes sufficient restaurant Portuguese to help you through the usual menu.

## In a bar/café

| I would like … | *Queria …* |
| a beer, please | *uma cerveja, por favor* (for types of beer, see *Drinks* below) |
| a sandwich, please | *uma sanduíche, por favor* (these almost always come as rolls filled with ham, cheese or mixed: *fiambre, queijo* or *mixta*) |
| mineral water, please | *uma água mineral, por favor* (*com gás* = carbonated; *sem gás* = still) |
| two coffees, please | *dois cafés, por favor* |
| some more coffee, please | *mais café, por favor* |
| the bill, please | *a conta, por favor* |

## In a restaurant

| For two, please | *Para dois, por favor* | dinner | *jantar* |
| The menu, please | *O menu, por favor* | dish of the day | *prato do dia* |
| Enough, thank you | *Chega, obrigado* | the wine list | *lista de vinhos* |
| lunch | *almoço* | | |

**Drinks** Coffee comes in many forms: *café com leite* = white coffee; *café bica* = small strong black coffee; *café galão* = white coffee served in a long glass; for more details, see page 56.

| tea | *chá* (*chá da Índia* = India tea; *chá de camomile* = chamomile tea) |
| fruit drink | *um sumo de frutas* |
| iced | *fresco* |
| house wine | *vinho da casa* (*tinto*, red; *branco*, white) |
| bottled beer | *cerveja de garrafa* |
| draught beer | *cerveja de pressão* or *fino* or *imperial* |

# Fish (*Peixe*) See also *Appendix 3*, pages 268-70.

| | | | |
|---|---|---|---|
| clams | *ameijoas* | salmon | *salmão* |
| common sea bream | *pargo* | salted cod | *bacalhau* |
| forkbeard | *abrotea* | sardine | *sardinha* |
| horse mackerel | *chicharro* | shellfish | *mariscos* |
| lobster | *lagosta* | shrimps | *camarão* |
| mussels | *mexilhões* | squid | *lula* |
| octopus | *polvo* | swordfish | *espadarte* |
| prawns | *gambas* | tunny fish | *atum* |
| red fish | *boca negra* | wreck fish | *cherne* |
| red mullet | *salmonete* | | |

## Meat (*Carne*)

| | | | |
|---|---|---|---|
| beef | *carne de vaca* | rabbit | *coelho* |
| chicken | *frango* | sausage | *salsicha* |
| chop | *costeleta* | smoked pork | |
| kid | *carne de cabrito* | sausage | *linguiça* |
| liver | *fígado* | spiced sausage | *chouriço* |
| loin | *lombo* | tongue | *lingua* |
| pork | *carne de porco* | veal | *carne de vitela* |

## Cooking methods

| | | | |
|---|---|---|---|
| baked/roasted | *no forno* | smoked | *fumado* |
| boiled or *pot-au-feu* | *cozido* | steamed | *suada* |
| fried | *frito* | stewed | *estufado* |
| grilled | *grelhado* | tinned | *conserva* |
| roast/roasted | *assado* | with a sauce | *com molho* |

## Azorean/Portuguese foods

| | | | |
|---|---|---|---|
| apple | *maça* | lemon | *limão* |
| beans | *feijão* | lettuce salad | *salada de alface* |
| beans with mixed | | lupin seeds (usually | *tremoços* |
| meats | *feijoada* | in a saucer on the | |
| beef | *bife* | bar counter) | |
| biscuits | *biscoitos* | mixed salad | *salada mista* |
| bread | *pão* | olive oil | *azeite* |
| bread soup | *açorda* | olives | *azeitonas* |
| butter | *manteiga* | omelette | *omelete* |
| cabbage soup | *caldo verde* | orange | *laranja* |
| cake | *bolo* | peanuts | *amendoins* |
| caramel custard | *flan* | potatoes | *batatas* |
| chicken | *galinha* | rice | *arroz* |
| egg | *ovo* | sauce | *molho* |
| fruit | *frutas* | soup | *sopa* |
| fruit salad | *salada de frutas* | sugar | *açúcar* |
| garlic | *alho* | tomato salad | *salada de tomate* |
| honey | *mel* | yoghurt | *iogurte* |
| ice cream | *gelado* | | |

## HEALTH

| | | | |
|---|---|---|---|
| casualty department | *banco de socorros* | diarrhoea | *diarréia* |
| | *(SAU – Serviço de* | to hurt (or ache) | *doer* |
| | *Atendimento* | doctor | *médico* |
| | *Urgente)* | ill | *doente* |
| hospital | *hospital* | fever | *febre* |

## OTHER USEFUL WORDS

| | | | |
|---|---|---|---|
| battery | *pilha* | mountain | *montanha* |
| book | *livro* | night | *noite* |
| change | *câmbio* | nothing | *nada* |
| child | *criança* | on the beach | *na praia* |
| church | *igreja* | rain | *chuva* |
| currency | *devisas* | sea | *mar* |
| enough | *bastante* | shop | *loja* |
| hill | *colina* | small | *pequenho/a* |
| house | *casa* | to swim | *nadar* |
| lake | *lago* | too much | *demais/demasiado/a* |
| large | *grande* | town | *cidade* |
| a little (not much) | *pouco/a* | travellers' cheques | *cheques de viagem* |
| a lot (very, much) | *muito/a* | village | *aldeia* |
| market | *mercado* | you | *você* (polite, formal), |
| money | *dinheiro* | | *tu* (familiar) |

**LANGUAGE COURSES** The University of the Azores (*Rua da Mãe de Deus, 9500 Ponta Delgada;* ✆ *+351 296 650 000;* e *cursoverao@alf.uac.pt; www.uac.pt*) offers summer Portuguese-language courses at beginner, intermediate and advanced levels on São Miguel. There are also courses in Azorean culture, society and art on São Miguel, Terceira, Faial and Pico. Courses run for two to five weeks between June and July. Accommodation is provided in university hostels and fees include costs of field trips and social events.

# Appendix 2

## FLORA

Given that there are some 850 flowering plants and ferns in the Azores, the following 60 have been selected as those most likely to strike the eye of the visitor. Books that describe European flowers will identify most of the Azorean flora apart from the endemics, and the well-illustrated *Mediterranean Wild Flowers* by Marjorie Blamey and Christopher Grey Wilson, published by Collins, London, is helpful. The most difficult plants to identify confidently are the evergreen trees and shrubs. As always, the one plant you really would like to name will not be included!

The Latin name is given in italics, followed in brackets by the Portuguese vernacular where known, and by the common English name if there is one, and then the family.

### EVERGREEN TREES AND SHRUBS

**Myrica faya (faia) Myricaceae** Evergreen shrub or small tree up to 8m. Leaves lanceolate, leathery, dark green, margins often toothed towards the apex and frequently rolled backwards. Flowers are unisexual and borne on axillary catkin-like spikes, male and female on the same plant; overall colour olive-green, withering to brown. Fruit small, rounded and very hard. All Azores islands, Madeira, Canaries and Portugal. Often a coastal shrub, but found up to 700m. At higher altitudes a member of the laurisilva association. Can form pure stands, but is often out-competed by alien *Pittosporum undulatum* and you can frequently see the two species fighting for dominance. Makes a good shelter hedge and was once used around orange orchards. Isolated trees make good garden specimens.

**Ilex perado ssp. azorica (azevinho; Azorean holly) Aquifoliaceae** Tree up to 5m, with a smooth grey bark. Leaves dark and glossy, stiff, elliptic-oblong, sometimes with a few spines. Madeira and the Canaries also have their own subspecies. Usually found above 500m, and an important member of the laurisilva forest; can be seen as isolated specimens or in hedgerows. Formerly encouraged by farmers for winter cattle feed. On all the islands apart from Graciosa.

**Laurus azorica (louro; Canary laurel) Lauraceae** Dark, glossy green, evergreen tree up to 10m, sometimes taller, with a dense crown. Young shoots clothed in dense brown downy hairs. Leaves alternate, varying between five and 15, 3–7cm, broadly lanceolate-elliptic, hairless above, softly hairy beneath at least when young, strongly aromatic when crushed; in the axils of the midrib and main veins are tiny, gland-like projections. Flowers creamy yellow, fruit ovoid, 1–2cm, broadly ellipsoid,

green turning to black when ripe. Usually grows above 500m and a key member of the laurisilva forest.

***Picconia azorica (pau-branco)* Oleaceae** Evergreen tree or shrub, leaves opposite, leathery, without hairs, two to three times as long as broad, with small white flowers on inflorescences from the leaf axils. Found mostly between 300m and 600m, once widespread and used for house building, its presence now rather scattered. Endemic to the Azores, but not found on Graciosa.

***Frangula azorica (sanguinho)* Rhamnaceae** Large deciduous shrub or small tree with a wide spreading crown; branches little divided and leafy only towards the end. Leaves broadly elliptic, up to 15cm long with distinct parallel lateral veins. Flowers small, yellowish, in clusters from the leaf axils. Generally around 500m and up to about 1,000m altitude it is a member of the laurisilva forest, and also remnant hedgerows. On all islands except Graciosa and Corvo, now extinct on Madeira.

***Prunus lusitanica* ssp. *azorica (ginja;* Azores cherry laurel) Rosaceae** Evergreen small tree to 4m, leaves somewhat leathery, to 10cm, oval and tapering at each end, dark green and shiny above, paler beneath, possibly finely toothed, leaf stalks red when young, the whole plant without hairs. Flowers rounded, white, in racemes of up to 20–30 from the leaf axils. Fruit cherry-like, oval to almost round, turning red at first, finally ripening purplish black. Above 500m in deep ravines or in dense laurisilva forest. Endemic and rare.

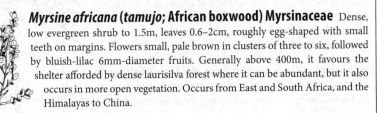

***Myrsine africana (tamujo;* African boxwood) Myrsinaceae** Dense, low evergreen shrub to 1.5m, leaves 0.6–2cm, roughly egg-shaped with small teeth on margins. Flowers small, pale brown in clusters of three to six, followed by bluish-lilac 6mm-diameter fruits. Generally above 400m, it favours the shelter afforded by dense laurisilva forest where it can be abundant, but it also occurs in more open vegetation. Occurs from East and South Africa, and the Himalayas to China.

***Persea indica (vinhático)* Lauraceae** Evergreen tree up to 15–20m tall, with a broad, rounded crown. Shoots finely hairy when young. Leaves without glands, 10–20 x 3–8cm, elliptic, leaf stalks up to 3cm, reddish; whole leaf becomes reddish when old. Inflorescence on stalks shorter than the leaves, flowers small, whitish. Fruit about 2cm. Ellipsoid, bluish-black when ripe. Found above 200m, introduced long ago (from the Canaries?), now naturalised. *Persea americana* is the avocado.

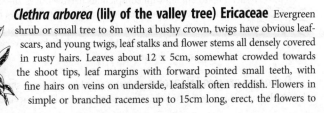

***Clethra arborea* (lily of the valley tree) Ericaceae** Evergreen shrub or small tree to 8m with a bushy crown, twigs have obvious leaf-scars, and young twigs, leaf stalks and flower stems all densely covered in rusty hairs. Leaves about 12 x 5cm, somewhat crowded towards the shoot tips, leaf margins with forward pointed small teeth, with fine hairs on veins on underside, leafstalk often reddish. Flowers in simple or branched racemes up to 15cm long, erect, the flowers to

8mm, nodding, white, cup-shaped, scented. Endemic to Macaronesia (Madeira), probably introduced into São Miguel where it has rapidly naturalised on the hills above Furnas.

### *Pittosporum undulatum (incenso;* Victorian box, orange berry) Pittosporaceae Vigorous tree to 14m, leaves 10 x 3cm, narrowing to a point, shiny dark green above, pale beneath, young leaves yellow-green, margins wavy. Flowers bell-shaped, about 1cm diameter, creamy-white in clusters, sweetly scented, February. Fruit orange when ripe, the pale brown seeds very sticky. Native of southeast Australia, it was introduced as an ornamental and used as a hedging plant to shelter the orange orchards but is now widely naturalised throughout the archipelago and is a major and aggressive component of the tree cover, especially on Santa Maria and Pico.

### *Hedera helix* ssp. *canariensis* (Canary ivy) Araliaceae The familiar plant with climbing or creeping woody stems and evergreen leaves with three to five short, triangular lobes. Yellow-green flowers in many flowered umbels, fruit rounded ripening black. Widespread between 100m and 1,100m, most common at mid altitude, and most luxurious in laurisilva forest. Also found in Madeira, Canaries, Portugal and northwest Africa.

### *Viburnum tinus* ssp. *subcordatum (folhado;* Azorean laurustinus) Caprifoliaceae Evergreen shrub with oval leaves and small white to pink flowers in large terminal convex clusters, spring. Fruits are at first a vivid deep metallic blue, turning black as they mature. Associates with laurisilva forest, but can be seen in remnant hedgerows on Pico; generally above 400m and up to 900m. *V. tinus* is native of southern Europe, with a closely related species in the Canaries, but absent from Madeira. The Azorean subspecies differs from the mainland species by its more vigorous habit, more glossy leaves and larger inflorescences.

### *Vaccinium cylindraceaum (uva da serra)* Ericaceae Deciduous shrub generally less than 2m tall, with 20–50mm-long finely toothed, narrowly oblong leaves; when young these are attractively red-tinged. Flowers borne in clusters, yellow-green tinged red; just how red the flowers are varies, partly due to age, and the combination of young red leaves and good red flowers in June puts this among the most attractive of the Azorean endemic plants. Grows generally above 400m and is conspicuous among the laurisilva forest, and often may be seen in old hedgerows. Occurs on all the islands. Fruits locally harvested for preserves.

### *Euphorbia stygiana* Euphorbiaceae Many-stemmed soft wooded shrub up to 2m tall with conspicuous narrow leaves 10–15cm long, apple-green and waxy with prominent pale midrib. Flowers terminal, yellow-green. Most easily seen in association with laurisilva, where it is moist and the surrounding vegetation provides shelter. A very noticeable plant of attractive form. Endemic.

### *Daboecia azorica* Ericaceae Dwarf, heath-like evergreen shrub less than 15cm tall with alternate leaves to 8mm long. Flowers in terminal loose racemes, nodding, bell-

shaped, ruby-red. Mostly above 500m, can be found in grassland but is most spectacular on the upper slopes of Pico, where it forms magnificent carpets with *Thymus caespititius* in midsummer. Endemic.

### *Erica scoparia* ssp. *azorica* (urze; besom heath)
**Ericaceae** Stout, evergreen shrub or small tree with narrow 4–7mm-long leaves in whorls. Insignificant reddish-brown flowers in interrupted terminal groups. Grows from sea level up to about 2,000m on Pico, at its best above 500m when part of the humid laurel forest. Long used for fuelwood, fencing poles, and woven shelter screens and brooms. Endemic, on all the islands, but large old specimens now rare.

### *Juniperus brevifolia* (*cedro-do-mato*) **Cupressaceae** This endemic conifer was
once a major tree in the laurisilva forests, producing a superb timber from trunks 40–60cm in diameter; these may still be seen as roof beams in old buildings. Today they are small trees or mostly shrubs with crooked stems affected by exposure and are to be found in remnant cut-over forest associated with other laurisilva species or sometimes surviving in hedgerows or as forlornly isolated specimens. The branches are short and numerous, densely foliate with needle-like leaves in whorls of three with two white stomatal (breathing pore) bands on the upper surface. Found usually above 500m, but also lower and on Pico they reach up to 1,500m. On all the islands except Santa Maria and Graciosa.

### *Arceuthobium azoricum* (*espigos-de-cedro*; dwarf mistletoe) **Viscaceae**
A genus of partly parasitic mistletoe found on conifers. The whole plant is yellowish-green with scale-like leaves and grows upon *Juniperus brevifolia*. At first difficult to find, the rather sickly colour of the small bunches of tangled stems becomes apparent from among the dense green leaves of its host. Above 600m altitude, it is found scattered in large laurisilva stands and is most easily discovered on Pico. An intriguing curiosity, it can be cultivated by taking cuttings of infected juniper when, after three years or so, the parasite will develop from the host tissue.

### *Lantana camara* (*cambará*; shrub verbena) **Verbenaceae**
Evergreen shrub to 2m, leaves oval, shortly pointed at apex, up to 6cm long, margins toothed, surface wrinkled, rough to the feel with a strong, pungent, lemony smell. Flower in hemispherical heads to 3cm across, yellow to orange or red often with a brighter 'eye'. Native to tropical America, this attractive flowering shrub has escaped from gardens and is naturalising and becoming a pest as it has in so many other places worldwide; poisonous to cattle.

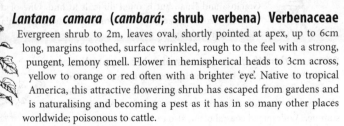

### *Solanum mauritianum* **Solanaceae** Large shrub or small tree up to
4m tall with foetid, softly hairy leaves ovate-elliptical, pointed at apex, up to 30cm long. Flowers up to 2cm across, violet-blue with yellow anthers, in many-flowered heads. Fruits round, 1.5cm across, deep yellow. Native of Central America, it is frequently found near habitation and on waste ground.

# HERBACEOUS PLANTS
## Rocky coastal areas, formed by variously aged lava flows or volcanic ash

### *Crithmum maritimum (perreexil-do-mar;* rock samphire)
**Umbelliferae** A short, bushy plant with fleshy, hairless, once- to twice-divided greyish leaves. Flowers yellowish-green in umbels 3–6cm across. Usually seen growing alone or with few other species in lava close to the sea and tolerant of sea spray. Britain and western Europe.

### *Gnaphalium luteo-album (perpétua-silvestre;* Jersey cudweed) **Compositae**
Shortish, white-woolly annual. Clustered yellow-reddish flowers. In sandy soils and lava cliffs. Rare in Britain, occasional in Europe, and in warm temperate regions worldwide.

### *Solidago sempervirens (cubres)* **Compositae**
Fleshy with leaves ending in small broad points at the tip. Flowers yellow in a closely branched panicle. Found as a coastal plant and occasionally elsewhere, particularly noted on the sea cliffs of Flores. Native of northeast America, and spread to the Azores in prehistory times.

### *Tolpis succulenta (visgo)* **Compositae**
Perennial herb with a woody base and becoming shrubby with age. Up to 30cm but can be as much as 100cm. Leaves narrow to broadly elliptic, often toothed, somewhat succulent. Flowers yellow, late summer/autumn. Grows near the coast on sea cliffs and gravelly places, as scattered individuals. To be found on all the islands, but in few localities, and on Madeira.

### *Azorina vidalii (vidalia;* azorina) **Campanulaceae**
Soft-wooded shrubby perennial with a main stem and branches to 50cm. Young plants form ground-hugging rosettes. Leaves dark green, often shiny, narrow, edged with forward-pointing rounded teeth, the whole plant somewhat sticky. Flowers nodding, bell-shaped, waxy, greenish-white to white to pink in an elongated raceme. Coastal plant in rock crevices and sandy places – even grit on the edge of asphalt roads. Most abundant among the rocks and sand below the airstrip on Corvo where it gets frequent sea spray. On all islands except Graciosa and Faial, but is often difficult to find. One of the loveliest endemic Azorean species, it is becoming increasingly popular in Britain as a tender garden plant.

### *Silene uniflora (bermin;* seacampion) **Caryophyllaceae**
Hairless, prostrate, much-branched perennial herb up to 30cm. Leaves without a stalk and often covered with a waxy bloom. Flowers with a bladder-like calyx, petals white, from March to late summer. Widespread coastal plant, also on Madeira, and in west and northwest Europe. Also found around the summit of Pico, but this may be a subspecies.

### *Plantago coronopus (dia-belha;* buck's-horn plantain) **Plantaginaceae**
Small herbaceous annual, biennial or perennial plant with rosettes pressed closely to the ground. Leaves somewhat fleshy, usually 2–6cm, linear-oblong, not lobed or with a few teeth or often twice-lobed. Flowers yellowish-brown, 3mm, borne in long, dense spikes on

curved stems that are longer than the leaves. Very common in coastal habitats and an early coloniser. Can also be found inland on dry, waste ground.

***Juncus acutus* (sharp rush) Juncaceae**  Tall, up to 150cm, robust grassy perennial making dense prickly tussocks with stiffly pointed stems and reddish-brown flowers in a compact inflorescence. Although a widespread species – Madeira, Mediterranean, Britain, North America – it is included here because it is a typical plant of the coast.

***Festuca petraea* (*bracel-da-rocha*) Graminae**  Grass with narrow, stiff leaves 30–50cm tall, flowers in whitish-green panicles. Coastal plant on cliffs, on lava and in sandy places often exposed to sea spray. Forms pure colonies but these are now rare because of human interference along the coast and this species is found commonly mixed with other species. Endemic to the Azores and found on all the islands.

## In laurisilva forest and at habitats generally above 400m
***Leontodon filii* (*petalugo-menor*) Compositae**  Perennial herb with up to five 20cm conspicuous, more-or-less elliptical leaves, toothed and hairy, bearing one to five yellow flowers on a branched stalk. Associated with the laurel forest, it likes wet, open places, often in grassland, usually above 600m, lower on Flores. Endemic, but not found on Santa Maria or Graciosa.

***Senecio malvifoliius* (*cabaceira, figueira-brava*) Compositae**  Perennial herb up to 120cm with rounded, lobed leaves 10–15cm, often found growing among shrubs which provide support. Flower colour varies from pale purple, bluish to white all on the same inflorescence, summer. An attractive plant usually growing in wet shady places, but I have seen it in a sunny hedgerow on São Miguel. Endemic, but not on Graciosa or Flores and Corvo.

***Tolpis azorica* Compositae**  Perennial herb up to 70cm, leaves crisp-looking, hairless, oblong, up to 15cm, margins deeply toothed. Flowers yellow on a branched inflorescence. To be seen in laurel forest and on constantly moist grassy slopes where it is conspicuous, generally above 600m. Endemic, but not on Graciosa.

***Erigeron karvinskianus* Compositae**  Perennial, stems slender, flat on the ground with erect tips. Leaves to 3cm, flowers varying from white through pink to red-purple. A pretty little daisy from Mexico that has escaped from gardens in numerous temperate places worldwide; in the Azores it is adaptable to different habitats.

***Cardamine caldeirarum* Cruciferae**  Included here because it is endemic and widespread in the Azores above 400m (but not on Graciosa). In northern Europe it has bittercress relatives that are the weeds and curse of garden centres. Herb up to 50cm tall, basal leaves with five to six pairs of leaflets, flowers white. Likes wet places.

***Centaurium scilloides* (perennial centaury) Gentianaceae**  Low, spreading perennial with non-flowering decumbent (flat, tips turning up) shoots, found usually above 400m. Upper leaves lanceolate, about 1cm long. Flowers white, solitary or just a few together in summer. Likes moist habitat, often with grasses. Could once easily be seen at several viewpoints, but seems to be disappearing, maybe due to visitor trampling. *C. scilloides* occurs in western Europe, generally with pink flowers, but some authorities classify the Azores plants as subspecies *massonii*, in which case they would be endemic. Francis Masson, Kew Gardens' first professional plant hunter, collected in the Azores in 1776 and this became one of the first plants from the Azores cultivated in England.

**Hypericum foliosum Guttiferae** Deciduous shrub to 0.5m with crowded narrowly ovate leaves and conspicuous yellow flowers 2–5cm diameter in terminal inflorescences. Normally above 400m, a member of the laurisilva forest but survives where this has been destroyed, and can also be found on steep grassy slopes. Endemic, on all the islands.

**Thymus caespititius (erva-úrsula) Labiatae** Dwarf, mat-forming plant with woody growth and upright flowering shoots to 5cm. Leaves to 6mm, narrow, spoon-shaped. Flowers in lax, small heads varying in colour from white through rose to almost lilac. Grows from low altitude to high on Pico, often in crevices on lava flows and on sandy banks. On the upper slopes of Pico it makes a spectacular summer display with *Daboecia azorica*.

**Anagallis tenella (bog pimpernel) Primulaceae** If you are looking at this in detail you will either be bored or very keen. Mat-forming, slender perennial with mostly opposite rounded to elliptical leaves. Flowers pink to whitish pink, somewhat bell-like on slender stalks, opening fully only in sunshine. Around 500m in wet or moist places, often near lakes. Western Europe.

**Lysimachia nemorum ssp. azorica (palinha; yellow pimpernel) Primulaceae** Evergreen herb with procumbent stems, quickly creeping and rooting at the leaf joints. Leaves opposite, more or less egg-shaped. Flowers solitary on slender stalks. A pretty, modest plant most often found in moist grassland and happiest above and around 500m. *L. nemorum* is found from Britain through to the Caucasus, the endemic subspecies *azorica* is found throughout the archipelago.

**Ranunculus cortusifolius (bafo-de-boi) Ranunculaceae** A handsome buttercup being an erect, up to 1m-tall herbaceous perennial, with slightly leathery basal leaves, lobed, rounded and heart-shaped up to 21 x 30cm. Flowers shining yellow up to 50mm diameter in a branched inflorescence. Usually above 500m but lower on Flores in permanently moist areas especially in the shelter of laurisilva forest in ravines, and occasionally in roadside gullies. Also found on Madeira and the Canaries.

**Polygonum capitatum Polygonaceae** Prostrate perennial with rooting stems, often forming large ground-covering carpets. Leaves 2–5cm oval, green with purple V-shaped band, often covered with glandular hairs. Flowers pink in dense, stalked, more or less globular heads. Native to the Himalayas, it was introduced and has escaped on many of the islands, happily colonising young lava flows, stone walls and waste places.

### *Rubia peregrina* (*rapa-língua*; wild madder) Rubiaceae

Distinctive, trailing or scrambling, hairless, rampant evergreen perennial. Stems square and rough with downturned prickles, leaves in whorls of four to six. Flowers yellowish-green, 4–5mm, forming a leafy inflorescence. Fruit rounded, ripening black and fleshy. Widespread, also in west and south Europe and North Africa.

### *Luzula purpureo-splendens* Juncaceae

This charming woodrush is a perennial, leaves grass-like, wide and up to 60cm long with fine hairs along the margins; flowers brown-purplish in clusters. Found usually between 500m and 1,100m altitude, preferring a moist grassland habitat, often on slopes, and among moss carpets around remnants of laurisilva forest, but also can withstand drought. Endemic, on all islands except Santa Maria and Graciosa.

### *Platanthera micrantha* (Azores butterfly orchid) Orchidaceae

Basal leaves two, about 10 x 4cm, erect to spreading. Stem leaves two to six, much smaller. Flowers in a rather dense narrowly cylindrical inflorescence, 8–13cm high and about 1cm across. Individual flowers numerous, small, yellow-green. Found between 200m and 1,000m but mostly above 600m in moist places in full sun to semi-shade; most often seen it grass on roadside verges. The plant's characteristics are variable and some authorities recognise a second, similar species *Platanthera azorica* that is more stocky with larger leaves and a more lax inflorescence of whitish-green flowers. Of the orchids recorded for the Azores' *P. micrantha* is the species most likely to be encountered; the other is a Tongue orchid.

### *Trachelium caeruleum* (throatwort) Campanulceae

Perennial herbs up to about 50cm tall with numerous small slender blue or lilac flowers in much-branched, leafless, broad flat inflorescences. In walls, roadside verges, etc, São Miguel, Terceira and Faial, west and central Mediterranean.

### *Arundo donax* (*cana*; giant reed) Graminae

A tall (to 5m) perennial rhizomatous grass, leaves 60 x 6cm, grey-green. Flowers in large terminal, feathery inflorescences, autumn. Introduced long ago, it thrives in volcanic sands around the coast and is used widely for shelter hedging. Strongly invasive, it quickly spreads if not strictly controlled. When grown in ideal conditions in the south of France the canes are supplied to make the reeds for musical wind instruments.

## FERNS

### *Asplenium marinum* (*feto maritime*; sea spleenwort) Aspleniaceae

A coastal, tufted, plant with a short, thick rhizome with dense blackish-brown scales, the whole growing tightly in among the rocks. Leaves 20–30cm long, pinnate, mid green and glossy above, dull and paler below, thickened and rather stiff; tolerant of salt spray. Madeira, Britain to western Mediterranean.

### *Blechnum spicant* (hard fern) Blechnaceae

Evergreen fern forming attractive crowns of long, sterile, pinnate leaves with a herring-bone appearance lying close to the ground; the young leaves are flushed red. The fertile fronds have a longer stalk, are much narrower, and are erect.

Widespread in northern temperate lands, it is one of the commonest and most distinctive ferns in the Azores, usually above 300m.

### *Woodwardia radicans* (chain fern) Blechnaceae

Found from the Azores to Java, this fern is one of the most attractive of the archipelago's fern flora. The fronds are 1–2m long and up to 0.5m wide and often hang down over gullies and banks. The fronds produce bulbils towards the apex and these form new plants, hence the common English name. Usually found above 400m in moist places.

### *Culcita macrocarpa* (*feto-do-cabelinho*) Dicksoniaceae

Conspicuous large fern with strong erect stems up to 100cm tall. The frond is triangular in outline, often shiny and frequently of a yellow-green colour. Found mostly above 500m but also down to 150m. It is associated with laurel forest and can be readily seen between the tree stems on the lava flows of Pico, but it also survives the loss of forest cover and can be found beyond the laurisilva. It has a prostrate rhizome covered with hairs, which were once collected and used for stuffing cushions, etc. Found on all the islands except Santa Maria and Graciosa, it is native to Macaronesia and the Iberian Peninsula.

### *Lycopodium cernuum* (*clubmoss*) Lycopodiaceae

A distinctive curiosity of a plant and a fern ally, its long creeping, looping stems rooting at intervals often spread over several square metres. Overall colour is yellowish-green and the tiny leaves are spirally arranged along the stems. The fertile leaves (sporphylls) are arranged in terminal cones (strobili). Generally found above 400m, frequently associated with laurel forest, but often also on steeply sloping banks where it can be a pioneer species on recently exposed surfaces. Also occurs by hot-water springs. On all islands, except Santa Maria and Graciosa. In central Europe the strobili of clubmosses used to be collected, dried, and the fine yellow spores kept for use as a medicated talcum powder; sensitive to pollution, they are now rare and strictly protected there.

### *Osmunda regalis* (*feto-real*; royal fern) Osmundaceae

Large tufted fern with upright fronds up to 1m tall and 30cm broad, pinnate. Sporangia produced on some of the terminal pinnae of the fertile fronds. It has a distinctive, short, massive, erect rhizome and a tangle of wiry roots, once popular in mainland Europe until mid last century as compost for growing orchids. Growing in wet places, often in water, and found on all islands except Graciosa.

### CULTIVATED PLANTS

### *Agapanthus praecox* Liliaceae

Perennial herb forming dense clumps from strong fleshy rootstocks with long strap-like leaves and large heads of blue flowers on leafless unbranched stems up to 60cm tall. Seeds black when ripe, borne in pendulous capsules. Native to South Africa, widely planted in towns and along roads, often naturalising.

### *Amaryllis belladonna* (*beladona*; belladonna lily) Amaryllidaceae

South African bulbous perennial with strap-shaped leaves in two ranks. Large funnel-shaped pink flowers produced in late summer before the leaves appear, six or more together on stout 60m stems. Frequently planted in public gardens and along roadsides, also naturalised.

***Abelia x grandiflora* Caprifoliaceae** Attractive semi-evergreen shrub to 2m with long arching branches, the young leaves at first markedly bronze-pink; flowers tubular, five-lobed, in clusters, pink to white, flowering over an extended period from summer. Frequently planted on road verges.

***Aloe arborescens* Liliaceae** Perennial succulent from South and East Africa with 60mm long grey-green leaves having sharp forward-pointing teeth. Inflorescence unbranched to 80cm, flowers tubular, 4cm, scarlet tipped greenish-white. A good ornamental thriving in hot dry places in private gardens and public places.

***Acacia melanoxylon* (blackwood) Mimosoideae** Fast-growing Australian tree with leaves modified to reduced simple, flattened leaf stalks up to 14 x 2.5cm. Flowers in nearly spherical heads in branched racemes, very pale yellow, late winter. A much-desired timber tree for high-value products. Seedlings are abundant on disturbed land, mature trees in gardens and woodland.

***Metrosideros excelsa* Myrtaceae** Dense evergreen tree that in maturity develops massively heavy branches and trunk with many aerial roots swinging from its branches. The dark leathery leaves are silvery on their undersides, and in summer terminal flowers burst into a spectacular show of scarlet-stamened pin cushions, seldom all over the tree but in large patches. Called *pohutukawa* by the Maoris, in its native New Zealand it often begins life as an epiphyte and is commonly found on sea cliffs. Very tolerant of salt spray, this tree is often to be seen in public gardens and squares on most of the islands.

***Melia azedarach* (Persian lilac) Meliaceae** This tree has many local common names around the world where it has been widely planted, but originally it came from northern India and China. Deciduous, spreading tree with an open crown and handsome twice-pinnate leaves to 80cm somewhat like the European ash. Flowers violet-blue in loose sprays 10–20cm long, often with the new foliage, followed by 1–5cm-diameter round fruits ripening yellow, wrinkling and turning brown with age remaining on the tree long after the leaves have fallen. Planted as a street tree and in public gardens.

***Araucaria heterophylla* (Norfolk Island pine) Araucariaceae** A stately conifer endemic to Norfolk Island attaining 20m or more, with spreading branches in whorls. Leaves scale-like to 1cm, somewhat triangular, overlapping like roof tiles. Planted widely throughout the islands, they are all protected and special permission is necessary before they can be felled. Captain Cook on his second round-the-world voyage in the 1770s discovered them and enthused about their potential use for ships' masts but sadly the wood proved too spongy and heavy. In their natural state they grow to 60m with a trunk circumference of over 8m on dry but fertile shallow volcanic soils. This drought tolerance the Victorians soon realised made it an ideal house plant when young, and it is again coming back into fashion. Dating back to the Jurassic period 225 million years ago, they were browsed by dinosaurs, but in the Azores they are vulnerable to lightning strikes.

# Appendix 3

There are some 50 species of fish found in the waters around the Azores that can be eaten. Those more likely to be found in the islands' restaurants are detailed below in alphabetical order according to their Azorean common name. Resilience is an indication of how much exploitation a species can tolerate and how long a minimum population takes to double in time. Very low = more than 14 years; Low = 4.5–14 years; Medium = 1.4–4.4 years.

**ABROTE** Greater forkbeard *Phycis blennoides*. Commonly up to 45cm, max size 110cm long, max weight 3.5kg. Found over sand and mud bottoms, a deep-water fish 10–800m, usually seen in caves, very shy, gentle fish; young more coastal. Feeds on crustaceans and fish. Eastern Atlantic, Iceland down to West Africa, and the Mediterranean. Resilience medium. Served as transverse steaks or filleted.

**ATUM** Tuna or tunny. Three different ones are commonly eaten in the Azores: *Thunnus obesus* is mostly squeezed into tins while albacora, yellowfin tuna, *Thunnus albacares*, and Bonito, skipjack tuna, *Katsuwonus pelamis*, are served under Atum in restaurants. The yellowfin tuna reaches a max size of around 230cm and weight of about 180kg, and the skipjack 90cm and 23kg.

**BADEJO** Island grouper *Mycteroperca fusca*. Max size 80cm, max weight 3kg. Subtropical, found above rocky areas, depth down to 200m. Azores, Madeira, Canaries and Cape Verde Islands. Resilience low. Served stewed, maybe grilled or baked in the oven.

**BICUDA** Yellowmouth barracuda *Sphyraena viridensis*. Max size 128cm, max weight 8.2kg. Depth 0–100m. Tropical, eastern central Atlantic. Feeds on fish, cephalopods and crustaceans. Resilence low. Eaten best as a transverse steak, also whole baked in the oven.

**BOCA NEGRA** Blackbelly rosefish *Helicolenus dactylopterus*. Max size 47cm, max weight 1.5kg, reportedly living for around 40 years. Depth 50–1,100m. Deep-water fish found in soft-bottomed areas of continental shelf and upper slope, feeds on crustaceans, fish, cephalopods. Venomous. Eastern Atlantic Iceland to South Africa, western Atlantic. Resilience very low. Served whole, good grilled or fried.

**BODIÃO VERMELHO** Ballan wrasse *Labrus bergylta*. Max size 65cm, max weight just over 4kg. Found around rocks and offshore reefs to a depth of 50m. Feeds on crustaceans and molluscs. Eastern Atlantic. Born first as female, then changes sex after four-plus years old. Resilience low. Served grilled.

**CHERNE** Wreckfish *Polyprion americanus*. Max size 210cm, max weight 100kg. Deep water (40–600m), solitary, likes caves and shipwrecks. Feeds on large crustaceans, cephalopods and fish. Wide distribution, eastern and western Atlantic, southwest Pacific. Resilience low. Best served as transverse steaks, when thick and simply grilled a gastronomic highlight.

**CHICHARRO** Blue jack mackerel *Trachurus picturatus*. Max size 60cm. Depth to 270m, a schooling species favouring shallow coastal waters of islands, banks and sea mounts, feeds on crustaceans. Eastern Atlantic, Bay of Biscay down to Tristan da Cunha. Resilience medium. Eaten small, about 10cm, fried really crispy they are quite yummy.

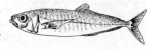

**ESPADA** Silver scabbardfish *Lepidopus caudatus*. Max size 2m, max weight 8kg. Depth 100–600m. A deep-water school-forming fish found usually over muddy or sandy bottoms and migrates into midwater at night, when it is most often caught. Eastern Atlantic France to South Africa, southern Indian Ocean, southwest and southeast Pacific. Feeds on crustaceans, squid and fish. Resilience medium. Eaten as fillets.

**ESPADARTE** Swordfish *Xiphias gladius*. Max size 4.5m, max weight 650kg. Depth 0–800m. Oceanic, occasionally in coastal waters. Migrates to temperate or cold waters in summer, returns to warmer waters in autumn. Feeds on fish, also crustaceans and squid, using their sword to kill prey. Atlantic, Indian and Pacific oceans. Resilience low. Usually served as a transverse steak, too often cut measly thin; like a good beefsteak, it should be thick.

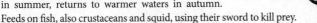

**GAROUPA** Blacktail comber *Serranus atricauda*. Max size 43cm. Depth 1–90m, found over hard bottom; carnivorous, distributed eastern Atlantic. Resilience low. Served whole, usually grilled.

**GORAZ** Garapau or Peixão blackspot seabream *Pagellus bogaraveo*. Max size 70cm, max weight 4kg. Inshore waters to a depth of 700m, feeds on crustaceans, molluscs, worms and fish. Eastern Atlantic. Resilience low. Served grilled or baked in the oven. Locally regarded by some as 'horrible'.

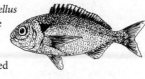

**MERO** Dusky grouper *Epinephelus marginatus*. Max size 150cm, max weight 60kg. Depth 8–300m, subtropical, likes reefs and rocky bottoms, solitary and territorial, feeds on crabs,

octopus and fish. Eastern Atlantic and western Indian Ocean, and western Atlantic. Resilience low, endangered. Served as fillets rather than steaks but also good poached or cooked in the oven.

**PARGO** Common seabream *Pagrus pagrus*. Max size 91cm, max weight 7.7kg. Depth down to 250m. Subtropical, found over rock or sandy bottoms, feeds on crustaceans, fish and molluscs. Eastern Atlantic north to the British Isles, western Atlantic, down to Argentina. Resilience medium, endangered. Served whole or as transverse steaks. Excellent covered with sea salt and oven baked.

**ROCAZ** Large-scaled scorpion fish *Scorpaena scrofa*. Max size 50cm, max weight 2.9kg. Depth 20–500m. Subtropical, solitary, sedentary over rocky, sandy or muddy bottoms, feeds on fish, crustaceans and molluscs. Venomous. Eastern Atlantic. Resilience low. Very expensive but very nice! Served whole, grilled or poached.

**SALMONETE** Striped red mullet *Mullus surmuletus*. Max size 40cm, max weight 1kg. Depth less than 100m. Found over rocky places and also sand and soft bottoms, feeds on shrimps, molluscs and fish. Eastern Atlantic. Resilience medium. Eaten whole.

**SERRA** Atlantic bonito *Sarda sarda*. Max size 90cm, max weight 11kg. Depth range 80–200m, subtropical schooling species, cannibalistic, feeds on squid, shrimps and fish. Widespread Atlantic. Resilience medium. Served as fillets or transverse steaks.

# Appendix 4

**MAPS** *Azores* published by Turinta in their regional series. Folded map, scale 1:75,000. A topographical map of the islands with tourist information, lots of detail and easily readable; £8.95

**BOOKS** There are numerous publications on technical topics about the Azores, but they are almost all in Portuguese. In English there is virtually nothing readily available that is specific to the Azores, but there are several coffee-table books for sale in the local shops, together with outline guides with lots of pretty pictures. One exception is the guide to Flores:

Bragaglia, Pierluigi *Flores–Azores–Walking Through History* Author's publication, 2009; www.argonauta-flores.com

Nemésio, Vitorino *Mau tempo no Canal* (1944), translated as *Stormy Isles: An Azorean Tale* (1998). Nemésio's novel provides an intriguing window into early 20th-century Azorean life and society, with coastal whaling at times a prominent feature. It is a story of unrequited love and two warring families in locations on Pico, Faial and São Jorge, and the intervening channels, and may still be available in Ponta Delgada bookshops.

## Nature

Bento, Rita and Sá, Nuno *Diving Guide Azores* Ver Açor, Ponta Delgada. Available from the Centre for the Arts and Marine Sciences, Pico. A 192-page guide with photography by Nuno (265 photos). A total of 53 diving sites are described.

Cas, R and Wright, J V*olcanic Successions* Springer, 1987

Clarke, Tony *Birds of the Atlantic Islands* Christopher Helm, 2006. The first comprehensive field guide to the birds of the Macaronesian islands – Canaries, Madeira, Azores and Cape Verde. Illustrated by Chris Orgill and Tony Disley.

Rodrigues, P and Michielsen, G *Birdwatching in the Azores*. Detailing habitats and distribution with many excellent colour photos and illustrations. Pbk, published by Azores Tourism but currently out of print.

Scarth, Alwyn and Tanguy, J-C *Volcanoes of Europe* Terra, 2001

Schäfer, Hanno *Flora of the Azores* Margraf Verlag, Weikersheim, 2002. In English, with 380 colour photographs and brief descriptions of 650 native and introduced species.

Soares de Albergaria, Isabel *Gardens and Woodlands of the Azores Islands*. Pbk, published by Azores Tourism but currently not for sale. In the format of a travel guide the 692 descriptions are liberally illustrated by excellent small photographs, old postcards and engravings, together with location maps and opening times. Most interesting and informative is the introduction in which the historical and social background sets the scene for the intriguing snippets appearing in the individual garden descriptions.

# General reading

Abdo, Joseph C *On the Edge of History* Tenth Island Editions, 2006. The story of the Dabney family, American consuls to the Azores during the 19th century.

Ashe, Thomas *History of the Azores or Western Islands: Containing an Account of the Government, Laws and Religion, the Manners, Ceremonies and Characters of the Islands* Kessinger, 2009

Birmingham, David *A Concise History of Portugal* Cambridge University Press, 2003

Boid, Edward *A Description of the Azores: Or Western Islands from Personal Observation* London, 1835. Kessinger Legacy Reprint.

Gordon, J S *A Thread Across the Ocean* Simon & Schuster, 2002. A fascinating account of entrepreneurial determination to lay the first Atlantic cable.

Robertson, Ian *A Traveller's History of Portugal* Cassell, 2002

## ARTICLES

Alfrey, P 'American vagrants on the island of Corvo, Azores', 2005, Birding World 18(11): 465–74

## WEBSITES
### Tourism

www.visitazores.com Site in English and Portuguese giving details of travel agents, accommodation, etc, run by the Azores Tourism Authority.

www.azores.com User-friendly site run by Portugal Online Corp, a company promoting Portugal on the internet.

www.azores.gov.pt Official website of the Government of the Azores, which gives up-to-date information about the Azores and government activities and, under 'About the Azores', tourist information.

www.casasacorianas.com Owners of rural accommodation website, giving property details and booking online.

www.hostels.com/pt.az.html Azores youth hostels.

www.destinazores.com Simple 'guidebook' in English, German and Portuguese giving very limited background information plus some accommodation and eating places.

www.azores.com Information on travel, hotels, tours, etc.

www.azoresinfo.com Details of restaurants, local agents offering activities, and other useful information.

www.atlanticoline.pt Inter-island ferry services.

www.meteo.pt All you need to know about the weather in the Azores, including a ten-day forecast.

www.azoresairlines.pt For direct flights from the UK and inter-island flight schedules.

www.flytap.com For flights throughout the year via Lisbon to the Azores.

www.noonsite.com/Countries/Azores/ Yachting information.

http://news.bbc.co.uk/weather Under 'search', type in 'Azores' for a five-day forecast.

www.meteo.pt/en A fascinating site from the Instituto de Meteorologia Portugal giving all the information and more about the weather in the Azores, seismology, marine meteorology and atmosphere.

www.allyoucanread.com/azores-newspaper-portugal/ Online newspaper.

## Activities

www.teatromicaelense.pt For programme details of the theatre in Ponta Delgada.

www.cineclube.org For information on films being shown in the Horta theatre; see page 197 for details.

www.angrajazz.com For details of the jazz festival on Terceira.

**www.trails-azores.com** Government site giving details and updates on all the official walking trails.

**www.montanheiros.com** Website of the Sociedade de Exploração Espeleológica whose headquarters are on Terceira.

**www.azoresweb.com/diving_azores.html** Details of diving companies.

**www.marinasazores.com** Official website of Sea Week.

## Natural history and conservation

**http://parquesnaturais.azores.gov.pt/en/index** Gives details of all the nature parks.

**www.spea.pt** SPEA: the society for the study and conservation of birds in Portugal.

**www.birdingazores.com** Excellent website, initialised in 2004 by two Swedish birders to collect information and describe the bird fauna of the Azores, and to create a source of information for visiting birders. Gives birding sites, bird photos, trip reports, checklist and more.

**http://azoresbs.weebly.com** Records bird sightings and disseminates interesting bird news from the Azores.

**www.wdcs.org** Whale and Dolphin Conservation Society, the world's most active charity dedicated to the conservation and welfare of all whales, dolphins and porpoises.

**http://whale.wheelock.edu/whalenet-stuff/Azores** Shows satellite-tagging observation maps for sperm whales in the Azores, part of a programme to monitor migration of selected species.

**www.ospar.org** For the past 40 years OSPAR has been identifying threats to the marine environment and has organised programmes and measures to combat them. Their Biological and Ecosystems strategy aims to restore, where practicable, marine areas adversely affected, and to create marine protected areas.

**www.azoresbioportal.angra.uac.pt** An important and wonderful working tool providing a database for about 5,000 species, often accompanied by images. Groups include lichens and fungi, bryophytes, flowering plants, marine invertebrates, arthropods, and vertebrates.

**www.horta.uac.pt** University of the Azores, Department of Oceanography and Fisheries.

# Index

## INDEX OF ADVERTISERS

# NOTES